Epistemological and Social Problems of the Sciences
in the Early Nineteenth Century

Epistemological and
Social Problems of the Sciences
in the Early Nineteenth Century

Edited by

H. N. JAHNKE

and

M. OTTE

The Institute for the Didactics of Mathematics,
Bielefeld University

D. Reidel Publishing Company

Dordrecht : Holland / Boston : U.S.A. / London : England

Library of Congress Cataloging in Publication Data
Main entry under title:

Epistemological and social problems of the sciences in the early nineteenth
    century.

        Papers from a workshop held at the University of Bielefeld, Nov. 27–30,
1979, and sponsored by its Institute for the Didactics of Mathematics.
        Bibliography: p.
        Includes index.
        1. Science–History–Europe–Addresses, essays, lectures.   2.   Science–
Social aspects–Europe–Addresses, essays, lectures.   3.   Knowledge, Theory
of–History–Europe–Addresses, essays, lectures.   4.   Science–Study and
teaching–Europe–History–Addresses, essays, lectures.   I.   Jahnke, Hans
Niels, 1948–   . II. Otte, Michael, 1938–   . III.   Bielefeld.
Universität. Institut für Didaktik der Mathematik.
Q127.E82E64   509.4   80–27919
ISBN 90–277–1223–9

Published by D. Reidel Publishing Company
P.O. Box 17, 3300 AA Dordrecht, Holland

Sold and distributed in the U.S.A. and Canada
by Kluwer Boston Inc.,
190 Old Derby Street, Hingham, MA 02043, U.S.A.

In all countries, sold and distributed
by Kluwer Academic Publishers Group,
P.O. Box 322, 3300 AH Dordrecht, Holland

D. Reidel Publishing Company is a member of the Kluwer Group

Printed in The Netherlands

TABLE OF CONTENTS

Editorial remark   ix

H.N. Jahnke, M. Otte and B. Schminnes
Introduction   xi

I   SCIENCE AROUND 1800: COGNITIVE AND SOCIAL CHANGE

M. Heidelberger
Some Patterns of Change in the Baconian
Sciences of the Early 19th Century Germany   3

P. Buck
From Celestial Mechanics to Social Physics:
Discontinuity in the Development of the Sciences in the
Early Nineteenth Century   19

C. Salomon-Bayet
1802 - "Biologie" et Médecine   35

P. Gajdenko
Ontologic Foundation of Scientific Knowledge in
Seventeenth- and Eighteenth-Century Rationalism   55

C.-U. Moulines
Hermann von Helmholtz: A Physiological Approach to the
Theory of Knowledge   65

H.N. Jahnke and M. Otte
On "Science as a Language"   75

S.R. Mikulinsky
The Historical Conditions and Features of the
Development of Natural Science in Russia in the First
Half of the 19th Century   91

S. Turner
The Prussian Professoriate and the Research Imperative,
1790 - 1840   109

B.M. Kedrov
European Natural Science.
(The Beginning of the 19th Century)   123

L. Laesker
Science, Knowledge, and the Reproduction of the Social
Capacity For Labour   141

II SCIENCE AND EDUCATION

R. KUENZLI
Teaching Method and Justification of Knowledge:
C. Ritter - J.H. Pestalozzi   159

D.K. Mueller
Possibilities and Limits of the Prussian School Reform
at the Beginning of the 19th Century   183

B. Rang-Dudzik
Qualitative and Quantitative Aspects of Curricula in
Prussian Grammar Schools During the Late 18th and Early
19th Centuries and Their Relation to the Development of
the Sciences   207

W. Langhammer
Some Aspects of the Development of Mathematics at the
University of Halle-Wittenberg in the Early 19th
Century   235

A.C. Lewis
Justus Grassmann's School Programs as Mathematical
Antecedents of Hermann Grassmann's 1844
'Ausdehnungslehre'   255

G. Schubring
On Education as a Mediating Element Between Development
and Application: The Plans For the Berlin Polytechnical
Institute (1817 – 1850)   269

III   MATHEMATICS IN THE EARLY 19TH CENTURY

L.J. Daston
Mathematics and the Moral Sciences: The Rise and Fall
of the Probability of Judgments, 1785 – 1840   287

J.V. Grabiner
Changing Attitudes Toward Mathematical Rigor: Lagrange
and Analysis in the Eighteenth and Nineteenth Centuries   311

W. Scharlau
The Origins of Pure Mathematics   331

I. Grattan-Guinness
Mathematical Physics in France, 1800 – 1835   349

J.W. Dauben
Mathematics in Germany and France in the Early 19th
Century: Transmission and Transformation   371

H. Mehrtens
Mathematicians in Germany Circa 1800   401

Name Index   421

List of Participants   430

EDITORIAL REMARK

Vom 27. bis 30. November 1979 fand im Zentrum fuer interdisziplinaere Forschung der Universitaet Bielefeld eine Arbeitstagung zum Thema "Epistemologische und soziale Probleme der Wissenschaftsentwicklung im fruehen 19. Jahrhundert" statt. An ihr nahmen Wissenschaftler unterschiedlichster Disziplinen teil. Die Tagung war vom Institut fuer Didaktik der Mathematik (IDM) der Universitaet Bielefeld organisiert worden, um bestimmte inhaltliche und methodologische Orientierungen weiterzuentwickeln, die die Grundlage eines am IDM durchgefuehrten und von der Stiftung Volkswagenwerk finanziell gefoerderten Projekts zur Geschichte der Mathematik in der ersten Haelfte des 19. Jahrhunderts darstellen.

Der vorliegende Band dokumentiert diese Tagung. Er enthaelt in ueberarbeiteten Fassungen die Mehrzahl der Papiere, die vorgelegt und diskutiert worden sind. Die Diskussionen wollen wir nicht im einzelnen darstellen, sondern wir beschraenken uns darauf, in Form eines Vorworts eigene Orientierungen fuer eine weitere Arbeit in diesem Bereich zu entwickeln, die unser ganz subjektives Resuemee darstellen.

Wir moechten an dieser Stelle den Mitarbeitern des oben genannten Projektes "Mathematik im Wissenschafts- und Bildungsprozess des fruehen 19. Jahrhunderts" am IDM: Bernd Bekemeier, Ingrid Lohmann und Bernd Schminnes, die uns bei der inhaltlichen und organisatorischen Vorbereitung der Tagung sowie bei der Arbeit der Herausgabe des Bandes unterstuetzt haben, unseren herzlichen Dank sagen. Wir bedanken uns auch bei der Vielzahl der Kollegen und Institutionen der Universitaet Bielefeld sowie bei der Stiftung Volkswagenwerk, die uns alle auf mannigfache Weise unterstuetzt haben. Insbesondere sei darauf hingewiesen, dass der Text mit Hilfe des am Rechenzentrum der hiesigen Universitaet entwickelten Systems 'EUMEL' erstellt worden ist.

Unser besonderer Dank gilt Maria Ahrend, Ingrid Kootz und Christa Vorwerk, die den Text unter auesserst schwierigen Bedingungen hergestellt haben.

Wir danken schliesslich dem Verlag D. Reidel Publ. Comp. in Dordrecht fuer die freundliche Kooperation.

Die Herausgeber

EDITORIAL REMARK

From the 27th to the 30th November 1979 a workshop was held in the Center for Interdisciplinary Research at Bielefeld University under the title "Epistemological and Social Problems of the Sciences in the Early 19th Century", in which scientists from many varied disciplines participated. The Institute for the Didactics of Mathematics (IDM) had arranged the conference in order to further develop some specific orientations, which formed the basis for a project concerned with the history of mathematics during the first half of the 19th century. This project is being carried out in the IDM and financed by the Volkswagen foundation.

This conference is reflected in the following pages which contain the revised editions of the majority of the papers which were presented and discussed at this workshop. It is not our wish to document the discussions individually, but in the subjective introduction we have merely summarized them, elaborating on concepts for further development in this field.

At this point we would sincerely like to thank our colleagues in the above mentioned project, "Mathematics in the Development of the Sciences in the Early 19th Century", from the IDM: Bernd Bekemeier, Ingrid Lohmann and Bernd Schminnes, who have helped us in both preparing and organizing the conference, and given us their full support in editing this volume. We would also like to thank the many other colleagues and institutions of Bielefeld University, also the Volkswagen foundation, who have all given us their manifold support. Particular reference is made to the text which was produced with the aid of the "EUMEL" system, developed by the computer center at the local University.

Special thanks also to Maria Ahrend, Ingrid Kootz and Christa Vorwerk, who produced the text under extremely difficult conditions.
Finally our thanks to the publishers D. Reidel Publ. Comp. in Dordrecht for their kind co-operation.

The Editors

Hans Niels Jahnke, Michael Otte and Bernd Schminnes

INTRODUCTION

I. Some Characteristic Features of the Passage From the 18th to the 19th Century

1.

The following notes grew out of reflections which first led us to send out invitations to, and call for papers for, an interdisciplinary workshop, which took place in Bielefeld from 27th to 30th November, 1979. The status and character of this preface is therefore somewhat ambiguous: on the one hand it does not comment extensively on the articles to follow, on the other hand it could not have been conceived and written in the way it was without knowledge of all the contributions to this volume – which contains revised editions of papers for the workshop – nor without the cooperation of the participants in the above mentioned symposium.

Furthermore, although the following may sound slightly programmatic and summary, we hope that it will be sufficiently explicit to provide some key words and concepts useful for further scholarly work. Perhaps the most important result of our efforts is the very structure of these notes: it is aimed at providing methodological orientations for the investigation of what turned out to be a very peculiar period in the history of science.

H. N. Jahnke and M. Otte (eds.), Epistemological and Social Problems of the Sciences in the Early Nineteenth Century, xi–xlii.

Although we were primarily interested in the development of mathematics during the first half of the 19th century we soon realized that a broader approach encompassing all the scientific disciplines in their interdisciplinary relations and their relations to other areas of knowledge and social and cultural development would be more appropriate to that particular historical period. Even the term "culture" as an independent noun signifying an abstract process or the result of such a process dates from the first half of the 19th century. A semantic analysis shows generally that in contemporary public discussions wider and up to then separate areas were dealt with as a whole and in their context. The social idea of culture was worked out and introduced into English thinking. Cultivation was to be taken as the highest observable state of man in society. "What in the 18th century had been an ideal of personality ... had now, in the face of radical change, to be re-defined, as a condition on which society as a whole depended" (Williams 1977, p. 77).

Of course our conception of the symposium at first met with some scepticism from historians of science, of education, from sociologists and others. But it appealed to most participants since it was "unusual to take on several topics over a short period rather than one or two topics over a long period, which is usually the case at a historical meeting."

This characterization given by one participant, kind though it is to us, also expresses, in our opinion, an "objective" demand that arises when one is trying to cope with the problems of our particular period in the history of science, namely the early 19th century.

Characterizations of the situation at the turn of the 18th century by historians of science usually draw a picture of dramatic change and dazzling complexity, with the French Revolution as the outstanding landmark. Consider, for instance the following remarks made recently by E. Mendelsohn: "If the scientific vision of the 18th century remained ordered and unchanging, the nineteenth century was forced to deal with change. Nothing seemed stable and in place. Order was challenged and often disintegrated. Authority

became tenuous and often changed hands. Traditions of long
duration were set aside; the very manner in which humans produced
goods and distributed them were altered. Social, political,
economic and religious institutions all underwent significant
transformations. But perhaps most importantly, the day to day life
of many individuals exhibited marked alterations from the
generation of the immediate past ...

The French Revolution set the pattern for one way of changing
society and indeed gave a new meaning to the term 'revolution'.
Drastic, violent change on a broad scale became the definition
associated with the 1790s in France. The fact that the next fifty
years or so witnessed repeated attempts to overthrow political
regimes and social orders provides a specific background to all
intellectual developments that took place" (Mendelsohn 1978).

There is evidence (see Lepenies 1978, pp. 106ff) that
contemporaries generally had a similar vision of their time, thus
justifying the argument that "at the turn of the 18th century it
was especially appealing to draw a connection between the history
of the sciences and contemporary history - the unforgotten event
of the French Revolution appeared as a model for political as well
as scientific upheaval" (Lepenies 1978, p. 107).

But the situation looks paradoxical indeed. On the one hand one is
tempted to say: The message is clear enough. Science is a social
activity and this fact has to be taken into account above all
else. But when concrete questions are approached, then every
single detail, every phenomenon seems controversial and it is
necessary first of all to develop a concept of knowledge and
especially of scientific knowledge which allows for those social
aspects.

Within the sociology of knowledge this problem has also been
worked on. It is no accident that Durkheim, for instance, in his
sociology of religion had to give a corresponding form to the
'concept' itself in order to accomplish his purpose. At first it
could be asked whatever a theory of concept has to do with a
sociology of religions.

But even more is desirable. Related to the social description of knowledge and beyond that, a coherent description of the scientific field as a whole seems desirable; a description in proper relation to the historical period in question and to the self-conception of that period.

2.

One peculiarity of the scientific field is the fact that science, although it is only one subsystem of the social system, must to a certain degree express and represent the very general. Science is related to historical objectivity. This problem is governed by a special dialectic. In order to understand or describe the nature or essence of something (the 'general') as something of its own, one must portray this nature as a form. Two remarks on this:

First, the above mentioned objectivity is itself governed by its own particular and general rules and conditions.

For instance, there are quite different theories of generalization discussed in science. All are based on the concept of contrast or opposition of knowledge as a source of generalization. But some emphazise the plurality of the social process and its implicit manifold objectives and purposes; others base generalization on the diversity of aspects which a certain thing can show when it is reflected in knowledge. However, insofar as there is a commitment to reach the objective 'general' in the scientific field, the two branches cannot be completely separated. Bourdieu (1975) in particular tried to depict the respective connection. Considering the problem central for both history and theory of science, one accordingly obtains two 'part-descriptions' of the development of science. One is focussed on the question of "Who determines types and standards of scientific achievement? Who decides on the relevance of scientific questions or the adequacy of solutions suggested for scientific problems?" The other arises from Stegmueller's modification of Kuhn's conception of the dynamics of theories: "Which theory achieves more within the framework of legitimate measures, i.e. which commands the higher explanatory potential?" Both aspects of the development of science indicated in these questions are inseparably and circularly connected. The dependence of the second on the first is obvious and has been extensively discussed since the days of L. Fleck's "Entstehung und Entwicklung einer wissenschaftlichen Tatsache" as a substitution for the positivistic, cumulative conception of science. But in the reverse, not every 'knowledge' can achieve the generality of scientific knowledge at any point in time.

Scientific knowledge is not synonymous with social knowledge just because the study of science is an activity pursued by acting and interacting human beings. Such a vague usage of the term 'social' would fundamentally miss the specific nature of the scientific field which is "the specificity of the politics of truth in our society". And it is this last feature which enables science as a human activity to "take on a general significance" (Foucault 1977). This is the reason for characterizing science as, on the one hand a concrete sub-area of social activity, and on the other hand a part of the social system, but a part which nevertheless finds its fundamentals in the 'general', namely the problems of true knowledge.

All reflections aiming at a characterization of science (its development, its links with other historical processes etc.) are either of a methodological or a social order. But what we have tried to promote above is the social nature of the methodological and the methodologic aspects of the social side.

These dialectics can be found in real life and are not merely analytic constructions. There are certain real processes and problems which directly illustrate the two above mentioned components of science as an object of scientific reflection and analysis. The problems of communication, of general education, and of teaching are some of these as they demand on the one hand an explicitness that presupposes consciousness (methodologic reflection) and on the other hand set limits to this aspect of awareness, because they always re-integrate science into the social process as a whole. It is therefore not surprising that in early 19th century Germany the debate on matters of education (and education theory) led to the formulation of conceptions of the form and function of knowledge in a manner most comprehensive and rich in aspects. (We shall come back to this in part II.)

We have seen that in order to characterize the scientific field we have to represent scientific knowledge (its objectivity, its generality etc.) as form. But that is not enough. It is not even sufficient to describe theoretical concepts as at the same time abstractions and collective representations (Durkheim). There are limits to explicitness in the methodologic field and therefore limits to the adequate representation of the 'objective', the 'general', the 'essence' as form. Expressing 'objective reality' is the privilege of society as such, characterized as "consciousness of consciousnesses" (Durkheim).

3.

The relationship between scientific knowledge and empirical knowledge, between science and other cultural forms attains a particular relevance at a certain point in the dynamics of history. Foucault's case studies in the history of science illuminate this development admirably, especially the marked shift in his point of view when he was trying to cope with the problems of the situation around 1800.

In his "Les mots et les choses", he emphatically demonstrates the discontinuities and disruptions in the epistemology of the sciences between 1775 and 1825 (pp. 229ff. Note the similarity to the descriptions quoted above).

In "The Archaeology of Knowledge", the methodological 'supplement' published three years later, Foucault says that in 'Les mots et les choses' "the absence of methodological signposting may have given the impression that my analyses were being conducted in terms of cultural totality" (p. 16). And with regard to the situation itself, in almost subdued tones: "Archaeology disarticulates the synchrony of breaks, just as it destroyed the abstract unity of change and event. The period is neither its basic unity, nor its horizon, nor its object. ... Thus the French Revolution — since up to now all archaeological analyses have been centred on it — does not play the role of an event exterior to discourse, whose diversive effect one is under some kind of obligation to discover in all discourses; it functions as a complex articulated describable group of transformations that left a number of positivities intact, fixed for a number of others rules that are still with us and also established positivities that have recently disappeared or are still disappearing before

our eyes" (pp. 176f.). Nevertheless, the French Revolution does
mark the end of the "classic age" and shows the 'limits of the
representation'.

To carry our investigation of Foucault further we should like to
pick out one particular formulation of the 'part-whole' problem we
used above in describing the specification of the scientific field
('essence as form'). This formulation involves the concept of
'text'. It is a central methodological term in Foucault's work;
in addition to that we consider it as being of some relevance to
the historical period in question, therefore we should like to use
the concepts of 'text' and 'text reception'.

Taking this concept serious amounts to abandoning questions like,
"What did the author really mean?" or "What is being said in what
is said?". Texts have to be accepted as autonomous and immediate.
In order to be understood they must be taken literally, not
metaphorically. But on the other side then it is usually not
admissable to take a text at face value; it must be interpreted
intelligently. There must be some idea about the message of the
text or an advance organizer.

So what is a text? What is an appropriate unit for investigation
in the field of scientific history? Where must the line be drawn?
Foucault says: "I was suspicious of such unities of discourse as
'the book' and 'the oeuvre' because I suspected them of not being
as immediate and self-evident as they appeared ..." (p. 135).

The field we are looking for is described by the term 'knowledge'.
"Science (or what is offered as such) is localized in a field of
knowledge and plays a role in it" (p. 184). "Instead of exploring
the consciousness/ knowledge(connaissance)/science axis (which
cannot escape subjectivity), archaeology explores the discursive
practice/knowledge(savoir)/science axis" (p. 183).

The discursive practice/knowledge/science axis also hints at the
'material component' of the field of knowledge, at its material
artefacts, because discursive practices are not simply ways of
producing discourse. They are embodied in means and forms of human
social activity (tools, organizations, institutions, techniques of
communication). If the limits of mere analysis are to be overcome
- analytical decomposition, after all, necessarily emphasizes the
more formal aspects - a third concept must be introduced, namely
the epistemologic and social subject (see Foucault 1977).

These, then, are our three central concepts – to be found implicitly or explicitly in most of the contributions to this volume –: the 'knowledge/science' relation; the concept of 'material aspects of the field of knowledge'; the 'differentiations of the epistemologic and social subject'.

II. Science and Education

1.

The above reflections imply that even the most differentiated epistemological characterizations will not suffice to characterize what is really new in the history of science in the 19th century. This becomes evident in virtually all those contributions to this volume which try to point out differences in the sciences of the 18th and the 19th century. Epistemological conceptions and standpoints efficient and valid in the 18th century were not suddenly inadequate or outdated in the 19th. It was rather that the efficiency and applicability of epistemological concepts was limited and specified, in a differentiated manner, to certain objective social and institutional contexts. At the same time, highly general concepts like 'education', 'culture', 'civilization' become operative for the self-conception of the sciences. And with that the social plane becomes of immediate significance for the analysis of the development of the sciences at the turn to the 19th century. It proves necessary to take the social-historical subject of the production and application of knowledge into account, if differentiation and connection of diverse forms of science are to be comprehended. The crux of this new type of rationality seems to be the ensuing importance of the connection between epistemology and social theory. In this sense, the close connection of scientific and social development lived in the consciousness of contemporaries especially at the beginning of the 19th century. "But perhaps this demand (for realizing the living connection of all science) will never be more urgent than at the present time, now that everything in science and art seems to press more powerfully towards unity, now that even the seemingly most distant things in their fields touch; now that every vibration that occurs in or near the centre continues quicker and more immediately, so to speak, to the outer parts and a new organ of contemplation forms more generally and for almost everything. Never can such a time pass without the birth of a new world which inevitably buries those who do not take an active part in it into nothingness" (Schelling 1803, p. 213).

Within these general conceptions, we consider the analysis of education of paramount importance. This is true historically-concretely for an investigation of the development of science in the period of time in question, as well as in a fundamentally methodological sense. Surely the fact is undisputed with historians of science that the establishment of a public education system was of great relevance for the development of science in Prussia and Germany. After all, the universities with their seminars and laboratories represented the essential institutional site of scientific research. This can also be asserted for France, if to a lesser extend, while a similarly great significance of the educational system cannot be assumed for England. Admittedly, the connection of science and education has up to now usually been considered from organizational or institutional points of view; the question of whether, and if so which, repercussions on the methodological self-conception of the sciences resulted from their implementation into a public education system, has been contemplated less frequently. Yet as early as 1900, A. Harnack, in his history of the Prussian academy of the sciences, remarked on the characterization of the difference between the sciences in the 18th and 19th centuries: "Universal knowledge in a scholar could no longer be achieved - whosoever tried all the same was doomed to fail. But a new sort of universal accomplishment of a more intensive kind was set up as a marvellous ideal. ... Not knowledge but education and cultivation are the ultimate objective of even the scholar; ..." (Harnack 1900, I.2., p. 630).

The qualitative change in the scientific and educational system which took place during the early 19th century can also be realized from the fact that in the late 18th and early 19th centuries almost half of the then existing universities in Germany ceased to exist, while some important new universities were established. This was done under the aspect of a far-reaching reform of the scientific and educational system. Especially in the conception of Berlin university, the most influential intellectual

minds of Prussia participated. In France, a similar process of
destroying old and establishing new educational institutions took
place, only in a more drastic form in the course of the French
Revolution. Within this process, the establishment of the Ecole
Polytechnique, for instance, resulted with regard to mathematics
not only in furnishing this discipline with a new locality of
operation and new prestige; it also led to a new style in studying
mathematics originating from there (See Felix Klein 1926; M. Paul
1980). It should also be remembered that a thorough reform of the
whole education system was an important motivation of early French
positivism. French positivism – in total analogy to the discussion
in Germany – saw the essential motivation for such a reform in the
necessity of counteracting the increasing disruption of knowledge
and the prevailing specialisticism: another vision of a "new
universal accomplishment of a more intensive kind" (See Cassirer
IV, p. 17ff.).

If one tries for a better understanding of the connection between
education and science, it must be realized that education
establishes above all else the individual's conscious and also
unconscious relationships to knowledge, produces ideas of the
unity and coherence of knowledge and furthers the methodolization
of knowledge. Education is connected in an essential sense with
the establishment of scientifically general, supra-disciplinary
concepts. Scientific education demands comprehensive images of
science within the social-historical process. The function of such
images or ideas of science includes that they are not merely
conceptions of knowledge pure and simple but that they rather
contain an image of man as an important point of reference. This
is very distinct in the educational theories of the early 19th
century. Something else becomes evident as well: the underlying
image of man can apparently not be separated from
social-theoretical conceptions. Whether the demand for a general
and universal education is deduced from a notion of human freedom
or from the insight into the dynamics and complex involvement of
social development, both arguments are reflexions of two
sides of one and the same state of facts. Education is thus
revealed as an important field in which the very connection
between epistemology and social theory becomes operative, which we

supposed above to be characteristic for the newly emerging
rationality type.

The pre-occupation with education did not constitute the sole
point of reference for reflexions on the unity and
coherence of knowledge, (the 'speculative', as it was called
in German philosophy). Natural philosophy or French Positivism
must surely be analysed in a wider context. We tried to
imply this above by giving equal status to the terms 'education',
'culture', and 'civilization'. In Germany, for instance, people
were definitely aware of the fact that here the demand for a
general education system was of more immediate interest for
social development than, say, in England where the function of
establishing a conscious connection between different social
activities was excercised by an active civic public. On the other
hand, one must realize (and this leads back to the basic problem
of the new rationality type) that after the introduction of points
of reference like 'education', the problem of the coherence of
knowledge was no longer discussed on a metahistoric level related
to the absolute, but was qualified with reference to the
social-historic context. As against the antinomy of purely
object-related or purely subject-related classifications of the
sciences there emerges a real basis and a real point of reference
for intermediate positions in which subject and object related
principles of classification can complementarily "co-exist".

2.
Education is orientated not so much towards the mere acquisition
of knowledge as towards a distinction of a relationship or an
attitude towards knowledge. Such an education leads to the result
that beside the reflexion on the coherence of knowledge a second
aspect is strongly emphasized and made explicit: the aspect of
form. 'Form', after all, means nothing but the relations the
social individual may establish to knowledge, the way knowledge is
represented or taken on by an individual. For the reflexion on the
forms of knowledge, on 'formal education', the early 19th century's
educational thinking was an important driving power which promoted
methodological reflexion. In Gemany this is true for more or less
all academic disciplines from older philologies to mathematics.
Essentially, the more comprehensive reflexion on the forms of

knowledge amounts to a greater awareness of the means and
methods of scientific research and of the representation of
knowledge; it implies a more profound contemplation of the
status of theoretical knowledge. In this respect, the
'methodolization' stimulated by educational thinking constitutes
an essential aspect in the process of the 'theorization of
knowledge', which is pointed out as characteristic for the early
19th century (in various contributions to this volume).

The process of theorization of knowledge, insofar as it goes with
a greater explication of the formal aspect and a higher awareness
of form, naturally had the most lasting consequences for
mathematics. This becomes evident already in the early 19th
century from the fact that mathematics was (apart from chemistry)
the one science that underwent the most comprehensive change of
its methods and style. In the curricular debate, the status of
mathematics was particularly controversial. There were those who
denied it any educational value at all, because they identified
this science to a large extent with a principleless practicism of
18th century science (which they opposed); on the other hand,
however, the paradigmatic role of mathematics for the process of
theorization of knowledge was particularly emphasized. In France,
this position is nearly uncontested, but in Germany, too, this
opinion was advocated by influental scholars. To name some eminent
pedagogues who in connection with the education problem attached a
central role to mathematics, there are Pestalozzi and Herbart.

The different demands made on mathematics out of the various
institutional contexts are exemplified in the works of the then
famous author of textbooks, Martin Ohm, brother of the physicist
Georg Simon Ohm. In his "Kritische Beleuchtungen der Mathematik
ueberhaupt und der Euklidischen Geometrie insbesondere" (1819) he
writes that the adherence to the one, the Euclidean method was no
longer compatible with the progress in mathematics which had been
achieved by our French neighbours in the development of analytic
geometry from their more practical point of view. At the same
time, there must not be an 'either – or question', i.e. the
alternative of either Euclidian or analytic geometry is wrongly
put. The question should rather be, "under which conditions must
the geometry of the elders be preferred and under which conditions

an analytical treatment of geometry? In this we answer. In schools, where the main objective must be a harmonic cultivation of a pupil's every talents and in which this objective is to be achieved through every subject matter pursued, the purpose would be definitely missed, if the calculus (i.e. analytic geometry) was to dominate mathematic tuition. A pupil on his lowest level of education clings only to the tangible and the school's objective must be to slowly draw him away from that, to 'elevate' him from the particular to the general" (p. 11). Euclidean geometry suits this purpose. "If, however, not the education of a human being, but rather science itself is the objective of geometrical activity ... then the calculus undoubtedly attains predominance. Science must always strive for the highest and most general standpoint and unscrupulously uses that method which admits the most effective approach to its objectives. This means is the calculus. With generality and as quick as lightning it penetrates irresistably to the holiest of holies of knowledge and often achieves in an atom of time what a study of the geometry of the elders cannot achieve in a thousand years" (pp 12f.). Ohm's statements also illustrate that the formal element of knowledge was not thought of as static codification, but that its explorative functions were viewed as pre-eminent. This is true for the methodological reflexion in the early 19th century in general.

The emphasis attached to the formal aspects is not introduced in the sense of developing standardized and fixed patterns. It is rather the plurality and variability of the forms of knowledge according to the multitude of relationships towards knowledge in society that are relevant. Thus the imparting of forms of knowledge and their transformation into one another becomes the crucial problem. In this sense, the early conceptions of the role of the formal in science and education aim more at the explorative aspect which concentrates on expanding the range of possible applications of theories. The formal is not seen as a static pattern. However, both ways of interpreting and using formalism have become effective because of the real-life development of the education systems. While in the early phase of reform a dynamic conception of formality set on expansion of the intended applications and of mediation between the various social contexts was undoubtedly predominant and operative, later formal education increasingly becomes a static interpretation aiming at social stratification and leaving the question of the applicability of knowledge aside.

In a twofold sense education is revealed as an essential driving power in the process of the theorization of knowledge: The problems of education lead on the one hand to a strengthened awareness of methodology and theory and with that to an emphasis on 'knowledge as form': 'Consciousness' as expansion of methodological reflexion. On the other hand, the problems of education set limits to this methodological reflexion inasmuch as they show that science possesses only relative independence from culture and society. Scientific knowledge is only real in the context of culture and society and if it can be related to other forms of knowledge.

Of course the problem of education is only one - if, in our opinion, essential - factor in the process called 'theorization of knowledge' here. The more general issue seems to be the independence and autonomy of the question of the applicability of scientific knowledge. Application becoming a problem in its own right is the decisive aspect of the development of science in the early 19th century. The application of theoretical knowledge does not only represent 'cognitive' or 'intellectual' achievement; it also proves full of pre-conditions and consequences in the social sense above all. The terms introduced above, 'material aspects of the field of knowledge', 'relation of knowledge and science', and 'differentiation of the epistemologic and social subject', mark dimensions which must be taken into account in a socio-historical study of the application problem.

This problem and the theorization of knowledge are closely related. This is true insofar as the application reference is connected with a greater field specification of scientific theories and methods. As opposed to universalist conceptions of the method of scientific work and non-historic conceptions of the apriori of scientific cognition the field specification and context dependence of scientific methodologies become increasingly evident. The circularity in the relationship between the formal

and the substantial, between method and subject matter, poses
problems which no longer could be solved once and for all with the
help of a great metaphysical construction. It rather emerges as a
time and context dependent problem which must be solved in
different ways according to the respective fields of science and
applications of scientific knowledge. In the course of the 19th
century epistemologies emerge which in their statement of the
problem and their method are oriented towards individual
scientific disciplines. This also means that the phenomenon of the
self-reference in the establishment of scientific theories, which
is being discussed in contemporary philosophy of science in terms
of 'theory loadedness of the observational language' or
'theoretician's dilemma' and the like, becomes a general problem
encroaching on all sciences.

3.
If our considerations up to now are related to the question of
what is really new in 19th century science, the following emerges:
Both in the field of science and in the field of education before
the 19th century, there are two streams, tendencies, or branches
which exist in relative isolation and are handed down independent
from each other. In the field of science one branch of tradition
can be characterized through the names of Bacon and Locke, the
other through that of Descartes. One branch emphasized the role of
experience and experiment and the practical usefulness of the
sciences. The other accentuated mathematical deduction and the
metaphysical, speculative construction of a 'Weltbild'. Descartes
formulated physics as geometry and criticized Galileo because the
latter believed he could have scientific generality on an
empirical-experimental basis. Accordingly, there are two
traditions in the field of education, which can be called material
and formal education respectively and which can be connected with
the names of Rabelais and Erasmus. This 'antinomic character' of
science in the 17th and 18th centuries has something to do with
the unseparable identity of the planes of philosophical and
scientific discourse. The argument between Clarke and Leibniz is
one expression of this. During this time, of course, attempts have
constantly - and especially in the 18th century (Euler, Diderot) -
been made to reconcile all occuring dichotomies. But only when in

the 19th century the philosophical meta-level of scientific knowledge gained greater distance and independence from this knowledge itself and had therefore become flexible in its relationship to the scientific plane, only then did the epistemological discussion gain new possibilities of dealing with epistemologic and methodologic questions.

This development can be demonstrated with the example of geometry itself and its changing status as subject matter and methodological basis of mathematics. In the 18th century geometry was still object and method (logics) in immediate identity. It embodied at the same time method and theory. The term 'geometric' was very often synonymous with logical, rational, and in this sense geometric truths and moral certainties were set side by side in the 'Vernunftlehre' (doctrine of reason) for instance (see Ebert 1796; Diderot 1774).

This identity had its own problems. It was ultimately connected with the 'antinomic rationality type' of that period, which in fact expressed the 'logic of mechanical motion'. "That the truths of geometry are 'necessary' in some sense which is not merely factual or experiential, and that geometry does formulate relations between properties of bodies, were two conclusions which seemed inescapable and at the same time difficult to reconcile. The various philosophies of classical rationalism, classical empiricism, and Kantianism, were alternative heroic attempts to establish some sort of uneasy balance between them. What is common to them all is the view that the geometry systematized by Euclid is the definitive science of space or extension" (Nagel 1939, p. 143). Since 1800 we find a definite and marked shift in point of view. Geometry loses its status as universal method (and the Euclidean method its status as universal logic) in the sense that theory and method gain relative independence from each other and a multitude of dialectic connections between the two develops: subject matter specification of the methodologic debate and development of the forms of knowledge in relation to the multitude of social and objective aspects and purposes.

Within the process of overcoming this 'antinomic rationality type'
Condillac's "La Logique" constitutes a first attempt to counteract
these antinomies through identifying the respective sides with one
another. In France, for instance, an identitiy of the methods of
research and of presentation in the sciences is assumed on the
basis of Condillac's "La Logique". Progress here lies undoubtedly
in the fact that the problem of the relationship of the two is
discussed in a systematic way for the first time. The further
development, however, leads to more differentiated conceptions
which assume that particularly on the basis of a systematic
distinction, the relationship of the two can become a topic for
scientific enquiry. Admittedly, this relation can no longer
be treated in the form of a universal theoretical conception, it
must be related to the social and institutional context in
question.

III. The Antinomical Character of Science Questioned – A Case
      Study on the Historiography of Chemistry

1.
The above described antinomical character of science before 1800
also appears in the main issue of science during that time, namely
the problem of 'mechanical motion', insofar as this conception is
related to the questions of space and matter, of geometric form
and substance, of kinematics and dynamics. The differences of
practical vs. rational mechanics, of experience vs. theoretical
speculation etc. can also be found here. The problem of mechanical
motion sets an archetype, inasmuch as the real logical structure
of scientific thinking in the 17th and 18th centuries was
paradigmatically determined by this problem and the conceptions
connected with it. Scientific analysis concentrating on this
problem is of general importance for the study of the history of
science, of epistemology, and of knowledge in general. It is
therefore suitable to resolve the much discussed dichotomy of
rational reconstruction vs. historical narrative (There have been
numerous attempts at analysing the problem of mechanical motion.
For the 18th century see especially Cassirer II, chapter 2;
and concerning Hamilton's conception and later that of quantum
mechanics, see Kedrov et al. 1967 or Bohm 1977, p. 383).

This splitting of the scientific and epistemologic thinking of the
'classical age' (Foucault) into two more or less independent
self-contained opposite sides is connected (since the end of the
18th century) with the names of F. Bacon and R. Descartes
respectively. The two positions are usually referred to as
Baconian vs. Cartesian science or thinking. On the other hand
these names can be regarded as representing the social and the
methodological view on science.

To show the essence of all the oppositions described above in the
sciences of the classical age, especially the controversy about
theory as opposed to common practice, it is profitable to consider
the question of the relation of knowledge to activity. This
question can be pursued in various ways. For instance, by means of
- a characterization of knowledge as complementary, both
  subjective and objective, both method and subject matter (see
  Jahnke 1978; Otte 1980), and related to that as transition from
  thinking of objects to relational thinking. This is a transition
  which, according to Cassirer's description, was in preparation
  at the end of the 18th century and which, in certain scientific
  disciplines, has been partially accomplished only today.
  (Bourdieu 1980, p. 12). Or
- as a characterization of the relationship between scientific
  knowledge and meta-knowledge (paradigms, regulative principles
  of science, philosophy) (see, e.g., Amsterdamski 1975, p. 168).
And it is this second characterization that we would like to
investigate again in part IV, because it helps to elucidate the
connection of methodological and social aspects of the development
of science.

What is of special importance in the context of this volume is the
fact that the essential identity of the different
characterizations just described was a new component in the way of
thinking in a transitional period between the 18th and 19th
centuries. Since about 1775 the differentiation and change in the
relationship of science and philosophy, of knowledge and
meta-knowledge gives the duality of Baconian vs. Cartesian
thinking a quite different quality. The eclectic, dichotomic,
or even contradictory character is transformed into newly
established relations of method and theory, of science and

philosophy. This leads to a new dynamic flexibility in many
methodological questions about the sciences and their social
organization without necessarily producing final answers to these
questions. What one should look at is a process, not a conclusion.
A process whose transitory character was expressed by a typical
clear-sightedness, heterogenous plurality and instability of that
period. In his well-known analysis "Das 18. Jahrhundert", W.v.
Humboldt characterized his own time as a transitionalory time, but
then he added: "Only he who stands in the middle between two
different epochs is a really valid witness of their transition"
(W.v. Humboldt 1969, p. 401).

2.
We will try to illustrate what was said above by describing a
study of the history of science of that time. 1803 - 1806
J.B. Trommsdorf published what is, in contemporary estimation,
the first German work on the history of chemistry "in
which the development of chemistry is treated
historically-pragmatically and in connection with the general
history of culture and of the mind" (Struwe 1965). Trommsdorf
himself characterized the specificity of his enterprise somewhat
differently. He regarded his work as the first history of
chemistry as a science. For him, the scientific character of the
historiography of the sciences resulted from that very reference
to the general development of culture and society. This demands an
overall conception of scientific development. "The fates of the
sciences depend on the spirit of the age. The common history of
scholarship and scientific culture represents the spirit in a
general way and draws only general conclusion from it. But each
science also originated from specific events, - originated, grew,
and disappeared, according to the way things went. To interpret
these events, to deduce the scientific standpoint from the related
spirit of the age, ... that is the purpose of a general history of
the science as science" (Trommsdorf 1965, preface).

First of all, however, some personal data: Johann Bartholomaeus
Trommsdorf was a pharmacist and analytical chemist. He was born in
Erfurt in 1770 and died there in 1837.
He has been praised as one who "made an end to the unscientific
character, the uncertainty, the pedantry and the charlatanism in

the house of pharmacy" and he did this by "installing scientific
chemistry as legislator" and "at the same time raising the
standard of knowledge and the whole class of his professional
colleagues to a higher level". In 1794 he founded the Journal of
Pharmacy. "The first pharmaceutic journal in the world soon became
the meeting place of all scientific endeavours in the field of
pharmaceutic sciences.... When, in 1834, he retired from
editorship it was no less a person than Justus Liebig who, in his
Annals of Pharmacy, created a worthy continuation of the Journal."
The Annals of Chemistry later emerged from Liebig's Annals.
Trommsdorf is said to have written 160 books, many of them
"textbooks and handbooks of the highest scientific standard". As
early as 1795 "he, with his own means and in his own house,
established a pharmaceutical education institute" out of which
came "in the course of 33 years no less than 300 capable students
who later became apothecaries, doctors, professors, and
manifacturers." His private initiatives for practical laboratory
training of analytical chemists, which were later systematically
developed by Liebig into a training method that has become famous
all over the world, were unique in contemporary Prussia (Heinig,
p. 105). In the first edition of the Brockhaus Encyclopaedia of
1837/41 the fact is still praised that he, after having closed his
pharmaceutical teaching institute in 1828, continued to provide
"tuition in chemistry, physics and technology for the tradespeople
of Erfurt free of charge". In 1813 he founded one of the first
pharmaceutical factories, which "grew rapidly and became the
ancestor of the famous Trommsdorf Factory in Erfurt". Trommsdorf
also received many honours during his life time. Since 1823 he was
director of the Royal Academy of Utilitarian Sciences in Erfurt
and since 1834 he was Secret Privy Counsellor (Quotations are
from the articles under the respective entries in "Allgemeine
deutsche Biographie 1894"; "Brockhaus-Enzyclopaedie" 1837 –
1847, 1. ed.; and the "Allgemeines Konversationslexikon" of
1838.)
Trommsdorf develops the history of chemistry on the basis of a
productive use of the circular connection of knowledge and
meta-knowledge. On the one hand he states that "the change of the
course of the sciences had to start from an improvement of
philosophy, an assessment of tenable principles ...; the
revolutions in the history of science have always evolved from the

alteration of the prime foundations of thinking ..." (part II,
p. 58). On the other hand he simultanuously uses chemistry as a
yardstick for philosophical (methodologic and epistemologic)
systems and programs. He stresses again and again that in this
sense philosophy is an auxiliary science. Still, "the period of
those 'who thought for themselves' ("Selbstdenker") should not be
replaced by the period of the 'observers', the wholesome use of
reason - wherever there are truths - must not be neglected while
its infinite strivings were to be kept in reins" (part III,
pp. 193f.). As this circle cannot be broken by speculations, all
aspects of the 'antinomical character of the Cartesian rationality
type' are important for Trommsdorf's history of chemistry. Above
all, the theory-practice problem: chemistry develops with the
extension of the range of its applications from alchemistic
experiments to medicine, metallurgy, the mining industry, and
finally agriculture, and trade. But he sees this relationship
quite dialectically. The too-close link with medicine, for
instance, also hindered chemistry, because it was continually
drawn into the argument of the quacks and because the
manufacturers of medicines were more set on filling apothecary's
purses. Only when chemistry had ceased to be the 'girl servant'
of pharmacy and metallurgy did it become a science in the true
sense.

As already mentioned, the problem of the antinomical character of
science runs through Trommsdorf's entire history of chemistry and
is connected with the names of Descartes and Bacon. Both strove to
reach the same objective, but "what Bacon solved in the realm of
reality, Descartes tried to establish by fixed points in the realm
of possibility. - The philosophy of the latter is no method for
the practicioner, as the rules of the practicioner could not be
taken for the theorist's final principles" (part II, p. 62). Both
of them for Trommsdorf are really great geniuses who cannot be
explained from their time. "Bacon's writings were not produced by
his age, he was the teacher of his age who drew from his own
genius and disdained the teaching of his contemporaries." As
Trommdorf sees it, both ways have the following features:
eclecticism vs. systematic character; practice vs. theory; the
dangers of empirical superficiality vs. the dangers of theorizing

speculation; induction vs. deduction; apodictic and antididactic explanations vs. systematical ones. For the one system, man is no more than a chemical stove, for the other a mechanical edifice or a hydraulic machine (at least before 1720).

The antinomical character is on the one hand connected with the relationship of natural sciences and philosophical meta-knowledge. On the other hand it is reflected in chemistry itself which ultimately connects the development of chemistry to the development of the philosophical meta-systems.
Another important point which historically places Trommsdorf within his time is the emphasis on the fundamental hierarchical unity of the sciences. The interdisciplinary coherence of the sciences is necessary in order to regulate the relationship between knowledge and meta-knowledge in a reasonable way. that is why progress in physics, which had been much more thoroughly considered by philosophers, was of such great importance to him. Newton's achievement, too, is seen within the framework set up by the names of Bacon and Descartes and is above all estimated as an important help in overcoming the antinomical character of the spirit of that time in its effect on chemistry. "There is no part of the natural sciences which could exist in isolation; all must rise towards the philosophy of nature and from there obtain the attestation of a common origin. Progress in chemistry begins with the time of Lavoisier, for since that time the attitude towards chemical studies altered. This science has been more intimately linked with the other natural sciences and has been philosophically developed in all its parts. ... The critical method of philosophical thinking (especially Kant; author's interpolation) will not be ousted by a hyper-critical one: the path which has also been opened for chemistry by the latest revolutions in philosophical thinking gives us hope for the most productive consequences for chemistry and physics and after a thorough revision of its laws, science will not strive against philosophically based innovation, if it is of the modest kind and does not threaten to devour science, and dictate the laws of nature from the lecturing-desk ..." It becomes obvious that "a philosophical consideration of theory coupled with profound practical knowledge is spreading, to the advantage of

science ... Excellent hints for the treatment of natural science
came from Schelling's philosophy, and when the heat of the newer
ones has burnt itself out, when sectarian antagonism has
transformed into peaceful community for really scientific purposes
and when the good and useful, purified from over-hasty application
to things for which it is not meant becomes adequately effective,
only then will the new natural philosophy show itself worthy of a
grateful remembrance within the history of chemistry" (part III,
pp. 133-140).

Trommsdorf's book contains numerous and very differentiated
opinions of the influence of the state, of economy, of the
education system, of communicative techniques etc., on scientific
development. Education, for instance, became a progressive element
for Trommsdorf only when letterpress printing was available to a
greater extend. "In all the European countries, scientific
education raised its prestige [during his time] and the
collective strength of scholarly education had found a common
point in the widespread book trade, which put an end to all
useless rovings on already better used roads" (part III, p. 59).
On the other hand, the first great teacher of chemistry, Sylvius
(1614-1672), who was said to be one of the most eminent physicians
of his time and who had just opened the medical field of
application for chemistry, was still remarked upon as follows: "It
was a new way of shaking science, but not always the better way
which from now on was trodden by several people who wished to win
effect and prestige [through lecturing; the author]. ... it sets
up unchecked authorities, chooses young men as admirers, and
brandishes the flag of the sect amongst an easily inflammable
crowd." Thus Sylvius had, according to Trommsdorf, inherited from
the philosophy of Descartes the mind for innovations and the mania
for hypotheses, and he supported his innovations with the power of
his eloquence. His system had to win from the lecturing-desk, had
to convince by oral communication; he seems to have known the
defects of his system. Therefore he was not inclined to publish
his writings and what did appear publicly was printed without his
permission and he often resisted this only way of reaching
certainty and inviting the acumen of the observers, because he
feared to fall victim to doubt" (part II, pp. 88f.).

xxxiv H. N. JAHNKE ET AL.

From the point of view of today's concept of science Trommsdorf can be seen as a typical as well as a transitional phenomenon difficult to assess. If his work is compared either to its immediate antecedents - e.g. J.F. Gmelin's "Geschichte der Chemie" of 1797/99 - or to its not-too-distant successors - e.g. "Entwicklungsgeschichte der Chemie" by A. Ladenburg, 1st edition 1869, 4th edition 1907 - then one gets the impression of a suddenly erupting clear-sighted awareness, which seems to have quickly faded and was forgotten. Already around the middle of the 19th century a change occurred in the relationship of science and philosophy (meta-knowledge). Accordingly, Ladenburg's purely descriptive history of ideas in chemistry no longer even contains the name of Trommsdorf; even though H. Kopp (1817-1892) is supposed to have continued Trommsdorf's conception of history in his famous four volumes of "Geschichte der Chemie" (1843/47).

IV. The Present Relevance of the Considered Period: The Concept of
    'Rationality Type'

1.
In the following, we will try to further develop the relationship between methodological and social aspects of science with the help of the circular relation of knowledge and meta-knowledge.

As long as science is only understood as a form of knowledge or portrait of the world, no rational reconstruction of the process of scientific development evolves. The 'theorization of knowledge' is determined by methodology and its respective limitations, by the limits to the awareness of the scientific process (a limit to explication, to codification, to formalization, to operationalization etc.). In other words, foundational problems in the sciences, if treated in a manner independent of time, always lead to contradictions, paradoxes, or to the problem of infinite regress. Questions of foundation and development of science are therefore inseparably connected. "The regulatory principles deriving from philosophy are considered at one point as the product of the evolution of cognition, and at another as its indispensable condition. ... If knowledge without presuppositions is impossible - since in our opinion it is not

provided either by experience or by the mind - then how is the evolution of knowledge, founded on the systematic criticism of its own assumptions, possible?
I can see no other answer to this question then ... - that our knowledge never constitutes a closed and coherent system. It would be a closed system if, in the first place, all the assumptions actually accepted at a given moment were accepted explicitly and, secondly, if the criticism of these assumptions itself was possible without any assumptions. It would constitute a coherent system if all the (implicitly and explicitly) accepted assumptions were noncontradictory. In the light of Goedel's theorem, we know that even a mathematical system of knowledge cannot escape incompleteness and internal contradiction" (Amsterdamski 1975, p. 175).

As a second decisive problem, however, there remains the question of how the historic dynamics itself is conceived, from where it is given structure and substance, how the circular self-reference of scientific knowledge can be related to the evolutionary process and the dynamics of this process. Although one could in a very general, methodological way describe the problem of closed loops mentioned above as a paradox of subsystem vs. system relation, this is not sufficient. Not only is the real historical dynamic an essential aspect of every scientific knowledge, but the process/structure dialectic involved asks for a description of that dynamic which is specific to the object field. In this respect the cognitive interests of the various disciplines concerned with knowledge differ. Artificial Intelligence (AI) refers to the function mechanisms of neurons and of hardware (see Hofstadter). Epistemology refers to the principal importance of physics or of formal logics, sociology and historiography of science refers to tools, means of communication and social institutions or other so-called 'permanent elements'. Last but not least, the history of ideas may refer to certain key words or 'key concepts' and their transformation in history or stress their corresponding to the most universal properties of things. Only the fact that the individual disciplines in their specific ways reduce the relationship of structure and process to a 'point of balance' elucidates the fact that the patterns, the texts, the theories can retain an explorative and anticipatory beside their descriptive function (cf. part II). Naturally, every such 'point of balance' refers somewhere to the physical or the social field and thus, in the final analysis, to the relation between these two fields. Every methodological analysis of the process of scientific development must therefore also include the differentiations and developments of the epistemological and social subject (confer in contrast to this Turchin 1977, p. 320).

2.

Of course it depends on the theoretical basis of reduction, on the projection of the theme on this basis, on the methodological orientation, on the scientific-historic subject etc., whether the early 19th century is regarded as the perfection of the type of rationality of the 17th century scientific revolution, or as the beginning of a new rationality type, which is often supposed to become fully visible in the writings of Planck, Einstein, Bohr, and Heisenberg.

In any case, at the beginning of the 19th century there is not only the (in part I. described) multitude of characteristics and epiphenomena of a situation changed in detail as compared with the 18th century that is to be noted. The antinomical rationality type established by the scientific revolution of the 17th century entered the consciousness of the period itself in various ways.

To illustrate this we come back to the development of mathematics (Goedel's theorem, Russell's theory of types, Zeno's paradoxes etc.). Paradoxes and vicious circles have "interested philosophers of all periods, but until the middle of the nineteenth century the paradoxes were almost always regarded as mere sophisms which could be removed with little trouble. In the last hundred years they have been taken very seriously", and have moved to the status "of the very source of mathematics itself" (Salmon 1970, p. 8; Wilden 1972, p. 124). Concerning the 18th and 19th centuries, the development of geometry shows this most distinctly. But the described 'circularity' becomes essential only when the question of the application of scientific knowledge grows into a central problem. Explicitness, explicating theories into coherent systems, and the limitations of such an endeavour, become important only where problems of co-operation are involved. We therefore take the seriousness with which paradoxes have been treated in mathematics as an expression of the question: 'How can mathematics develop as a science and as such gain the status of an instrument of society and social practice in general?'

To analyse questions of the historic development of the sciences and of the rationality type in the different historical periods and thereby to point to the tangled hierarchies of knowledge (as has been done above) means to point out this problem; there are social and objective reasons for this as well.

An individual may act intuitively and without regard to rules, but in order to 'organize' social activity as a whole one needs rules, and then rules on a higher level to justify the rules and then rules ...(see above). As Durkheim puts it, society is "the consciousness of the consciousnesses. Being placed outside of and above individual and local contingencies, society sees things only in their permanent and essential aspects, which it crystallizes into communicable ideas. At the same time that it sees from above, it sees farther; at every moment in time, it embraces all known reality; that is why it alone can furnish the mind with the moulds that are applicable to the totality of things and which make it possible to think of them. It does not create these moulds artificially; it finds them within itself; it does nothing but become conscious of them.

Attributing social origins to logical thought is not debasing it or diminishing its value or reducing it to nothing more than a system of artificial combinations; on the contrary, it is relating it to a course which implies it naturally. But this is not saying that the ideas elaborated in this way are at once adequate for their object. If society is something universal in relation to the individual, it is nonetheless an individuality itself, which has its own personal physiognomy and its idiosyncrasies; ... Therefore collective representations also contain subjective elements, and these must be progressively rooted out, if we are to approach reality more closely" (Durkheim 1965, pp. 492f.).

As already mentioned, the aspect of "consciousness of the consciousnesses" plays a prominent role, especially in societies which are behind their time, because explicitness fulfills anticipatory functions. Some objections might be raised against the connection we see between science and application: the emergence of 'pure' science at the beginning of the 19th century; the influence of German Idealism on the 'self-conception' of the sciences; the then current polemics against the 'utilitarianism of Enlightenment' etc.. We believe, however, that these objections should rather be seen as evidence in favour of our proposition, and not as counterarguments. There is hardly any scientist of that period insisting on the independence of 'pure' science who neglects to point out that its applications will benefit from this very fact. The historical facts summed up in the following quotation may therefore receive a new and different interpretation: "It is, however, unmistakable that the often cited underdeveloped state of Germany in this time is not least documented by the fact that 'here science was still allowed to interpret itself chiefly from the perspective of speculative philosophy, as pure science'. It is against this background that the neo-humanistic thought of 'universal human education' – finally formulated by Humboldt and based in Idealism – which, merging with the ideas of idealistic philosophy, becomes the 'idea of an education through science'. This idea becomes institutionalized in the new type of university. This idealist idea of education and the idealist concept of science are the decisive image from the institutionalization of which results the separation of 'pure' science and practice-related technology" (P. Weingart 1976, pp. 118f.). J.v. Liebig formulated the objective in correlation to this: "A really scientific instruction should impart ability and susceptibility of each and every application, and with the knowledge of the principles and laws the applications are easy, they simply follow. Nothing is more disadvantageous and harmful as when materialism or the principles of usefulness take root in an educational institution ..." (quoted after Weingart 1976, p. 121).

Application-mindedness is incompatible with a science that is based on pre-established, fixed, invariable principles guarding the determination of its object. Rather, the very foundations of science must be conceived as 'variables', because they are inseparably linked with the applications. Theories, then, represent dynamic models. They do not depict their objects comprehensively and as such, they rather introduce 'limits' to the scope of 'application' of a theory. Theories are never models of

the universe as a whole. This means that, beside the congruence of
theory and reality, the difference between the two becomes a
constitutive factor for the concept of theory. This entails no
effacement of the object reference but rather the necessity to
reflect continuously and manipulate this reference. In this
respect, the epistemology of modern science at the beginning of
the 19th century (in Germany), rooted in the tangled hierarchies
of empirical claims, theoretical knowledge, and meta-knowledge, is
essentially new compared to the irresolvable eighteenth-century
antinomy of rationalism and empiricism. The separaton of 'pure'
and 'applied' sciences is the organizational expression of this
development in its social and objective aspects.

3.
Here we would like to recapitulate the problems elaborated on in
the form of a definition that does justice to the
interdisciplinary character of scientific-historical study as well
as to the particular relevance of the period which is considered
in all contributions to this volume. We use the, repeatedly
informally used, above concept of the "rationality type of a
historic epoch". This concept appears with various authors under
different terminologic names (cf. Amsterdamski 1975, pp. 168–176;
Churchman 1968; 'Man, Science, Technology' 1973, pp. 297; Zeleny
1974, p. 371). A "rationality type' is defined in terms of the
following three dimensions:
a) the assumed ontological structure of reality or the ontology of
   the body of knowledge belonging to the given rationality type;
   the basic set of categories and methodologies;
b) the conception and nature of the theory-practice relation; the
   forms of social practice reflected in the given rationality
   type; and
c) the nature of the relation of descriptive vs. evaluative
   propositions, of factual statements and value judgements.

We believe to be justified when, in conclusion, we describe a
category which has not been elaborated in detail, but which seems
to reflect something like a collective experience of the science
of sciences.

References

Amsterdamski, S.:   Between Experience and Metaphysics, Boston
                           Studies   in   the   Philosophy of Science, Vol.
                           XXXV, Dordrecht, Boston 1975
Bohm, D.:   Science   as   Perception-Communication, in:
                           Suppe, F. (ed.): The Structure of scientific
                           Theories, Urbana 1977, 2d ed., Session IV
Bourdieu, P.:   Le sens practique, Paris 1980
Bourdieu, P.:   The Specificity of the Scientific Field and
                           the Social Conditions of the Progress of
                           Reason, in: Soc. sci. inform 14 (1975),
                           pp. 19-47
Cassirer, E.:   Das Erkenntnisproblem in der Philosophie und
                           Wissenschaft der neueren Zeit, vol. II, Darm-
                           stadt 1971, and vol. IV, Stuttgart 1957
Churchman, C.W.:   Challenge to Reason, New York 1968
Diderot, D.:   Bildungsplan fuer die Regierung von Russland
                           (1774/75), Weinheim, Berlin, Basel 1971
Durkheim, E.:   The Elementary Forms of the Religious Life,
                           New York 1965
Ebert, J.J.:   Unterweisung   in   den   philosophischen und
                           mathematischen Wissenschaften, Leipzig 1796
                           4th ed. (5th ed. 1810)
Foucault, M.:   The Archaeology of Knowledge, London 1972
Foucault, M.:   Les mots et les choses, Paris 1966 (engl.:
                           Order of Things. An Archaeology of the Human
                           Sciences, New York 1970)
Foucault, M.:   The Political Function of the Intellectual,
                           in: Radical Philosophy 17 (1977), pp. 12-14
Goedel, K.:   Ueber   formal   unentscheidbare Saetze der
                           Principia Mathematica und verwandter Systeme
                           I, in: Monatshefte fuer Mathematik und Physik
                           38 (1931), pp. 173-198
Harnack, A.:   Geschichte   der   Koeniglich   Preussischen
                           Akademie der Wissenschaften zu Berlin,
                           3 vols., Berlin 1900

Heinig, K. (ed.):		Biographien bedeutender Chemiker, Berlin 1970

Hofstadter, D.R.:		Goedel, Escher, Bach, Hassocks 1979

Humboldt, W.v.:		Das 18. Jahrhundert, in: Gesammelte Werke, vol. I, Darmstadt 1969

Jahnke, H.N.:		Zum Verhaeltnis von Wissensentwicklung und Begruendung in der Mathematik – Beweisen als didaktisches Problem, Bielefeld 1978 (Materialen und Studien, vol. 10) (Diss.)

Kedrov, B.M. et al.:	Analyse des sich entwickelnden Begriffs, Moskau 1967

Klein, F.			Vorlesungen ueber die Entwicklung der Mathematik im 19. Jahrhundert, part 1 a. 2, Heidelberg 1979 (Repr. Berlin 1926f.)

Kopp, H.:			Geschichte der Chemie, Hildesheim 1966 (Repr. Braunschweig' 1843)

Lepenies, W.:		Das Ende der Naturgeschichte, Frankfurt/Main 1978

Man, Science, Technology. A Marxist Analysis of the Scientific-Technological Revolution, Moscow 1973

Mendelsohn, E.:		The Continuous and the Discrete in the History of Science. Lecture held November 21, 1978 in the Center for Interdisciplinary Research, Bielefeld (unpubl. manuscript)

Nagel, E.:			The Formation of Modern Conceptions of Formal Logic in the Development of Geometry, in: Osiris 7 (1939), pp. 142–224

Ohm, M.:			Kritische Beleuchtungen der Mathematik, Berlin 1819

Otte, M.:			On the Question of the Development of theoretical concepts, in: Communication & Cognition 13 (1980), pp. 63–76

Paul, M.:			Gaspard Monges "Geometrie Descriptive" und die Ecole Polytechnique – Eine Fallstudie ueber den Zusammenhang von Wissenschafts- und Bildungsprozess, Bielefeld 1980 (Diss.)

Russell, B.:		Mathematical Logic as based on the Theory of Types, in: American Journal of Mathematics 30 (1908)

Sadovsky, V.N.:   Probleme einer allgemeinen Systemtheorie als
                       einer Metatheorie, in: Ratio 16 (1974),
                       pp. 29-45

Salmon, W.C.:   Zeno's Paradoxes, Indianapolis, New York
                       1970

Schelling, F.W.J.:   Vorlesungen ueber die Methode des
                       akademischen Studiums (1803), in: Anrich, E.
                       (ed.): Die Idee der Deutschen Universitaet,
                       Darmstadt 1964, pp. 1-217

Stegmueller, W.:   Theorienstrukturen und Theoriendynamik,
                       Probleme und Resultate der
                       Wissenschaftstheorie und analytischen
                       Philosophie, vol. II/2, Berlin 1973

Stegmueller, W.:   Theorie und Erfahrung, Problem und Resultate
                       der Wissenschaftstheorie und Analytischen
                       Philosophie, vol. II/1, Berlin 1970

Struwe, W.:   Vorwort zum Nachdruck, in: Trommsdorf (1965)

Trommsdorf, J.B.:   Versuch einer allgemeinen Geschichte der
                       Chemie, Leipzig 1965 (Repr. Erfurt 1806)

Tuomela, R.:   Theoretical Concepts, Wien, New York 1973

Turchin, V.F.:   The Phenomenon of Science, New York 1977

Weingart, P.:   Wissensproduktion und soziale Struktur,
                       Frankfurt/Main 1976

Wilden, A.:   System and Structure, London 1972

Williams, R.:   Culture and Society 1780 - 1950,
                       Harmondsworth 1977

Zeleny, J.:   Kant, Marx and the Modern Rationality, in:
                       Boston Studies in the Philosophy of Science,
                       Vol. XIV (1974), pp. 361-376

I

SCIENCE AROUND 1800

COGNITIVE AND SOCIAL CHANGE

Michael Heidelberger

SOME PATTERNS OF CHANGE IN THE BACONIAN SCIENCES OF THE EARLY 19TH
CENTURY GERMANY

Gillispie once made the remark that the Encyclopedists boasted of
having liberated science from metaphysics and that the generation
succeeding them after the French revolution completed this
emancipation by taking away from science even ontology – and not
only that; any claim to grasp reality beyond controlled
observation, experience and experiment became utterly impossible.[1]
For the generation of the philosophes science still was the source
of gaining knowledge of the objective reality and, in turn, this
knowledge was taken as the source for the enlightened perfection
of man. In the postrevolutionary phase no effort was spared to
make the sciences the dynamic motor of human history and social
development. The claims that science gains knowledge in the old
sense of the word are becoming to be forgotten, sometimes they are
redefined and often even negated. The ideal of an enlightenment
through knowledge and cognition undergoes a profound change and it
turns into the vision of progress by prediction and control. This
redefinition of the task of science is a direct result of the
French revolution.

In France, this change manifests itself as a relatively marked
rupture. The new point of view came into force through the
foundation of novel institutions and through the abolishment of
old ones as well as in the subordination of the sciences and their
representatives under the pedagogical aims of the state.

3

H. N. Jahnke and M. Otte (eds.), Epistemological and Social Problems of the Sciences in the Early Nineteenth
Century, 3–18.
Copyright © 1981 by D. Reidel Publishing Company.

In Germany, Prussia, no doubt, had the strongest intention of all nations to imitate and to even excel the French model. After the battle of Jena, Friedrich Wilhelm III declared that the state had to make up with mental power for the loss in physical one.[2]

Between 1825 and 1836 polytechnical schools and Technische Hochschulen were founded according to the model of the Parisian école polytechnique of 1794 in almost all the German states.[3] But for several reasons the vision of progress could not find expression in Germany as distinct and as quick as in France. Still, the universities set the intellectual standards. The peculiar German ideal of Wissenschaft again was brought home and programmatically formulated, though in a reformed way, through the foundation of the Berlin university in 1810 and also to some extent of the university of Bonn in 1818. Only with great reservations one could say that the German ideal of Wissenschaft is determined by the enlightenment in one way or other. But one can say unreservedly that originally it had nothing to do with the vision of progress as advocated by the French revolution.

Now, one could make the objection that science is science whether it serves enlightenment or philosophical idealism, whether the national state or technocracy. And one could further say that the backward state of science in Germany compared to France was not caused by slow and hesitating implementation of the revolutionary vision; rather that the pernicious influence of the Naturphilosophie of Schelling and others is responsible for that. According to a popular topos in historiography the few real scientists were virtually starved. True science was not promoted. Instead, philosophers could freely persue their pseudoscience creating nature out of concepts in a most speculative way while disdaining observation and experiment.[4] Only after Alexander von Humboldt's return to Berlin in 1827 and with Hegel's death in 1831 the nightmare was over and the few genuine scientists who were left could presume their work It is regarded as a curious and happy coincidence that there were some Naturphilosophen who contributed to 'real' science, as Ritter, Oersted, J.R. Mayer and others.

A closer look seems to suggest that during the reign of Naturphilosophie the difference between the 'few genuine scientists' and their naturphilosophischen counterparts was not very great if one compares the norms, methods, and values which guided their scientific work. I do not deny that there is a great deal of difference between the contents of the views they actually asserted about nature nd its phenomena.

I wish to argue that the most important change of science in the first half of the 19th century Germany is not to be described as liberation of science from the yoke of Naturphilosophie. Rather, both Naturphilosophie as well as its alleged genuine counterpart had to be transformed jointly. This transformation takes place when the theoretical method of French science, as I sketched it in the beginning, comes to be recognized.

But what about Leibniz and Euler, Tobias Mayer and the Bernoullis? Did not they start or continue to make science theoretical in Germany before the French revolution? This is certainly true but their theoretical accomplishment is not related to the realm counted as Naturlehre in Germany. It is rather concerned with rational mechanics and their theoretical offshoot in mathematical astronomy, geometrical optics, theoretical hydrodynamics and so on - all sciences which were called 'applied mathematics' and which were often regarded as a priori sciences.[5] In the same way as geometry is a science a priori mechanics for Kant is a science which determines the properties of time synthetically a priori. The history of these applied mathematical sciences went on in a different way from the history which I am concerned with here. My remarks refer to those sciences which then counted as sciences synthetically a posteriori, as Naturlehre. This class of sciences agrees well with what Kuhn calls the 'Baconian sciences'.[6]

In the beginning I characterized rather briefly the theoretical turn of the sciences as it took place in France by its most important cause and its most important consequence. For the German development I would like to go further into detail and to show the constitutive elements of the Baconian sciences and how they changed. If I concentrate on the cognitive aspect of this change and if I refer only very indirectly to the social aspects of this change then this is not to be taken programmatically.

As my main example of a Baconian science I choose the science of electricity which was especially popular in the early 19th century Germany. I would like to deal with Georg Simon Ohm (1789-1854) and the way in which he made electrical science theoretical. With his little book of 1827 Die galvanische Kette, mathematisch bearbeitet and other short contributions from about the same time electrical science started to undergo a theoretical change which is in many ways typical for the Baconian sciences in general.

1. Change in Ontology

At the beginning of this paper I mentioned a remark by Gillispie that the French revolution has taken away even ontology from science. By an ontology let us understand the sets of those entities whose existence are stipulated by the theory. Then there were two ontologies prevalent in the electrical theory before Ohm: on the one hand the atomistic one according to which electricity consists of finest imponderable corpuscles which act on each other by central forces at a distance, and on the other hand the dynamistic conception of romantic Naturphilosophie that conceives electricity as the interaction of pure forces and energies. Both conceptions have in common that they reduce the electrical phenomena to one or more entities which themselves rest unexplained. This way of reduction belongs, as so many things, to the vast stream of Newtonian tradition. In this way, Newton explained chemical affinity by forces acting at a distance between corpuscles without being able, to his very regret, to arrive at a final and unequivocal causal explanation of these forces. One can immediately see how the atomistically oriented scientists employed this mode of halfway explanation, so to speak, to electricity. But the dynamical view can in this respect also be subsumed under the Newtonian tradition. In the same way it was very common among the French physiologists of the 18th century while explicitly referring to Newtons method to reduce the phenomena of life to a vital force or to a similar attribute, principle or energy without giving a further cause or explanation of these forces.[7]

This was not the only thing the two groups of scientists had in common. They both were convinced that it was not a mere way of hypothesising when one talked about the entities (atoms, resp. forces) underlying the electrical phenomena. Rather, the entity was taken as a principle whose existence is unequivocally demonstrated by known phenomena. However, the real nature, the essence, of the entity was left open. But one was convinced, much the same way as Newton with his gravitational force, that in not a too distant future conclusive experiments will make evident the essence and the cause of these principles.

Ohm, on the other hand, went along the lines of Fourier's Théorie analytique de la chaleur of 1822 which one could almost regard as the manifesto of the abandonment of ontology by French science. An often cited quotation goes like this: "The truth of these equations is not founded on any physical explanation of the effects of heat. In whatever manner we please to imagine the nature of this element, whether we regard it as a distinct material thing which passes from one part of space to another, or whether we make heat consist simply in the transfer of motion, we shall always arrive at the same equations, since the hypothesis we form must represent the general and simple facts from which the mathematical laws are derived."[8]

One could say almost the same words about Ohm's work. Ohm's theory on electricity does neither deal with corpuscles nor with forces as its primary entities, i.e. its ontology. Instead, Ohm deals with the phenomena of the distribution of electricity in the electric circuit, that is, with measurable effects only. Ohm's theory is also completely neutral in respect to the then very prevalent controversy over the origin of the electromotive force, whether it is to be explained in chemical terms or by the contact theory of Volta. In 1841, the Royal Society put a lot of stress on this neutrality[9] when it awarded the Copley medal to Ohm. By this, it enabled Wheatstone and Daniell who tended to the chemical hypothesis to make use of Ohm's theory in their practical work in spite of the fact that some Germans claimed Ohm's theory for the Voltaic hypothesis.

2. Change in the Standards of Theory Formation

The conception of the ontology of a scientific theory changed simultaneously with the criteria by which one evaluated the quality of a scientific theory. Naturphilosophen as well as their contemporary counterparts were united in the opinion that a theory can be valuable only if it establishes a connection between the actual observable phenomena and the basic underlying entities in an anschaulich (intuitive) way. In this sense, theory is only a provisional aid to give man an empirical intuition (empirische Anschauung, in Kant's sense) of a domain which is not yet directly intuitive. Accordingly, Johann Salomo Christoph Schweigger for example, physicist and editor of an important science journal, wrote in 1828: "Any theory ... basically has no other purpose than to comprise the known phenomena under one single point of view which makes it possible to delightfully contemplate [beschauen] ... them." [10]

Naturphilosophen and their counterparts – Schweigger was one of them – agreed together that any element in theory formation which does not increase the Anschaulichkeit (intuitive clarity) has to be abandoned. Since according to Kant a mathematical construction yields only the forms of intuition, that is, of sensual perception, it can never be origin of the content of the empirical intuition. But this should be the foremost subject of the natural sciences as far as they are a posteriori! The Naturphilosoph, physicist and mathematician Georg Friedrich Pohl, who reviewed new scientific books in a literary journal coedited by Hegel, wrote about Ohm's book: "The claim that only mathematics is the way to a clear intuition of the physical phenomena is equal to the claim that the evaluation and the understanding of a painting has to start with the knowledge of the chemical and technical nature of the pigments which constitute the work of art." [11]

The alternative to the mathematical way is envisaged by Pohl in the "thorough training of a genuine concentrated intuition".[11] Similarly, the physicist Christoph Heinrich Pfaff who, as an adversary of Naturphilosophie, was in continuous quarrel with Pohl over electrical matters, came to the same conclusion: "Physical explanation ... penetrates further than ... a mathematical explanation. Physical explanation strives to exhibit the phenomena in their great general connection with the whole life of nature and it attempts to render an account of the qualitative aspect in the appearences by tying even higher the given data which are the basis for mathematical construction to the Wesen [essence] of the natural forces."[12]

As much as the Naturforscher (inquirers of nature) agreed in the beginning of the 19th century that knowledge of nature can never be reached through mathematics, as much they become discordant over the question what ultimately can count as clear intuition of the qualitative. Everyone tried to achieve an experimentum crucis, a Fundamentalversuch (fundamental test) which could intuitively clear up the true nature of electricity with one stroke and which could confirm the theory by making it superfluous. But as Schweigger complains in continuation of the quote above: "If now a great many phenomena appear this will lead to the formation of new groups and therefore new points of view, i.e. new theories, will come up automatically."[13]

The accepted method brought about an increasing inflation of perceptions and intuitions without reducing the complexity of the appearences anymore. In electrical theory, Ohm was the first one who just brushed aside this muddled situation. Having a solid mathematical background at his disposal he was clear on it from the start that "any theory of a class of natural phenomena which is based on facts and which in its form of representation can not bear mathematical completeness of detail is imperfect."[14] Instead of giving a solution of the topical problems Ohm simply ignores them. His axiomatical and analytical treatment of the galvanic circuit is a completely new way of theorising which 'drains' the treated domain of all its intuitive content, so to speak. Both groups, Naturphilosophen and their adversaries, not in accordance what can ultimately count as intuitive agreed together

nevertheless that the analogous transformation of Fourier's theory
of heat conduction to the conduction of electricity is in no way
intuitive and therefore to be regarded as bad physics. The
abstract model which underlies Ohm's theory is regarded as
genuinly hypothetical as distinguished from the basic conceptions
of its predecessors. It is not at issue whether the idealised
entities as they are described by the model actually exist or not.
As soon as the theory has been developed one can free oneself of
all models without loosing anything of the theory's content
proper. In contradistinction, grasp of theory always means
intuitive grasp of the primary conception, whether this follows
atomistic or naturphilosophisch - dynamistic lines. According to
the new theoretical physics any conception whatsoever is allowed
as a hypothetical instrument as long as it is a construirbare
Vorstellung [constructible conception], to use a famous word of
Gauss,[15] irrelevant of the question whether it can be grasped
intuitively or not.

3. Change in the Standards of Concept Formation[16]

The formation of a scientific theory naturally depends on the kind
of concepts one allows. It should be clear by now that the
Naturforscher at that time conceded to quantified concepts only a
very inferior position. Qualitative concepts however which could
vividly express the empirical intuition were most important.
Oersted's concept of the 'electrical conflict' by which he named
the interaction of electrical forces in a current carrying wire is
a good example; also the concept of polarity which was searched
for as an intuitive principle in the whole of reality. Comparative
use of concepts was not barred, that is, one could speak of a
stronger or weaker power of a certain effect under changing
conditions. But quantitative concepts are irrelevant for the
science of electricity or, at best, premature anticipations of
something which has first to be prepared and carried out by a
proper formation of qualitative concepts. Pfaff, for example,
writes that there could be no "absolute measurement" of
electricity as long as electricity "has not yet been developed in
its pure form."[17]

Ohm, on the other hand, disregarded all these vagaries. In his above mentioned work on the galvanic circuit he writes for example: "We will call ... the sum of the electroscopic manifestations ... the quantity of electricity without presupposing anything about the material constitution of electricity." And he continues: "The same remark applies to all pictorial expressions introduced without which our language, perhaps with good reasons, cannot exist."[18] Ohm then introduces each of his concepts by specifying methods of measuring them, some of which are direct methods and some are derived ones.

These words of Ohm must have been a shrill sound in the ears of all German Naturforscher who in philosophy had at least studied Kant. Had not Kant taught that concepts without intuition are empty and that it is necessary to make concepts sensuous, that is, as he put it: "ihnen den Gegenstand in der Anschauung beifuegen"[19] (to attach to them the object in intuition)? And now, there comes a scientist and admits even voluntarily that his concepts are only pictorial and do not deal with any intuitive aspect of reality. No wonder that Pohl qualifies Ohm's theory as a "mechanical composition", as a "game with mathematical formulas and empty hypothetical forms without purpose for science" and as an "abstraction of an abstraction".[20]

4. Change Through Quantifying and Metricizing

There have been, on the other hand, those physicists who were busy to interpret Ohm's theory for their own needs in the same way as Coulomb's operational achievement was seen as supporting the atomistic conception. Many of the followers of Volta succumbed to this temptation, especially Pfaff. In Ohm's theory they thought to have found a good weapon against the chemical theory, even against Faraday! Also, Ohm presented his theory as the final confirmation of Volta's theory. Ohm's theory was regarded as the proof that the intensity of the current depends solely on the geometrical circumstances of the conducting elements in the circuit and not on the intensity of some obscure chemical affinity of the substances in the Voltaic cells as the chemists maintained. But in accepting Ohm's theory the Voltaists overlooked for some time that Ohm had changed the meaning of some basic concepts by having metricized them in a way which depended on the acceptance of some other theoretical presuppositions laid down in his theory. I want to illustrate this with the concept of Spannung (electric tension). Spannung, also called Intensitaet was an electrostatic concept which, according to the old theory, one could detect at the poles of an unclosed cell or other source of current with the help of an electroscope. But as soon as this source becomes part of a closed circuit the tension is believed to disappear completely. For Ohm, tension is a magnitude which is also present in a closed circuit and which is interpreted as the difference of the elektroskopische Kraft (electroscopic force), as he terms it, which originates at the poles of the current source. Up to 1847, this magnitude could, for the electrodynamic case, be measured only indirectly by comparing two sources with each other. Spannung was thus a derived magnitude whereas the electroscopic force is a fundamental magnitude in the static case. It was not before 1849 that Kirchhoff interpreted Spannung as potential difference.[21] At least up to this time the concept of Spannung had to appear highly suspect even for the most willing contemporary of Ohm.

This example also shows that by metricizing his concepts Ohm does not comply with the traditional classification of the sciences. Instead of dividing the appearences into those of static and those of dynamical electricity as one universally did since Ampère, Ohm mixes the two classes together without making clear how his theory has to be related to electrostatics and -dynamics. Only with the mentioned paper by Kirchhoff one could theoretically clarify the relation of Ohm's theory to electrostatics.

There is a third factor which was influenced by the process of metricizing, namely the conception of current flow as it was tacitly assumed as basic by the atomists. This was the idea that the flow of a current through a conductor is to be seen analogously to the loss of electricity which a charged ball suffers along its isolating suspension. This, in turn, is to be set in analogue to the friction of a body which is sliding down an inclined plane. Instead of these analogues Ohm takes the Fourier model of heat conduction as a constructible model of current flow whereby resistance is not anymore the mechanical resistance of friction but a magnitude defined by tension and intensity without an intuitive interpretation.

Finally, as a forth condition of metricizing there is a change in the quality of the theory's domain. The domain of the theory receives a completely novel organisaton, it undergoes a gestalt switch. The traditional divisions in the textbooks: closed chain, open chain, further subdivided relative to the different possible sources of current, they all can be subsumed now under the single category of the electric circuit. The nature of the source becomes irrelevant, the concept of the electric circuit is such a wide and fruitful principle that all these cases which appear very heterogeneous before are comprised as well as many other phenomena.

5. Change in the Attitude Towards Experiment

We now come to a very controversial point, the value of observation and experiment for the Naturlehre in that time. One can often find the assertion that Naturphilosophie tried to do science in the arm-chair. This view has some merit, but the reason for this has also been that the practical means for experimenting and for instrumental observation have been very limited in Germany at that time - many could not experiment even if they wanted to. But mainly responsible for this view was the generation of scientists, immediately succeeding the Naturphilosophen, who had gathered on polemical grounds and joyfully cited some anti-empirical quotations by Schelling and others which had been taken as exemplary for a whole generation of scientists influenced by Naturphilosophie. However, experiments and observations were of course of importance, for both groups of scientists alike. But they played a completely different role and were employed in a way different from Ohm's theoretical method. In the first place, experiments and instrumental observations were the medium for revelations about nature, in the literal sense of the word. Experiments are artifices of man by which he makes nature speak where she is silent - by an experiment one finds new sources for immediate empirical intuition by which all the theories and all theoretical hypothesizing about nature becomes superfluous. For a long time, Oersted's experiment of 1820 which showed the magnetic effect of a current carrying wire was regarded as being such a Fundamentalversuch (fundamental try) which made clear immediately and intuitively that all forces of nature depend on each other, interact with each other, and operate together in unity. Pohl, for example, wrote still in 1826: "By the discovery of electromagnetism science has received a solemnity which ... will in spirit and in truth raise it to the cloudless intuition of the vivid unity of all appearences of nature."[22] Any further experimentation could function only as a try to make even clearer the intuition of nature through the finding of heretoforth unknown effects and to expand the intuition to all areas of nature and all effects of forces. Null-methods as well as such experiments which actually were comparisons of effects were not forbidden and were regarded as useful preparatory work for other Fundamentalversuche. In the whole, however, they played an inferior role in the consciousness of the scientists.

But how different are Ohm's experiments! In the understanding of his predecessors they are not experiments anymore, but pure measurements. For Ohm, the determination of physical quantities in an experiment is a trial, a touchstone, for a theory set up in advance. There is no word of a direct, unmediated access to experience, no intellectual intuition (in Kantian terms). Instead, there is thought, theory, construction – all factors which dim and modify intuition.

6. Change in the Attitude Towards Technical Utilisation

It is well known that for a long time Ohm's work did not find any appreciation. Science acknowledged it in the end because it could be used in technical applications. But at first the practical applicability of the theory was even more impeding than advantageous. For the Naturphilosophen as well as for their contemporary colleagues the technical utilisation of the theory did not count as a confirmation of its likely truth. Practical utility was regarded as useful but one did not see any epistemological value in it. The following quotation from Pohl is commonplace and could have also been said by his adversaries. He writes that one can admit the Vermittlung (mediation) of mathematics and physics only as "a formal extension of knowledge ... which, comprising only quantitative characteristics as the most superficial aspect of the appearences, is to be welcomed for extrascientific interests, but for the Erkenntnis (knowledge, cognition) of the qualitative, on which physics chiefly and foremost depends, it is of only limited and subordinate influence."[23] Very soon, some investigators suddenly grasp that Ohm's law is indispensable for telegraphy. They do not worry about Anschauung, Erkenntnis und so on, not even about the incompatibility of Ohm's theory with electrostatics and -dynamics. They use his concepts in a careless way even if they have to admit sometimes that they are not fully clear on their meaning. The theory serves only for calculations which are necessary for building telegraph lines and for similar applications. Even Gauss belongs to this group. He made use of Ohm's law when he, in 1833, together with Wilhelm Weber, tried out an electrical needle-telegraph for the first time in history, over a distance of 2.8 km.[24]

The difference between the 'technical' and 'scientific tradition' of electrical theory was still distinctly to be felt even in the late 19th century. In 1883, Lord Kelvin remarked that electric measurements, as founded by Ohm and W. Weber among others, had only recently found their way into the laboratories of the universities and similar institutions. But for the electrical engineers of the submarine cable industry those measurements were daily practice since the beginning of this industry in 1858.[25]

We can conclude that the acceptance of Ohm's law went hand in hand with a gradual redefinition of the concept of scientific knowledge and cognition. To put it as a somewhat simplified slogan: Erkenntnis was not any more the enterprise of achieving an adequatio rei et intellectus, or, to speak with Schelling, an identity of subject and object, but Erkenntnis in natural science became tantamount to predictability and controllability. We know that, at least in Germany, this new view did not make its way all of a sudden. It was never accepted in its pure form but only with strong revisions as a compromise with the mechanistic world view,

which one can probably see as a faint and distant concession to
the scientific values of Naturphilosophie. Ohm's disparity with
his contemporaries is the first and shrillest form of a leitmotiv
which can be heard throughout the rest of the 19th century in
Germany. The transformation and reinterpretation of the conception
of scientific knowledge formed one of the grand debates of the
19th century.[26] And perhaps it has come to an endpoint with
Kirchhoff's Vorlesungen ueber Mechanik in 1876 and Hertz's
Prinzipien der Mechanik in 1894. Others say that the real debate
commenced all the more and that it even became the fundamental
problem of even a new subject, philosophy of science, which has
not yet ceased to deal with it until today.

The six patterns of change which I wanted to illustrate with an
episode in the history of electricity could be found, at least in
part, in all the other Baconian sciences, if one takes into
account modifications necessary for each individual subject. This
is a far reaching and perhaps too audacious a claim of which I
cannot furnish any proof here. But I hope that I succeeded in
demonstrating a significant cognitive change at least for one
Baconian science.

References

1 See Gillispie, C.C.: Science and Technology, in: Crawley, C.W.
(ed.): War and Peace in an Age of Upheaval 1793 – 1830, in: The
New Cambridge Modern History, Vol. 9, Cambridge 1965, pp. 118–145,
here p. 118.
2 See Harnack, A.: Geschichte der Koeniglich Preussischen
Akademie der Wissenschaften zu Berlin, Vol. I, pt. 2, Berlin 1900,
p. 556.
3 Other parallel foundations were: Madrid 1802, Prag 1806 and
Wien 1815.
4 This claim can be found as a common place in numerous
presentations, e.g.: Harnack, A., see ref. 2, pp. 728ff.; Winter,
H.J.J.: The Reception of Ohm's Electrical Researches by his
Contemporaries, in: Philosophical Magazine 35 (1944), pp. 371–386;
or: Gerlach, W.: Fortschritte der Naturwissenschaften im 19.

Jahrhundert, in: Mann, G. (ed.): Propylaeen Weltgeschichte, Vol. 8, Berlin 1960, pp. 235-277.

5 See for example Laudan, L.: Theories of Scientific Method from Plato to Mach, in: History of Science 7 (1968), pp. 1-63, here p. 28.

6 See Kuhn, Th.S.: The Function of Measurement in Modern Physical Science, in: Isis 52 (1961), pp. 161-190; and by the same author: Mathematical vs. Experimental Traditions in the Development of Physical Science, in: Journal of Interdisciplinary History 7 (1976), pp. 1-31. Both articles are reprinted in: Kuhn, Th.S.: The Essential Tension. Selected Studies in the Scientific Tradition and Change, Chicago 1977 (German translation: Die Entstehung des Neuen, Frankfurt/Main 1977).

7 See Hall, Th.S.: On Biological Analogs of Newtonian Paradigms, in: Philosophy of Science 35 (1968), pp. 6-27.

8 Fourier, J.B.: Théorie analytique de la chaleur, Paris 1822, p. 432 (English translation by Freeman, A., New York 1955, p. 464 and German translation by Weinstein, B., Berlin 1884, p. 457).

9 As documented in the Proceedings of the Royal Society 4 (1841), p. 336.

10 Schweigger's Journal fuer Chemie und Physik 52 (1828), p. 65.

11 Jahrbuecher fuer wissenschaftliche Kritik 1 (January 1828), Nr. 11-14, p. 94 and (July-September 1829), p. 445.

12 Pfaff, Ch.H.: Der Elektro-Magnetismus, Hamburg 1824, p. 201.

13 As ref. 8.

14 Ohm, G.S.: Die galvanische Kette, mathematisch bearbeitet, Berlin 1827; repr. in: Lommel, E. (ed.): Gesammelte Abhandlungen, Leipzig 1892, pp. 61-186, here p. 106.

15 See Gauss, C.F.: Werke, ed. by the Koenigliche Gesellschaft der Wissenschaften zu Goettingen, Vol. V, Goettingen 1877, p. 629 in a letter of Gauss to Wilhelm Weber, dated March 19, 1845.

16 This passage and the following on the change through metricizing is treated in more detail in my article: Towards a Reconstruction of Revolutionary Change. Ohm's Theory as an Example, in: Studies in the History and Philosophy of Science 11 (1980).

17 Pfaff, Ch.H.: [article on] Elektrometrie, in: Gehler's Physikalisches Woerterbuch, neu bearbeitet von Brandes, H.W. et al., Vol. III, pt. 2, Leipzig 1827, p. 681. Note that 'absolute measurement' is used by Pfaff in a sense wholly different from

Gauss' and Weber's.

18 See ref. 14, p. 109.

19 Kritik der reinen Vernunft, A 52 (introduction to transcendental logic).

20 Jahrbuecher fuer wissenschaftliche Kritik 1 (January 1828), Nr. 11-14, p. 102 and p. 96.

21 See Poggendorff's Annalen der Physik und Chemie 72 (1849), pp. 506-513.

22 Pohl, G.F.: Der Process der galvanischen Kette, Leipzig 1826, p. 32.

23 See ref. 2, p. 94.

24 See Goettingische gelehrte Anzeigen 9 (August 1834); repr. in: Werke, Vol. V, Goettingen 1877, p. 525.

25 See Thomson, W. [Lord Kelvin]: On the Electrical Units of Measurement, in: Popular Lectures and Adresses, Vol. I, London 1883, p. 76.

26 Ludwig Boltzmann gives a vivid description of this change as it continues in the later 19th century, in a talk of 1899: Ueber die Entwicklung der Methoden der theoretischen Physik in neuerer Zeit, in: Populaere Schriften, Leipzig 1905, pp. 198-227.

Peter Buck

FROM CELESTIAL MECHANICS TO SOCIAL PHYSICS: DISCONTINUITY IN THE DEVELOPMENT OF THE SCIENCES IN THE EARLY NINETEENTH CENTURY

Statistics textbooks for social scientists describe sound mathematical practices as having the power to reveal and then neutralize distortions resulting from biased research strategies, biased sampling procedures, biased researchers, and the like. Cliched though these claims may seem, their import is not trivial. They raise the possiblility of an escape from the tangle of social structural constraints, ideological commitments, and clashes of selb-interest that ordinarily impair people's understanding of society and politics. More specifically, they place statistics in a crucial position relative to the interactions of social and political life with science. The incorporation of statistical methods into the social sciences becomes a sign of success in realizing one of the enduring promises of scientific knowledge, namely that it contains within itself compelling imperatives regarding its proper social uses. The expectation is that the construction of genuinely quantitative social sciences will permit a scientific answer to the vexed question of the proper connection betwen scientific theory and social practice. The relationship of knowledge to action will then be a strictly cognitive problem, susceptible to strictly analytic solution. In transforming problems of the relationship between theory and practice into epistemological questions, social scientists aim to make them less urgent by stripping them of their immediate behavioral and social consequences. While in everyday life people quite naturally judge

19

H. N. Jahnke and M. Otte (eds.), Epistemological and Social Problems of the Sciences in the Early Nineteenth Century, 19–33.

ideas on normative as well as logical grounds, systematic
theorists anticipate that quantification and abstraction will
permit the removal of value considerations from the formulation of
policy. Depending on their predilections, they may attempt to
distinguish questions of means from questions of ends, and then
turn to abstract mathematical analysis for objective judgments
about which means will best serve which ends; or they may even
argue that quantitative methods have the capacity to reveal an
objective ordering of ends as well as means. But either way, they
measure their achievement as social scientists by the extent to
which they can divorce considerations of fact and analysis from
considerations of value in their work.

The natural sciences are customarily cited as providing the
relevant warrant for believing that the pursuit of knowledge can
be usefully separated from normative issues, that the knowledge in
question is ultimately sustained by being grounded on empirical
evidence, and that abstraction and quantification are the soundest
procedures for acquiring true and useful understandings of
reality. An important part of the aura that association with the
natural sciences imparts to these propositions comes from the
implicit presumption that they constitute the constellation of
background assumptions that has governed scientific work for some
three hundred years. The crucial premise is that the natural
sciences have presented social theorists with a single,
unambiguous model of research and explanation to accept or reject.
That belief makes it seem reasonable to answer questions about
how, why, and with what consequences statistical habits of mind
have taken hold in the social sciences by appealing to a record of
continuing efforts since the seventeenth century to cast the study
of society, politics, economics, and indeed all of human behavior
into an immutable framework set by concepts and methods drawn from
the successful interpretation of nature.

The unity radiated by this account of the natural and social
scientific past is specious. Even in the natural sciences,
abstraction, empirical data, and objectivity have not always been
conjoined in the same fashion. There is no historical basis for
the comfortable assumption that the powerful methods of modern
science arose when people ceased to look to nature for guidance

about their own affairs. The architects of seventeenth century natural philosophy did not assume that they were neutral observers. Nor did they believe that the objects under observation were without ethical significance. In the orderliness of nature they saw manifestations of God's Will and expositions of the principles of His Justice.[1] The slogan of the Scientific Revolution, that the natural philosopher through his observations glorified God and advances the human condition, presumed that questions of utility, divinity, and validity were coextensive. Knowledge which was not of divine origin, or not useful, or not rooted in empirical observation was false; and a natural philosophy which did not encompass social and political phenomena was unsatisfactory on its face.

Current views of the relationship between the natural and the social sciences are based on the quite different premise that observation can be separated from both analytic and value judgments. Contemporary scientists, whether social or natural, postulate a hierarchy of method in which the low level activity of the data gatherer is independent of and refined by the abstract and mathematical powers of the scientist. They also assume a hierarchy of practice in which improvements in human affairs depend upon the extension to society and politics of quantitative and analytic procedures whose purchase on generalized reality is not open to question. This dual vision of mathematics as controlling both observation and action derives from conceptions of quantification and its uses that belong to the early nineteenth century and are rooted in a specific understanding of the relationship between natural regularities, social order, and social change. As social scientists, it is with Adolphe Quetelet, not seventeenth century natural philosophers, that we share assumptions. Like Quetelet, we believe that explicating the principles of social order is the precondition for effecting rational social change. Like Quetelet, we also assume that the foundation for comprehensive knowledge is the ordered collection of data. But again like Quetelet, we believe that the order in question is external to the observer, both in the usual sense of not being his creation and in the more restricted sense of its apprehension being beyond the reach of purely empirical

investigation. Our crucial premise, and Quetelet's, is that the
discovery of order, but not its fabrication, requires the use of
analytic processes based in mathematics.

The structure and background of Quetelet's "social physics"
suggests the range of issues at stake in this view of the
relevance of mathematics to the understanding and control of human
affairs. His "Treatise on Man" combines epistemologically and
politically tendentious arguments in equal parts. In the interest
of subordinating value considerations to the logic of scientific
progress, the essay reduces problems of social order and social
change to questions about the relationship of observation and
analysis to judgement, but it does so by making ostensibly
technical conclusions regarding proper statistical methodology
depend on assumptions about the nature and consequences of social
progress.

Quetelet's model for scientific analysis was celestial mechanics.
When he began the "Treatise on Man" by urging social theorists and
"friends of humanity" generally to concentrate their energies on
elucidating the causal laws governing social reality, he did so
with a confident assurance that astronomy and its practitioners
had already developed the requisite mathematical means for
demonstrating that "man is born, grows up, and dies according to
certain laws." In part the argument was broadly rhetorical. Having
"observed the progress made by astronomical science" in
explicating the principles of the heavens, "why should we not
endeavor to follow the same course in respect to man," he asked;
for it would surely "be an absurdity to suppose that, whilst all
is regulated by such admirable laws, man's existence alone should
be capricious." [2]

The analogy between celestial mechanics and social physics was
also pursued in the Treatise on a more fundamental level.
Quetelet's argument turned on the significance he attached to the
"remarkable constancy" exhibited by observations of "moral
phenomena." This regularity showed that "human actions are
regulated by fixed causes", because it showed that "moral
phenomena, when observed on a great scale,... resemble physical
phenomena," in that "the greater the number of individuals

observed," the more "individual peculiarities" are "effaced," leaving only "the general facts by virtue of which society exists and is preserved."[3]

As might be expected, the parallel between physical and moral phenomena was not so straightforward as Quetelet would have had it. His salient assumption was that taking observations "on a great scale" meant observing a great number of individuals. But in the celestial mechanics that served as his model, observing on a great scale meant taking a great number of observations. That Quetelet saw no significant difference between these two activities places him on the near side of a major social and intellectual divide separating the naturalized social statistics of the nineteenth century from the rationalist expectations that informed Enlightenment programs for building sciences of man, society, and nature on probabilistic foundations.

Quetelet's primary point of reference was Laplace's discovery that in astronomy observations of planetary and stellar positions and motions are distributed in a regular fashion, according to the law of error. For Laplace that finding was important because it allowed him to maintain a determinist view of the physical world in the face of apparent randomness, by ascribing observed disorder to errors of observation.[4] He built the point into the famous passage in the "Philosophical Essay on Probabilities" where he contrasted how "the phenomena of nature" are apprehended by the human mind with the way in which the universe would appear to "an intelligence which could comprehend all the forces by which nature is animated and the respective situation of all beings who compose it." Such an intelligence would be able to devise a single formula that would embrace all the motions of the universe, from those of "the greatest bodies" to those of "the lightest atom." But men encountered the physical world under quite different conditions. Natural phenomena, Laplace wrote, present themselves for human inspection "enveloped by so many strange circumstances, and so great a number of disturbing causes mix their influence, that it is very difficult to recognize them."[5]

Given the contrast between what would be revealed to an omniscient intelligence and what was presented to the human mind, the uses of probability theory were clear. As Laplace explained, the calculus of probabilities showed men that they could arrive at "the phenomena of nature" by "multiplying" their observations "so that the strange effects finally destroy reciprocally each other, the mean results putting in evidence those phenomena and their diverse elements". More precisely, probability theory provided grounds for concluding that constant causes were at work when, as in celestial mechanics, the multiplication of observations could be shown to lead to the kind of reciprocal destruction that eliminated "strange effects".[6]

To make this argument, Laplace turned to Bernoulli's theorem on the relationship between the probability of an event's happening and the frequency of its actual occurrence. He interpreted Bernoulli as having established that if a particular observation has a given probability of being made, then it will appear with a frequency approaching that probability, as the number of observations increases. With his radical distinction between phenomena and observations in hand, Laplace was then in a position to add the significant further remark that the probability of a particular observation's being made is fixed, only when the phenomenon being observed is itself completely determined. It followed, from the converse of Bernoulli's theorem, that the presence of statistical regularity at the level of observational data implied the operation of constant causes at the level of observed events.

The implications for celestial mechanics were immediate, obvious, and precisely what Laplace had wanted. Astronomers could draw two important inferences from the fact that their data were distributed according to the law of error. First, astronomy was a science that dealt with observations distorted by "strange circumstances," not a science concerned with phenomena disordered by "disturbing causes." Second, in reasoning about events in nature, it was both possible and proper for astronomers to give pride of place to causal explanations. Theirs was a science that proceeded from the mathematical analysis of statistically regular empirical findings to an understanding of the constant causes that determined the phenomena of nature. It was a science in which progress was possible and equivalent to the eradication of error by means of a rationally directed process of reciprocal destruction.

Quetelet's social physics incorporated these conclusions about the meaning of statistical regularity, the centrality of causal considerations in scientific thinking, and the nature of progress. But the "Treatise on Man" was not simply a reprise on the main themes of the "Philosophical Essay on Probabilities", and for good reason. Applied directly to the study of man, Laplace's general line of interpretation would have only permitted social scientists to take the mean of repeated observations of an individual's height, for example, as equal to his true height - hardly an interesting result and not at all the point Quetelet sought to establish. In fact, he extended the argument in a quite different direction, substituting measurements taken of a large number of individuals for repeated measurements of a single individual. The two sets of observations, he found, were distributed according to the same law, the law of error, and from this he concluded that it was appropriate to speak of a "social man" or "average man," who would occupy the same position in social physics as the mean observation did in normal physics. "Social man" was what emerged when "individual peculiarities" were "effaced"; he was "the center around which oscillate the social elements," a "fictitious being for whom everything proceeds conformably to the medium results obtained for society in general." It was this being whose fortunes had to be examined in "establishing the basis of social physics," because the object of the enterprise was to determine the "variations which the whole system undergoes," a matter of following "the progress of the centers of gravity" in each of its parts.[7]

With this formulation of social physics and its program, Quetelet had systematically confounded observations and events; entirely abandoned was Laplace's central distinction between a strictly deterministic phenomenal world and the human mind's uncertain knowledge of it. In its place Quetelet set a quite different pair of dichotomies, between simple empiricism and causal analysis, on

the one hand, and between human actions and their social
determinants, on the other. The result was a sweeping redefinition
of the conditions for effective social reform, in which the
manipulation of causes was given absolute priority over mere
tinkering with effects. Or as Quetelet remarked in a justifiably
famous passage, it might be disconcerting to find that it is
possible to "predict annually how many individuals will stain
their hands with the blood of their fellow-men, how many will be
forgers, how many will deal in poisons."[8] Yet the discovery was
ultimately "consolatory," demonstrating as it did that the
incidence of crime is but an example of "regular effects,"
produced in a given society "resting under te influence of certain
causes," and consequently open to modification when and insofar as
the causes are changed.[9]

Social physics was thus a science of reform, oriented toward
showing the "friends of humanity" where the determinants of change
lay and having for "its object to leave this important subject no
longer to a kind of empiricism."[10] But social physics was equally
a science of ends, explicitly committed to defining the proper
aims of reform. Here too Quetelet's identification of observations
with phenomena had decisive consequences. It allowed him to
transform what Laplace had regarded as an essentially
epistemological question — how can knowledge be improved and its
adequacy estimated — into a socially normative judgment. Where
Laplace had used probabilistic arguments to show that in astronomy
observations which depart from the mean are only errors, Quetelet
applied the same considerations to man, contending that deviant
individuals are likewise "errors," to be eliminated with the
growth of civilization, just as erroneous observations are
corrected by the progress of science, "The perfectibility of the
human species," he wrote at the end of the Treatise on Man,
"results as a necessary consequence from all our researches." Not
only was it true that "defects and monstrosities disappear more
and more from the physical world"; social physics also
demonstrated "one of the principle facts of civilization," that
its advance inexorably "contracts the limits within which the
different elements relating to man oscillate. The more knowledge
is diffused, so much the more do the deviations from the average

disappear; and the more consequently do we tend to approach that which is beautiful, that which is good."[11] Perfection, in other words, was a stable state where human differences did not simply balance out but were erased.

There were, of course, elements in the Laplacean oeuvre that could be made to fit Quetelet's line of argument. Vital statistics had an important place in Laplace's early work on probability theory, for example, and the conclusions he drew from his population studies seem to point unmistakeably toward the analogy between celestial and social phenomena elaborated in the "Treatise on Man". The "small variations" displayed in the proportions of annual births to the population, of marriages to births, and of male births to female births all showed that "results due to moral causes" were not exempt from the "general law, namely, that the ratios of the acts of nature are very nearly constant when those acts are considered in great number." It followed that "history treated from the point of view of the influence of constant causes would unite to the interest of curiosity that of offering to man most useful lessons."[12]

But the lessons in question were not exactly the ones Quetelet drew. Laplace's overriding aim in applying the calculus of probabilities to the political and moral sciences was to bring human affairs more into line with "the eternal principles of reason, justice, and humanity." He saw that as a question of translating "the inevitable effects of the progress of knowledge" into changes in "the moral world," and he believed that the example of celestial mechanics was relevant to the undertaking. But his argument linking the sciences of nature to the sciences of man hinged on the way that probability theory allowed men to improve their understanding of natural phenomena, not on the way that those phenomena were themselves determined by the laws of nature. What the rationalization of society and politics seemed to require, and what the calculus of probabilities promised to provide, were procedures for dealing with the political equivalents of the natural philosophers' disordered observations: "testimonies, votes, and the decision of electoral and deliberative assemblies, and the judgments of tribunals."[13]

In placing those topics at the center of his moral and political concerns, Laplace was in effect locating the respective subject matters of the natural and the social sciences on opposite sides of the boundary dividing the "system of the universe" from the "system of human knowledge."[14] That was consistent with his understanding of how and why "the method which has served us so well in the natural sciences" was to be extended to society and politics. His guiding premise was that "our institutions and the usages to which we have already so long conformed" lent themselves to his calculus for precisely the same reason that our representations of events in the physical world did: they were based on probabilities, in the sense that they stood in the same relation to the principles of reason, humanity, and justice as observations of natural phenomena did to regular and constant causes. [15] The survival over time of established social and political practices showed that they were sustained by "the favorable chances ... constantly attached" to rational conduct, chances that, "like those favorable to lotteries, always end by prevailing." [16]

Such considerations had no meaning for Quetelet, because they drew their political force from conceptions of social order and social change that he did not share. The issues associated with the credibility of witnesses, the decisions of assemblies, and the judgments of tribunals that Laplace addressed were standard fare in eighteenth-century treatises on probability theory. But they owed their prominent position in his "Philosophical Essay" to the emphasis that Condorcet had placed on their relevance to what he regarded as the central political problem raised by contractualist social theory: how to make "the decision of the majority" genuinely express "the common will of all." Condorcet's proposed solution to the problem involved transforming majority rule from a practice designed solely to "place authority where the force was" into a method of "avoiding error and acting according to decisions based on truth." He assumed that the common will was rational, and he set himself the task of showing that, in societies where political issues were settled by representative bodies, it was possible to devise "rules" that would lead them to act "only to sustain decisions that conform to the truth."[17]

Laplace accepted Condorcet's equation of the will of all with reason. He too was convinced that the way to rationalize society and politics was to devise procedures for distinguishing the collective will from the "many passions and particular interests." Like Condorcet, he also assumed that the place to start was with the question of how "to understand and to define the desire of an assembly in the midst of a variety of opinions of its members"; for, as Condorcet had hoped, the calculus of probabilities offered "some rules in regard to this matter." Indeed, it essentially dictated the best way for deliberative bodies to do the two things most commonly required of them: choose among several candidates for a position or among "several propositions relative to the same subject." In both cases, the particular "mode of election" indicated by probability theory could be counted on to produce a true "order of preference."[18]

This was not an argument for applying the calculus of probabilities directly to specific questions concerning public affairs. Laplace was persuaded that the substantive matters on which judgments had to be passed simply could not be resolved on quantitative grounds, because they were complicated by too many "passions, diverse interests, and circumstances."[19] That is, his political mathematics, like Quetelet's social physics, was designed to remove value considerations from the formulation of policy by transforming political issues into epistemological ones. But where Quetelet regarded that problem as itself susceptible to purely statistical solution, in Laplace's scheme the prerequisites for the rationalization of politics remained irreducibly institutional: deliberative assemblies, organized and operated according to the dictates of probability theory and endowed with authority, in Condorcet's phrase, to "dispose of the public power."[20]

These explicit institutional presuppositions disappeared from the intellectual tradition linking Condorcet and Laplace to Quetelet as the political calculus resting on them lost its power to offer either plausible alternatives to or convincing analyses of the realities of French social life. In the 1780s, when Condorcet was applying probability theory to decisions taken by majority vote, the subject had at least the appearance of potential practical

political significance, because of the prominent role that his
mentor, Turgot, had assigned to representative assemblies in his
program for reforming the administrative structure of the "ancien
regime".[21] But by the 1810s, when Laplace was marshalling his
findings, there was no comparable reference point in the real
world of French politics for arguments about the proper
organization and operation of such deliberative bodies. During the
intervening years, the French Revolution had altered the political
landscape in ways that the calculus of probabilities, as Laplace
understood it, simply could not illuminate. On the subject of
"sudden changes," all that he could extract from his applications
of probability theory to the moral sciences was an abstract,
universal injunction against them, on the grounds that "in the
moral world as in the physical world" they always occasioned "a
great loss of vital force."[22]

Quetelet's social physics generated equally abstract and universal
conclusions. But they gave him a rather greater intellectual
purchase on such "deviations from the average" as the French
Revolution, just as yet another set of quantitative results did
for his English contemporary, Thomas Robert Malthus. Neither
theorist saw any reason to suppose that the way to arrive at
scientific judgments concerning 1789 and its aftermath was to hand
over the relevant observational data for some sort of
institutional review. Objectified and reified knowledge provided
both with frameworks in which observation and judgment emerged as
non-problematic activities by virtue of being separated from each
other. With fixed laws and constant causes governing the whole of
reality, diversity and error could be equated, and the definitions
of natural philosophy taken as both normative and determinant.

For Malthus, observing events in France from across the English
Channel, the revolution was an aberration doomed to failure
because it was committed to ideals incompatible with the now
identical and equally mathematical laws of human and natural
populations. In an industrializing England, those laws were
"great", "restrictive", and by 1798 confirmed directly by
"experience, the true source and foundation of all knowledge."[23]
On the continent, several decades later, where the tangible
failure of the French Revolution had been experienced, as well as

observed, the foundations of knowledge seemed equaly secure and
the upheavals of 1789 equally marginal in their effects on the
progress of the centers of social gravity. But to a French
educated Belgian statistician, sound knowledge and failed
revolution, when conjoined, were not only mutually explanatory but
also prescriptive of the conditions for bringing social change
under rational control. Where Malthus explored the fixed causes
which inexorably limited the power of reason to shape society in
its own image, Quetelet turned to causal analysis as the means for
rational intervention. The good society became one in which
deviations from the norm were minimized, and a natural science
whose laws had the twin virtues of simplicity and elegance became
the model for sound social theorizing.

As social scientists, we have doubtless long passed the point of
being beguiled by the specific details of Quetelet's vision of the
good society, in part because our statistical techniques have a
different focus from his. But the general program built into his
social physics has proved compelling. The history of the sciences,
social as well as natural, that we have constructed for ourselves
describes social and scientific progress along precisely the lines
of the "Treatise on Man". It legitimates the particular way of
transforming cognitive rules into normative principles exemplified
by the line of development from Laplace's law of error to
Quetelet's normal curve; it asserts that there is no other way of
deriving principled actions from observations, except through the
intermediary of mathematical method and abstract analysis.

Our sense for the power of quantification is bound up with our
belief that the important lines of influence linking the natural
sciences to social theory and social theory to social action all
run in one direction, from the first to the second and then from
the second to the third. Here the contrast between Quetelet and
his predecessors was pronounced and decisive: such inventors of
social statistics as John Graunt and William Petty had not
regarded natural philosophy as an already essentially completed
model for programs of social research; they saw their work as a
necessary preliminary to the reform of the natural sciences
themselves. [24] Similarly, while Laplace was convinced of the
reality of scientific progress, his mathematical ambitions were

predicated on thoroughly skeptical premises about the possibility of comprehensive knowledge. Yet only a few decades after the "Philosophical Essay on Probabilities", Quetelet found it reasonable to portray the natural sciences as so internally coherent and rigorously established that his adoption of their statistical method for social physics could at no point alter their future course of development.

This vision of the natural sciences as immutable and socially autonomous was so attractive to all manner of nineteenth-century social critics, from Mill to Marx, from St. Simon to Durkheim, from Freud to Weber, that twentieth century heirs to the most diverse theoretical traditions have accepted it entire. It is a measure of how far we continue to accept it, that we conceive the possibilities for social order and social change within limits set by observed regularities and by the results of quantitative, causal analyses. Like our predecessors, we define the social theorist's claim to scientific status by making social theory logically necessary for and logically prior to reasoned social action. When we consider the ways in which scientific knowledge is relevant to social change, we locate our alternatives on a spectrum running from Quetelet to Malthus, not from Laplace to Quetelet. The critical tension we seek to resolve is between the competing promises of science to enhance our power as active, controlling agents in the world, and to explicate the inexorable natural laws to which we are subject.

References

1 See, for example, McGuire, J.E.: Boyle's Conception of Nature, in: Journal of the History of Ideas XXXIII(1972), pp. 523-42.
2 Quetelet, L.A.J.: A Treatise on Man and the Development of His Faculties, Edinburgh 1842, p. 9.
3 Ibid., p. 6.
4 Gillispie, C.C.: Probability and Politics. Laplace, Condorcet, and Turgot, in: Proceedings of the American Philosophical Society CXVI(1972), p.6.

5 Laplace, P.S. Marquis de: A Philosophical Essay on
Probabilities, trans. Frederick Wilson Truscott and Frederick
Lincoln Emory, New York 1951, pp. 4, 73.

6 Ibid., p. 73.

7 Quetelet, Treatise on Man (ref. 2), p. 8.

8 Ibid., p. 6.

9 Ibid., p. vii.

10 Ibid., p. 7.

11 Ibid., p. 108.

12 Laplace, Philosophical Essay (ref. 5), pp. 61-3.

13 Ibid., pp. 2, 108, 190.

14 Ibid., pp. 2f.

15 Ibid., pp. 107f.

16 Ibid., p. 2.

17 Condorcet, M.-J.-A.-N. Caritat Marquis de: Essay on the
Applications of Mathematics to the Theory of Decision-Making,
translated in: Baker, K.M. (ed.), Condorcet: Selected Writings,
Indianapolis 1976, pp. 34-6.

18 Laplace, Philosophical Essay (ref. 5), pp. 126-31.

19 Ibid., p. 190.

20 Condorcet, Essay on the Applications of Mathematics (ref. 17),
p. 36.

21 Gillispie, Probability and Politics (ref. 3), p. 17. See Keith
Michael Baker, K.M.: Condorcet. From Natural Philosophy to Social
Mathematics, Chicago 1975.

22 Laplace, Philosophical Essay (ref. 5.), p. 108.

23 Malthus, Th.R.: An Essay on the Principle of Population, ed.
A. Flew, Harmondsworth 1970, p. 72.

24 See my: Seventeenth Century Political Arithmetic. Civil Strife
and Vital Statistics, in: Isis LXVIII(1977), pp. 67-84.

Claire Salomon-Bayet

1802 - "BIOLOGIE" ET MEDECINE

La transition est un terme rhétorique qui désigne l'art de passer
d'un raisonnement à un autre, de lier les parties d'un discours.
Elle se ménage, elle peut être brusque ou insensible. Son emploi,
ici, est à la fois métaphorique et contraignant. Parler des
"sciences pendant la période de transition du XVIIIème siècle au
XIXème siècle", c'est transposer ce qui est de l'ordre du
discours, éventuellement historique, dans l'ordre des choses et du
temps, en utilisant des repères chronologiques conventionnels.
Avec ou sans transition en effet, le temps passe et le temps fuit.
Mais cette métaphore est contraignante, dans la mesure où
l'histoire des sciences est l'art de présenter la logique d'une
évolution et non celui d'écrire la chronique d'une accumulation.
Elle est un discours et relève donc d'une rhétorique, qui peut
utiliser des artifices aussi bien pour persuader que pour
comprendre: l'idée de révolution dans les sciences en est un ,
l'idée d'une transition entre deux siècles en est un autre, leur
point commun étant l'affirmation d'un changement radical dans un
cas, progressif dans l'autre.

Notre problème nait de la juxtaposition de deux faits: il y a
toujours eu quelqu'un - sorcier ou médecin - pour soigner le
malade. L'acte thérapeutique est l'objet de l'histoire de la
médecine, art, savoir, science, consciente à la fois de son
pouvoir et de ses limites. La science du vivant, en revanche,

35

H. N. Jahnke and M. Otte (eds.), Epistemological and Social Problems of the Sciences in the Early Nineteenth
Century, 35–54.

détournée du souci thérapeutique, même si elle lui est finalement ordonnée, donne lieu à une autre histoire, qui passe par le laboratoire de chimie, par la table de dissection, par l'expérimentation physiologique. Au lit de l'homme malade se substituent le microscope et la lamelle: changement d'échelle, changement d'objet, changement d'attitude définissent l'objet d'une autre histoire, l'histoire de la biologie.

Or le siècle a deux ans lorsque le terme "biologie" apparait. C'est un bon prétexte pour s'interroger, à cette date, sur l'entrecroisement des deux histoires, les prises de conscience des spécificités des disciplines; pour mettre en question certaines idées reçues qui font coincider le début du siècle, les acquis révolutionnaires et l'innovation scientifique. Notre exploration se limitera à la France, mais elle ne se veut pas exclusive.

1795-1820: Les Nouveaux Savoirs

Ce n'est pas une illusion d'historien de lier à ces dates - 1795-1820 - l'avènement d'une nouvelle médecine: la médecine d'observation, le néo-hippocratisme, est désormais institutionnellement médecine hospitalière, armée et instrumentée de la percussion médiate, de l'auscultation et du stéthoscope, unifiée par le champ théorique que représentent l'anatomie pathologique et le concept de lésion, quantifiée par l'introduction de la méthode numérique, c'est-à-dire par le dénombrement des cas que permettent la structure hospitalière et la médecine aux armées. La naissance de la clinique[2] a superbement analysé cet espace de temps pendant lequel la médecine s'est constituée en termes positifs: elle se détache de la métaphysique et de la doctrine en offrant, dans l'ouverture des cadavres, les signes visibles, tangibles et lisibles de la maladie, en structurant par le langage et le regard le symptôme en signe, et le signe en cause.

On peut néanmoins chicaner sur le radicalisme de la novation à la date de 1795. S'agit-il, à partir de 1795, de l'apparition de nouveaux savoirs, ou du temps d'installation, de diffusion de notions et de pratiques déjà nées? A tout prendre, le traité

d'Auenbrugger (1722-1803) qui préconise la percussion date de
1763; traduit initialement par Rozière de la Chassaigne en 1770,
il l'est de nouveau par Corvisart en 1808, sous le titre "Nouvelle
méthode pour reconnaître les maladies internes" de la poitrine. Le
traité de Morgagni, "De sedibus et causis morborum", qui fonde
l'anatomie pathologique, paraît à Venise en 1761 et ne cesse
d'être invoqué dans la littérature médicale et dans les textes des
naturalistes de la fin du siècle. C'est dans les hôpitaux de
marine, à Brest et à Toulon que Dubreuil, médecin à l'Ecole de
Brest, a commencé à penser la clinique en terme numérique, bien
avant 1795, sur des populations homogènes, de même sexe, d'âge
moyen et vivant dans des conditions identiques. Si l'on peut
parler de nouveaux savoirs et de ruptures épistémologiques, c'est
l'histoire d'avant 1795 qui prépare les ruptures épistémologiques
dans la continuité et c'est l'épithète "épistémologique" qui donne
tout son sens à l'expression.

On peut aussi chicaner prospectivement sur les dates. E.H.
Ackerknecht[3], par exemple, propose une périodisation plus longue
dans "Medicine at the Paris Hospital" qui ne changerait en rien -
sinon dans la quantité des titres recensés - la nature du savoir
médical: 1794-1840. C'est pour lui, le temps de vie de l'école
médicale de Paris, c'est-à-dire de la perfection de la clinique
française.

Que l'on adopte la période longue, de 1795 à 1840, ou la période
courte, de 1795 à 1820, le propre de ceux qui détiennent le savoir
médical, convaincus de porter un immense espoir en même temps que
conscients des limites de leur efficacité (sur ce point, a
l'exception de la vaccination jennerienne, les médecins font plus
grande confiance à l'action des hygiénistes qu'à leur propre
thérapeutique) est de ne pas soupçonner ou de très peu soupçonner
qu'en dehors de la médecine, des disciplines qui en modifieront
radicalement la nature et la portée sont en train de se
constituer; en même temps de récuser une des figures négatives de
l'histoire de la médecine, Broussais, qui, dans tous les excès et
les échecs, fonde néanmoins une médecine des réactions
pathologiques et non plus des maladies classées. E. Ackerknecht
comme M. Foucault[4] reconnaissent à Broussais d'avoir promu, à
contre-courant, une médecine de l'organisme, en réarmant la

vieille notion de sympathie, en réactivant la notion hallérienne
d'irritabilité et en reprenant le thème brownien de monisme
pathologique. Entre l'inconscience et l'excès, force est de
reconnaître que la révolution anatomo-pathologique, positiviste
d'essence, n'a pas transformé radicalement la thérapeutique en la
rendant plus efficace. C'est la théorie cellulaire, avec R.
Virchow, la chimie, avec Ehrlich et Pasteur, la voie expérimentale
avec C. Bernard, qui accompliront la positivité médicale, dans
l'efficacité d'une étiologie et d'une intervention, préventive ou
thérapeutique, dans la désignation précise du fonctionnement et du
dis-fonctionnement. La médecine de laboratoire - expression qu'il
faut saisir à sa date dans toute sa puissance paradoxale- succède
à la médecine de l'Ecole de Paris et lui donne une autre
positivité. A la médecine physiologique de Broussais s'ajoute et
se substitue une "physiologie expérimentale appliquée à la
médecine", pour reprendre le titre de la série de cours donnée en
1855 au Collège de France par Claude Bernard, alors suppléant de
Magendie

Dans l'histoire des "nouveaux savoirs", le retournement est
symboliquement accompli, sinon effectué, par Francois Magendie[5]
(1783-1855) qui, succédant a Laënnec, médecin de l'Ecole de Paris,
en 1826, dans la chaire de médecine du Collège de France, demande
à la stupéfaction de tous ses collègues, médecins et non-médecins,
l'installation d'un laboratoire. Ni entièrement clinique, ni
totalement hospitalière, la médecine à cette date commence d'être
aussi une médecine de laboratoire. Mais alors, comment entendre la
nouveauté des savoirs médicaux, entre 1795 et 1820, si dès 1826,
une nouvelle dimension de la médecine se fait jour? S'agit-il de
deux "révolutions" successives, toutes les deux aussi "vraies"
l'une que l'autre, ou bien l'une moins que l'autre?

1795-1820: Une Révolution en Médecine?

Le terme révolution n'est ici ni un anachronisme ni un hasard. Il
est employé a sa date et au sens que lui donnent aujourd'hui les
historiens des sciences par P. Cabanis, dans un texte écrit en
1795 mais publié en 1804: "Coup d'oeil sur les révolutions et la
réforme de la médecine."[6] Sur la révolution conceptuelle se greffe

très consciemment la volonté de réforme de l'enseignement et de la
pratique qui accomplit et prolonge la période révolutionnaire
entendue politiquement. Quel sens donner à cette richesse de sens?
ou plutôt à quoi tient cette multiplicité de sens? d'abord, à la
nature mixte, ambigüe aujourd'hui encore, de ce que l'on appelle
médecine. A la fois art, savoir, discours théorique, intervention
pratique, le médecin obéit à l'impératif thérapeutique; la
médecine, le médecin appartiennent très fortement au tissu social,
ne serait-ce que par la médicalisation ou par la sacralisation de
l'attitude médicale devant les grandes constantes de la vie
collective, la naissance, la maladie et la mort. Aussi une
histoire de la médecine ne peut-elle utiliser le concept
proprement historique de révolution qu'avec la plus extrême
prudence: révolution théorique, changement brusque dans la
pratique, innovation thérapeutique, efficacité quantifiable,
modification des politiques de la santé?

La transformation du champ du savoir médical ne change pas ipso
facto la pratique ni la thérapeutique. Dans l'histoire de cette
discipline, le paradigme de la révolution astronomique ne
fonctionne pas de manière satisfaisante. Il ne peut en être
autrement si l'on adopte par provision la définition kuhnienne
d'une révolution scientifique, une communauté qui change de
paradigme. La communauté dite médicale n'est pas homogène, le
paradigme lui-même s'éclate dans des directions qui n'ont rien de
commun entre elles. Il faut un long temps pour qu'une révolution
théorique, par exemple la théorie harveyenne de la circulation, la
notion de tissu ou le concept de cellule, définissent un nouvel
art de guérir. Inversement, une pratique efficace comme celle de
la vaccination jennerienne attend plusieurs décennies pour
trouver, avec Pasteur, son fondement théorique.

Ces préalables méthodologiques posés, la question peut être plus
précisément formulée: les "nouveaux savoirs" qui se font jour de
1795 à 1820 constituent-ils une révolution en médecine, comme en
ont eu conscience les contemporains, comme ils l'ont écrit? ou
bien s'agit-il d'une simple contamination du vocabulaire, d'un
glissement du politique à la science?

La réforme de la médecine se situe entre les deux rapports de
Fourcroy qui aboutissent à la loi du 14 frimaire An III (4
décembre 1794), puis à celle du 19 ventôse An XI (9 mars 1803). La
première crée les trois écoles de santé de Paris, Montpellier et
Strasbourg dans le cadre très général de l'Instruction publique et
lie formellement, explicitement l'enseignement à la clinique,
c'est-à-dire à la structure hospitalière.

Réforme donc incontestable: les machines à guérir sont aussi des
machines à enseigner et à chercher, sur fond de constitution du
regard clinique et d'exploration due à l'anatomo-pathologie, dans
l'urgence toutefois de pallier les insuffisannces numériques du
corps médical et "l'anarchie et le brigandage" qui prolifèrent
naturellement sur ces insuffisances. Mais y-a-t-il alors
révolution dans le savoir médical et dans l'art de guérir? Que
signifie en fait l'extraordinaire floraison des traités, des
revues, des écoles de l'extrême fin du XVIIIème siècle au tout
début du XIXème siècle?

Il faut procéder par énumération. Non que l'énumération réponde
d'emblée à la question posée, mais elle apporte, par son abondance
même, la certitude que, quels que fussent ces "nouveaux savoirs",
ils étaient alors perçus comme scientifiques et comme nouveaux. La
publication est, on le sait plus nettement aujourd'hui, un critère
tangible de la production scientifique. La littérature médicale
produite sur ces trois décennies progressivement isole, décrit,
dénomme non plus des entités nosologiques mais soit des ensembles
de symptômes - des syndrômes -, à partir desquels se dégagent des
pronostics constants - c'est-à-dire des déductions statistiquement
probables; soit des méthodes d'exploration qui sur le vivant
substituent l'examen à l'observation, qui post mortem comparent ce
que donne à comprendre la dissection des organes et des tissus.
Entre l'induction et la déduction du phénomène morbide, le savoir
médical se déploie désormais dans un espace causal diffus certes,
approximatif, mais qui ouvre la voie à l'intervention
thérapeutique efficace dans la chaîne des causes.

Dans les dernières années du siècle, la littérature médicale ouvre
cette voie avec X. Bichat, "Recherches physiologiques sur la vie
et la mort" (1800) et avec Pinel, qui transforme déjà la vieille

nosographie en la pensant "philosophique", c'est-à-dire positive
et différentielle (1798, Nosographie philosophique). G.L. Bayle
(1774-1816) en 1801 publie les "Remarques sur les tubercules" qui
précisent l'appréhension du phénomène cancéreux, et en 1810-1812,
ses 'Recherches sur la phtisie', chef-d'oeuvre de la clinique. La
méthode d'exploration de la cage thoracique par la percussion -
mise au point par Auenbrugger en 1763, présenté au public français
en 1770 - se diffuse derechef par la traduction de Corvisart en
1808. Dix ans plus tard, sur le plan de la méthode, c'est
l'auscultation médiate qui triomphe avec Laënnec. De 1806 à 1814,
J. Alibert (1768-1837) décrit les maladies de la peau. Au même
moment, en 1803, le baron Portal (1742-1832), dont la longévité
traverse tous les régimes, donne la somme de son expérience
d'anatomie clinique dans les trois volumes d'"Anatomie clinique".
En 1808, le grand Broussais, du côté de la doctrine et non de la
théorie, publie l'"Histoire des phlégmasies chroniques", tandis
que J.N. Corvisart (1755-1821) fait paraître l'"Essai sur les
maladies et les lésions du coeur", 1806. Au même moment le
chimiste Berzélius met en évidence la présence du fer dans le
sang. En 1813, Petit et Serres traitent de la fièvre
étéromésentérique. En 1811, Le Gallois avait localisé le centre
respiratoire dans le bulbe. En 1817, Chaumel fait paraître les
"Eléments de pathologie générale". La même année, Parkinson isole
la paralysie tremblante qui désormais porte son nom. En 1819,
Laënnec traite de l'"Auscultation médiate". On retrouve la même
année Serres dans l'analyse des hémorragies méningées et de
l'épilepsie partielle. En 1818, à Genève, Mayer s'intéresse aux
bruits du coeurs du foetus. En 1821, C. Itard public un "Traité
des maladies de l'oreille et de l'audition". En 1822, Bayle le
neveu, c'est-à-dire Antoine-Laurent, décrit la paralysie générale,
rend caduque la distinction classique de la manie et de la
mélancolie dans sa thèse de Doctorat "Recherches sur l'arachnitis
chronique". En 1817, du sel d'opium que Delorme avait isolé en
1803, Serturner extrait la morphine. Enfin, pour sacrifier au rite
de la numération par dix, en 1820, Pelletier et Caventoux dans la
série des alcaloïdes isole la quinine, un remède parfaitement
efficace.

Tous ces titres - quelques-uns tirés de la masse - sont le fait de
médecins praticiens, qui trouvent à l'hôpital les conditions de la

clinique, le malade, la maladie et la mort. Aussi significative
que leur prolifération est la succession des revues médicales,
expression d'un certain nombre de sociétés et d'écoles,
rétrospectivement désignees sous le terme générique d'Ecole de
Paris. Dès l'An IV apparaît la Société Médicale d'Emulation avec
Bichat, Larrey et Alibert; le mot de Bichat souligne le
retournement de la nouvelle médecine: "les sciences accessoires
deviennent essentielles; la médecine les a conquises". La même
année 1796, la Société de Médecine de Paris se crée; en 1808,
l'Athénée Médical; en 1810, le "Bulletin des Sciences Médicales".
Au-delà des années 20, la Société Médicale d'Observation, fondée
par trois élèves du Dr. Louis (1830-1832); Jules Guérin, en 1830,
lance la "Gazette Médicale de Paris", avant de lancer l'expression
de médecine sociale en 1848; en 1828, c'est la "Lancette
française"; enfin, en 1848, la Société de Biologie va établir la
médiation entre la médecine et la médecine expérimentale.

On a l'impression d'assister à une véritable inflation des savoirs
médicaux, du côté des doctrines comme du côté de ce phénomène tout
nouveau qu'est le développement des "spécialités". Savoirs
nouveaux, savoirs précis. Mais l'oeuvre de l'école clinique
française s'accompagne-t-elle d'un développement analogue du
pouvoir médical? La médecine peut-elle guérir plus efficacement à
la mesure de ce qu'elle sait? En fait, tant qu'il ne s'agit pas
d'intervention chirurgicale, le pouvoir médical reste
thérapeutiquement très limité. Pourtant, il y a un pouvoir du
médecin, mais il est alleurs, du côté de la notabilité, de
l'hygiène et de l'économie. Des textes littéraires, comme "Le
médecin de campagne", "Le Curé de village", qui datent des années
35 sont éloquents sur ce point. Que font ces médecins? Ils
développent une région, en pensent l'économie et en équilibrent
les forces sociales. Dans "Le médecin de campagne", on ne relève
que trois interventions proprement médicales: une intervention
préventive, qui consiste à isoler un crétin pour qu'il ne procrée
pas, intervention socio-médicale plus que médicale d'ailleurs; une
auscultation à l'oreille et une percussion au doigt d'un enfant;
la constatation d'un décès. Symétriquement, Balzac voit le pouvoir
médical en ville, non plus du côté de l'économie et de l'hygiène,

mais du côté de la politique et de la libre pensée: littérairement l'influence économico-politique du médicin est plus évidente que son efficacité thérapeutique.

Les contemporains sont parfaitement conscients de l'impuissance médicale, accompagnée de tant de savoirs. Ce pouvoir ne peut être affirmé que par les charlatans .... Les prospectus médicaux sont probants sur ce point. Par exemple, dans un prospectus pour vendre un livre de Portal, "Observations sur la nature et le traitement des maladies du foie", on lit: "C'est là qu'on apprendra à bien connaître les maladies du foie, à ne plus les confondre avec d'autres affections dont les symptômes sont plus ou moins semblables et à leur opposer un traitement sinon toujours efficace, du moins constamment rationnel. Il n'est pas un praticien qui ne voudrait avoir dans sa bibliothèque cet excellent traité et ne désire en posséder un du même genre sur toutes les maladies."[7] Sont ici présents les quatre éléments de l'acte médical, praticien, malade, diagnostic et traitement; mais dès qu'il s'agit de qualifier le traitement, il n'est "pas toujours efficace"; si la guérison intervient, c'est "par hasard" ou selon les vues déconcertantes de la nature, non de l'art; il est néanmoins "rationnel", c'est-à-dire conforme à la doctrine et aux faits.

Sacerdoce et Magistrature

En 1797, le médecin Pierre Cabanis écrivait dans "Les degrés de certitude en médecine": "Sous certains aspects, la profession de médecin est une espèce de sacerdoce. Sous d'autres, c'est une véritable magistrature."[8] Il est significatif que le pouvoir de guérir, qui, dans les mentalités, se transforme très spontanément en obligation de guérir, ne soit pas mentionné par Cabanis et à cette date, c'est-à-dire vingt cinq ans avant le prospectus que je viens de commenter, comme étant le propre du médecin. Celui-ci tente de guérir, mais il n'y parvient ni toujours ni toujours complètement. On ne peut que relever cette constante, et interroger sur ce qui la rend possible et tenter de comprendre comment et à quel moment elle a pu cesser d'être.

Cabanis est une bonne reférence, puisqu'il a été pour une part
l'inspirateur des lois qui de 1794 à 1805, ont défini
l'enseignement et l'exercice de la médecine pour un bon
demi-siècle.[9]   Pour lui, la guérison du malade vient de surcroît,
s'ajoute à l'exercise d'un art médical, instinct perfectionné par
l'habitude, garantie contres les charlatans et prise de décision
d'un homme investi de la confiance du malade et d'un certain
savoir.[10] Investi de la confiance du malade et d'un certain savoir
- lié au divin Hippocrate -, c'est en cela que le médecin exerce
un sacerdoce. Rempart contre les charlatans, il exerce une
véritable magistrature au sein de la cité.

Pour Cabanis, positiviste avant la lettre comme le sont la plupart
des Idéologues dans leur référence à Condillac, ce savoir est un
savoir des faits, non des causes: de là, une limite de principe de
l'intervention, donc de l'efficacité. Les surprises thérapeutiques
sont de règle, non que l'idiosyncrasie d'un organisme soit tel
qu'à tel médicament, un organisme réagit d'une façon ou d'une
autre, mais parce que récuser la possibilité d'atteindre les
causes transforme la pratique médicale en constatation de
régularités, non de règles.

Scepticisme thérapeutique et nouveaux savoirs posent à l'historien
un problème: qu'est-ce qui va rendre possible la suite,
c'est-à-dire le renversement dont la seconde moitié du XIXème
siècle est le théâtre, renversement qui lie une indéniable, puis
spectaculaire efficacité thérapeutique à l'étiologie? La réponse,
me semble-t-il, est doublement paradoxale. Ce qui va rendre
possible l'efficacité thérapeutique n'a pas nécessairement une
origine médicale, premier paradoxe, et n'est pas immédiatement
l'objet d'une reconnaissance médicale, second paradoxe. Il suffit
d'une part de rappeler Pasteur, chimiste, qui démontre
expérimentalement l'existence des micro-organismes et pour
certains, leurs actions pathogènes spécifiques, dans une
succession de recherches d'abord axées sur les épizooties et sur
les fermentations. De l'autre, de rendre hommage à la mémoire du
médecin praguois I. Semmelweis, mort fou d'avoir mis en lumière le
fait et la cause de la fièvre puerpérale et de n'avoir pas pu
obtenir du personnel médical qu'il reconnaisse le fait et se plie
aux règles qu'il préconisait.[11]

D'où la nécessité de faire intervenir, dans l'histoire de la
médecine, avant même la période contemporaine, l'histoire de
disciplines non strictement médicales. Aux "nouveaux savoirs" se
juxtaposent et parfois se mêlent des recherches qui n'ont pas pour
objet le malade, mais le vivant, détournées de toute visée
thérapeutique immédiate. Le phénomène pathologique n'est ni le
premier ni le seul travaillé, et le cadre de ces recherches ne se
confond ni avec la structure hospitalière ni avec la pratique
médicale. L'efficacité thérapeutique ou les stratégies préventives
relèvent alors de l'application d'une science autre à l'art, au
savoir médical. Dans le domaine qui est le nôtre ici, la
physiologie, la médecine, la chimie, la physique, l'urbanisme se
sont trouvés alors dans ce rapport incessant de provocation,
d'incitation. Le phénomène n'est d'ailleurs pas nouveau, certaines
institutions y ont répondu.[12]

Des Nouveaux Savoirs à la Positivité d'une Rationalité Proprement
Biologique

Tous les historiens des sciences inexactes connaissent la date de
naissance du mot "biologie", depuis longtemps repéré: 1802. Les
dictionnaires les plus classiques la mentionnent, Littré donne des
références précises et exactes, sous la rubrique étymologie, aussi
bien dans le "Dictionnaire de la langue française" que dans le
"Dictionnaire de médecine". C'est une date qui néanmoins reste
très irritante, car tout le monde s'y réfère et personne ne
l'analyse. Pourtant, l'esquisse d'une analyse devrait pouvoir
éclairer la nature de cette "rationalité proprement biologique"
qui chemine à côté de la médecine et à un moment donné, lui
fournit les conditions de sa positivité propre et de son
efficacité. Ce "savoir nouveau" fait partie des "nouveaux savoirs"
dont la médecine a dressé le catalogue pour la constitution de son
histoire et l'affermissement de son pouvoir; pourtant il s'en
distingue. C'est à déterminer les grandes lignes de ce "savoir
nouveau" qu'en dernier lieu nous nous attacherons.

On connaît les sources: "biologie" est un mot forgé et proposé
simultanément par Lamarck dans l'"Hydrologie" et dans ses
"Recherches sur l'organisation des corps vivants"[13] et par

Tréviranus, à Goettingen, dans "Biologie ou Philosophie de la
nature vivante pour les naturalistes et les médecins", six volumes
publiés de 1802 à 1822 et restés inachevés.[14] Il y aurait une
troisième référence, indiqué par le Pr. M. Klein, renvoyant à K.F.
Burdach, mais je ne l'ai pas utilisée. L'histoire commence avec
l'écrit: au sens strict, il n'y a d'histoire de la biologie qu'à
partir de 1802. Avant, on ne peut employer pour désigner son
territoire sans anachronisme que ce qui en désigne des parties -
anatomie, physiologie, histoire naturelle, philosophie naturelle
ou expérimentale, physique, médecine, observations et expériences,
- et non ce qui en constitue l'unité.

La tentation est donc grande de faire commencer le siècle sur une
notion désignée par un terme attesté. Mais l'illusion est non
moins grande de confondre un terme et le sens auquel il répond
explicitement à sa date de création avec la richesse de ses
connotations ultérieures. Le problème est très nettement posé par
le rapprochement de deux phrases que j'emprunte à un article de G.
Canguilhem. Mais à ma connaissance, le problème n'a pas été
exploré en tant que tel. Dans cet article consacré au singulier et
à la singularité en épistémologie biologique: "Pas de biologie
avant et sans Bichat, avant et sans Lavoisier, même si ceux qui
inventent le terme, Lamarck et Tréviranus, ne se réclament ni de
l'un ni de l'autre". Et dix pages plus loin: "Le XIXème siècle a
deux ans lorsque meurt Bichat et que naît conceptuellement la
biologie"[15]. Lamarck et Tréviranus sont-ils les fondateurs du mot
et du concept, si par concept on entend non un terme mais un
procédé opératoire ou exploratoire appartenant à une théorie
toujours soumises à une réfutation... possible? S'ils ne sont les
créateurs que du mot, quel est le contexte théorique, puisqu'à la
même date - humor plus que ruse de l'histoire - naît
conceptuellement la biologie, au sein d'une lignée théorique toute
autre? De cette lignée relèverait le savoir nouveau qu'on peut
appeler biologie, que les fondateurs eux-mêmes désignent plus
volontiers comme une physiologie expérimentale, dont la
physiologie de l'homme malade est un cas particulier, que d'autres
appellent médecine. Préciser le sens, le did et le non-dit
constitue en enjeu non négligeable, à l'entrée d'un siècle
positiviste d'accent, qu'on le veuille ou non: la biologie dans
l'ordre encyclopédique occupe la position éminente qui rend

possible la sociologie, joue le rôle de modèle et fonde les
emprunts conceptuels qui, à i'intérieur des disciplines ayant pour
objet le vivant, le milieu, le social, n'ont cessé depuis de les
constituer.

La création du terme - ce qui appartient en propre à Lamarck et à
Tréviranus - est le fait de "naturalistes-philosophes"
(l'expression est de Lamarck): "Quelle peut être l'origine des
corps vivants pour un naturaliste-philosophe? ... La vie n'est pas
un être particulier, un principe quelconque que possèdent les
corps vivants ... La vie est un ordre et un état de choses dans
les parties de tout corps qui la possède, qui permettent ou
rendent possible lui l'exécution du mouvement organique et qui,
tant qu'ils subsistent, s'opposent efficacement à la mort"[16].
"Biologie" pour Lamarck, pour la Naturphilosophie, désigne un type
de réflexion et de spéculation sur les formes vivantes dont le
répertoire a été l'oeuvre du XVIIIème siècle, oeuvre dont le but
est de vouloir rendre compte de l'échelle des êtres observés et
perçus dans l'espace et le temps. Temps et espace, là réside
l'innovation: le XIXème siècle peut se caractériser par
l'utilisation systématique, par la variation rigoureuse de ces
deux ordonnées. L'ambigüité du texte de Lamarck, l'espèce de
issonnance qu'y perçoit le lecteur moderne tiennent à cette double
appartenance: d'une part la classification et la nomenclature
propre au XVIIIème siècle, dont il se défend d'ailleurs[17]; de
l'autre, une spéculation hardie, dont la limite, radicale, est la
non-expérimentation - ce que relève Cuvier dans un "éloge"
académique, qui est un contre-éloge.[18] Mais cette spéculation
hardie ne sera accomplie en même temps qu'infirmée qu'en 1859,
avec l'Origine des espèces: au mot "biologie" répond alors un
concept, celui d'évolution, qui opère suivant les deux axes du
hasard et de la nécessité.

Du côté du concept non nommé oeuvrent un chimiste et un
anatomo-physiologiste, Lavoisier et Bichat. Ils appartiennent à
une longue histoire qui n'est pas strictement celle de la médecine
- même si Bichat est un des médecins de l'Hôtel-Dieu, un
professeur de la Faculté de médecine de Paris -, mais plutôt celle
de la physiologie[19]. On sait qu'avec Lavoisier se substitue à la
mythologie des rapports du microcosme au macrocosme l'étude des

rapports du vivant et de son milieu, l'étude des échanges
quantifiables qui aboutissent à la mise en évidence de la nature
des grandes fonctions de la vie animale. La science du vivant peut
être une science exacte - quantifiée, expérimentée -, par la
médiation de phénomènes appartenant au monde inorganique. Bichat,
qui insiste sur l'instabilité fondamentale des processus vitaux,
n'en demande pas moins de penser rationnellement et spécifiquement
les phénomènes communs à tous les êtres vivants, pour atteindre
les lois générales d'une "vie" dont le propre et de n'être jemais
atteinte que médiatement. La vie est un résultat, non une cause,
elle est "l'ensemble des fonctions qui résistent à la mort. Elle
est en effet le mode d'existence des corps vivants, que tout ce
qui les entoure tend à détruire ... bientôt ils succomberaient
s'ils n'avaient en eux un principe permanent de réaction. Ce
principe est celui de la vie; inconnu dans la nature, il ne peut
être apprécié que par ses phénomènes."[20] Citation célèbre à
laquelle il faut ajouter l'apport de l'"Anatomie générale
appliquée à la physiologie et à la médecine" (1801) et du "Traité
des membranes" (1800). L'anatomie classique distingue les organes,
auxquels répondent les fonctions. L'anatomo-physiologie de Bichat
cherche à mettre en évidence, à reconnaître et à spécifier les
éléments qui constituent les organes, la texture, le tissu,
auxquels n'appartiennent pas nécessairement un seul type de
fonction.

De l'histologie à la cytologie, de Bichat à R. Virchow, le chemin
est ouvert vers ce qui est l'objet d'une "biologie" au sens
moderne du terme, la science du "vivant élémentaire", dans ses
deux sens, soit du plus simple organisme vivant - l'unicellulaire
-, soit de l'élément qui constitue tout organisme complexe vivant
- la cellule -, dans un ordre double de structure et de fonction.
La biologie, comme l'écrit Littré quelques soixante ans plus tard,
est bien une science abstraite et générale: abstraite, elle
retranche pour atteindre le simple - selon les lois et les limites
de l'analyse; générale, elle peut affirmer que tout organisme
vivant est constitué par des éléments de ce type. Car "tous les
systèmes complexes connus qui contiennent des macromolécules et
sont capables de se reproduire appartiennent au monde vivant ...
la plus petite unité de l'intégration, de coopération et de
reproduction est la cellule ... il est essentiel de savoir que le

terme cellule s'appliqué à deux catégories différentes de système:
la partie dépendante de l'organisme multicellulaire et l'organisme
unicellulaire independante"[21]. Ce texte, qui appartient à la
science d'aujourd'hui permet d'apprécier l'enjeu de ce qui s'est
noué, avec Bichat, en 1802: à une définition agonistique de la vie
– logiquement vicieuse comme le remarque Magendie – répond la
recherche du vivant élémentaire, totalité organisée ou élément
spécifique d'un tout organisé, objet et fin de ce savoir d'un type
nouveau que les naturalistes ont appelé alors, mais a côté,
biologie.

Il faut maintenant conclure ce long périple, en reconnaissant les
termes qui, appartenant ou n'appartenant pas au domaine de la
médecine, émergent et constituent une bonne part de ce qui rend
possible l'innovation médicale, plus tard, après 1820, la
transformation de sa pratique avec des marges d'incertitude
moindres. A l'intérieur de ces dates, 1795-1820, l'interrogation
sur les "nouveaux savoirs" a conduit de l'Ecole de Paris aux
tables de dissection et aux laboratoires dans lesquels s'élabore
un savoir expérimental de l'organisme. En retour, le savoir
expérimental de l'organisme, qui n'a pas alors pour nom celui de
biologie, réservé aux spéculations des naturalistes, permettra
ultérieurement à la médecine de conquérir des titres de
positivité, ceux-là même dont Bichat contestait la possibilité; ce
sera l'oeuvre, encore, en France, d'un physiologiste Claude
Bernard et d'un chimiste Pasteur, pour ne citer que des
noms-repères, oeuvre préparée par la réflexion d'un
mathématicien-philosophe, Auguste Comte.

L'histoire – en l'occurence l'histoire de la médecine – participe
de cette métaphore du voyage: elle n'est pas plus linéaire que ne
l'est le périple, quand on la concoit comme une histoire des
concepts, des filiations et des emprunts, et non comme une
description des pratiques et des écoles. Au-delà des vogues et des
mandarinats, à travers les pratiques, les idéologies et les
conceptualisations théoriques, l'histoire progressive de la
médecine met en jeu, autour de l'idée expérimentale, des
disciplines qui semblent étrangères au précepte hippocratique,
soulager et ne pas nuire. Les détours peuvent en être symbolisés
par la multiplicité des institutions médicales et non médicales

que, dans ce rapide survol d'une époque, nous avons évoquées:
l'Hôtel-Dieu avec Bichat, fondateur de la discipline histologique
et de l'unité de la science du vivant; le Muséum, avec Lamarck,
créateur du terme dont Bichat fonde le concept, biologie; du
concept à l'idéologie (à la philosophie) de la discipline, c'est
l'Ecole Polytechnique et Auguste Comte; de l'Ecole Polytechnique
au Collège de France, Magendie, successeur de Laënnec, lui-même
"pur" médecin de l'Ecole de Paris. Mais en 1821, la création du
"Journal de physiologie expérimentale" peut symboliser l'exigence
institutionnelle d'une discipline positive, qui identifie la
pensée du vivant à une recherche fondamentale dont le "savoir
médical" bénéficie, peut bénéficier autant qu'il y participe.
Quant au pouvoir médical, qui ne saurait totalement s'identifier
au savoir, il ne peut que relever le cri de guerre de Magendie,
singulièrement limitatif: "la médecine n'est que la physiologie de
l'homme malade". Plus tard, il faudra aller rue d'Ulm, à l'Ecole
Normale Supérieure, pour y trouver Pasteur, retour de l'Université
de Lille et de la brasserie Bigot, Roux et Grancher; au
laboratoire de la Préfecture de la Seine et aux services de santé
militaire du Val de Grâce, entre Laveran et Miquel, pour se
retrouver, en 1894, dans les salles des diphtériques à l'Hôpital
des Enfants Malades et à l'Hôpital Broussais, et dans les
laboratoires d'analyse du tout nouvel Institut Pasteur.

Notes

1 Doublement métaphorique, vocabulaire astronomique, temps de
révolution d'un astre; vocabulaire médical, mouvement
extraordinaire des humeurs. Cette source double, qui joint à
l'idée d'une chronologie l'idée d'une crise, rend compte du sens
nouveau apparu dès la fin du XVIIème siècle, du changement brusque
dans les affaires du monde.
2 Foucault, M.: Naissance de la clinique, une archéologie du
savoir médical, Paris 1963.
3 Cf. Ackerknecht, E.H.: Institut d'Histoire de la Médecine de
l'Université de Zurich, 1967.
4 Cf. Foucault, Naissance (ref. 2), ch. X, La crise des fièvres,
et Ackerknecht, E.: Broussais as a forgotten medical revolution,

in: Bull. Hist. de la Méd. 27 (1953), pp. 320–343.

5 Les premiers textes de Magendie sont de 1809 et 1816.

6 Cabanis, P.: Oeuvres Complètes, éd. critique, vol. II, Paris 1956; Cf. Salomon-Bayet, C.: L'institution de la Science: un exemple au XVIIIème siècle, in: Annales E.S.C. 5 (1975).

7 Liste des prospectus de la maison Bechet jeune, qui est le libraire de la Faculté de médecine, dans la quatrième édition des 'Recherches physiologiques sur la vie et la mort de Bichat' (1822); les prospectus indiquent la manière de présenter ce qui est à vendre et ce qui va être acheté.

8 Du degré de certitude en médecine, t. I, p. 99 (note 2) ad finem. Ce texte publié en 1789, a été réedité en 1797.

9 Cf. Foucault, Naissance (ref. 2), ch. V., et Salomon-Bayet, C.: L'institution (ref. 6).

10 Dans le 'Journal de la maladie et de la mort de Mirabeau', dont Cabanis était le médecin et l'ami, toutes ces composantes sont admirablement analysées.

11 I. Semmelweis (1818-1865), dans les hôpitaux de Prague, saisit la réalité du vecteur de l'agent de la fièvre puerpérale, c'est-à-dire les mains des médecins qui passent, sans lavage, de la salle de dissection à la salle d'accouchement. La thèse de médecine de Louis-Ferdinand Céline – Docteur Destouches – porte sur ce cas d'obstacle épistémologique.

12 Cf. Salomon-Bayet, C.: L'Institution de la science et l'expérience du vivant. Méthode et expérience à l'Académie royale des sciences (1666-1793), Paris 1978.

13 Lamarck, J.B.A. de: Recherches sur l'organisation des corps vivants, et particulièrement sur son origine, sur la cause de ses développments et des progrès de sa composition, et sur celle qui, tendant continuellement à la détruire dans chaque individu, amène nécessairement la mort. Précédé du discours du cours de Zoologie, donné dans le Muséum National d'Histoire Naturelle, l'an X de la République, Paris an X, 1803.

14 Ces volumes de Tréviranus n'existent ni à la Bibliothèque Nationale, ni à la Bibliothèque Centrale du Muséum. Ils ont été consultés à la Widener Library, Cambridge, Mass. Le terme se retrouve sans périphrase, avec la simple traduction d'équivalence, dans le titre du volume de M. Fodera, en 1826, Baillère, Londres. 'Discours sur la biologie ou science de la vie' suivi d'un tableau des connaissances naturelles envisagées d'après leur nature et

leur filiation. En 1836, dans la 40ème leçon du 'Cours de philosophie positive', A. Comte développe l'histoire de la "rationalité proprement biologique". En 1862 encore, dans le 'Traité sur l'enchaînement des idées fondamentales dans les Sciences et dans l'histoire', A.A. Cournot écrit que "pour mieux prévenir toute équivoque (entre les sciences physiques et cosmologiques, les sciences naturelles et l'histoire naturelle), il faudrait sans doute accepter définitivement la dénomination de sciences biologiques qui déjà commence à s'accréditer" (éd. Lévy-Bruhl, p. 235).

15 Canguilhem, G.: Etudes d'histoire et de philosophie des Sciences, Paris 1968, pp. 215 et 225.

16 Recherches sur l'organisation ..., Partie II, pp. 68,71.

17 Ibid, p. 4: "Il (le naturaliste) ne doit pas consumer son temps, ses forces et sa vie entière à fixer dans sa mémoire les caractères, les noms et les synonymes multipliés de cette innombrable multitude d'espèce ... Cette entreprise exclusive ne serait propre ... qu'à étouffer son génie, et qu'à le priver de la satisfaction de concourir à donner à la science l'impulsion et la véritable direction qu'elle doit avoir pour remplir son objet."

18 Au point que les enfants de Lamarck ont tenté d'en suspendre la publication. Baron Cuvier: Eloge de Lamarck - 1831-1832, p. 13: "Ainsi, pendant que Lavoisier créait dans son laboratoire une chimie nouvelle, appuyée d'une suite si belle et si méthodique d'expériences, M. de Lamarck, sans expérimenter, sans même aucun moyen de le faire, en imaginait une autre ... dès 1802 ... il eut une physiologie à lui, comme dans ses Recherches sur les causes des principaux faits physiques, il avait eu une chimie."

19 Littré, 'Dictionnaire de médecine', article 'biologie', ... "la biologie, qui dépend de la physique et surtout de la chimie, envisage les êtres organisés sous deux faces 1o. statiquement c'est-à-dire aptes a agir; 2o. et dynamiquement, c'est-a-dire comme agissant ... Au point de vue dynamique la biologie comprend, la physiologie; les actions réciproques du milieu (physique, chimique ou social) sur l'être vivant, et de celui-ci sur le dernier, point par lequel la biologie touche à la science des sociétés (cf. Sociologie). Contrairement à l'histoire naturelle, la biologie est une science abstraite et considère à un point de vue général les corps organisés qu'elle étudie"...

20 'Recherches physiologiques sur la vie et la mort', 1800.

Magendie réédítant en 1822, ce texte, commente: "Le mot de vie a
été employé chez les physiologistes en deux sens différents. Chez
les uns, il désigne un être de raison, principe unique de toutes
les fonctions que présente un corps vivant. Chez d'autres, il
désigne simplement l'ensemble des fonctions. C'est dans ce dernier
sens que Bichat l'emploie. Il a eu tort seulement d'y faire entrer
l'idée de mort, car cette idée suppose nécessairement celle de
vie." (note p. 2).
21 Lwoff, A.: L'ordre biologique, Paris 1969, pp. 14-15.

Abstract

Two new facts guide the examination of epistemological problems
raised by life sciences at the beginning of the 19th century: in
the medical field, the birth of the clinic, the realisation of
"new knowledge" contemporary of new times; apart from the
hospital, the creation by naturalists - at the same date in France
and Germany - of the term "biology" which defines an additional
object of knowledge apart from the "ill man" and an additional
preoccupation than the therapeutical preoccupation. But does this
really mean a "revolution" in life sciences?

We are trying in this text to show how by the analysis of new
knowledge proposed by the clinics and by the examination of the
meaning of the term "biology" in 1802 - and contrary to the
popular belief, this is not the meaning that was defined around
1860, which approaches the modern meaning - the heterogeneity of
the scientific community (doctors, practitioners, doctrinarians,
naturalists and laboratory staff) forbids the explanatory plan of
the substitution of one paradigm for another.

On the one hand, "new knowledge" has not resulted in a
transformation of medical practice of a further guaranteed
efficiency; on the other, the term "biology" used by Lamarck and
Treviranus in 1802, illustrated a type of consideration and
speculaton on living forms - in time and in space - which will be
substituted in 1859 by the term "evolution" and Darwin's theory.
In order to find the origins of a general science of the organism,
of the elementary life that we now call biology, we should not
turn to the inventors of the term, but rather to those from Bichat
to Virchow, who abandoned the hospital for the laboratory. Later
it is in the laboratory that the history of medicine will cross
the history of biology.

P. Gajdenko

ONTOLOGIC FOUNDATION OF SCIENTIFIC KNOWLEDGE IN SEVENTEENTH- AND EIGHTEENTH-CENTURY RATIONALISM

For the philosophy of the 17th and of the first half of the 18th century, a contrast existed between scientific and non-scientific thinking: This contrast really reached back to antiquity: even Anaxagoras had contrasted the philosophy of a rational way of explaining the world with mythology and religion. And since the 17th century traditional scholasticism is set against the scientific approach to reality. As evidence, one only has to remember Galilei's criticism of Aristotlelism, Bacon's exposure of all the prejudices of non-scientific thinking, or the radical Cartesian "doubt".

But the most remarkable fact of all is the fact that despite our general conviction of its gnoseologic character being the substance of the "new" philosophy since the 17th century, the dichotomy of scientific and non-scientific cognition is explained here ontologically. Scientific knowledge is knowledge that discovers the true structure of the world, non-scientific knowledge is regarded as a delusion which is created by the subjective qualities of human perception. Francis Bacon described these qualities in a vivid metaphor as "the roughness, unevenness" of the mirror that is to reflect the real objects.

So, as the result of an ontologic foundation of the theory of cognition, the problem of the subjective qualities of human perception was considered mainly in connection with the question

H. N. Jahnke and M. Otte (eds.), Epistemological and Social Problems of the Sciences in the Early Nineteenth Century, 55–63.

of the nature and origins of the delusion. I.e., it was not asked
how true knowledge is possible but how delusion is possible.
This is quite legitimate in an ontologic foundation of knowledge,
because instead of asking about the possibility of true knowledge
it asks: What is the world? What is being? It's epistemology is a
theory of delusion and the problem of true knowledge is
substituted by an essentially ontologic question: How is the world
arranged, in which way does it exist?
This was a very deep-reaching and general assumption of
philosophical thinking in the 17th and the first half of the 18th
century so that Kant had to take great pains over questioning it.
This assumption was actually based in the conviction that clear
and distinct thinking understands being itself and that the true
nature of scientific thinking lies in this very comprehension of
being. Cases in which non-being (the non-existing) is thought,
i.e., where thinking is deluded, are abnormal and pathological.
And a theory of cognition is intended to reveal the origins of
this very pathology.
About the conditions for a possibility of true, i.e. scientific,
thinking no special question is necessary: it would be nonsense
because then the only basis on which we could ever put any
question would be destroyed. If this unshakable basis was ever
doubted, we could no longer think about anything: there must,
after all, be a final 'referee', an "arbitrum extremum", and the
very 'thinking-which-thinks-being', i.e. ontological thinking is
such an arbiter. And an investigation of this thinking could not
have any other form than that of an analysis of being itself, i.e.
has to be ontological itself.
At a superficial glance, the Cartesian doctrine seems to
contradict our above conclusions. After all, it was Descartes
himself who introduced the well-known principle of subjective
assessment into the new philosophy in that he put the
investigation of the human capabilities of knowing before the
analysis of being.
In reality, however, this subjective Cartesian assessment is based
on the ontological proof of existence of God: this very proof
warrants the "cogito ergo sum"; and this final truth, assessed by
means of the proof of the existence of God, constitutes the
foundation of the entire structure of Cartesianism.
The ontology (or doctrine of substance) built on this foundation

again confirms, from another point of view, the possibility of true knowledge which has been doubted at the beginning. The essentially epistemological problems, although playing an important role in Cartesian philosophy, appear as a sort of propaedeutic which is to prepare the grounds for the construction of ontology.

Witness Descartes' own considerations: "... Because quite to the contrary, I clearly realize that more reality is contained in the infinite substance than in the finite, and that accordingly the concept of the infinite in a certain sense precedes that of the finite, i.e. the concept of God precedes that of myself. However should I otherwise understand that I am doubtful, that I desire something, i.e. that I am lacking something and that I am not quite perfect, if no idea of a more perfect being was in me through comparison with which I recognize my own imperfection?"[1] Thus even the doubt with which Descartes begins his metaphysical meditations has its foundation in the infinite substance.

The nature of thinking lies in its ontologism, because thinking means thinking of being - this thesis is the essential point of Cartesian doctrine. It can also be formulated in a different way: thinking is determined by what is thought, by its object. With Descartes, this is most clearly and distinctly expressed in the following excerpt: "... The second objection", he writes, refuting the arguments against his foundaton of true knowledge, "is: it does not follow from my having the idea of a more perfect being than I that this idea is more perfect than I, and even less that what is envisioned by this idea does exist. To this I answer that here is an ambiguity in the word 'idea', for one can understand it either in a material sense (materialiter) as an activity of my intellect, and in this sense one cannot pronounce it more perfectly than I, or in an 'objective' sense (obiective) as the object represented by this activity, and even if one does not assume it to exist outside my intellect, it can still be more perfect than I because of its nature."[2]

Spinoza expressed the ontologic character of knowledge even more distinctly: his entire system is set out in a way that bases the theory of cognition on the doctrine of substance (ontology). For the thesis that it is not the subjective mentality but the structure of object and being that determines the contents of thinking, Spinoza found an apt formula: "Truth exposes itself as well as lies." Here we see his anti-psychological conviction that the nature of thinking lies in its ontologic character. According to Spinoza, the possibility of true knowledge need not be proved, on the contrary — it is the possibility of delusion that must be explained.

Kant and the Gnoseologic Foundation of Knowledge

Only with Kant epistemology advances to a fundamental and logically principal position in the philosophic system. Kant fundamentally changes the assumption of the earlier philosophy by regarding cognition as an activity following its own rules and making these rules the object of investigation. For the first time the manner of cognition is not determined by nature and structure of the recognizable substance but by those of the knowing subject, and the latter creates the object of cognition itself, as well as the means and method of its construction.

In contrast to the rationalists of the preceding period Kant does not ask how delusion can arise but asks the question of the possibility of true knowledge. This meant a radical change in philosophical thinking. Such questions, it is true, had been asked before Kant — by the empiricists, particularly in Hume's scepticism — but it was Kant who made them the principle of the construction of a positive epistemology, while with Hume it played a rather negative part as evidence for the impossibility of general and necessary scientific knowledge.
In consequence of this new question, the structure of the cognitive process as well as its source, direction and objective are to be considered from a new point of view. If from the point of view of ontology everything subjective seemed in the first place an obstacle, something that distorted and "darkened" the true state of things, then Kant undertakes to ascertain the difference between the subjective and the objective in the knowing subject itself and in its activity. For this purpose Kant introduces the difference between the empirical and the transcendental subject.

A subject, whose activity constructs the material world according to the determined principles and makes objective, i.e., according to Kant, scientific, knowledge possible, is a transcendental subject. The products of its activity are of a general and necessary nature - quite different from the products of an empirical subject's activity.

But even though Kant radically changed the conditions for a philosophical contemplation of science he remains true to the natural scientific thinking of his time in that he transfers the characteristics of substance defined by Newton to his own transcendental subject. Newton's absolute space and absolute time appear with Kant, though somewhat transformed, as a priori conceptions of the transcendental subject. In this way Kant succeeds in not only preserving the achievements of contemporary physics, i.e. of Galilei's and Newton's classical mechanics, he also gives them a philosophical foundation. But at the same time Kant qualifies this physics with an important reservation: the weltbild of classical physics did certainly not represent the portrayal of things as such.

As a compensation for thus restricting natural science, which according to Kant finds its subject only in the world of appearences and not in the world of actual things, he promises this science protection from every kind of scepticism by establishing its general and necessary character within the limits of experience.

Thus furnished with a new foundaton and interpretation the entire contents of classical physics was preserved. The most important elements of Kant's epistemology are: the unity-demanding reason, the intellect which realizes this demand and achieves a pure function of the unity, and lastly the variety which is to be transformed into unity and which in the activity of the intellect is represented by space and time as pure forms of variety. Without this representation a variety devoid of form would remain completely indeterminable (chaos, apeiron, what Plato called 'non-being'). In this case it could never be synthesized by the concept of reason. Kant understands synthesis in its most general meaning as "the activity of adding different conceptions to one another and comprehending their variety cognitively".[3]

In the Kantian system, space and time constitute an intermediate
link between the completely undetermined variety and thinking in
categories.

The Kantian transcendental subject thus receives an unhistoric
structure and this very structure becomes the main reason why
neither the world of experience nor the science attending to this
world — mathematical natural science above all — are merely an
empty logical construction devoid of reality. If only the
principle of unity was functioning as regulative axiom, a set of
logically thinkable worlds could be constructed (cf. Leibniz). But
these worlds would lack something which our world has — existence.
As Kant is convinced that science investigates an existing world,
it can definitely not restrict itself to the mere logical means of
knowledge. According to Kant, thinking is an empty shell if it is
not supported by material evidence, i.e. if it does not attend to
the variety outside itself. "Concepts without illustrative
material are empty."

In this manner Kant reproduces the radical difference between
scientific and non-scientific knowledge on a new basis. Kant's
teachings excercised powerful influence on another development of
the philosophical reflexion of science. But is was not so much his
solution to the problem of true knowledge but his way of putting
this problem, which transferred the emphasis to the subject of
scientific knowledge.

For the later German Idealism this restriction of philosophical
research to the subjects, to the principles of transcendental
subjectivity, has already become a matter of fact. Fichte and
Schelling concentrated their whole attention on the
epistemological subject that means they adhered to the Kantian way
of putting the question even though they opposed the Kantian
answer to the question. It can be said without exaggeraton that
nearly all post-Kantian philosophers, who contemplated the problem
of true knowledge and worked within the framework of the condition
introduced by Kant, rejected the earlier ontological foundation of
science.

And at the same time almost every philosopher who worked under
Kant's condition and called his own philosophy transcendental —
from Fichte and Schelling to Dilthey and Husserl — rejected the

Kantian solution of the problem. Thus the structure of transcendental subjectivity was reviewed, and that in very different ways.

German Idealism and the Ontologization of Transcendental Subjectivity

One of the schools in which Kant's teachings were revised at the beginning of the 19th century is represented by Fichte and Schelling who attended to the problem of foundaton of scientific knowledge.

According to Fichte and Schelling, the Kantian conception of the structure of transcendental subjectivity must be revised because it is determined by Kant's orientation on natural science and especially on the physics and mechanics of the 17th and 18th centuries. This is why, so Fichte and Schelling, Kant gave the knowing subject such a rigid, non-historic structure: it was intended to serve the purpose of supplying a foundation for the science of that time; other kinds of knowledge – art, myth –, however, were contrasted with natural science and not regarded as true knowledge.

In contrast to Kant, later idealism, especially with Schelling and Hegel, rather constitutes a criticism of natural science (as formed by Galilei and Newton). This fact easily explains the negative attitude of some 19th century natural scientists towards post-Kantian idealism as well as a growing interest in it which can be observed in several twentieth-century scientists during the crisis of classical physics.

This post-Kantian German Idealism, especially Hegel's, assumed a historical character for the knowing subject. But as here mankind as a whole appeared as the epistemological subject, the structure of the consciousness of mankind is considered historically determined. Now one could no longer speak of the rigid forms of transcendental subjectivity – these forms were described as developing. Now they were considered as objective forms of culture itself, not as the structure of a non-historic transcendental subject.

In concequence, some important principles which guided Kant and his predecessors were altered. Firstly, the old and, for seventeenth- and eighteenth-century thinking, undoubted dichotomy of scientific and non-scientific knowledge was resolved. Science was no longer contrasted with pre-scientific forms of knowledge: the latter were now recognized as its forerunners and science is a product of the development of these mythological pre-scientific forms. In the diachronic profile, science is compared with myth, in the synchronic, with the forms of knowledge existing within science, like art, religion, philosophy. The distinction of science and other kinds of knowledge, which had been essential for Kant and pre-Kantian rationalism, was already irrelevant for Schelling and Hegel. According to Schelling they have all basically equal rights, art has even an advantage over science because it can comprehend truth immediately and is therefore a more perfect kind of knowledge than science.

For Hegel, however, science is more adequate, but the general assumption of all kinds of knowledge being in a way equal is made as well.

Secondly, as the knowing subject is regarded as historical from now on, the opposition of true and false in the Kantian and pre-Kantian interpretation is removed as well. It was, after all, closely connected with the dichotomy of scientific and non-scientific knowledge. The problem of true and false knowledge was now transferred onto the historic plane. A new principle, unknown to the earlier rationalist philosophy, was formulated: "it is true for its time". Thus the concept of 'relative truth' is introduced.

Thirdly, as classical German philosophy regards history as the epistemological subject, the Kantian distinction between the empirical and the transcendental stages of observation is introduced into history: from now on we see two kinds of history: a factual, empirical history on the one hand and one that is, in Hegel's words, understood "in its concept", i.e. in its truth, on the other hand. The latter is really a certain speculative construction which had the same significance for German post-Kantian philosophy as the doctrine of substance had for pre-Kantian rationalism.

So it is on the basis of transcendental subjectivity that yet another special ontology develops in the form of a speculative

reconstruction of history - a subject ontology, so to speak.
History as the mode of being of the subject (of course, this is no
individual but a general subject) meant the same to Fichte,
Schelling, and Hegel as nature as the mode of being of the object
meant to Bacon, Descartes, and Spinoza. The speculative pattern of
the historical process in Fichte's, Schelling's, Hegel's idealism
appears as a new ontology: this very pattern constitutes the
standard in comparison to which the cultural-historical material
is analysed and understood - it is the principle of unity of the
historical variety.

This transition from the pre-Kantian ontology of object or nature
to the new ontology of subject or culture of post-Kantian German
Idealism entails the transfer of the philosophical emphasis from
the natural sciences (physics, mechanics, chemistry etc.) to the
cultural and historical sciences (the histories of art, religion,
mythology, states, science, and philosophy). These last provided
the basis of the new ontology.
It is also noteworthy that German Idealism regarded natural
science, too, as an element of cultural history, an element whose
development was not determined by the external world of objects
but by the logics of the historical process.

Thanks to this transfer of philosophical interest from the objects
of knowledge to the knowing subject German Idealism has removed a
defect characteristic of all earlier modern thinkers including the
materialists, a defect which, according to K. Marx, consisted of
the fact that "the object, reality, sensuousness were only
conceived in the form of the object or the conception ...; but not
as sensual human activity, practice; not subjectively."[4]

References

1 Descartes, R.: Meditationen ueber die Grundlage der
Philosophie, transl. A. Buchenau, Hamburg 1954, p. 37.
2 Ibid., p. 4.
3 Kant, I.: Kritik der reinen Vernunft, p. 77.
4 Marx, K.: Thesen ueber Feuerbach, in: Marx/Engels: Werke, vol.
3, p. 5.

Carlos-Ulises Moulines

HERMANN VON HELMHOLTZ: A PHYSIOLOGICAL APPROACH TO THE
THEORY OF KNOWLEDGE

0. Introduction

The philosophy of logical positivism, which so influenced the
epistemology and philosophy of science of the last decades,
certainly did not arise in a historical vacuum: everyone knows
that it has its ancestors. Among its historical antecedents, Hume,
Mach, the rise of modern logic, the early Wittgenstein, and the
great revolutions in physics are most often mentioned. I do not
intend to deny the significance of those influences; however, it
seems to me that they do not cover the whole prehistory of logical
positivism. Too often a further important element is ignored: the
influence of the great developments in the physiology of the
senses of the 19th century on ways of expressing problems and
conceptions in the Vienna Circle and related groups. This
influence can be clearly traced in the phenomenalism of the
twenties – its clearest expression being Carnap's first major
work, 'The Logical Structure of the World'. It is quite surprising
for a modern reader to see how much effort and detailed work
Carnap devotes to problems, concepts, and hypothetical constructs
of the physiology and psychology of sensorial perception –
especially if one remembers Carnap's subsequent development. I
take this brand of phenomenalism to be nothing but a
physiologically elaborated theory of knowledge. Moreover, it is a
theory of knowledge whose methodology proves to contain Kantian

65

H. N. Jahnke and M. Otte (eds.), Epistemological and Social Problems of the Sciences in the Early Nineteenth
Century, 65–73.

elements. Carnap's 'Structure of the World' owes more to the Kantian tradition than it is likely that its author would have liked to avow.

Of course, Carnap's and other similar attempts within the first phase of logical positivism could be traced back to Mach. Mach's 'Analysis of Sensations' is a curious melting-pot of physiological as well as epistemological issues. However, Mach's theory of knowledge, in turn, came from a tradition that emphasized the epistemological consequences of modern sense physiology and its connections with Kant. This tradition was especially strong in the German-speaking world and showed two features which were not present in the theory of knowledge of empiricism proper: first, a connection with special, experimental research in the field of sensorial perception, and secondly, a detailed and critical analysis of Kant's epistemology. Mach's so-called "empiriocriticism" cannot be well-understood without taking into account his own psychophysiological investigations, as well as those of such scientists as Hering, Fechner, and, above all, Helmholtz. In this respect, Mach belongs to a quite definite development in the history of ideas: to an epistemological program aiming to base all kinds of genuine human knowledge on a careful philosophical analysis of concrete empirical results of the study of the physiology of the senses. This historical development has its predecessor in Kant, its pioneers in Johannes Mueller and his collaborators, its radical continuation in Mach's and Avenarius' empiriocriticism, and its culmination in Carnap's phenomenalism; its central figure is Hermann von Helmholtz. Historically as well as methodologically, Helmholtz can be regarded as the crucial figure in the evolution of this program of basing a theory of knowledge upon the physiology of the senses. What I intend to do in the following is to discuss the essential features of Helmholtz' contribution to that tradition.

1. How a Natural Scientist Became an Epistemologist

In a letter to Fick, Helmholtz defined the aim of philosophy, as he understood it, in the following words: "I think that the only way to help philosophy to move on again is to get her seriously and eagerly devoted to the investigation of the processes of knowledge and the scientific methods. ... However, above all an exact knowledge of the processes of sensorial perception belongs to such a critical investigation".[1]

This strong impulse to use scientific (in this case physiological) results and concepts in order to clarify general epistemological questions characterizes the lifelong work of Helmholtz. Such a theory of knowledge was not for Helmholtz a "hobby", but a serious matter, closely related to his scientific work. It is this attitude which makes of him not only a great physicist, mathematician, and physiologist, but also an outstanding philosopher.

Now, we may ask ourselves: How was it that such a physicist and physiologist as Helmholtz, in spite of not having any special training in academic philosophy, devoted himself with such an eagerness to the elaboration of a general theory of knowledge?

In addition to Helmholtz′ personal virtues (like his almost unbelievable capacity for work and his intellectual energy), there are two sorts of historical factors which might explain his strong impulse to jump from highly specialized scientific research to the deepest epistemological questions. The factors of one sort are of a general kind, the others are more specific. Let us describe them briefly.

In his always stimulating history of European ideas in the 19th century, Theodore Merz very clearly depicted the extent to which all scientific activities in Germany (especially during the first half of the 19th century), in contradistinction to other European countries, were influenced by genuine philosophical, even metaphysical reflections and discussion. The whole of that cultural life was permeated by philosophical discussion. During the second quarter of the century, the controversies about the issues of vitalism and materialism were particularly lively. Helmholtz′ intellectual development took place in this atmosphere. Of course, this factor alone is not enough to explain his philosophical career. Nevertheless, it determined its framework.

Within this general frame of influences, the special relationship between philosophy and the physiology of the senses played a particularly important role. The second quarter of the 19th century was the great time of Johannes Mueller and his school. Helmholtz belonged to this school. Mueller's and his collaborators' interests were not restricted to specific physiological questions. Mueller was a convinced Kantian and thought that his "law of the specific energies of the sense nerves" had provided an experimental foundation for Kant's theory of knowledge. His contemporaries did not regard this as an esoteric evaluation of the philosophical consequences of his own work. A genuine Kantian such as Friedrich Lange felt similarly: "The physiology of the sense organs is the developed or revised form of Kantianism and Kant's system can be seen as a program directed to the new discoveries in this field".[2]

This identification was obvious for Helmholtz, too. In the beginning, when still under Mueller's strong influence, he regarded himself as an experimental Kantian - as a natural scientist who aimed at showing by means of specific physiological research that Kant's general scheme was in principle correct. In his later work, Helmholtz deliberately detached himself from Kant's philosophy. However, this was largely due to his analyses of the foundations of geometry rather than to the development of his physiological investigations. The "revised form of Kantianism" (to employ Lange's phrase) was for him nothing but the physiological interpretation of the epistemology of the criticist school, and as such it was still valid. The "revised form of Kantianism" is the view which arises when philosophy and physiology are combined. In a lecture that Helmholtz gave around the middle of the century in memory of Kant, he said: "The point of closest contact between philosophy and the natural sciences is the discipline of the sensorial perceptions of human beings".[3] And also: "The physiology of the senses is the border field wherein the two big areas of human knowledge, usually distinguished under the names of natural and cultural sciences, overlap; it is where problems pile up ... that can be solved only through the cooperation of both fields".[4]

Such a physiologically interpreted philosophy is the field which Kant had foreseen, but he was unable to really establish it because of a lack of the required empirical findings. Kant set out the program and it was carried out by the physiology of the 19th century. This is how Mueller and Helmholtz saw their relationship to Kant; and in the present context it is completely irrelevant to ask whether their interpretation of Kant was correct or not. The interesting question is rather: to what extent did the physiological reconstruction of Kant's program determine Helmholtz' lifelong work as a philosophical physiologist?

Helmholtz considered the law of specific energies which Mueller had discovered and which he himself had further developed to be as significant for a general philosophical worldview as Newton's law of gravitation.[5] But, according to him, the law of specific energies is nothing but a systematic application of Kant's principle of the a priori forms of intuition to the forms of perception which are determined by each single sense organ, or even sensorial nerve.[6] The principle which Kant had advanced in general terms and without experimental foundation was supposed to be carefully justified and interpreted through the physiology of the senses. This idea occurred to Mueller only as a vague project; for Helmholtz, it became a whole philosophical system.

2. The Basic Elements of Helmholtz' Theory of Knowledge

The philosophical interests of the natural scientists of the time, the physiological training with Mueller and the consideration of Kant's theory of the a priori forms of intuition - all these constituted the background of the elements out of which Helmholtz was to build his own theory of knowledge. I would like to comment briefly on the organisation of these elements into a coherent conceptual structure.

A careful analysis of Helmholtz' epistemological approach reveals the three following components to be the most significant ones: symbolism, structural realism, and epistemological activism. Undoubtedly, these components, in particular the first and the third, can already be found in a more abstract form in Kant. On

the other hand, in Helmholtz' physiological version they
constitute the first step towards empiriocriticism and Carnap's
phenomenalism. These theories are nothing but more precise and
developed forms of the theory of knowledge inaugurated by
Helmholtz - if one puts aside the presupposition of any sort of
substantive realism.

Of the three components mentioned above, symbolism is the most
important, since it is the conceptual precondition of the other
two. Helmholtz takes for granted that the detailed investigations
carried out by Mueller, himself, and other in the field of the
physiology of the senses have shown that the nature of differences
of modality within sensorial perception can be directly reduced to
qualitative (physiological) differences among the different sense
organs and the different single nerves - and not, say, to the real
differences among external stimuli. Mueller had advanced this
thesis first of all only for the "big" differences which allow us
to distinguish between different senses (let us say, for the
difference between vision and hearing). Helmholtz extended the
principle to single qualitative differences within one and the
same sense (say, differences between two color sensations).

The philosophical danger which Helmholtz wished to avoid with
respect to this view was that of total subjectivism in the theory
of knowledge. The first step in this attempt was his symbolism. In
opposition to naive realism, symbolism frees us from the idea that
sensations are pictures of external objects. Sensations need not
have anything in common with their external sources. From this,
however, one should not infer, as in subjectivist idealism, that
there are no sources of the sensations independent of the subject.
Sensations are certainly not pictures of, but symbols for external
reality: they are signs of an independent "something". Or, in the
words Helmholtz himself used in a concrete example: "Sensations of
light and color are only symbols for some relationships in reality
..., we do not know anything about the real nature of the external
relations they denote".[7]

This doctrine is certainly a familiar one in the history of
philosophy. Nevertheless, the point to emphasize here is the fact
that the physiologist Helmholtz considered that his own (and his

collaborators') empirical results had proven beyond doubt that this philosophical doctrine is simply true.

Though each single sensation is nothing but a sign of the external object carrying to essential similarity to it, an assembly of a certain number of interconnected sensations might build a structure that is not a mere sign any more, but is rather a true picture of something external, objective. The depicted something is then not a single external state of affairs as a source of single sensations, but rather the lawlike structure, the frame of objective relations into which each one of the unknown sources is inserted. Though we can not be realists with respect to the single pairs sensation-object, we are justified in assuming another sort of realism - a realism at a higher level, if your wish: realism with respect to the depicted structures.[8] This idea leads direcly to a methodological consequence which was systematically elaborated by Carnap many years afterwards: the idea that the proper objects of scientific knowledge are sensorial structures and not single objects. Needless to say, at that time Carnap did not speak of realism any more.

For Helmholtz, on the other hand, realism was an essential component in a scientific theory of knowledge. Furthermore, he considered that epistemological realism could and should be grounded not on purely philosophical arguments, but upon physiological results which showed the active character of epistemic processes. The physiologically proven fact that the human processes of acquiring knowledge do not occur in a purely passive way, but rather contain active constructive aspects, was for Helmholtz the scientific premise of philosophical realism: "The efforts of philosophical schools to justify the belief in the existence of a reality had to remain without success as long as their starting point was only the passive observer of the external world; ... they did not see that the actions originated in the human will constitute an indispensable part of our sources of knowledge".[9]

The active aspect of the epistemic process consists, according to Helmholtz, in the human ability to modify or adjust sensation aggregates of his experience by means of so-called innervation, i.e. through the arbitrary stimulation of the motor nerves.[10] Helmholtz calls the class of all sensation aggregates that can occur through innervation at a given time the class of the presentabilia ("Praesentabilien") at that time.[11] This class is primarily something which has been constructed by the subject. However, there is something which the subject cannot determine at will through his motoric activity: the empirical fact that at a different time and with respect to the same innervations, a different class of presentabilia will be given. In general, it will be impossible for the subject to reproduce exactly the same class as occurred previously. This, according to Helmholtz, is the concrete empirical meaning of realism: the fact that at different times different classes of presentabilia occur and that the active innervation of the knowing subject can modify the elements of each class at will but not the classes themselves. The existence of these different classes is independent of innervation.

Symbolism, structuralism, activism: these are the elements that Helmholtz put together so as to get a particular kind of epistemological realism - a realism which originated in the physiological results of the second quarter of the 19th century. The next stage of this historical evolution is represented by such physiologically interested philosophers as Avenarius and philosophically-minded physiologists like Mach. It led to the transformation of Helmholtz' realism into a pure empiricism. This, however, is another chapter of the story.

Notes

1 Quoted in: Hoerz, H. and Wollgast, S.: Einleitung ..., p. XXVI.
2 Lange, F.: Geschichte des Materialismus, vol. II, p. 409.
3 Helmholtz, H.v.: Ueber das Sehen des Menschen, in: Philosophische Vortraege und Aufsaetze, p. 48.
4 Helmholtz, H.v.: Vortraege und Reden, vol. 1, p. 16.
5 See Kahl, R.: Introduction ..., passim.
6 See Helmholtz, H.v.: Goethes Vorahnungen kommender naturwissenschaftlicher Ideen, in: Philosophische Vortraege und Aufsaetze, p. 358f.

7 Helmholtz, H.v.: Vortraege und Reden, vol. 1, p. 30.

8 See Helmholtz, H.v.: Die Tatsachen in der Wahrnehmung, in: Philosophische Vortraege und Aufsaetze, p. 256 and passim.

9 Helmholtz, H.v.: Goethes Vorahnungen..., in: op. cit., p. 362.

10 See Helmholtz, H.v.: Die Tatsachen..., in: op. cit., p. 257.

11 See ibid., p. 259.

References

Carnap, R.: Der logische Aufbau der Welt, Hamburg 1961, 2. ed.

Helmholtz, H.v.: Philosophische Vortraege und Aufsaetze, ed. by Hoerz, H. and Wollgast, S., Berlin 1971

Helmholtz, H.v.: Vortraege und Reden, Braunschweig 1903

Hoerz, H. and
Wollgast, S.: Einleitung, in: Helmholtz, H.v.: Philosophische Vortraege und Aufsaetze, Berlin 1971

Kahl, R.: Introduction, in: Selected Writings of Hermann von Helmholtz, Harvard 1971

Lange, F.A.: Geschichte des Materalismus und Kritik seiner Bedeutung in der Gegenwart, 2 vol., Leipzig 1908, 8. ed.

Mach, E.: Die Analyse der Empfindungen, Vienna 1911, 6.ed.

Merz, J.Th.: A History of European Thought in the Nineteenth Century, Dover 1965

Mueller, J.: Handbuch der Physiologie des Menschen, Coblenz 1837

Hans Niels Jahnke and Michael Otte

ON "SCIENCE AS A LANGUAGE"

I.

We shall offer some remarks concerning the philosophical debate on science at the turn of the 18th century, especially on the concept of science as a language, and relate these remarks to some characteristic features in the development of mathematics. Other disciplines will thus not be referred to directly. Indirectly, however, one can learn something for a better evaluation of their development from studying that of mathematics. Mathematics (with the possible exception of chemistry) is the one science for which the hypothesis of a breach in its epistemological and ontological conceptions at the turn of the 18h century can be most easily verified. We are taking this as evidence for the assumption that the development of mathematics at that point of time was particularly dependent on the development within the overall context of the sciences in general, and of the way mathematics was integrated into these. It should thus be possible, from an analysis of the mathematics science of that time, to obtain questions and problems providing promising access to an investigation of this context.

We should like to begin with a proposition which is, above all, of methodological importance for the historiography of the sciences, but which at the same time implies a statement on the developmental logic of modern science as a whole. This proposition

75

H. N. Jahnke and M. Otte (eds.), Epistemological and Social Problems of the Sciences in the Early Nineteenth Century, 75–89.

reads: The further development and modification of the concepts pertaining to the object of scientific theories provide the essential yardstick for an analysis of the development of science. This does not only concern the knowledge of subject matters, but also the changes in its social and institutional context.

This proposition assumes that the relationships between scientific theories and their object or application fields, and the concepts which historically develop by means of these relationships, are the key problem for an analysis of modern science, starting from which studies concerning history of science, philosophy of science, sociology of science, and psychology of science can be meaningfully related to one another. In a way, this contradicts the points of view brought forward by Kuhn, among others.

In our opinion, the relative difference between scientific presentation and object of science, between sign and signified, should be systematically included among the components of an analysis of scientific development. Seen in the light of our above proposition, this distinction seems to be extremely important. In particular, this proposition says that within dynamically developing modern science, any increase in differentiation of the object field and application field is accompanied by an increase in differentiation and and explication of the scientific system in its social, institutional, methodological, and literary components.

In order to clarify this matter, it will be useful to show on a more general level how the methods of scientific concept formation have developed in modern science. An additional advantage of this procedure is that it will illustrate the importance of mathematics and its understanding of scientific generalizations. In this context, we should like to refer to the presentation of this problem in Cassirer's "Substanzbegriff und Funktionsbegriff", which is very clarifying indeed. Cassirer asks how it is possible that scientific concepts can reproduce a multitude of empirical details despite the fact that they were produced - at least according to classic logical self-conception - by increasingly omitting specific properties. He subsequently shows that this paradox can be understood, as modern science tends more and more

towards an understanding of concepts as no longer substance
concepts in the classical sense, but as relation or function
concepts. He shows how the mathematical concept of variables in
particular is brought into play here. According to that, concepts
are not names or designations of things, but of relationships
between things. Accordingly, a concept designating, for instance,
one characteristic feature of a thing, does not only refer to this
feature, but to the relationships between it and the totality of
characteristic features to which it belongs. This totality,
however, remains implicit in the respective designation, and
represents that knowledge which is specific for the social and
communicative context in question. Thus it becomes possible for
the more general concept, to be the one richer in content.
Differentiated object-references in a theory thus lead to
differentiations in the structure of knowledge.

Beyond that, Cassirer shows that the rejection of the traditional
substance concepts, and the development of modern relation and
function concepts fits into the temporal frame chosen for this
conference. The tendency itself, of course, belongs universally to
modern science as a whole, but this particular process had a
definite peak in the time between 1750 and 1850.

To characterize the modern scientific method of abstraction as the
development of relation concepts - and here we come to our second
main proposition - will serve us to describe, in terms of
scientific theory, those problems which, in our opinion,
constitute the main characteristics of the development of science
at the turn of the 18th century (that is between 1770 and 1850).
We mean the education problem and the problems of applying
scientific knowledge.

For didactics, for instance, it is obvious that the didactical
problem in its deeper sense, that is in the sense that it is
necessary to work on it scientifically, is constituted by the very
fact that concepts will reflect relationships, and not things.
Analogously, we may state for the problem of the application of
science that it will become a real problem only where the
relationship between concept and application is no longer quasi
self-evident, but where to establish such a relationship requires

an independent effort. In this, we agree with Wussing, who has observed, in an essay on Bolzano, that all the efforts concerning foundation problems of mathematics at the beginning of the 19th century were, basically, aimed at enhancing the teachability and applicability of mathematics (see Wussing, 1974).

The point of these thoughts concerning the independence of the problem of applying and teaching scientific knowledge is that these are indeed problems which can be described and characterized cognitively, but that to solve them is not only a theoretical problem, but a deeply practical, political, and organizational problem as well. This is the very reason why it has become the object of systematical, empirical research. This is how we should like to interpret Saint-Simon's remark: "The philosophy of the 18th century was revolutionary; the philosophy of the 19th must organize." Summarized, our second proposition thus reads: The fact that application and teaching of scientific knowledge is independent and obeys to laws of its own becomes the decisive aspect at the turn of the 18th century.

It is evident that a statement so highly general is of a strongly explorative character, and cannot be simply "proved".

II.
Let us now visualize some of the basic features of the conception of science and mathematics in the 18th century, in particular those of the French Enlightenment.

In their criticism of Cartesian Metaphysics, the French representatives of the Enlightenment aim mainly at developing the foundations of an "application-oriented science", which is no longer concerned with deducing the world's diversity from mathematics, that is from a few predetermined principles, or with making it "vanish" altogether into mathematics. Rather, they imagine a science which allows its development to be optimally regulated by empirical facts and data, and adapts to these as closely as possible. The Enlightenment emphasizes the world's immense diversity, and the real reason for the popularity of English empiricism in France is that it was hoped to achieve a

breakthrough for that very principle, i.e. that science must be
guided by empirical reality, and not by preconceived notions.
D'Alembert says: "What we have to put into the place of all these
foggy speculations, is a metaphysics which has been created more
for ourselves, and which keeps more closely and more immediately
to earth: a metaphysics the applications of which will extend to
the sciences, and above all to geometry, and to the various
branches of mathematics." (quoted from Cassirer, 1974, p. 414).

Encyclopedists, like Diderot, develop an enormously differentiated
conception of the world, and visualize a huge universe of details
in continuous movement. Goethe is said to have remarked: "When we
heard somebody talking about the Encyclopedists, and opened one
volume of their huge work, we felt as if walking among the
innumerable moving bobbins and weaving looms of a vast factory.
Upon hearing all that buzzing and clanking, on being confronted
with this mechanism confusing eye and mind with the
incomprehensibility of that most intricately interlocking
institution, considering all these things necessary to produce a
piece of cloth, you feel as if developing a dislike for even the
coat you are wearing." (quoted from Cassirer, 1974, p. 565).

The conception of science as a language is probably the most
influential concept of science developed by the French
representatives of the Enlightenment, with which they attempted to
conceptualize the unity of human reason, as opposed to the
diversity of things in the world. This conception, which was
primarily attached to mathematics, and still is of great
importance for this science today, contains essentially two
aspects: Firstly, this conception is to express that preoccupation
with the diversity of empirical reality we have just described.
Secondly, and this is certainly just as important, the conception
of science as a language refers to the social-communicative
function of science and recognizes that function as an essential
element of its development.

The most detailed elaboration of the conception of science as a
language was achieved by Condillac. His "Logics" (first published
in 1780) was written at the request of the Polish Educational
Council and was intended for use in the national schools in

Poland . But in France, too, the book was very widely spread and became highly renowned . In 1795, 1400 copies were acquired for distribution to the new students admitted to the Ecoles Normales . "Logics" had become a standard textbook in France, and remained so for many years to come (see Albury, 1972, p . 27) . Without exaggeration, Condillac's book can be considered the most influential methodological work of the late 18th century .

Condillac attempts to derive the development of the human mind systematically from two sources: from sensual experience, and from the use of signs . Condillacs essential proposition says that every language is an analytic method, and every analytic method is a language (see Condillac, 1780, part II) .

Condillac thus continues an understanding of analysis which has been important for the entire methodology and self-reflection of modern science . The analytic method accepts an unknown, yet unexplored object or problem as given, and separates it, by means of sucessive experimental or logical methods, into (known) components, with subsequent reconstruction . In mathematics, specifically, this means we must assume an unknown, sought quantity as given, and reduce it, by the help of all the relationships and relations this quantity must satisfy, to known quantities . The analytical method is thus opposed to establishing principles concerning the object of research beforehand, and to deduce the object's properties from these by inference . This is made particularly clear in Condillac's "Logics" where he deals with the role of definitions in science . Condillac will have definitions understood only as indications towards the object in question, and not as a principle or a complete determination of the object from which all properties of the object can be derived . This is why he pokes fun at the efforts of some mathematicians to define the concept of the straight line, a problem which was widely discussed in contemporary mathematics . With regard to this problem, Condillac takes the rather modern position of accepting the "straight line" as an undefined basic term of a theory, which will attain definiteness and content only as the theory develops . It is evident that on the basis of this conception the use of signs acquires universal significance in science. Signs emerge as representatives of the yet unexplored objects. After that, the use of signs has had a predominantly explorative function.

The analytic method, as presented and justified by Condillac, was understood by contemporary scientists, not only as a method of developing new knowledge, but also as the appropriate method of scientific teaching. This is made evident by Lavoisier who based his chemistry textbook on Condillac's logic. This influence is also reflected in the intense efforts Lavoisier made to develop an adequate terminology in chemistry, and to introduce a systematic use of signs. It is impressing to behold how Lavoisier consciously considers the problems of terminology and the use of signs not under a static-classifying angle, but from the viewpoint of developing new knowledge on the basis of the explorative function of signs. The scientific revolution in chemistry, which undeniably took place during that period, is thus inseparably linked to Condillac's conception of science as a language.

There is a third element which is important in Condillac's conception. This is the insight into the genetical connexion between primitive sign language and sophisticated symbolic calculus. In his study titled "The Language of Calculating", Condillac derives arithmetic and algebra genetically from the primitive calculating activity with the fingers. Analogy, he says, is the principle guiding the development of algebra. The linguistic signs are linked to their meanings by relationships of similarity. "Analogy, which can always be discerned, in algebra visibly leads from one expression to the next... If algebra is a language shaped by analogy, then the analogy which shapes the language, shapes the methods, too; or rather: the method of invention is only analogy itself." (Condillac 1798, p. 122).

The following characteristics must be noted in Condillac's conception of science. First, he goes beyond the dichotomy of "sensation" and "reflection" still contained in Locke's empiricism by practically objectifying reflection, which Locke still conceived of as inborn. He does this by emphasizing the constitutive role of signs in the development of science. Instead

of being regarded as an internal skill of the individual, the
ability to think becomes an intersubjectively controllable
element, and a component of social reality. Thus the problem of
communicating and disseminating knowledge is given its
constitutive role in the development of knowledge. Secondly,
Condillac links science genetically to the cognitive activity of
man, and thirdly, the concept of science as a language expresses a
universal turn of science towards empirical, factual reality, and
thus lastingly questions metaphysical objectivism which adheres to
a mechanistic view of the world.

For mathematics, the conception of "science as a language" has
been particularly influential. The process of general
reorganization of the relationships between arithmetic/algebra on
the one hand and geometry on the other, which began towards the
end of the 18th century, is in its initial stage most closely
connected with this philosophical concept. This is evident, in
geometry, among other things. C.B. Boyer, who has done extensive
work on the history of analytic geometry, shows that analytic
geometry, in the tradition of Descartes, remains, despite the use
of arithmetic/algebraic helps, still aligned to the guiding
principle of solving problems by means of geometrical
constructions. On the other hand, so Boyer says, there has been
since Fermat an opposing tradition in analytic geometry, which
placed the emphasis on defining curves by means of algebraic
expressions. It is only towards the end of the 18th century that,
promoted by the work of Monge and Lacroix (who took advantage of
the conceptual progress achieved by Euler and Lagrange before
them), an analytic geometry comparable to present-day conceptions
emerges within a relatively short time. It is based on a stricter
separation of algebraic/arithmetic methods and geometric methods,
as well as on a more general conception of geometric objects.
These are now considered independent of the possibility of
constructing them geometrically. Boyer, who stresses that this
"revolution" in analytic geometry was brought about by two
pedagogues (i.e. Monge and Lacroix), compares this development
(justly, we think) with the "chemical revolution" initiated by
Lavoisier. (See Boyer 1947, p. 152). Indeed, these two
developments may be compared in the very aspects we have
highlighted as being essential for Condillac's conception: the

emphasis on and the development of the explorative function of
signs, and the concurrent recognition of the dominance and
independence of the empirically-objectively given.

The question how the conception of science as a language proposed
by the Enlightenment should be evaluated in the light of our
initially formulated proposition concerning the independence of
the application and teaching problem in the early 19th century,
may be answered as follows: This conception was an important step
towards a conception according to which the development of the
sciences aligns to their applications. Perhaps it may even be said
that this has remained the most sophisticated general
theoretical-philosophical concept of application-oriented science
to this day. On the other hand, however, this concept is
insufficient insofar as it fails to perceive, because of its very
universalism, the independency of the application problem. It
develops a notion of application-oriented science so-to-speak only
intellectually, in the mind. "Science as a language" implies that
application of knowledge becomes something almost automatic,
raising no problem at all as long as the language developed is
sufficiently good, clear, and reasonable. In Condillac's work, the
necessary variability of standpoints, views, and objectives, which
enters the process of cognition, and which is prerequisite to
ensure that knowledge can be variably applied, is still seen as a
purely pragmatic element, which needs not be justified, but is
simply subjective.

The stronger emphasis on the foundation of the apriori of sciences
is typical for those theoretical approaches going beyond the
conceptions of the Enlightenment. Consequently, epistemological
conceptions prove more and more discipline-specific and are
specifically developed on the bases of the individual sciences.
The application problem and the teaching problem are no longer
considered solvable exclusively in the realm of theory; their
practical, political, and organizational dimensions are recognized
as well. The introduction of a general educational system, and the
theoretical debate referring to it, are prominent landmarks in
this development. The reflections of Condorcet und Comte in
France, of Schleiermacher in Prussia may be seen in this

connexion, however incomparable they may seem with regard to the
content of their assumptions, and to the concrete historical
situation they referred to.

III.

Any attempt to really understand the change in the object
understanding of mathematics which began to prevail at the turn of
the 18th century requires first of all a consideration of the
problem and the context of the "arithmetization of mathematics".
It must be said at once that this arithmetization did not only
aim, as it is often supposed, at founding infinitesimal calculus
anew, but at transforming and reformulating mathematics as a
whole. The crux of what we will term arithmetization here, may be
described, in first approximation, as follows: Whereas in the 18th
century numbers, in their inseparable linkage to the quantity
concept, represented the essential object of mathematics, and
algebra, or the symbolic calculi of mathematics, were considered
merely as a language in which the relationships between numbers
and quantities respectively could be expressed in an easy and
suggestive manner, this state of affairs was reversed in the 19th
century. Algebra and geometry now immediately contain the
mathematical relationships as such, which constitute the object of
investigation, whereas arithmetic, for its part, becomes the
language of algebra or rather, of mathematics as a whole, by which
and in which all mathematical facts must be expressed. This
process of arithmetization finally culminates, towards the end of
the 19th century, in the consistency of mathematics being seen as
due to the consistency of arithmetic. This establishes arithmetic
as the true foundational science of mathematics. Hilbert's
program, which aims at reducing mathematics as a whole to finitist
combinations of signs and numbers, is only an extreme expression
of these efforts, which finally lead to Goedel's arithmetizing the
logical system of the "principia mathematica".

Arithmetic as the foundational science of mathematics does not
mean that arithmetic is the true object of mathematics. It rather
means that numbers are no longer interpreted as objects, but as
pure symbols, as "markers", as a means to objectify mathematical
thinking, in other words, as a language. This shall be illustrated

by quoting a statement by H. von Helmholtz, which although it belongs to the second half of the 19th century, nevertheless very poignantly expresses a conception which began to prevail at the beginning of the same century: "I consider arithmetic, or the theory of pure numbers, as a method based on purely psychological facts, which teaches the logical application of a symbolic system (i.e. of the numbers) which has unlimited extent and unlimited possibilities of refinement. Arithmetic notably explores which different ways of combining these symbols (calculative operations) lead to the same final result ... Beside the proof of the inner consistency of our thinking thus furnished, such a method would naturally at first be pure play of our acumen with imagined objects ... if it did not permit so many useful applications." (v. Helmholtz, 1897, p. 303/304). The strict separation between the object of theory ("useful applications") and the level of representation ("a method based on purely psychological facts") advanced here becomes typical for the entire mathematics in the 19th century, a fact for which there is multiple evidence. We shall quote two statements by Gauss, which are of further interest because they contradict a widespread notion, which, however, in our opinion fails to see the core of contemporary understanding of the concept of mathematics. These statements concern the concept of the complex number, which is usually said to have been created by Gauss by his having illustrated it on the number plane. Gauss sees that differently. He conceives of the representation of complex numbers on the plane in a purely symbolic sense (see Gauss, 1831) and stresses that the essence of complex numbers should be conceived of in a much more general sense (we should say: in an explorative sense). Gauss writes to Drobisch: "Only the representation of imaginary quantities in the relations of points in plano is not their essence itself, which must be conceived of as being higher and more general, but rather the example of its application purest to man, or perhaps even the only entirely pure example." To Hansen, he writes: "The true meaning of $\sqrt{-1}$ is very vivid in my mind, but it will be very difficult to put into words, which will always only be able to give a vague image floating in the air ..." (Both quotes taken from Schlesinger 1912, p. 56).

The complementarity of the concept's simulative and explorative function which emerges here plays also an important part in the

metamathematical reflexions of Bolzano. For a historical study of
the metamathematical conceptions prevalent during the first half
of the 19th century, Bolzano is a central figure, as he
comprehensively read and assimilated the literature existing in
his time. He distinguishes between "making certain"
(Gewissmachung) and "foundation" (Begruendung). While "making
certain" means a mere formal demonstration or subjective
illustration, "foundation" aims at establishing the objective
connection between the various truths. "Therefore I demand that
any tuition that wants to be called strictly scientific does not
only give certainty about the truths it establishes, but that it
also gives us as much insight as possible into the objective
connections these truths have to one another. ... Since
consideration which lead to both of these belong to the class of
proofs, one could call such proofs objective proofs or
'foundations' to distinguish them from others which lead only to
one and not at the same time to the other. ... Proofs, however,
which only make certain without giving the objective reason of a
truth, could be called mere 'making certain' or subjective
proofs". (Bolzano 1830-48, p. 83/84). Conscious reflexion of the
difference between level of content and level of representation,
which is hinted at here, is deeply engrained in Bolzano's
philosophical thought. As far as we know, he is the first
philosopher to introduce the concept of "textbook" as a
constitutive component into his fundamental philosophical
definition of science and thus to attempt to conceptualize the
independence of the representation and teaching problem. (see his
"Theory of Science" § 393/394)

Like many other mathematicians of his time, Bolzano considers the
relationship between science and teaching, for instance, when
within the context of his reflexions on the arithmetization of
mathematics he insists on a careful separation between theory of
numbers and theory of quantities, but observing, on the other
hand, that he would not recommend such a distinction for
children's tuition. The great importance which set theory notions
attain in Bolzano's mathematical thought also seems to be
connected to the problems of representation, and with resulting
requirements which must be met by a theory of mathematical
concepts. Set concepts, in Bolzano's understanding, lead to a

structure of knowledge and to an "order of presenting scientific knowledge" which consist of the principle that "the simpler truth should always come before the composite truth, and, in case of equal degree of compositeness, the more general truth should always come before the specific truth."

On the basis of the set concept, a theory of concepts can be built up which understands the concept as a relation concept, as opposed to the substance concept of old. Especially the method of "definition by abstraction" which Bolzano discusses at length, and which classifies objects according to an equivalence relation corresponding to the object of cognition and subsumes them under one concept, illustrates the fact that subjective purposes and objectives of cognition will enter concept formation itself. The conventionalist element contained in this implies that concepts can no longer be understood in the sense of a negative concept realism.

Within the tendency to arithmetize mathematics, Bolzano has made an important contribution in his works concerning the quantitiy concept and function theory. A particularly striking example is his proof of the intermediate value problem, as well as his realization that this is actually a theorem requiring proof. The necessity of proving this theorem becomes evident only from the point of vantage offered by the program of arithmetizing mathematics.

On the other hand, however, the history of the function concept in the early 19th century also shows that a purely algebraic-operative foundation of analysis, as it had been attempted by Lagrange, is not possible. It was shown that the constructive and descriptive aspects of mathematics cannot be traced back to each another, but only in their interplay will they represent the "life" of a mathematical theory, and of the function concept in particular.

An observation made by Weyl on the twofold origin of the function concept seems to be helpful in this connexion. (see Weyl 1917, p. 34/35). Weyl says that our modern function concept has, on the one hand, a constructive origin stemming from arithmetic-algebraic operations, but that it has emerged, on the other hand, from our notions concerning the natural dependencies prevalent in the world. To us, this suggests the interpretation that geometry, at the beginning of the 19th century, becomes the bona fide representative of the objectified-objective in mathematics. This, however, would mean that the emerging complementarity of algebraic-arithmetic constructions and geometric-continuous notions, which is most salient in connexion with the development of the function concept, is deeply linked to the insertion of mathematics into the overall system of experimental empirical acquisition of knowledge. The shaping and systematization of experimental methods, as well as the genesis of new empirical sciences, would then be an important factor for the development of the reformulation of the relationships between algebra and geometry. At the same time, it must be kept in mind that the relative separation of algebraic and geometrical methods is also a result of the broad discussion of the problems of presenting knowledge, particularly in connexion with educational efforts. The statements we quoted will give only an imperfect impression of this debate's real extent.

References

Albury, W.:   The Logic of Condillac and the Structure of
                       French Chemical and Biological Theory, 1780
                       – 1801, The John Hopkins University, Ph. D.
                       1972.
Bolzano, B.:   Groessenlehre (1830–1848), Stuttgart 1975.
Bolzano, B.:   Rein analytischer Beweis des Lehrsatzes,
                       dass zwischen je zwey Werthen, die ein
                       entgegengesetztes Resultat gewaehren,
                       wenigstens eine reelle Wurzel der Gleichung
                       liege (1817), in: Kolman, A.: Bernhard
                       Bolzano, Berlin 1963.
Boyer, C.B.:   Cartesian geometry from Fermat to Lacroix,
                       in: Script. Mathematica XIII(1947), pp.
                       133–153.

Cassirer, E.:   Das Erkenntnisproblem in der Philosophie und
                     Wissenschaft der neueren Zeit, vol. 2,
                     Darmstadt 1974.

Cassirer, E.:   Substanzbegriff und Funktionsbegriff (1910),
                     Darmstadt 1976.

Condillac, E.B. de: Logik, first published 1780; repr.: Klaus,
                     G. (ed.): E.B. de Condillac. Die Logik oder
                     die Anfaenge der Kunst des Denkens, Die
                     Sprache des Rechnens, Berlin 1959.

Diderot, D.:   Zur Interpretation der Natur (1754), Leipzig
                     1976.

Gauss, C.F.:   Theoria Residuorum Biquadraticorum
                     Commentatio secunda, in: Goettingische
                     gelehrte Anzeigen 1831, April 23; also in:
                     Werke, vol. II, Hildesheim, New York 1973
                     (Repr. Goettingen 1863), pp. 169–178.

Helmholtz, H.v.:   Zaehlen und Messen, erkenntnistheoretisch
                     betrachtet (1887), in: Hoerz, H. and
                     Wollgast, S. (ed.): H.v. Helmholtz,
                     Philosophische Vortraege und Aufsaetze,
                     Berlin 1971, pp. 301–335.

Schlesinger, L.:   Ueber Gauss' Arbeiten zur Funktionentheorie
                     (1912), in: Gauss, C.F.: Werke, vol. X/2,
                     Hildesheim/ New York 1973 (Repr. Berlin
                     1917–1933).

Weyl, H.:   Das Kontinuum, Berlin 1917, repr. in: Das
                     Kontinuum und andere Monographien, New York
                     1973.

S. R. Mikulinsky

THE HISTORICAL CONDITIONS AND FEATURES OF THE DEVELOPMENT OF NATURAL SCIENCE IN RUSSIA IN THE FIRST HALF OF THE 19TH CENTURY

The first half of the 19th century in the history of science is usually viewed either as a direct continuation of the processes characterizing the development of science in the second half of the 18th century, or, more often, is not singled out from the 19th century as a whole. Meanwhile, science of the first half of the 19th century is notable for such features, which in our opinion, give every reason to consider it a special period in the history of natural science. This period is marked by discoveries and generalizations, which conciderably changed not only ideas in separate fields of knowledge, but also science itself, its subject, goals and methods, and paved the way for the old world picture to be replaced in the second half of the 19th century by a new one.

This period is rather peculiar. It is not distinguished by a revolutionary change; it is of transitional kind. Natural science of that time had already gone far from the mechanistic picture of the world, predominant in the 18th century, but had not produced a new one. This was not a revolution in science, its time had not come yet but old theories could not already explain a great number of newly-discovered facts. The old metaphysical world outlook, the idea of the world as of something created in former times and for ever unalterable was undermined by a torrent of new knowledge, was going through a crisis which it failed to overcome. The crisis,

91

H. N. Jahnke and M. Otte (eds.), Epistemological and Social Problems of the Sciences in the Early Nineteenth Century, 91–107.

the break-up of the metaphysical world outlook was accompanied by the change in the idea about the purpose of science. Science passed more and more from the description of objects and phenomena to the recognition of natural processes and laws of their realization. All the above shows that it is necessary to regard the first half of the 19th century as a separate period in the history of science in order to reflect the qualitative changes in science of that time.

Owing to the efforts of Laplace and Herschel, earth and the whole solar system appeared not as if they had been created or had come into being at once, but as phenomena which had developed in time. In chemistry the discoveries of that time included a common principle of explaining chemical phenomena and the structure of chemical compounds on the basis of atomism (Dalton), the dependence of chemical properties on the number and the arrangement of atoms in molecules (Avogadro, Berzelius, Gay-Lussac), the relationship between chemical affinity and electrical phenomena (Davy, Berzelius), chemical sources of electricity (Galvani and Volta).

The theory of the steam-engine served as an impetus for the development of the kinetic theory of heat and of the idea that molecular, statistical, irreversible processes are unreducible to mechanics; the relationship between thermal and mechanical work was discovered, thermodynamics arose. The idea of conservation of mass and energy was one of the sources of the concept of the electromagnetic field as a physical reality. The foundations of electrodynamics, which showed the possibility of conversion of mechanical work into electrical one and vice versa, were established then.

There were important and distinctive changes in mathematics. Mathematics of the first half of the 19th century is notable for the interest in physical problems proper. This was a period of vigorous development of mathematical physics and - which is closely connected with the above - of some large fields of analyses (trigonometric series, multiple integrals, complex functions). On the other hand, a number of difficulties and contradictions, partly revealed already in the 18th century, entailed deep reorganization in the grounds of mathematics themselves, which was necessary for the successful development both of its applications and its key branches. The result of such reorganization was the beginning of the reform of classical analysis and the rise of new disciplines: non-Euclidean geometry, the theory of groups, non-commutative algebra. All this led to considerable changes in mathematical thinking and was big with far-reaching consequences for natural science and scientific method as a whole. These important changes in the development of mathematics are characterised by the works of C. F. Gauss, A. Chauchy, N. I. Lobachevsky, E. Galois, W. Hamilton, J. Grassmann and B. Riemann. The comparison between the works of Gauss and L. Euler might be one of many examples explaining and illustrating both continuity and deep difference between mathematics of the 18th century and mathematics of the first half of the 19th century.

Mechanics, namely analytical mechanics of the first half of the 19th century, paved the way for an instrument, which became a universal instrument of physics. Such were, in particular, variational methods and principles of least action, later transferred from mechanics to physics.

It was shown in physiology that laws and methods of physics and chemistry could be fruitfully applied to the explanation of processes of vital activity of organisms; and in the struggle with vitalism, the idea of physiology as of physico-chemistry of the living had become firmly established by the middle of the 19th century. The first quarter of the century saw the origin of comparative anatomy. Its advancements made it possible to ascertain not only likeness in the structure of different species, but also, in many cases, such similarity in their organization, that it naturally made one arrive at the idea of deep connection between organisms and of their unity. There began systematic studies of fossil relicts of the ancient, long-extinct animal and vegetable world. Palaeontology arose, and a more and more distinct connection between the now existing species of animals and plants and the extinct organic world of the past geological epochs came to be recognized (disclosed).

In the late 1820s K. Baer established the major types of embryonic development and proved that all the vertebrates – this group including a great number of various species – developed according to a single pattern. Comparative embryology of animals was founded. In 1838-1839 T. Schwann and M. Schleiden formulated the cellular theory, revealing the unity of the elementary structure of all the organic forms and bridging plants and animals.

During the 1830s the foundations of the historical geology were laid down, which ensured the establishment of the continuity of geological transformations of the earth surface and the comparability of the major factors, which determined such transformations in the remote geological past, with factors acting nowadays. Since that time, owing to Ch. Lyell, in particular, the historical approach to the transformation of the earth surface and the principle of actualism, put forward in order to explain the driving factors of this process, had been gradually gaining more and more supporters in science. At the same time, more and more data contradicting the doctrine of constancy and independent origin of species were obtained in biology. Although the doctrine of evolution of the organic world, suggested by J.B. Lamarck in 18o9, seemed to have been forgotten by the majority of scientists as an extravagant scientific semi-poetry, the idea of evolution forced its way in various aspects throughout the first half of the 19th century, revealing itself , sometimes in the form of natural philosophic surmises about universal development, sometimes in the form of particular empirical generalizations concerning variability of animal and plants and their being timed to certain conditions of existance.

Still predominant in the first half of the 19th century, the old views on Nature had been completely undermined. Kant's nebular hypothesis, Ch. Wolff's "theory of descent", J. Hutton's theory of origin of the Earth's surface, Lavoisier's oxygen theory and other achievements of the second half of the 18th century, made the breaches in metaphysical world outlook even more wide. Essentially new ideas, contradicting the conception of invariablility of Nature, began to form, the ways of transition from one series of elements to another were anticipated and, in accord with the above, the ideas of the unity and the development of Nature began to take shape. The end of the period saw the establishment of such broad conceptions in natural science as the law of conservation and conversion of energy and Darwin's theory of evolution.

The principle of conservation and conversion of energy was the broadest generalization of the discoveries in natural science of the first half of the century. It went beyond the frames of mechanics, became a physical principle, gave rise to the classical theory of heat, electricity and light and penetrated into chemistry and biology. By the middle of the 19th century, atomistics had developed into the kernal of the chemical and physical doctrine of matter.

Darwin's work "On the Origin of Species" was published in 1859, 50 years after the first broadly developed conception of evolution had been put forward by Lamarck. The theory of evolution which was formulated and grounded there put an end to the idea of the organic world being invariable, and in the second half of the 19th century entailed fundamental changes not only in biology but also in the nature of biological thinking itself. It represented the triumph of the historical principle in nature, a conclusive proof of the whole Nature being subject to a universal system of natural laws and causal relationship, and exerted a great influence on the further development of natural science and philosophical ideas. Its fundamental significance lay not only in grounding the principle of evolution of the organic world, but also in the fact that statistical objective laws governing the evolution replaced the Laplacean mechanistic determinism and the purely dynamic approach to the explanation of causality.

This trend in the development of natural science was determined in the long run by the demands of social development; although, of course, science can meet the demands of the society only if scientific prerequisites for the resolution of the problems, facing it, have matured in science itself. Manufactory production could be to a certain extent satisfied with simple descriptions of phenomena and empirical generalizations; machine industry required that laws governing physical, chemical and other processes be discovered. Otherwise, neither machines, nor, all the more, machine industry was possible. Steam-engine designing required unterstanding of the relationship between steam pressure and temperature and the discovery of the laws of thermodynamics. The necessary quality of metals could not be obtained and their production could not be increased without insight into physical and chemical phenomena. The creation of electric motors called for the development of the theory of electromagnetism and electrodynamis. Without scientific interpretation, empirical knowledge alone could not provide a sharp growth in agricultural produce, the demand for which was constantly increasing.

With the increase in the need of deeper insight into the laws of nature and with the accumulation of new data and theoretical conceptions contradicting old theories, the need of new research methods, of a new approach to the study of the surrounding world, and, above all, of new ideas concerning Nature and its cognition became more and more manifest. Although still predominant in science, metaphysical ideas came in an ever-increasing contradiction with obtained facts, which were beyond explanation within the frames of old theories. Hence is the great interest, that scientists and philosophers of the first half of the nineteenth century had in the problems of the method of research into Nature and in other general scientific problems. The creation of a new scientific world outlook became urgent. Having been long divorced from each other and following nearly never-crossing ways, the scientific search of an adequate reflection of Nature's laws and the attempts to comprehend general laws of being and thinking had united, by the end of that period, in the philosophy of K. Marx and F. Engels. It was in their doctrine that for the first time philosophy was provided with scientific basis and turned into science itself. Guided by the whole of the knowledge, accumulated by mankind, Marx and Engels developed a truly scientific, dialectical-materialistic method of research into the laws of Nature, society and thinking.

This period brought rapid changes in the theoretical foundations of natural science, the corner-stone of which was represented by the principles of mechanics used by scientists for the explanation of the qualitative variety of natural phenomena. The mechanistic picture of the world was gradually replaced by a new idea of nature, with its basis formed by the principles of conservation and conversion of energy, determinism and atomistics, the doctrine of the historical development of the Earth and the organic world. "The new conception of nature was complete in its main features: all rigidity was dissolved, all fixity dissipated, all particularity that had been regarded as eternal became transient, the whole of nature shown as moving in eternal flux and cycles."[1]

The majority of European countries saw the break-down of old metaphysical, mechanistic conceptions. This process manifested itself distinctly in France, England, Germany, and gave rise, on the one hand, to a rapid spread of natural philosophy, particularly in Germany, and, on the other hand, it caused the search of a strictly scientific explanation of the objective laws of nature, and the attempts to combine experimental research and precise observations with sweeping generalizations. This is characteristic of the works of Laplace, S. Garnot, Lamarck, Geoffroy Saint-Hilair, Magendie, Claude Bernard in France, J. Mueller, Schleiden, Schwann, Helmholtz in Germany, Prochaska, Purkyne in Czechoslovakia, Lyell and Darwin in England.

The characteristic features of the period of the decay of old conceptions and the quest for a new scientific view of the world manifested themselves also in Russia where science developed in close interaction with science of other European countries. Apart from the struggle involving general theoretical problems of natural science, scientific view of the world obtained a particularly important position in Russia in the first half of the 19th century and was notable for its particular acuteness.

Here we come across a historical situation, very interesting when viewed in theoretical aspect. In the first half of the 19th century, for a number of reasons discussed later, Russia was behind scientifically developed European countries in many experimental fields of natural science. At the same time Russian science kept pace with world science in a number of general theoretical fields, and even surpassed it in some of them. This feature of Russian natural science of the 18th and 19th centuries was observed by the famous Russian plant physiologist K. A. Timirjasev already in the end of the past century. In 1894 he said

the following: "In what fields of knowledge during these two
centuries has the Russian intellect given the most obvious
evidence of its maturity, independence and fruitful creative work?
Not in the accumulation of innumerable data of meteorological
diaries, but in the discovery of the major laws of the history of
the development of organisms; not in the description of mineral
resources of its country, but in the discovery of the major laws
of chemical phenomena — it is there mainly that Russian science
has claimed its equality, and sometimes even superiority."[2]

Even if only the first half of the 19th century is taken, the
feature in question can be clearly shown on a large number of
examples. Let's indicate some of them. Already in 1816, the
Russian physician I. E. Djadkovsky (1784-1841) developed an
advanced (for his time) conception of vital functions of the human
organism, coming up to conscious philosophic materialism.[3] A
student and later a professor of the Moscow University, K. F.
Rouillier (1814-1858) created in the 1840s-1850s a sound theory of
the development of the organic world, which was the greatest
achievement of the world doctrine of evolution in the period
between Lamarck and Darwin.[4] While the Schellingian natural
philosophy was welcomed with enthusiasm in German Universities,
many Russian scientists were vigorously opposed to it. They wrote
that such important problems as the idea of the development and
universal relationship between phenomena which occupied a
prominent position in the Schellingian natural philosophy, had
been worked out in the erroneous idealistic basis; therefore the
Schellingian philosophy provided a distorted reflection of the
reality and though some of its propositions deserved
consideration, on the whole led scientists astray.

This situation might seem rather paradoxical. Let's try to analyse
it.

The second half of the 18th century is a period when the feudal
economy system began to decay in Russia, as well as in many
European countries. The 19th century saw a considerable extension
and acceleration of the process. There was a rapid growth of the
commodity production within the economy based on serfdom. The
turnover of the home market increased, indicating the decay of the

natural economy. New technology was applied to agriculture, the number of enterprises equipped with machinery was constantly increasing, and new branches of industry were founded.

In 1805 the steam-engine was first employed in Russian cotton industry. Since 1809 flax-spinning machinery had been employed, and in the 1820s a switch-over to the machine printing and weaving set in. The production of riverine steamers began in 1813, and soon riverine navigation was inaugurated on the Neva-, the Kama-, and the Volga-rivers. In 1820s-1830s several rolling-mills were mounted, a series of experiments with hot blowing during iron casting was conducted and a number of agricultural-machine-building plants arose. The reorganization of Russian industry is illustrated by the steadily increasing import of machines and tools. Thus, in 1815-1816 it made 83 000 roubles, and in 1825 it came already to 828 000 roubles, in 1840 to 3 500 000, and in 1850 to 8 397 000 roubles.[5] These figures indicate not simply a growth of industry, but also the fact that its new basis was forming. Although greatly hampered by serfdom preserved in Russia, this process was steadily progressing, with a corresponding increase in the demand for competent experts in various fields of knowledge. Universities were opening one after another – in Derpt (1802), Vilno (1803)[6], Kazan (1805), Kharkov (1805), Petersburg (1819), Kiev (1834). Besides, in Moscow and Petersburg higher medical schools, medical and surgical academies were founded. Lyceums – the Demidov Lyceum in Jaroslavl (1806), the Tsarskoselsky-Lyceum near Petersburg (1810), and the Richelieu Lyceum in Odessa (1817) – were organized as a kind of higher schools. In 1804, the Military School of Mines was founded in Petersburg. In 1866, it was reorganized into the Institute of Mines, which played an important role in training highly educated geologists. 1810 was the year of the foundation of the Petersburg Institute of Railway Engineers. It was in that period that a number of military engineer and naval academies was organized.

The Petersburg Academy of Science had extended the sphere of its research. However, it ceased to be the only scientific centre of the country. Universities had assumed the leading role not only in training specialists, but also in promoting science. Dozens of prominent scientists – N. I. Lobachevsky, M. V. Ostrogradsky, P.

L. Chebyshev, A. A. Voskresensky, N. N. Zinin, A. M. Butlerov, and others among them - studied at the universities during the first half of the 19th century.

A uniform system of education was introduced in the early 19th century. The country was divided into educational districts with a corresponding university at the head. However, the organization of and control over the educational process, as well as the appointment of teachers and the heads of schools, was exercised not by universities, but by guardians of educational districts, who were appointed by the government among civil and military officials of rank. For the most part they saw their task not in promoting education, but in barring free-thinking. Class restrictions had been strictly observed up to 1861; serfs by birth, i. e. the majority of the people, were completely refused admittance into high schools and universities. Even during short-term "liberal" periods, the tsarist government considered the spreading of education to be a great danger and sought to make it purely pragmatical and law-abiding.

The Church pursued the same policy. Thus, the State suppressed the development of the creative scientific thought and restrained the development of science though it was forced by economical necessity to allow a certain expansion of education and even to make some steps in this direction. However, having set in once, the process could not be stopped, and even severe restrictive measures taken in the end of the reign of Alexander I and later in the reign of Nikolai I could only hamper the development of science and education but not stop it.

The second half of the 1830s was marked by the increase in the number of university chairs and by a considerably higher standard of teaching and demands upon students. The master's and the doctor's degrees were introduced; standing for a corresponding degree became obligatory to fill the position of an assistant professor or of a professor in a university. The research work in universities became more intensive, although its resources were more than limited in the first half of the 19th century Funds alotted by the government were scanty, and professors had to overwork themselves with teaching.

The rise of scientific societies and appearance of new scientific journals can serve as an important indicator of the growth of science in Russia of the early 19th century. In the 18th century there was only one scientific society in Russia and only some 20 scientific journals were published; in the first half of the 19th century already more than 10 scientific and medical societies were actively functioning, and about 60 scientific and popular-scientific journals were published.

Such scientific societies as the Moscow Society of the Researchers of Nature (founded in 1805), the Russian Geographical Society (1845), the Mineralogical Society (1817) played an important role in the study of the animal and vegetable world, of natural conditions and mineral resources of Russia, in the development of scientific research and training expert researchers. In the first half of the 19th century their contribution to this field was no less important than that of the major universities. The increase in the number of scientific societies and scientific periodicals in the early 19th century indicated the process of formation of the scientific world and the strengthening of contacts between scientists.

The 1820s were the period when the progressive people of the country were painfully and ardently seeking a way out of the deep social crisis Russia experienced at that time. P.I. Pestel, the Decemberist, defined this period as an epoch of "the seeth of minds". The Decemberists' movement awoke the progressive people of Russia.

The years following the defeat of the Decemberists' uprising, (1825) were not the years only of despair and embarrassment, as it used to be represented. The savage tsarist terror failed to suppress for a long time the discontent which had arisen in the country. Having caught the substance of the epoch very exactly, A.I. Herzen called this period "astonishing times of external slavery and inner liberation".

The number of peasant riots was constantly increasing. In 1826 they embraced 26 provinces. In 1830-1831, Russia saw a wave of "choleric riots" involving peasants and military settlers which

here and there developed into formidable revolts. In the period
1835 to 1844 there were on the average 22 cases of mass peasant
protest. Secret political societies and circles, in universities
as well, sprang up one after another. Russia was wakening from
sleep. In the 1830s–1840s 'raznochintsi' – a new and rather large
social stratum – entered the historical scene. The passionate
critical writings of V.G. Belinsky and A.I. Herzen were popular
all over Russia. They still very seldom reached the people
suffering from poverty and lack of rights, but they had an
ever-increasing influence, as well as fiction, on the educated
strata of the society.

Foreign political events also contributed to the mental ferment.
In July of the year 1830 the revolution in France put an end to
the dynasty of the Bourbons. The revolution in Belgium in August
of the same year brought national independence to the country. In
November 1830 an uprising in Poland broke out. Even the
representatives of the ruling clique began to realize that the
system of the government was to be changed in one way or another,
and that it was coming less and less possible to preserve the old
government in its entirety. The revolutionary storm over Europe in
1848 reminded of that once again.

A steady growth and aggravation of all the antagonisms of the
feudal economic system incited the progressive people of Russia to
searching the ways of the radical change in the whole of the
country's tenor of life. After the defeat of the Decemberists'
uprising, the necessity of a true revolutionary theory became more
and more apparent to the progressive Russian thinkers. They were
very far removed from the people yet and did not see the force
capable of implementing these reforms, and this made the search
for a true revolutionary theory especially difficult.

Under these circumstances, the primary task was to dethrone the
feudal, serfdom ideology which included religion and metaphysical
view on nature as its most powerful weapon. Literature and science
played an important role in achieving this goal under the
conditions of a fierce censorship and terror in the days of
Nicolai I. A serious social programme could not be worked out then
without a foregoing ideological, intellectual liberation –

liberation from the chains of feudal and religious world outlook. Intensification of class contradictions in the country resulted in aggravation of the ideological struggle. Many theoretical problems of general kind in natural science proved to be urgent problems of the ideological struggle. Such was the case in France on the eve of the Great French bourgeois revolution of the 18th century, and so it was in Russia in the first half of the 19th century.

The development of science is determined not only by economic requirements of the society. Besides the needs of economics and industry, it is influenced by the objective laws of the development of science, resulting from the continuity in knowledge, and also by cultural and scientific traditions, the number of scientists in the country and the level of their training etc. Without considering all these factors, it is impossible to reveal the real picture of the development of science, especially for a rather short period, and, the more so, in a particular country.

The ideological struggle represents an important factor influencing the development of science. Moreover, the significance of this factor may sharply increase in certain historical situations. Therefore it would be naive to expect an obligatory absolute correspondence between the level of science and that of economics, when studying the development of science in one country or another, or in this and that period. Some economically backward countries may surpass those highly developed in the promotion of this or that field of science.

When examining such cases one should, however, bear in mind the following two factors: first, the development of science in each country is indirectly, through the general state of the world science, influenced by economical and other demands of its own country and of other countries as well, and by the level achieved by science abroad; second, the effect of ideology on the formation of scientific theories often, and – which is more – chiefly manifests itself not in a direct form, but also mediately.

The broad interest in fundamental philosophical problems of natural science of the first half of the 19th century was heightened in Russia by the demands of the ideological struggle. Both science itself and life called for the resolution of these problems, and there was no ignoring them, they were to be solved. Consciously or spontaneously, scientists, nevertheless, responded to these demands of life.

That is why works on fundamental problems of general theoretical nature acquired primary importance at that time. The thing is, naturally, not in the ratio of descriptive and theoretical works, but in the elements of the new science of the first half of the 19th century.

In the historical situation that existed in Russia in the first half of the 19th century, the demand of science for new research methods, for a scientific world outlook, a new idea of nature, was much aggravated and stimulated by the intensive ideological struggle.

Many progressive Russian scientists of the first half of the 19th century proceeded from spontaneous materialistic views on the universe and adhered to the principle of evolution in their research; moreover, they opposed idealism as a philosophic world outlook and welcomed materialistic understanding of natural phenomena.

An important role was played here by the traditions laid by M.V. Lomonosov whose works on natural science were well known to scientists of the first half of the 19th century.

The resolute struggle carried on by progressive Russian scientists and thinkers against idealistic natural philosophy prevented them from following the Schellingian ideas. This struggle, in its turn, necessitated the development of major philosophic problems of natural science and served as an impetus to the extension of theoretical research mainly into the methods of studying Nature. Moreover, Russian scientists had to overcome not only the attacks of idealism of all shapes and shades, but also the impediments created by the police. The political enthusiasm evoked by the victory in the Patriotic War of 1812, peasant unrest, the increasing dissatisfaction with the autocratic regime among the progressive part of the nobility, caused in the middle of the 1810s, a savage reaction on the part of the tsarism. Education was affected as well. In 1817, the Ministry of Education was reorganized into the Ministry of Clerical Affairs and Education with the aim both of emphasizing the priority of religion as compared with education, and making education in fact subordinate to religious dogmatism. The tsar's manifesto issued on this occasion left no doubt concerning the purpose of this action. This was one of the first steps in realization in Russia of the principles of the notorious Holy Alliance which united European monarchs. The Kazan University was literally devastated in 1819. Even the attempts to teach mathematics, medicine, natural history without constantly citing the Holy Scripture were savagely persecuted. In 1820, the mathematician T.F. Osipovsky, one of the most prominent professors of the Kharkov University and a talented materialist thinker, was dismissed from the University, while his pupil M.V. Ostrogradsky, also a brilliant mathematician, was refused a candidate's degree. In 1821, the professors of the Petersburg University A.I. Galich, K.I. Arsenyev, and others were subjected to a disgraceful trial. As a result, the best professors were dismissed from the University, and their works were banned.

After the death of Alexander I and the Decemberists' uprising in 1825, the police means of influence became even more hard. Thus, teaching philosophy was prohibited, lectures even in natural sciences were put under a strict control, censorship became more severe, import of foreign literature was forbidden without special permit; if noticed to be involved in freethinking, professors were dismissed from universities and exiled; students were flung into prisons, exiled, recruited by force.

The development of Russian science in the first half of the 19th century was also influenced by deep social and economic contradictions of that time. On the one hand, the capitalist forms of economy, which were evolving in the depths of the feudal system, necessitated a more extensive study of natural resources and their application, and also the development of scientific knowledge. At the same time, a rather backward feudal economy of Russia, being fettered by relations of serfdom, hampered the development of scientific research impossible without material resources - laboratories, equipment, a sufficient number of specially trained personnel not engaged in any other work. All this resulted in the fact that, though behind in many experimental fields, Russian science of the first half of the 19th century kept pace with world science in the resolution of many fundamental theoretical problems of that time, and sometimes even surpassed it.

This, naturally, does not mean that Russian scientists of the first half of the 19th century were preoccupied exclusively by general problems and carried on no special theoretical and experimental research. It were Russian scientists of that period who made such important discoveries as the creation of non-Euclidean geometry (Lobachevsky), thermochemistry (G.I. Gess), and in the field of organic synthesis (Zinin) which served as a basis for organic dyes manufacturing, and it were Russian scientists who created comparative embryology (Baer), ecology and zoopsychology (Rouillier). The discovery of the electric arc and the creation of the largest - for those times - source of electricity (V.V. Petrov), and of galvanoplasty (B.S. Jacoby) was carried on by such important research as Ostrogradsky's works on mathematical physics, V.Y. Struve's research into astronomy etc.

The high level of theoretical research in Russian natural science created favourable conditions for the development of philosophic thinking in Russia and gave rise to a strong materialistic trend in it; this manifested itself in the outstanding works of A.I. Herzen. His "Letters on the Study of Nature" represented an unsurpassed example of materialistic generalization of philosophical problems in natural science of that period. Inspired by the progress in world science, its studies, and achievements, this work in its turn exerted a great influence on the following generations of Russian scientists.

References

1 Engels, F.: Dialectics of Nature, in: Marx, K. and Engels, F.: Collected works, vol. 20, p. 354.

2 Timirjasev, K.A.: Collected works, vol. V, Moscow 1938, pp. 41-42 (in Russian).

3 See Mikulinsky, S.R.: A History of Biology from Ancient Times to the Beginning of the 20th Century, Moscow 1972 (in Russian).

4 See Mikulinsky, S.R.: K.F. Rouillier as a Scientist, a Personality and a Teacher, Moscow 1979 (in Russian).

5 Ljashenko, P.I.: A History of the USSR National Economy, Moscow 1950, 2. ed., p. 519.

6 It was closed later in connection with the Polish Urprising of 1830 - 1831.

Steven Turner

THE PRUSSIAN PROFESSORIATE AND THE RESEARCH IMPERATIVE, 1790 - 1840

In Germany, unlike other European nations, the universities have traditionally been the major centers for the creation of academic knowledge as well as for its transmission. This was especially true in the first two thirds of the nineteenth century, when German scholarship, first in philology and history and later in branches of the natural sciences, rose to dominate world learning and to impose its university-centered pattern of institutional organization upon other nations. The ultimate cause of this burgeoning of German scholarship was the new and at that point uniquely German conviction that the professor's responsibility is not only to transmit academic learning but also to expand it, through criticism and research. This ideal of the professor's proper function can be called the "research imperative."

The notion of the research imperative can be approached historically in several different ways. At one level it was a professional and institutional ideal, which held that appointments and promotions within the university system should be based primarily upon the academic's achievement in specialized research and upon the prestige he had achieved thereby among his disciplinary peers. A corollary of this ideal was that the institution and the state should provide the tools prerequisite to research, be it seminar training libraries, research leaves, or laboratory facilities. I have argued in other papers that the

H. N. Jahnke and M. Otte (eds.), Epistemological and Social Problems of the Sciences in the Early Nineteenth Century, 109–121.
Copyright © 1981 by D. Reidel Publishing Company.

policy of university administration adopted by the Prussian Kultusministerium during the Vormaerz period shows a faltering but unmistakable adherence to this ideal, and that state action played an important role in establishing the research imperative as the norm of professorial life in Prussia.[1] Two developments prepared the way for the emergence of the research imperative in this sense. One was the decline of university corporatism and the emergence of a younger, more competitive, more mobile professoriate, whose ties were more to the discipline than to the institution and which was more diversified by age, rank, and specialization. Another was a decisive shift in Prussian state policy toward the universities that occurred during the reform period, a shift toward more consistent surveillance and a more opportunistic exploitation of the universities and their prestige for nationalistic ends. Both developments suggest how the new academic ideal owed its origin in part to social and political changes outside academia.

The research imperative also represented a moral and philosophical commitment. As such its classical formulations are to be found in the writings of Humboldt, Fichte, Schleiermacher, Steffens, and Schelling, who glorified academic creativity as the lofty, moral mission of the German scholar. Two comments should be made about these classical formulations of the so-called Wissenschaftsideologie. First, despite the radical-sounding overlay of neohumanistic and idealistic rhetoric, the aim of these treatises was conservative. They sought to defend the status and prestige of professors and universities against their many critics of the late Aufklaerung period, and as such their program, although not their rhetoric, was largely continuous with earlier defenders of the universities, notably those at Goettingen.[2] Second, the classical formulations of the Wissenschaftsideologie underwent a subtle but pronounced reinterpretation in the course of the Vormaerz period and later. The original synthetic, normative ideal of learning was increasingly reinterpreted so as to make room under its mantle of prestige for detail research, specialization, and the disciplinary fragmentation that set in during the Vormaerz period. The Wissenschaftsideologie was thus a rhetoric of justification, which reflected rather than shaped prevailing scholarly practices and aspirations.

A third, perhaps more fundamental historical approach to the research imperative seeks its origins in a profound change within the disciplinary communities themselves. During the early nineteenth century several disciplines of the lower faculty seem to have passed in succession through a transition that can be described as "professionalization" or "preemption."[3] The pattern of this transition varied among disciplines but showed some constant characteristics. The scholarly community - those who wrote, read, and judged serious works of scholarship - became associated ever more closely with schools and universities. Membership in the community - the right to publish and be heard - came to depend heavily on academic licensing procedures: membership in seminar or school, the dissertation, the Habilitation, progress through the ranks of the professoriate. "Serious research" became increasingly centered around the application of expertise, whether manuscript genealogies, archival explorations, or quantitative chemical analysis; "serious scholarship" addressed itself increasingly to the narrower range of problems accessible to expertise and tended to dismiss others as illegitimate, speculative, or popular. In this sense disciplines were "preemted" by their academic elite, and marginal contributors were read out of the enterprise or were reduced to the status of popularizers or dilettantes. The disciplines and their practitioners evinced a strong, sometimes fanatical concern with delineating their boundaries, defining their problems and methods, justifying their activities, and probing the philosophical and epistemological bases of their practice. The transition was therefore a social one, as it affected the composition and definition of the disciplinary communities, and an intellectual one, as it bore upon accepted scholarly values and research methods.

In other papers I have traced this pattern of professionalization and preemption for the one discipline of classical philology.[4] There the pattern showed itself in increasing numbers of specialized journals, the growing rigor of criticism, the proliferation of seminars and the kind of training they offered, and the shift of scholarly focus onto problems requiring expertise in the application of Hilfswissenschaften. Seen in this light,

philology's interminable wars of method appear as contests of
professional legitimacy, struggles to delineate the proper
objectives of a professional science aborning. A renewed concern
with legitimacy and foundations characteristic of the preemption
process appeared in philologists' efforts to establish their
discipline's institutional and philosophical independence of
theology, pedagogy, and philosophy and in their preoccupation with
hermeneutics and method.

Only individual studies of other disciplines will show the extent
to which they shared traits of this professionalizing process with
classical philology. Nevertheless, some evidence suggests that
history and some linguistic specialties like Germanic philology
entered the preemption phase between 1820 and 1840, and that
mathematics and the natural sciences embarked upon it between 1825
and 1845.[5] For all these disciplines professionalization
necessitated establishing their institutional and intellectual
independence from the upper faculties, as it had for philology.
For all it implied the acceptance of new scholarly values based on
specialization, academic licensing, and methodological expertise.

What events, social or intellectual, triggered these successive
transformations of the disciplines of the lower faculty? No
definitive answer to this question exists now, nor do we possess
many plausible hypotheses. I want to point out here, however, that
the professionalization of the learned disciplines showed a broad
similarity to changes in the traditional service professions that
had begun to occur in Prussia late in the eighteenth century. This
shift in the nature of Prussian professional life and practice in
turn reflected broad social changes within the Prussian
intelligentsia.

As late as 1750 the intellectual life of Prussia was monopolized
by the element denoted in contemporary social theory as the
Gelehrtenstand, the Gelehrtentum, or (later) the Gebildete. It
included jurists, doctors, the better clergymen, university
professors, and rectors and instructors in the urban Latin
schools. As a funtional group, therefore, it constituted Prussia's
stratum of learned professionals. But function, professional or
otherwise, had little bearing on the honorific distinction of

membership in the Gelehrtenstand. Status rather accrued to the individual as social acknowledgement of his exclusive possession of the common intellectual culture upon which all professional learning was based.

This intellectual underlay of early professional life has been described as the culture of late humanism with its dual ideal of pietas et eloquentia.[6] Possession of it presupposed oral facility, elegant latinity, moral seriousness, familiarity with the writings of the latin authors, the fathers, and the scriptures, and – most important – a living sense of the pride and social exclusiveness that followed from membership in the res publica literaria. These intellectual values and abilities (largely stylistic in nature) were instilled in the Latin schools of the larger towns and further inculcated by the universities. Indeed, the very ideal of academic learning to which the universities adhered reflected the intellectual values of the Gelehrtenstand. The ideal of Gelehrsamkeit connoted stylistic attainment, fitness for the style of life associated with a scholar, and a universal erudition hostile to specialization. A common commitment to these intellectual values and their social expressions gave to the Gelehrtenstand a cultural unity that transcended its internal differentiation by profession and income and that legitimized its claim to be an honorific estate in society.

Adherence to these values largely dictated the profoundly corporative and ceremonial nature of professional life in the early eighteenth century. The collegiate organizations the distinctive costumes, the network of sumptuary, legal and municipal privileges, the eximiert status guaranteed by Prussian law – these constituted as much the essence as the trappings of the professional dignity.[7] They surrounded the local practitioner with an aura of honorific distinction before which considerations of function or social utility paled.

Because professionalism was identical with learned distinction, it followed that learned expertise and the social status it brought, not functional expertise per se, constituted the highest ideal of professional life. The status of an educated man lay in what he knew or what his bearing testified he was, not in what he could do per se. The ability of a jurist to administer the law or a doctor to heal the sick was felt to follow unproblematically from erudite studies, or the method of delivering these services was felt to be known from tradition or corporative participation. This body of assumptions is difficult to illustrate explicitly, but it was subtly reflected in all the ways in which professional men were trained, tested, and rewarded. University education in a profession, for example, afforded little or no practical training, and the testing procedures employed by the Prussian state through much of the eighteenth century largely ignored functional expertise.

In a manner subtly different from later practice, the middle eighteenth century still drew no sharp distinction between professional training and general or liberal eduction. The three Fakultaetswissenschaften represented not bodies of functional expertise per se, but rather a single polyhistoric corpus of learning whose three main divisions were thought to embrace all knowledge possible to man, and to which all other disciplines served as mere auxiliaries. The education of a Gelehrter, regardless of career plans, culminated in the learning of a faculty science, and the higher faculties thus offered an education as much "liberal" or "cultural" as the lectures of the arts faculties. The drastic decline of the arts faculties at the end of the seventeenth century had ushered in a long period in which nearly all students of the larger Protestant universities matriculated directly into the upper faculties. In the absence of an ideal of functional expertise, this further blurred the distinction between general humanistic and professional study.[8]

These values also explain the monopoly of ostensibly professional learning over German intellectual life in the early eigtheenth century. At the Leipzig book fair as late as 1740 technical treatises in law, medicine, and theology still made up 44 percent of all titles.[9] Germany lacked the leisured and learned middle classes and the enlightened nobility that elsewhere fed the ranks of virtuosi, amateurs, philosophes, and literati. Because it lacked the social basis for a "popular" intellectual culture, its intellectual life remained closely tied to the schools and universities, the ideals they espoused, the positions in society to which they led, and the corpuses of knowledge they taught. The Gelehrtenstand thus played a double social role as Prussia's functioning class of trained professionals and as its sole intelligentsia.

In the second half of the eighteenth century the intellectual culture which had sustained the old Gelehrtenstand underwent a cataclysmic dissolution before the forces of the Enlightenment. The disciplines of the lower faculty revolted in succession against their old subordinaton to theology, law, and medicine. They asserted their own contradictory claims to be the principles of all learning, and in effect ate the parents by subsuming professional studies as special applicatons of their more universal principles. Not until the nineteenth century and the rise of the philosophical faculties did most of these disciplines actually establish their academic and institutional independence. These late institutional developments, however, mereley consolidated an eighteenth-century revolution in ideas which had deposed the Fakultaetswissenschaften from their position as the inevitable organizing principles of all learning.

The intellectual world of the Gelehrtentum was challenged as well by the rise of a new, popular intellectual culture largely indifferent to old humanist values and to the Fakultaetswissenschaften. The new culture manifested itself in new genres of popular literature, the explosion in the number of journals and newspapers; in the enthusiasm for pedagogical experimentation; in the springing up of reading clubs and other societies for a host of social and semi-political purposes; in the creation of a new and vigorous national literature; and in the rise of a semi-independent literati. The core of this new reading public was still professional men and functionaries, but their interests were secular, aesthetic, literary, practical, and moralistic; they were largely unconcerned with theology, erudite learning, latinate scholarship per se. Indeed, one principle theme of the late Aufklaerung was a mocking hostility toward traditional intellectual culture. Between 1750 and 1780 the very word Gelehrsamkeit was degraded to a term of satiric abuse.[10] The

learned ideal it had denoted gave way to new ideals: rational
common sense, emotional and aesthetic sensitivity, and the most
potent ideal of all, that of Bildung.

These developments naturally threatened the educated, professional
elements of Prussian society that had constituted the old
Gelehrtenstand. These elements had justified their prestige and
privileges through their possession of a particular intellectual
culture. As that culture ceased to command universal admiration
and consent, its representatives were forced to seek a new
consensus. Much of the literature of German idealism and
pedagogical theory is given over to this search, to the attempt to
redefine a set of universal intellectual values, the common
adherence to which would sharply delineate the educated stratum of
society from its potential competitors. The social and cultural
solidarity of the later Bildungsbuergertum - the
nineteenth-century counterpart of the old Gelehrtenstand -
testified to their success in defining new, universal values and
achieving their wide acceptance in society.[11]

The dissolution of the Gelehrtenstand and its values threatened
traditional social interests in another respect. Between 1780 and
1800 Prussians evinced acute social panic over the fear of excess
social mobility through the schools and universities and into the
learned professions. They believed that untalented and
poorly-educated boys from the lower classes were studying and
seeking professional careers, thus lowering standards and
disrupting traditional social patterns. Several historians have
remarked on this phenomenon recently, and some have invoked the
meager statistical evidence from the period to suggest that the
object of such fears was more imagined than real.[12]

These fears, however, did reflect one clear social fact: that
traditional criteria no longer sufficed to define the learned
stratum or to protect its social boundaries. These criteria for
acceptance into the old learned stratum had been social, personal,
and stylistic in nature; one was required to possess the outward
accoutrements of a learned man. Judgments based upon criteria like
these had inevitably been subjective and impressionistic. Worse,
they presupposed a consensus on such attributes that was rapidly

disappearing. Faced with the inadequacy of such criteria, contemporaries turned to more formal systems of academic licensing to define membership in the learned world. Proof of successful schooling replaced the appearance of learnedness as the criterion for acceptance into the Bildungsbuergertum. The Abitur and the development of the Berechtigungswesen during the Vormaerz period presupposed this subtle shift in the nature of learned values.[13]

The rise of these new values gradually but decisively remolded contemporary ideas about professional practice. Intellectual culture became increasingly bifurcated into popular and liberal learning on the one hand and professional knowledge on the other. In this process the Fakultaetswissenschaften took on increasingly the guise they possess today: that of separate, functional specialties, whose highest ideal is of service and performance. Intellectual cultivation per se was no longer the equivalent of professional status, and this blurred the boundaries of the traditional professions and opened them to encroachment by their semi-learned competitors.

The literature of the traditional professions in Prussia during the decades around 1800 reveals these tensions clearly. All the professions, except possibly the clerical, were challenged (ultimately without success) by rival groups which coveted their status and privileges: jurists, by practically and cameralistically trained officials; medical doctors, by learned surgeons; and Latin school professors by teachers of other school types. All the traditional professions evinced a new adherence to the ideal of functional expertise: pastoral theology and the image of the Pfarrer as Volkslehrer; clinical traning as the basis of medical education; cameralism as the basis of administration; and pedagogical theory as a body of expertise in its own right. The development of the Prussian state testing system and the nature of the examinations it established testify to the new ideal of functional expertise being imposed upon the professions in the later eighteenth century. In every case the testing system and the licensing procedure it made possible proved an effective tool in delimiting membership in the profession and thwarting encroachment by rival groups. Adopting the ideal of functional expertise,

therefore, could protect the interests of a professional group at
the same time it represented an unavoidable adjustment to a new
and more fragmented intellectual world.[14]

The dissolution of the Gelehrtenstand also altered the status of
the disciplines of the lower faculty. Classical philology, which
in its cultivation of the old languages had been closely linked to
the intellectual values of the Gelehrtentum, faced an acute
challenge to the traditional justifications of its activities.
History and the natural sciences, deprived of their secure if
subordinate roles as minor parts of a unified and integrated
culture, found themselves reduced to the dangerous and exposed
status of Hilfswissenschaften. This institutional status
conflicted sharply with the intellectual primacy over the faculty
sciences which they were seeking to establish. This dilemma forced
the disciplines to adopt new strategies in order to defend or
expand their place within the intellectual vacuum left by the
fragmentation of traditional intellectual culture.

Again, the nature of these adaptations varied from discipline to
discipline, but all conformed to the general pattern of preemption
and professionalization. All involved adopting new learned values
that had already served the traditional service professions with
success. These included a new stress on methodological expertise
by which to define legitimate questions and issues; systems of
licensing, to delineate clearly between members and non-members;
and acceptance of specialization as a necessary good.

As was suggested earlier, these disciplinary metamorphoses
provided a necessary if not sufficient condition for the emergence
of the research imperative in Prussia.[15] The reformed university
system provided the framework within which professionalization
could go forward; its seminars, degrees, and hierarchies proved
easily adaptable to the new demands of specialized training and
formal licensing. Its continued growth and diversification
absorbed the new professional practitioners and scholars being
trained. Conversely, the professionalization process altered the
nature of the scholarly activities which universities pursued.
Traditional kinds of activity yielded to new norms which placed
greater stress on specialization, expertise, and methodology, and

which reduced the range and diversity of problems, areas, and approaches deemed susceptible to legitimate scholarly treatment. What was new in the "research imperative" of the early nineteenth century was not so much the "imperative" – not so much the compulsion of the professoriate to engage in scholarship. Rather what was new was the concept of research itself, a concept born largely out of the disciplinary metamorphoses of the early nineteenth century and ultimately rooted in the changing nature of Prussian professional life.

References

1 Turner, St.: The Growth of Professorial Research in Prussia, 1818 to 1848 – Causes and Context, in: Historical Studies in the Physical Sciences 3 (1971), pp. 137–82 and Turner, St.: Prussian Universities and the Concept of Research, forthcoming in: Internationales Archiv fuer Sozialgeschichte der deutschen Literatur (IASdL).
2 Turner, St.: University Reformers and Professorial Scholarship in Germany 1760 – 1806, in: Stone, L. (ed.): The University in Society, 2 vols., Princeton 1974, vol. II, pp. 495–531.
3 H. G. Daniels introduces the term "preemption" in his: The Process of Professionalization in American Science. The Emergent Period, 1820 – 1860, in: Isis 58 (1967), pp. 151–66.
4 'Historicism, Kritik, and the Prussian Professoriate, 1790 to 1840', delivered to a colloquium, Sciences philologiques et traditions culturelles nationales au 19ieme siecle, held at the University of Lille, 30 September to 2 October, 1977; also see my Prussian Universities (ref. 1).
5 See The Growth of Professorial Research, pp. 137–48, and my unpublished manuscript: The Prussian Professoriate and the Research Imperative, pp. 293–344.
6 Roessler, W.: Die Entstehung des modernen Erziehungswesens in Deutschland, Stuttgart 1961, pp. 95–142. And see Thomas Nipperdey's review of Roessler, in: Goettingische Gelehrte Anzeigen 216 (1964), pp. 249–72.
7 Koselleck, R.: Preussen zwischen Reform und Revolution. Allgemeines Landrecht, Verwaltung und soziale Bewegung von 1791

bis 1848, Stuttgart 1967 (2. ed. 1975), esp. pp. 52-77.

8 Roessler, W.: Erziehungswesen (ref. 6), pp. 101, 119-20; Eulenburg, F.: Die Frequenz der deutschen Universitaeten von ihrer Gruendung bis zur Gegenwart, Leipzig 1904, pp. 189-212; Herrlitz, H.-G.: Studium als Standesprivileg. Die Entstehung des Maturitaetsproblems im 19. Jahrhundert, Frankfurt am Main 1973, pp. 96-99.

9 Jentzsch, R.: Der deutsch-lateinische Buechermarkt nach den Leipziger Ostermess-Katalogen von 1740, 1770 und 1800 in seiner Gliederung und Wandlung, [Leipzig 1912], Tables I-III.

10 Turner, St.: University Reformers (ref. 2), pp. 501-504.

11 O'Boyle, L.: Klassische Bildung und soziale Struktur in Deutschland zwischen 1800 und 1848, in: Historische Zeitschrift 207 (1968), pp. 584-608.

12 Herrlitz, H.-G.: Studium als Standesprivileg (ref. 8), p. 67 and passim; Heinemann, M.: Schule im Vorfeld der Verwaltung. Die Entwicklung der preussischen Unterrichtsverwaltung von 1771 - 1800, Goettingen 1974, pp. 228-33, 296-305; Jeismann, K.-E.: Das preussische Gymnasium als Schule des Staates und der Gebildeten, 1787 - 1817, Stuttgart 1974, pp. 102-18; Brunschwig, H.: Enlightenment and Romanticism in Eighteenth-Century Prussia, Chicago 1974 (Fr. orig.: Paris 1947), pp. 119-146; and Turner, St.: Social Mobility and the Traditional Professions in Prussia, 1770 - 1848, forthcoming in: Central European History.

13 The rise of educational licensing, its effects on mobility, and its political and social significance have been hotly debated recently. See the literature discussed by Lenore O'Boyle in: Education and Social Structure. The Humanist Tradition Reexamined, in: IASdL 1 (1976), pp. 246-57, and more recent contributions by Jeismann, K.-E.: Gymnasium (ref. 12), pp. 117-18, 216-20, 310-24; Mueller, D.: Sozialstruktur und Schulsystem. Aspekte zum Strukturwandel des Schulwesens im 19. Jahrhundert, Goettingen 1977, pp. 24-90, and Heinemann, M.: Schule (ref. 12), pp. 1-40.

14 Turner, St.: The Bildungsbuergertum and the Learned Professions in Prussia, 1770 - 1830. The Origins of a Class, forthcoming in: Social History/Histoire Sociale.

15 For other approaches to the problem compare Ben-David, J. and Zloczower, A.: Universities and Academic Systems in Modern Societies, in: European Journal of Sociology 3 (1962), pp. 62-84; Pfetsch, F. R. and Zloczower, A.: Innovation und Widerstaende in

der Wissenschaft. Beitraege zur Geschichte der deutschen Medizin, Duesseldorf 1973; Pfetsch, F. R.: Zur Entwicklung der Wissenschaftspolitik in Deutschland 1750 – 1914, Berlin 1974, esp. pp. 236–38, 244–48; and Plessner, H.: Zur Soziologie der modernen Forschung und ihrer Organisation in der deutschen Universitaet – Tradition und Ideologie, in his: Diesseits der Utopie, Hamburg 1966, pp. 121–43.

B. M. Kedrov

EUROPEAN NATURAL SCIENCE
(THE BEGINNING OF THE 19TH CENTURY)

The General Features of that Epoch

After the development, in the mid–19th century, by J. Kant of his
cosmogonical hypothesis, its further elaboration by P. Laplace
and the revolution in chemistry at the close of the 18th century,
natural science entered into a period when fresh theories and
hypotheses flung the doors wide open for study into the evolution
of nature and the universality of links between all its phenomena.
The first three decades of the 19th century, however, were still
dominated by the then prevalent mechanical notions of nature. The
supramechanical branches of science were yet to take root. On the
whole, however, a leadership change in natural science occurred
precisely at the dawn of the 19th century: the leader up to the
end of the 18th century was mechanics which was, at the beginning
of the following century, to be succeeded by a set of natural
sciences including physics chemistry, biology, geology and
astronomy.

Thus, natural science at the beginning of the 19th century was
largely transitional, characterised by a switch from the concept
of nature's absolute immutability (the 18th century) over to one
of nature's evolution (the 19th century). The latter, however, was
still in its infancy, manifesting itself only in remarkable
insights anticipating a future evolution theory.

123

*H. N. Jahnke and M. Otte (eds.), Epistemological and Social Problems of the Sciences in the Early Nineteenth
Century, 123–140.*
Copyright © 1981 by D. Reidel Publishing Company.

Natural sciences developed most rapidly in Britain and France, economically and socio-politically the most advcanced countries of that period. The former had its bourgeois revolution in the mid-17th century while the latter towards the close of the 18th. Britain's industrial and technological revolution occurred at the end of the 18th century and at the beginning of the 19th began to spread on to the continent. For this very reason, natural sciences, freed from the influence of natural philosophy, developed most rapidly in those two countries.

In Germany and partly in Russia, on the contrary, natural philosophy's concepts still had a strong influence on science. Italy was witnessing the development of empirical natural science whose foundations had been laid during the Renaissance and the subsequent period. Sweden, for its part, saw its science develop and emerge onto the international area, while in Denmark natural sciences had only begun to emerge.

At that period, the development of natural science was characterised by a direct link of many of its components with the needs of industrial production and technological development, since those components had owed their existence to the real needs of society at a particular stage in its historical development. The very nature of science began, from the beginning of the 19th century onwards, to change from an empirical and data-collecting discipline it was in the 18th century to an increasingly theoretical and "expository" science. Thus, while previously it had concentrated on the study and grouping of nature's objects, it now began to concern itself with the study of processes of changes of the same objects. In this sense one detects a complete transformation in the period from the Forties to the Sixties of the 19th century, with the beginning of that century setting a preparatory stage for the above radical change in the natural sciences themselves. In the process, natural philosophy, despite its artificiality, speculative nature and its departure from the empirical basis of natural sciences, despite the absurdity of some of its hypotheses, had, at the beginning of the 19th century, to its credit many brilliant ideas and insights of genius in the master of nature and its laws.

At that period, there arose and became increasingly acute a
disagreement between natural scientists thinking in empirical
terms and rejecting theory as pure speculation and a natural
philosophic exercise on the one hand, and scientists capable of
theoretical thinking and using this ability, on the other.

With this general backdrop, there arose, at the very beginning of
the 19th century, a hot debate on the fundamental issues before
natural scientists. Sometimes discussions raged among scientists
of the same country (for instance, France and Britain), and
sometimes various national schools of thougth were locked in
argument with each other (the controversy between the English and
the French schools, etc.).

This was made possible by the fact that the victory of capitalism
on the global scale (as a result of the French bourgeois
revolution of the 18th century and Napoleon's wars) had spurred up
the development of international contacts, including those by
scientists of different countries.

From the methodological point of view, the controversy was chiefly
around the following two sets of issues. The first was the pivotal
issue of how changes occur in natural objects - whether gradually,
continuously, or unevenly, intermittently. Depending on the
objects's nature or structure, the winner was that side in the
argument which was capable of providing a reflection of the most
characteristic or typical features of the given object. It was
only many years after, towards the end of the second third of the
19th century or even later - on the watershed of the 19th and the
20th centuries, that the side allegedly "defeated" could claim
having been vindicated, which resulted in a kind of unity of the
previously opposed sides. The problem, thus, was that, faced with
a "living", real contradiction in nature, scientists, failing to
reflect it immediately as such in their minds, had to dissemble it
into contradictory components to be studied as opposed to each
other. Hence, the collisions of two conflicting theories on each
contradiction, with the two alternately having the upper hand
depending on the character of the natural object itself. With the
further progress of natural science, however, the winning side
discreetly transformed itself into its opposite, thus making it

possible to bring to light the real contradiction to be studied - as the unity of both opposites which had hitherto fought each other.

The second set of issues covered the reciprocal links and reciprocal transitions as between different forms of motion and different fields of nature, whose study has helped establish contacts between different fields of natural science: mechanics and the science of thermal energy, the doctrine of electricity and that of magnetism, chemistry and electricity, geology and biology, etc.

We shall analyse the status of sciences and trends in their development at the beginning of the 19th century not by countries but rather by individual disciplines. Let us begin with chemistry which, relying on the "chemical" revolution of the end of the 18th century, had clearly taken the lead; that is why one could describe the 19th century as above all that of chemistry as opposed to the 18th as distinctly "pre-chemical".

The Advent of Chemical Atomism at the Beginning of the 19th Century

In France, the Lavoisier school continued its successful progress along the path of its founder who ended his days on the guillotine. Inside the school there arose a controversy among the proponents of the oxygen doctrine of Lavoisier on the chemical composition of substance - a controversy which lasted seven years (1801-1807). J. Proust argued that each chemical combination has a quite definite composition. It could be likened to a dot on the line expressing a percentage ratio of two components, of, say, oxygen and some metal or non-metal (carbon, sulphur, and nitrogen). If the given chemical element forms two or more oxydes, then transition from one oxyde composition to another proceeds like an abrupt leap. In other words, the transition is not gradual or continuous, it is abrupt shift from one point on the line to another far removed from the former.

J. Proust had an opponent in the person of C.L. Berthollet. The latter asserted that within certain limits the composition of chemical combinations is changeful, not constant, subject to continuous change. As evidence, Berthollet cites solutions, glass and alloys.

The controversy was thus about whether the composition of chemical combinations is constant or changeable whether the change is abrupt, by fits and starts, or uninterruptedly continuos from one extreme component ratio to another.

J. Proust eventually had the upper hand. As a result, the law of constant and definite proportions was established in chemistry. From the viewpoint of cognition, the victory was due to the fact that chemistry was then on the threshold of adopting the atomism doctrine which was to become the basis for the overall development of chemistry in the 19th century. For its part, atomism posed the need for recognising the "intermittent" relationships in the chemical composition of substances since only these relationships could provide an empirical basis for the very idea of the discrete structure of matter. That is why Berthollet's position was self-defeating, since it had come into a clear contradiction with the fundamental idea of chemical atomism.

The advent of chemical atomism at the beginning of the 19th century was due to the need to harmonize the seemingly completely different premises: the purely theoretical and sufficiently abstract notion of atoms retained by the then science from the natural philosophy of antiquity and the empirical results of the quantitative chemical analysis meant marrying a then nebulous theoretical idea with experimental data of analytical chemistry, i. e. adding an empirical approach to theory. The theory received in the process a solid factual basis, while the empirical approach − a correct orientation and a theoretical interpretation of its contents.

It was J. Dalton who carried out such a marriage of theory and empirical approach in chemistry. In general, however, it was Britain that provided the most fertile ground for the development of chemical atomism. There at the end of the 17th and the

beginning of the 18th centuries chemist R. Boyle and mechanical
physicist I. Newton were developing their atomistic ideas.
Lavoisier's oxygen theory provided a pre-requisite for a further
development of these ideas. It is true that J. Priestley, who had
discovered oxygen through an empirical approach, had remained to
his very death in 1804 a champion of "dethroned" phlogiston. He
was, however, one of the last of its champions.

In Britain towards the close of the 18th century, two scientists –
B. Higgins and W. Higgins had already put forward ideas close to
the fundamental provisions of chemical atomism, but only Dalton,
in 1801-1804, had managed to lay the real foundations of chemical
atomism.

In 1800 he studied the mutual diffusion of gases and the process
of water's evaporation into the atmosphere, which resulted in his
discovery of the law of independence of partial gases in a
mixture: a gas in a mixture with other gases behaves as if it were
in a vacuum (Dalton's law). In the process Dalton who favoured the
mechanical concept of gas diffusion and water evaporation, became
engaged in a controversy with the proponents of the chemical
concept of dissolution (Berthollet and other French chemists). The
latter asserted that the atmosphere acted as a dissolvent with
regard to water vapor. In 1801 Dalton debunked this view and
asserted his law.

He then began building models of mechanically mixing gases for
which he needed to determine the diameter of gas particles
surrounded by heat-generating envelopes. It was then necessary for
him to divide the gas volume by the number of its constituent gas
particles. This, in turn, led him to the establishment of the
particles' atomic (relative) weights by taking hydrogen atoms's
weight (H=1) as a reference point. Relying on the experimental
data of other chemists who had studied combinations of two
chemical elements in different proportions, he also discovered the
fundamental law of chemical atomism – the law of definite multiple
proportions. This law decreed that all chemical elements are
combined in both intermittent and whole-number proportions. This
was a direct substantiation of the idea of atoms as being
indivisible.

Dalton's discovery was interesting and revealing from many viewpoints. Firstly, it flung the doors wide open for theoretical thinking into chemistry: you cannot observe atoms under a microscope and you can manipulate them only in your mind. Secondly, in this case theory did not just trail empirics generalising and explaining its results - it also emerged as a hypothesis preceding, and setting a definite framework for experimental research, with the experiment serving as the criterion for verifying the hypothesis, i.e. the theory. Thirdly, thanks to atomism, the winner in chemistry proved to be the one of the two concepts that upheld the idea of intermittence and discreteness, with the result that the concept of uninterruptedness and continuousness was discarded in chemistry.

In 1804 Dalton decided to test his experimentally discovered law of definite multiple proportions through an analysis of two hydrocarbons: marsh gas (methane) and ethylene. As was to be expected, there was two times more hydrogen in the first than in the other. Previously, Dalton had never engaged in chemical experiments.

At about that same time he was visited by T. Thomson, author of a chemistry text-book. Dalton gave him a version of his discovery that differed from the real: that he had first, allegedly, analysed the two hydrocarbons, then saw a definite and multiple quantity of hydrogen per one and the same quantity of carbon (i.e. the discovery of definite multiple proportions), and, finally, explained the law using the notion of atoms ascribing them specific weights. Thomson did not take long to describe this version of the discovery in his text-book, and the legend that had come into being firmly established itself in the minds of chemists.

Dalton himself described the basic provisions of his atomism in the first two parts of volume I of his "New System of Chemical Philosophy" (Manchester) in 1808 and 1810.

The Further Development of Chemical Atomism at the Beginning of
the 20th Century

That the discovery of chemical atomism was ready to come to
fruition at the beginning of the 19th century precisely in Britain
can be confirmed by the fact that almost parallel with Dalton the
British chemist W. Wallaston had also come to the discovery of the
definite multiple proportions. Unlike Dalton who dealt with
gaseous substances difficult to analyse, Wallaston analysed solid
substances (different basic, neutral or acid salts) and on the
basis of these experimentally proved the above law. Following,
however, a narrow empirical approach which denied the role of
theoretical thinking, he did not resort to the notion of atoms to
try to explain the discovery he had arrived at.

Dalton's discovery was followed   up on in 1815 by the British
doctor and chemist W. Praut who came up with a hypothesis that the
atomic weights of all elements are multiple with regard to H=1
and, consequently, represent whole numbers. Hence, it followed
that hydrogen was primary matter ("protyl") and all the other
elements were formed on its basis. In such a mechanistically
lopsided interpretation there arose the idea of the development of
elements. It was based, however, on rough approximations of the
originally determined atomic weights. As the weights were further
specified, their deviations from whole number values became
increasingly obvious, and eventually Praut's hypothesis began,
despite its lure, to lose ground.

In about the same years (1808) in France J.L. Gay-Lussac, who had
previously stated the law of dependence of the volume and
temperature of gases, arrived at the law with regard to volumes of
chemically reacting gases. Thus, two volumes of hydrogen and one
volume of oxygen gave precisely two volumes of water vapor (at
constant pressure and temperature). The law of definite multiple
proportions manifested itself most clearly in this case. However,
Gay-Lussac himself had no respect for atomism, while Dalton
rejected the admission that in equal volumes of gases (in equal
conditions) there are equal numbers of atoms. At that time, the
notion of "molecule" was still non-existent, and mention was only

made of atoms. At first sight, Gay-Lussac's data contradicted
atomism since the impression was that the atoms H and O could
divide into two in order to produce two volumes of water vapor.

The solution to this contradiction was found by the Italian
scientist A. Avogadro: in 1811 he introduced the notion of
molecule consisting of atoms. Thus, hydrogen's molecule was H_2
while that of oxygen O_2. This made it possible for Gay-Lussac's
discovery to agree with atoms' indivisibility and molecules'
divisibility into atoms. In 1814 a similar idea was put forward by
the French physicist A. Ampère.

A major stimulus for the development of atomism was provided by
the Swedish chemist I. Berzelius. A brilliant analytical mind, he
determined in the most precise manner the atomic weights of many
chemical elements and rejected Praut's hypothesis. Starting from
1811, he analysed the composition of a number of organic
compounds, demonstrating applicability to them of the law of
definite multiple proportions. Getting somewhat ahead of this
narration, let it be pointed out that the Germain chemist F.
Woehler proceeded in his research along the same path. In 1828 he
artificially produced urea for the first time. Until then the
ability to form complex organic combinations had only been
ascribed to living organisms thought to possess some
"life-producing force"; this was the position held by chemists of
that time, including Berzelius.

In 1819 two discoveries were made which further buttressed atomism
being developed by Berzelius: the first was made in France by P.
Dulong and A.T. Petit and became known as the Dulong and Petit law
to the effect that the product of specific heat of elemental
bodies multiplied by the atomic weight is a constant value. The
second discovery was made in Germany: E. Mitscherlich stated the
law of isomorphism about the existence of dependence between the
crystalline form and the number of atoms in a complex particle.
These two discoveries stimulated a further specification of
combination formulas and the values of atomic weights.

In the first quarter of the 19th century there began the process of rapid discovery of new chemical elements: discoveries in Britain were — radium, palladium, osmium and iridium in 1803 (Wallaston and S. Tennant); in 1807–1808 alkali and alkaline–earth metals (H. Davy) (to be discussed below); in France in 1808 Gay–Lussac and L. Tennard discovered boron, and B. Courtois iodine. In 1817 and 1824 F. Stromeyer and Berzelius discovered cadmium, selenium, silicon and zirconimum and J. Arfvedson discovered lithium in Sweden in 1817, while H.C. Oersted in Denmark obtained aluminium in 1825. Other elements were also discovered in the form of oxydes.

The discovery of a large number of new elements provided an impetus to attempts at classifying them. In 1817, J. Dobereiner found that the "atomic weight" of strontium oxyde (SrO) represents precisely the arithmetical mean of the "atomic weights" of oxydes of calciums and barium (CaO and BaO). This was how the idea of triades with regard to similar elements had come into being which later provided the basis for the system of triades by Dobereiner.

Chemical atomism enabled chemists to tie together all the chemical combinations and represent from a general viewpoint all the chemical transformations as processes of combination, dissociation and shifting of atoms.

The Development of Physics at the Beginning of the 19th Century

As we have seen, the winner in chemistry has been the concept of intermittence or discreteness, since the simplest chemical combinations usually include a very small number of atoms, usually no more than 10. That is why the intermittence and, moreover, the whole–number nature of relationship are at their most evident here.

In physics, however, the picture is different. The number of discrete "particles" forming its objects — under study at that time— was so great that the continuousness of the changes in the physical objects clearly masked their intermittent nature. Thus, the beginning of the 19th century saw an eventual solution to the protracted controversy between proponents of corpuscular (intermittent) and wave (continual) hypotheses for the structure and propagation of light. The founder of the first hypothesis was Newton, of the second Huygens. Their argument was resolved in favour of the wave theory, thanks above all to the discovery of two optic phenomena: light diffraction and light interference. In France, A. Fresnel developed a clearcut theory of diffraction substantiating it in his accurate experiments (1818); he studied experimentally polarisation's impact in light interference; he also discovered the transversal nature of light waves. These and many other of his discoveries led, in the first quarter of the 19th century, to the development of the wave theory of light.

Thus, the scientific controversies in chemistry resulted in the establishment (for quite a long time, till the end of the 19th century) of the concept of intermittence, while in physics (in optics) of the idea of interruptedness.

But the mainstream in the development of physics at the beginning of the 19th century was the steady headway made by the idea of the unity of the forces of nature. In Schelling's German natural philosophy the idea was represented most vividly, exercising a strong influence on some of the groups of natural scientists.

One should point, above all, the attack of the British physicist B. Thompson-Rumford against the doctrine of the heat-generating substance: in the watershed between the 18th and the 19th centuries he discovered an unlimited emission of heat in the boring of gun tubes which contradicted the idea of the heat-generating substance and its emission during a mechanical treatment of bodies alleged to contain it. This promised the eventual establishment of a link between mechanics and the doctrine of heat (physics), with Rumford regarding heat as a type of motion. Later, at the beginning of the 19th century he opposed the resort to the heat-generating substance to explain optical phenomena. The idea of the kinetic nature of heat was also put forward by H. Davy in 1812.

But especially important discoveries were made in the field of electricity and its related areas - magnetism and chemistry.

In 1800 the Italian physicist and physiologist A. Volta reported on his discovery of "Volta's post", the first steady source of direct current. This discovery was prepared by the discovery of another Italian physiologist, L. Galvani, of "animal electricity". Volta proposed his "contact theory" to explain the appearance of electric current.

In 1803 the Russian physicist and electrician V. Petrov published his "Izvestie o galvani-voltovikh opitah" (Report about the experiments of Galvani and Volta), in which he described his discovery of electric arc and electric discharge in rarefied gas. H. Davy's discovery of electric arc in Britain came 6 to 7 years later. In 1800 Davy put forward his electrochemical theory, further developed by Berzelius. The result had been a protracted controversy between the two theories of the origins of electric current - the electrochemical and the contact. 1807-1808 Davy carried out an electrical analysis of caustic alkali and oxydes of alkaline-earth metals and for the first time obtained unassociated sodium, potassium, calcium, strontium, barium and magnesium.

Even before that, 1803, Berzelius and W. Hisinger used electric current to decompose water solutions of salts, with the bases settling at the negative end and acids at the positive. Hence, in 1812, Berzelius came to the conclusion about the electrical nature of chemical means and developed that conclusion in 1819. The result was Berzelius' electrochemical (dualistic) theory that held that electrical charges exist in atoms themselves as their poles, and do not come into being at the contact of the elements as was presumed by Davy. On this basis, Berzelius built the whole of his atomism as the theory of organic radicals, closely tying them up with electrochemism.

Those were the beginnings of the contacts with such forces of nature as electricity and chemism.

But perhaps the greatest impetus toward the recognition of the unity of the forces of nature had been given by Oersted in Denmark under the influence of the general ideas of Schelling's natural philosophy. In 1820 Oersted made public his discovery - the influence of galvanic current on magnetic hand, which led to the development of the doctrine of electrical magnetism as a special section of physics. But long before this, under Schelling's influence, he had attempted to find a link binding together light, heat, electricity and magnetism.

In the same year, 1820, A. Ampère, upon acquaintance with Oersted's discovery, formulated his own "bather's rule" to determine the direction of the deflection of the magnetic hand by current. A further study of the interaction between current and magnet led Ampère to stating the basic law of interaction of electric currents and developing the first theory of magnetism. Ampere divided the theory of electrical magnetism into electrical statics and electrical dynamics.

On the whole, physics at the beginning of the 19th century progressed through the establishment of pair links: between mechanics and the heat theory, between electricity and chemistry, electricity and magnetism - toward the establishment of a comprehensive idea of the unity of all the forces of nature.

The Development of Other Natural Sciences at the Beginning of the 19th Century

Biology and geology, studying more complex natural objects compared to chemistry and physics, came into being, for this reason, much later than the latter. The basic questions they were looking for answers to were the same as for chemistry, namely how changes occurred in the living and inanimate nature. Were the changes abrupt, intermittent or gradual, evolutionary?

As applied to biology, controversy in this sense began in France. With regard to geology, it later spread to Britain. At the same time, an important emerging problem was to explain the mutual

links between the two fields of knowledge – biology and geology.
In 1809 J.B. Lamarck published his "Philosophy of Zoology"
expounding his historical concept of the development of living
nature. This was a lop-sided quantitative doctrine based on the
recognition of only one graduality and excluding abrupt leaps from
the evolution of living things. Lamarck saw the explanation of the
evolution in teleological considerations because it was still
impossible to identify the genuine factors underlying the
evolution.

Three years later, in 1812, another French scientist, G. Cuvier,
published his "Discourse" about revolutions on the surface of the
globe, describing the Earth's history and the living creatures
inhabiting it from positions diametrically opposed to those of
Lamarck. He rejected any mutability of the organic species
regarding them as permanent. In the history of the Earth and its
surface he recognized only periodic catastrophes ("revolutions")
alleged to occur abruptly, without any evolutionary preparation.
According to his reasoning, these revolutions brought death to all
that lived on earth through an abrupt raising of the sea-beds and
ocean floors and the flooding of all the continents. After this,
the whole of the animal and vegetable world recreated itself.

Biology, thus, became the ground for a sharp conflict between two
opposed concepts. A similar conflict was maturing in geology,
since Cuvier's concept of abrupt explosions was above all
geological in its thrust. Later, beginning from 1825, Ch. Lyell,
in Britain, began expounding ideas opposed to those of Cuvier, and
in 1830–1833 published his "Fundamentals of Geology" in which he
expounded his theory of the Earth's slow and gradual development.
According to that theory, in the past the same physical factors
operated on our planet as the factors (or causes) operating now,
and thus there is no need to resort to any other "forces".
Discarding the explosion concepts in the spirit of Cuvier, Lyell
at the same time rejected any idea of qualitative changes presumed
to have been at work during the Earth's history. As a result, his
theory acquired a lop-sided mechanistic character. And still, like
Lamarck's theory in biology, it was of enormous interest compared
to the concept of immutability and abrupt revolutions.

to the concept of immutability and abrupt revolutions.
But in the other fields of both sciences, Cuvier doubtlessly had major accomplishments to his credit. He, thus, created paleonthology without which geology could not be put on a solid scientific foundation. Paleonthology gave geologists a technique for determining the age and the succession of the formation of geological strata using as the criterion the remnants of living creatures.

Cuvier's research was based on the principle of "correlation between the parts of the organism" according to which a living organism constitutes a single, whole, closed system all of whose inside parts mutually correspond to each other.

Cuvier developed a method of comparative anatomy making it possible to establish a genetic affinity between different organisms on the basis of their internal structure. This method made it possible to elaborate the theory of development in biology, i.e. the theory rejected by Cuvier himself.

In those years the comparative method penetrates both into biology and other natural sciences. Thus, in the field of physical geography, it was elaborated by the German natural scientist and traveller A. v. Humboldt. He has to his credit the development of the method of isoterms which specifies (as aplied to physical geography) the general comparative method of research.

Thus the idea of development and of the universality of links between natural phenomena had been gradually gaining ground in natural sciences in the first quarter of the 19th century. However, at the first stages, it not infrequently assumed a lop-sided mechanistic character emerging as a harbinger of future evolutionary concepts free from such limitations.

Philosophical Questions of Natural Sciences at the Beginning of the 19th Century

The philosphical-methodological-ideological aspect of the rapid progress of natural sciences emerged, from the very beginning of progressive theories and hypotheses in natural sciences. This was due to the very idea of development: if, for instance, all organic species emerged from one another in the process of the evolutionary development of all the living world, then there is no place for an external creator to be ascribed the alleged creation of eternal and immutable living things. This conclusion stemmed directly from Lamarck's doctrine. On the contrary, Cuvier's theory, which rejected evolution and introduced the notion of abrupt catastrophes with the subsequent creation of immutable organic species, led inevitably to the admission of multiple acts of divine "creation". True to style, Cuvier also attempted to interpret his principle of "correlation between parts of the organism" in the spirit of teleologism, invoking the instrumentality of the divine creator.

In a similar way, Lyell's theory of the Earth' slow development left no place for God in nature, and for this reason British geologists holding to religious positions received it with extreme hostility. A similar situation developed in other fields of natural sciences already penetrated, at the beginning of the 19th century, by the idea of development. Thus, the development of the cosmogonic hypothesis made it possible to banish the divine impulse originally introduced into science by Newton. It was replaced by the notion of the formation of the Sun and the planets from a revolving primeval nebulosity. Laplace, a founder of the hypothesis, asked by Napoleon why there was no mention in his "Treatise on celestial mechanics" of the divine creator, proudly replied: "Sir, I had no need for that hypothesis (Sire, je n'avais pas besoin de cette hypothèse)". That was the answer of the whole of natural science of that time.

In chemistry, atomism asserted materialism already by the fact that atoms were regarded material, as particles of matter. It is true that some scientists preferred to stick to the dynamic theory which, in the spirit of idealism, proclaimed matter to be the product of interaction of diametrically opposed forces. This prevented consideration of chemical combinations from positions of discreteness and closed the door to the development of chemical atomism and its laws. Thus, the German scientist E. Fischer, who championed dynamism and opposed atomism, in 1802, produced a table championed dynamism and opposed atomism, in 1802, produced a table of chemical equivalents but could not, because of his hostility to atomism, give it a rational explanation, thus barring himself the path from the law of equivalents to the discovery of the law of definite multiple proportions. Thus, dynamism led its own proponents into a blind alley.

Chemical atomism opened the door to chemistry not only for materialism but also for dialectics. The latter made it possible to explain the transition from one chemical combination to another as a result of addition to, or removal from, a given particle of a particular atom, consequently as a transition of quantitative changes into qualitative. The whole set of chemical transformations was interpreted by it as a reciprocal link between two diametrically opposed processes - addition and removal of atoms and, thus, as a unity of opposites.

Chemical combinations positioned in a line according to the degree of their complexity, and chemical elements in a line according to their growing atomic weights (according to Praut) expressed the idea of the development of matter. And the very introduction, alongside of the atom, of the notion of molecule according to Avogadro and Ampère, introduced into chemistry the same idea of development: instead of the concept of simple discreteness which was upheld by Dalton and Berzelius and which recognized only one microdiscrete form of matter - the atoms, the atomic and molecular hypothesis introduced two forms of which the more complex one (molecule) had developed from the simpler one (atoms).

The correlation of the two discrete forms, atom - molecule, is the beginning of its subsequent expansion both ways: towards more elementary, than atom, and towards more complex, than molecules, discrete forms of nature. But that was, however, to come much later. The beginning of the 19th century only marked putting in place of the first link in that future chain of discrete forms of matter, a chain expressing the idea of the development of matter properly.

In the field of physics, although the idea of the unity of the forces of nature was put forward in the idealist natural philosophy of Schelling and Hegel, it was basically and profoundly materialistic and at the same time dialectical: the idea reflected the more general principle of the universality of links between natural phenomena which opened to physicists the path towards the discovery of the law of preservation and transformation of energy. It thus led to the establishment of an inextricable link between preservation of matter and preservation of motion (energy).

So much for the state of the art in natural sciences of the 19th century and the trends in their further development. From the gnoseological viewpoint, we have seen, firstly, the difficult penetration of the ideas of dialectics in natural sciences through the stone wall of the old metaphysical concept which decreed an absolute immutability of nature and a complete "compartmentalisation" of its fields; and, secondly, the assertion of the position of materialism and atheism and a consistent banishing of idealism and theism from fields where they had entrenched themselves using the limitations of metaphysical approach.

Lothar Laesker

SCIENCE, KNOWLEDGE, AND THE REPRODUCTION OF THE SOCIAL CAPACITY
FOR LABOUR

The social effect of science, especially those applications which
have profoundly changed social life, are arousing great interest
in problems of its development. Which laws or regularities, it is
asked, make scientific results possible? We know from experience
that the application of these results is inevitable. This is not
only an economic interest in science; but economy forms the basis
in this respect, as in many others, and from the applications in
material production all other effects are derived. Thus the
question arises of how science becomes a productive force. A
satisfactory answer can be found only if consideration is given to
how science has emerged by differentiation from an originally
uniform social practice. This process of differentiation began
many thousand years ago with the first forms of the separation of
manual work from brain-work and with the beginning class society.
This process, however, is not completed; there are important
arguments in favour of the significance of those periods in the
history of science in which differentiation processes dominate
rather than the application of ready-made sciences. In order to
illustrate this thesis special attention should be devoted to the
first decades of the 19th century, because they seem to represent
a period of changing predominance: the development of modern
science initiating from the 16th century arrives at a process of
maturity reaching a high level in the 2nd half of the 19th
century. This level is represented in new industries (chemical
industry, electrical engineering above all).[1]

141

H. N. Jahnke and M. Otte (eds.), Epistemological and Social Problems of the Sciences in the Early Nineteenth
Century, 141–156.
Copyright © 1981 by D. Reidel Publishing Company.

In Germany, the conditions for a flourishing of science and its stimulating interrelation with highly developed industry have mostly been created in the years since 1806. Among the essential perequisites for this rapid advance are the social revolutions and the high standard of science in France and of the industrial development in England.

The essential features of what we regard as science today have emerged during those decades: typical institutions, forms of training, working methods, and disciplinary structures emerged in the context of the industrial revolution. These developments ran parallel to the development of capitalist conditions of production and include the changes in the relation between the knowledge necessary for production (e. g. in a factory) and the knowledge demanded of the workers in the process of work.[2] Both elements, the changes in the theoretical structure of science resulting from the work of Kopernikus, Kepler, Galilei, and Newton, as well as the later changes in the character of work, in instruments, knowledge and skills of the workers, are to be viewed in their interrelation if the development of science in the 18th and 19th centuries is to be described. One of the most essential tasks in the theory of science for whose solution analyses in the history of science are necessary consists in representing the concrete mediation of this interrelation.

At first sight, this task coincides with the demand to overcome the so-called internalist historiography of science by giving greater consideration to social influences in explaining the development of science. Whether this is the case depends on how one understands the implied assumption that science develops according to its own laws because asking about the influence of social factors on science presupposes its own integrity. Against a metaphysically interpreted autonomy of science, the thesis can be put forth that the functional relations in the system of social reproduction are constitutive for science. Hence, the integrity of science is not to be conceived as independence, as science existing in isolation. Only if this abstract thesis is made concrete may the processes be outlined whose result is science. The autonomy of science must be seen in the unity of its genesis

with the processes that result in the application of scientific
achievements. However, it must be borne in mind that the
application of scientific results must not be comprehended simply
as a reversion of the processes of its genesis.

The task is therefore to present the theory of social reproduction
as the basis for the theory of science and hence for the history
of science. If this task is accomplished, the relationships
between the theory of cognition and the theory of science also
become obvious. In particular it becomes obvious that a theory
which defines cognition as a function of the physiologically
definable organs of cognition, i.e. the sensorium and the brain,
and which comprehends language as the reality of thoughts encoded
in the brain according to the scheme of data stores, cannot meet
the demands of the theory of science. The biologically defined
individual is not the subject of cognition. The consequence of
this incorrect approach is related to the psycho-physiological
approach in the theory of cognition and has been carried to an
extreme in the positivist works of the twenties.[3] This tendency
does not only entail an empiricism leading to subjective idealism,
but also, and this is especially interesting to us here to the
separation of the cognitive process from work. Always a given
level of qualitatively determined capacity for labour of the
considered individuals is presupposed, and the capacity of
cognition is part of this level. On this level the objective of
real activities does already exist. Hence, the analytical or
individualising approach makes it impossible to ask how real
action, i.e. work as a material process generates knowledge. As a
result, the autonomy of science, too, is interpreted
metaphysically. Science is then understood as knowledge and
cognition as the activity through which scientists acquire this
knowledge.

When discussing this problem it is necessary to define the meaning
of the term "knowledge" more accurately. This involves the
suggestion of a methodological framework in which knowledge can be
defined in relation to social reproduction and the development of
science may be understood as an expression of social development
in a general form.

In all analytically oriented publications on scientific methodology science is mainly treated as language, and investigations are primarily concerned with the structures of this language on various levels. For a materialist approach difficulties arise in particular when, in the context of semantics, the question of the objective meaning of language is raised. Excluding the pointless attempts to leave the dimension of language for that of the real world by using language (finding the word that is no longer merely language), it remains necessary to bear in mind that not only the function of language is to be considered, but that language is to be taken as a function of real work.

Of course, the description again will remain within language. But it becomes possible to explain that the meaning relation attaches an abstractum to linguistic expressions, and that the question about objective truth can only be answered by analysing the production of these abstracta in context with the formation of real modes of behaviour and labour. The question involved is, which elaborations are necessary to the theory of science, if the production of these abstracts is to be included within its range. Whether an enlargement of the object of scientific theory is deemed necessary at all or not, will depend on the attitude adopted toward the previous attempts to treat the problem of truth. Presuming, as, for instance, Popper[4] does, that this problem has been solved in principle by the work of Tarski[5] , one will not see such a necessity. To him, meaning is reduced to a purely linguistic phenomenon; in consequence discussing the question of objective truth becomes impossible[6] . This, however, applies to all attempts which take the functioning of language as their precondition but at the same time exclude the very conditions necessary for language to function. This is even the case if reality is taken into account by viewing it as the set of objectively existing things, because thereby the structure of reality is presupposed to be nothing but a system of identifiable objects, properties and relations. Thus, no consideration is given to the fact that this structure can only be reflected in language because it has actually been produced by society and is maintained in a sufficiently stable form by social reproduction.

The   structure   of reality that is produced by social reproduction
and that maintains itself is a primary, not a passive, reflection.
It is rather a stage in a real evolutionary process. The objects,
in   becoming   objects   for   cognition,   need   to be formed in this
process. Therefore, science in the sense scientists understand it,
as   their   profession,   and   themselves   as   partial   workers of a
society, is primarily determined by the respective level of social
production.   The   possibilities   provided by a given level for the
next steps of development determine science as a productive force.
Only   that   can   be   thought   which   has   formerly been produced in
social   reproduction   as a material structure and is maintained in
social   reproduction.   This   means: social   reproduction   must be
appreciated   as a structure formation process, before the question
of   objective   meaning   and   truth   can further be deepened in the
sense of the 2nd thesis on Feuerbach.[7]

In   everyday   language,   reproduction   is   used   in   the   sense of
repeating   or   reestablishing   a   state.   But as early as the 18th
century,   "reproduction" in the works of Réaumur, Buffon, Quesnay,
and   others   began   to   derive   its   meaning   in   the   context   of
self-reproduction,   at   first   from   living   beings, and then from
social   wealth.[8]   With   these   questions   it   became   possible to
formulate as a theme the relation between parts (elements) and the
entireties   (systems)   which maintain themselves by the process of
reproducing   (reviewing,   reconstructing)   their   parts.   This
interrelation   between   the   renewal of parts (elements) and of the
entireties   (systems)   that are maintained thereby, has been spelt
out by Quesnay[9] for political economy, Buffon[10] for organisms, and
by Hegel[11] in a general philosophical   programme.   Its representation attains   scientific   importance   at   first   in   Darwin's evolutionary theory[12] and in Marx's theory of social reproduction[13]. In
both theories,   attention   is   focused   on   the   interrelation
between   elementary   processes and the structures by which they are
formed,   and   it   is   a   feature   common to both theories that the
ambiguity   expressed   in   this   interrelation is not eliminated by
reducing   it to one of its two sides. In the general definition of
reproduction   as   a   form   of   existence   of   systems maintaining
themselves   owing   to the fact that their constituent elements are
continuously renewed, structures are comprehended both as a result
of   the   interaction of the elementary processes (by which they are

formed) and as their prerequisite by coordinating them in such a way that the elements are renewed. Of special interest are systems in which the renewal of elements is brought about by their duplication or propagation. Reproduction comprises these duplication processes and the continuous renewal of the conditions in which this duplication can be brought about. In the biological literature, above all, reproduction is frequently identified with reduplication, and the essence of these duplication processes is seen in the duplication of nucleic acid molecules.[14] In fact, this is a modern form of reductionism, because reproduction is defined as a concept of the biological sciences with relation to populations.[15] The preservation of living conditions can be taken as a prerequisite, but it is also a result, a link in the "circulation of nature".

Supposing that both processes, the duplication of individuals and the preservation of their living conditions are functioning, then social reproduction can be represented as a circular process in which production appears as a real metamorphosis, and circulation emerges as a sequence of formal metamorphoses. The value is maintained by being transformed, according to the viewpoint in question, e.g., at first from money into commodities, labour power and working conditions, or from commodities into money. Production annihilates the object of work, uses up the means and tires the worker; the manufactured product is converted into a commodity, into money, and the circle has been closed. What had been a result has become a prerequisite. Each such circulation produces an invariant from whose metamorphosis it is created. This way of thinking has been prepared in the 18th century. However, it still remained unsettled how the existence of these invariants was to be represented: as a material substance, as a sensually perceptible property or as a spiritual essence. For social reproduction, this question was scientifically answered first as a result of the Marxian analysis of the capitalist mode of production: Value as an invariant of the circulation of capital exists as a commodity which hence embodies a social relationship. Insofar as a product or sign represents this relationship, it is value. Hence, the existence of value is related to the functioning of the circulation. But the circulation functions precisely, when the labour power is continuously reproduced (labour power, in this

case, not in its abstract determination as a commodity, but rather
in its concretion, as a capacity for performing labour, that is,
as a unity of subjective and objective conditions). This power
forms the substance of what then appears as value.[16]

The production of value is an objective process that must be
principally distinguished from its representation in signs of
value. In the transition from value to the sign of value, the
value is consciously and ideally reflected as the price. This
consciousness, which is different from knowledge formed and
realised in concrete work, originates as an element of actions of
exchange, hence in situations, where value appears as an exchange
value.[17] The partners act necessarily as individuals, and they are
not aware of how they represent their community in doing so.
Rather, they find their behaviour objectified in the relationship
of the things that they exchange.[18] The operations of abstraction
involved in this process have been analysed and described in
detail by Marx; and, socially acquired, they become a schematic
pattern or formula, so that at later stages of development the
representation of the value by the price can take place before the
product is converted into money. Thus, by emphasizing the
objectiveness of value, it is easily forgotten that even as an
objective phenomenon value is a product. Since social development
is an objective process in which the individuals can become aware
of the interrelations in the reproduction of the community only
from the viewpoint of the level attained (only post festum), the
process of cognition proceeds from the phenomena that appear at
the "periphery" of reproduction, in order to advance into its
"centre".[19] The "periphery" is formed by the circulation in which
real metamorphoses no longer occur. Rather, circulation appears as
a pattern describing changing forms of a substance. This substance
is not conceived as an invariant, i.e. as a result of the
circulation process, but rather as its prerequisite. Therefore, it
is possible to distinguish reproduction from the circulation that
represents its pattern. This distinction is important, if a
distinction is to be made between simple and identical
reproduction. If identity is meant in its logical sense, identical
reproduction can only be defined for the pattern of reproduction,
hence, it can only be a result of the abstraction from real,

simple, or extended reproduction. Simple reproduction "in reality" is never identical. But by simple reproduction abstractions are produced as real structures forming the object range of cognition.

If these continuous references to political economy convey the impression that the considerations on reproduction deal with a special field only distantly related to the development of science, then this is solely due to the fact, that the Marxian theory remains the farthest developed form of the theory of social reproduction. If, in the sense of dialectical materialism, one asks about the objective meaning of language and hence of the content of knowledge, then knowledge is determined by its relation to society. By social reproduction, i.e. by means of labour whose central link is this reproduction, the structures which form the object of observation and thinking of the individuals are produced. Like the value in trade by way of exchange, this structure is realized in communication and objectified in signs (on the basis of co-operation or as a mediating element of this kind of trade). Concomitant to this originating of consciousness is the formation of the capacity of universal behaviour (that is, behaviour, co-ordinated within the community), and thinking is the ability which establishes this behaviour. This behaviour becomes a relationship, that is, the objects become things, and activities are turned into patterns. Language is the individualized and objectified relationship. To the linguistic sign for a thing there belongs a pattern in which the behaviour is laid down. Hence, to speak of the objective meaning of language is to speak of its social function and to represent not only the function of language, but rather language itself as a function.

If we assume that social reproduction generates the material structures by which the objects of cognition are constituted, then it becomes possible to understand that the "homogeneity" of the structures forming the object of cognition, will have a determining influence on the structure of knowledge. In the medieval and early bourgeois forms of the division of labour, the different trades were mutually related only by the exchange of products; each trade constituted a relatively independent type of activity which reproduced itself both with regard to its future personnel and the working and living conditions. Related to the

immediate link with the objective working conditions, there was a
close personal contact, in work and in everyday life, that also
ensured the handing on of experience, skills, and knowledge. In
the imparting of labour skills, language as separated from
practical work played only a minor, subordinate role. As far as
languages were developed, they remained entirely context-related,
and communication beyond a workshop did not function. With the
overcoming of this narrow-mindedness through the transition from
handicraft to the manufactory and to large-scale industry, an
essential prerequisite was created for the development of modern
science . This process is certainly initiated in the 14th and 15th
centuries, but remains only local and limited to trades[20] ; mines,
mills and the building of churches[21] are the first undertakings in
which the experiences of various trades and local traditions are
integrated and are therefore gaining in universality. In the early
19th century, this development qualitatively arrives at a
temporary completion with the industrial revolution. The workers
are separated from the objective conditions of labour, and with
the machinery in large-scale industry, knowledge, too, is
objectified in the separation from the worker.[22] At the same time,
with the modern proletariat, labour power becomes universal. In
the form of mobility and disposability this constitutes a
prerequisite for the functioning of capitalist production.[23] This
universal labour power forms the prerequisite for the fact that
the "knowledge about production" can be organized in a general
manner and be integrated with "commercial knowledge" (i.e., with
mathematics, at first especially with arithmetic). To what extent
the combining of trade capital and industrial capital is involved
here, would need some further discussion. Here, the point is only
to state that with this development the object range of generally
applicable language was extended and insofar as "knowledge about
production" is represented in terms of language nature becomes an
object of science. At the same time (and this is only another
aspect) "knowledge about production" becomes amenable to teaching
in separation from work. Consequently, it becomes socially
necessary to organize science in a new form. The master in
medieval craft guilds embodied the treasure of experience and
skills of his trade; the graduate engineer in the factory of the
19th century had to employ the relevant knowledge from all
professions to solve the problems entrusted to him. Hence, there

arises a demand for science that makes itself felt immediately as
a demand for education, and therefore as a necessity for teaching
and for teachers. As a result, the reproduction mechanisms of
labour power are altered, and therefore the structure in which it
is laid down as knowledge in the form of language is changed. At
the same time, together with the historic mission of capitalism to
develop production for its own sake[24] , the innovative function in
the development of productive forces is transformed to an
independent field of activity according to the division of labour,
namely into science, as we have known it since the 19th century.

As is suggested by these considerations, in the development of
science the following two elements are operative: If social forms
of reproduction have been stabilized in such a way that knowledge
is laid down in language (in unity with the standardization of the
context in which it is valid), then results of scientific work
constitute prerequisites for its continuation on a new level; it
developes autonomously, and if only its results being laid down by
language are considered, scientific work is cumulative. Objective
truth is to be identified with logical truth (as consistency of
systems of affirmative statements). These conditions were attained
by the end of the 18th century and qualitatively completed for the
following decades by 1830.

But the entirety of social conditions that are continuously
reproduced, i.e., that must always be given to maintain the
objective meaning of language cannot be reduced to science and its
results. These entire conditions forming the context from a
theoretical point of view do not only play the role of
prerequisites that must be trivially assumed as given, but
otherwise have no influence on what constitutes the actual nature
of science. In my considerations, the thesis that the universal
labour power of the industrial proletariat formed the basis for
object ranges of natural sciences to become object ranges of
industrial production (i.e. objects of work) has a central
significance. The necessity of having recourse to normal language
when introducing basic concepts of theories on nature, suggests
such a connection. The difficulty in representing these
interrelations results above all from the fact that they can only
be comprehended under the precondition of the existence of

science. But then this interrelation is no longer represented
genetically, but analytically. The immediate practical meaning of
this interrelation becomes manifest in the problems related to the
creation of a scientific potential in developing countries. As far
as national industries and the national proletariat are lacking
the research conducted there is related in its content, and
therefore in its potential application, to the conditions of the
countries whose industry and experience of work form its basis.
Historically speaking, it is possible to understand why natural
science could not emerge as long as work in material production
was that of slaves or serfs only, since there was no necessity for
representing the experience of work as separate from its carriers.

On the basis of this conceptual approach, and in context with the
distinction of these two elements, further questions can be
discussed: What influence do social (mainly technological)
requirements have on the development of science and what role do
individuals (or personalities) play?

According to our previous considerations, it may be expected that
the interrelation between a requirement and a problem can be
defined differently; analytically under the assumption that the
requirement has been comprehended, i.e. laid down in terms of
language, and genetically, by defining the requirement and the
problem, as the results in relation to the one social reality
(i.e., in its historical concreteness), as basis. Now it is clear,
that this analytical interrelation only exists, if the object
range in reproduction is kept stable and therefore, if the
objective meaning is laid down. Hence, for the pattern of
reproduction, this interrelation is valid and must be understood
as the relationship between various manifestations of the
invariants which are formed by reproduction, that is to say, that
this interrelation is to be comprehended as a reversible
transformation (not as a real metamorphosis). Only under this
assumption does it make any sense to suppose a derivational
relationship. However, this derivational relationship does not
describe the process in which problems emerge. If it can be
represented, this only means a statement of adequacy: the problem
is adequate to the need, i.e., the solution of the problem will
open up possibilities for the satisfaction of the need. Then it

remains to explain how it can occur that conditions for such adequacy do emerge. They do by no means always come about: frequently, for social needs no problems can be formulated and no needs can be listed for existing scientific problems.
In my opinion, an explanation can be given, if science is functionally understood as a reproduction of the social labour power in its universal form, with the structuring of the object range as generated in social reproduction forming the basis of science. Thus, science has this basis in common with social practice.

Adequacy is obtained by evaluation: society promotes the science which corresponds to it, and the benefit for society forming the criterion can be greatly varied. But the applicability of scientific results in material production (possibility of transforming science into material production, possibility of reproducing the original) form the central criterion. By analogy to biology, consequently, science is not determined like the phenotype by the genotype, but it is determined rather like the genotype by the phenotype: it is the result of social development.[25] It is important to emphasize this point because of the widespread views that science and production are in relations of interaction. This is not only simplifying but basically wrong, as well as the abstract negation: that they have nothing essentially in common. Of course, this judgment applies only, if interaction is understood in the sense that the effect and the countereffect are of the same type of action. And that does not apply to the relationships under discussion here: the gene structure is not determined by a reversal of the gene expression, consumption is not the reverse of production, and likewise, the application of a cognitive result as a process is principally different from its obtention.

The form in which the capacity for work is maintained (i.e., reproduced), determines the possibilities of its development. If it remains represented as the experience, skills and knowledge of the workers who are naturally related with the objective working conditions as their property, then these possibilities will be different from when knowledge as a general element of labour power is available in the form of theories, so that it can be put into

more concrete forms according to any given particular features and
be applied in this specification. An essential advantage of this
consists in the fact that now individuals can perform general
work.[26] A result will be an achievement of scientific labour, if
it can be socially reproduced. The standardization of the context
and representation in a theory are the means that guarantee an
effective social reproduction. A result obtained by scientific
labour is what guarantees this reproduction (a stable
reproduction, maintaining the features of reality, being a
prerequisite). Thus, the question how the individual performance
of a piece of labour is related to the socially valid (scientific)
standard acquires a different meaning than, say, in handicraft.

In the product of scientific labour the element conditioned by
personality must be eliminated by definition. Personal opinions
become the direct opposite to scientific judgments. This shows
that great accuracy and reliability in reduplication are necessary
in order to ensure the stability of reproduction. At the same
time, in this context, individual variations are gaining
importance, they are either eliminated as mistakes, or errors, or
they begin to develop as personal views (opinions). Apart from the
social evaluation of science by which science is determined in its
development, obviously the evaluation of the individual
achievements, the repression or stimulation of variations in
personal methods of work and opinions also belong to the
functioning of science. The processes of evaluation and of gaining
practical recognition differ, which is an expression of the
relative autonomy of science.

Now, the question is of special interest whether and to what
extent experiences acquired in practical activity can become
scientific insights. The fact that in the natural sciences of the
late 18th and early 19th centuries numerous developments are
initiated by such experience, partially in a still not clearly
defined border region between practice in production and
scientific experiment, indicates in my opinion the suggested
genetic interrelation between experience from work and the
theories of natural science the autonomy of which is a result of a
differentiation process. In the context of the discussion of the
role of personality-conditioned variations in scientific

knowledge, it is therefore attractive to pose this question anew,
because possibly, via this connection, science is related to the
specific features of the given social conditions. These specific
features are conserved in the process of science to the extent to
which they represent the universal elements of labour capacity.
With their universality which they represent as scientific
propositions, another, namely the analytical relation to the
specific features is coming to the foreground: they are determined
as species united to form a genus by their common aspects. The
formation of features and recognition of their relevance are fixed
and follow a pattern which is different from the original process
of their emergence, of individual variation and of the obtaining
of general social recognition. The elaboration of these patterns,
their rationalization so that the individual acquisition of social
knowledge is effected with the utmost efficiency and reliability,
offering, however, a chance for general social recognitiion to
those variations that will prove useful to society, this process
is an essential integrating part of scientific work, a unity of
original production and of the application of results.

To summarize, from the viewpoint of the attempt to develop the
theory of science on the basis of the theory of social
reproduction, there results a twofold interest in science at the
turn of the 18th century: Firstly, at this time, basic thoughts
have matured affecting a general theory of reproduction (from
Buffon to Darwin, and from Quesnay to Marx), and secondly, with
the realization of the industrial revolution, in the process of
production a system based on the division of labour became
established, by whose reproduction the object range of modern
natural science was opened up.

References

1 For instance W. Lefevre inquires into this historical context,
in: Naturtheorie und Produktionsweise, Darmstadt, Neuwied 1978.
2 On these problems see: Marx, K.: Das Kapital, vol. 1, in:
Marx/Engels: Werke, vol. 23, pp. 356ff., pp. 382f.

3 For instance   Schlick, M.: Allgemeine Erkenntnislehre (1925), Frankfurt/Main 1979 (Repr.), in particular pp. 324ff.

4 Popper, K.R.: Objektive Erkenntnis. Ein evolutionaerer Entwurf, Hamburg 1964, pp. 57ff.

5 Tarski, A.: Papers, reprinted in: Logik-Texte, ed. by K. Berka und L. Kreiser, Berlin 1971; Der Wahrheitsbegriff in den Sprachen der deduktiven Diziplinen, pp. 356–359; Der Wahrheitsbegriff in den formalisierten Sprachen, pp. 445–559; Grundlegung der wissenschaftlichen Semantik, pp. 350–356.

6 For "gegenstaendliche   Wahrheit"   cf. in: Lenin, W.I.: Materialismus und Empiriokritizismus, in: Werke, vol. 14, Berlin 1964, pp. 96 und 132ff.

7 Marx, K.: Thesen ueber Feuerbach, in: Marx/Engels: Werke, vol. 3, p. 533.

8 The works by Réaumur and Buffon are   quoted by Jacob, F.: Die Logik des Lebenden. Von der Urzeugung zum genetischen Code, Frankfurt/Main 1972, pp. 82ff.

9 Quesnay, F.:   Oekonomische Schriften, vol. I, ed. by M. Kuczynski, Berlin 1971.

10 Cited in: Jacob, Die Logik (ref. 8).

11 Hegel, G.W.F.:   Enzyklopaedie   der   philosophischen Wissenschaften, ed. by F. Nicolin and O. Poeggeler, Berlin 1966, pp. 283 f.

12 Darwin, Ch.: Ueber die Entstehung der Arten durch natuerliche Zuchtwahl, ed. by J.V. Carns, Stuttgart 1876.

13 In the advanced form as the theory of reproduction in: Das Kapital, vol. I and II (ref. 2, 24).

14 Watson, J.D.: Molecular Biology of the Gene, 2d ed. by W.A. Benjamin, New York 1970.

15 Lewontin, R.C.: The Genetic Basis of Evolutionary Change. New York, London 1974.

16 Marx, K.: Grundrisse der Kritik der politischen Oekonomie, Berlin 1953, pp. 425ff.

17 Ibid., pp. 61ff.

18 Marx, K.: Das Kapital, vol. 1 (ref. 2), p. 85ff.

19 This reversal in the case of the theory of knowledge is discussed by J. Piaget: Die Entwicklung des Erkennens I, dazu: Das mathematische Denken, Stuttgart 1972, p. 271.

20 Dijksterhuis, E.J.: Die Mechanisierung des Weltbildes, Berlin, Goettingen, Heidelberg 1956, pp. 269ff.

21 Bernal, J.D.: Die Wissenschaft in der Geschichte, Berlin 1961, pp. 265ff.

22 Marx, K.: Das Kapital, vol. 1 (ref. 2), p. 391ff.

23 Marx, K.:   Zur Kritik der politischen Oekonomie, in: Marx/Engels: Werke, vol. 13, p. 18.

24 Marx, K.: Das Kapital, vol. 2, in: Marx/Engels: Werke, vol. 24, pp. 62f.

25 For the biological aspect cf. Waddington, C.H.: The Strategy of the Gene, London 1957, p. 109.

26 Marx, K.:   Kritik des Hegelschen Staatsrechts, in: Marks/Engels: Werke, vol. 1, p. 267.

II

SCIENCE AND EDUCATION

Rudolf Kuenzli

TEACHING METHOD AND JUSTIFICATION OF KNOWLEDGE:
C. RITTER – J.H. PESTALOZZI

Next to A. Humboldt, C. Ritter is considered the most important representative of classical geography and a rare example in the history of education of how pedagogics and didactics can become of constitutive importance for a scientific discipline. Ritter's geography theory can certainly only be understood when viewed in connection with his earlier relationship with Pestalozzi and his circle. This undisputable fact, however, needs further illumination – according to geography historian Beck.[1] Another[2] suggests that Ritter's views in geography have to be seen against the background that he was a pupil of Gutsmuths from whom he adopted the Pestalozzi way of seeing the earth. Ritter writes in 1815: "My entire geographic work is a portrayal of Pestalozzi's method".[3] That pedagogics are also able to show "new roads to entire sciences"[4] has repeatedly been observed with pleasure by various educationists without systematically interpreting the case. In the following I shall attempt an epistemological interpretation of this relationship.

Philosophers and historians of science usually did not pay much attention to questions of science teaching. This disregard also corresponds with the way most scientists see themselves. Teaching is not considered as a central phenomenon, but is treated as a

H. N. Jahnke and M. Otte (eds.), Epistemological and Social Problems of the Sciences in the Early Nineteenth Century, 159–181.

secondary problem of transmitting. The theoretical skill of the teacher and his personality are judged more important than the methodical structure of his presentation.

In this paper, however, the thesis of a convergency of "Lehre"[5], method and justification is supported and illustrated on the basis of the historic case of Ritter-Pestalozzi.

Purpose of this study is not to prove and consider in detail the influence of Pestalozzi on Ritter. I suggest an interpretation of the convergency of their thinking. Convergency is, in my opinion, more adequate to the relation of Pestalozzi and Ritter than influence. Ritter himself expressed this in his delight "to find that what he could imagine as sole scientific method in geography performed in the elementary course in Yverdon". And of Tobler, the collaborator of Pestalozzi, he says: "He is the indefatigable reviser of this method, he has in my opinion the verdict to have supplied a scientific basis for geography, a basis which it did not have so far."[6] Question here is as to the meaning of these statements; they are explained as arguments in favor of an interpretation of didactics within the constitution of a discipline. The didactic interest in epistemology is directed to the teachability and general accessibility of knowledge.

1. The Problem of Presentation

The problem of presentation is of special importance in geography and may be held responsible for its relatively high methodological level of discussion. There are two factors which especially shape the problem of presentation in geography: cartography as the core and the strained relation between history of discovery and the history of the geographic disciplines. Around 1800, a new solution to the problem of presentation became necessary for both factors.

Cartography (and travel report) tempt one to speak of a science of presentation. With reference to the etymology of the word, F.W. Lindner in 1806 insisted on an entirely topical geography and defined it as "the art of depicting the earth through lines".[7] It

is noteworthy that this is done with pedagogical intent and in a
pedagogical journal. In 1849 J.G. Luedde published an annotated
bibliography on the methodological discussion in the earth
sciences with 387 titles.[8] Although he differentiates between the
methodology of the science and that of (school) instruction, he
regards a separation of both as unfruitful and says "the dividing
lines between both are not easy to find".[9] As is shown
particularly by this bibliography, the history of the
methodological discussion in geography is inseparably linked to
the discussion about methods of instruction. This link is then
developed by Ritter in an exemplary way.

A special methodological accent is given to the presentation
problem in geography as a result of the tension between the
history of discovery and the history of science, between
discoverer and geographer. Accordingly an attempt was made to
describe the geographer in contrast to the discoverer as someone
who necessarily describes and writes, whereas the merit of the
discoverer - as the example of Columbus shows - is not dependent
on his own report of it. This comparison, in particular, of
discoverer and geographer seems to personify the relation between
research and presentation in an original way, or at least to
emphasize a striking problem. "While Spaniards and Portuguese were
successful in making important discoveries, it was the German
Renaissance geographers who methodically mastered the material
most efficiently".[10] The constitution of geography as a science
implies methodically mastering the material. On the other hand,
Kant's model of desk-geography - a reproach with which especially
Ritter was repeatedly confronted - is measured against the
travelling geographer. The methodological explosiveness of this
confrontation becomes evident in the importance of A. von Humboldt
who stands for the transition from mere educational journeys to
expeditions.

This connection of methodical possession of the material and its
secured extension is the decisive point of the new methodological
approach in geography in the beginning of the 19th century. In his
study "Das Ende der Naturgeschichte" W. Lepenies[11] spoke of

"pressure of experience"[12] ("Erfahrungsdruck") in sciences which demanded new forms of processing (scientific methods, techniques, theories) as an enormous quantitative widening of knowledge. Along with this pressure of experience goes a demand for empiricism.

However, the pressure of experience affected geographers for a long time and remained with them to a great extent up to recent times. Thus, for example, Varenius complains about "too many disconnected facts"[13] and Pfeifer states that as a consequence of the anthropo-geographic expansion "teachable methodology had to face more difficult tasks. It was no longer possible to present the material in clearly arranged textbooks".[14] C. Ritter made this problem of mastering the extensive matter his own and recognized in it the problem both of instruction and of the constitution of a discipline: "... this annihilation of the manifold and extensive material through the form seems to be the highest necessity of geographic science in its qualification for instruction which, from this aspect, lays far behind its other sisters of nature-describing sciences and, therefore, up to now remains the most unprofitable bulk for educative school instruction as well as for science itself unmastered by any kind of previous efforts".[15] The battle of form over material has not yet been won. The problem is often outlined like this and in similar formulations. Ritter's concern, i.e., raising geography to the rank of a science, was in his mind a task in solving the problem of presentation "for elementary as well as for scientific study (which coincide)".[16] Ritter emphasizes with this statement the convergency of the methodical (elementary) instruction problem with the science-methodological problem of presentation.

Until now I have talked about the problem of presentation in a somewhat vague, undetermined fashion as the difficulty to master a multitude of details, to integrate them into a clear relation. The problem has an aesthetic component. It also seems to have been recognized by Ritter as such, as can be assumed from his choice of words such as "Stoffvernichtung" (annihilation of material), "Herrschaft der Form ueber den Stoff" (domination of form over material) which calls Schiller's aesthetic theory to mind. But it is no longer the old unity of science and literature which is expressed by this. On the contrary, this unity was – at least in Germany – destroyed.[17] It is not the poetic character of the presentation, but the constructive element which becomes important in the new accentuation of the problem of presentation. Because, contrary to the narrative history of nature and the classifying compendium, the new presentation achieves two things: the unity of the narration shifts from the narrator to the narrated (less subjectiveness in favor of more historicism); the presentation is a reproduction of the presented which at the same time proves its reproducibility (methodization). This already implies the relation of the construct idea to the historical idea in Ritter's as well as in Pestalozzi's work which will be dealt with later.

The problem of presentation remains mainly a methodological one. Its treatment necessarily leads to methodology. This is where the methodical and meta-theoretical interest of Ritter is based. In 1810, he characterized his work as a "Kommentar zur Geographie"[18] (commentary on geography), and in his "Erdkunde" he banishes the elementary geographic material to the comments and annotations.[19] This also fits in with the above mentioned reproach about being a desk-geographer. Compared to Alexander von Humboldt, who "pursued his problems by means of special studies, in laboratories, herbariums, botanical gardens and observatories, with microscope and theodolite, in short: with all means available to exact research",[20] Ritter is necessarily pushed towards philosophy and methodology.

Ritter regards the task of "Begruendung einer mehr wissenschaft-lichen Behandlung der Erdkunde"[21] (foundation of a more scientific treatment of geography) expressed in an exaggerated and compressed way more as a problem of presentation rather than one of research. This comparison requires a conceptual clarification which I shall outline subsequent to the suggestions of the "Konstruktive Wissenschaftstheorie".[22] What seems important to me in this context is not so much the problem of a demarcation and definition of this relation but the fertility of the concept of presentation for the problem of didactics, i.e. "Lehre".

2. Research, Presentation, Instruction

The terms "research" and "instruction" stand for broadened forms
of, to begin with, everyday experience and practice in
organisation. We have experiences, compare them and thus arrive at
orientations for further action. Interest in successful and
appropriate orientations, tried experiences, is the basis for an
exchange of experiences in the form of narration and conversation
during which opinions are clarified and examined. The
"Konstruktive Wissenschaftstheorie" regards this common practice
of narration and conversation as the source of science the goal
of which is to provide approved orientations for action. The
securing of action-orientations affects two characteristics of
social experiences. On the one hand, everyday experiences are
highly accidental and we only learn, as the saying goes, through
experience. On the other hand, they are dependent on the situation
and their validity is limited by the social context in which the
experience is had. The transition from everyday narration and
conversation practice to a scientific securing of
action-orientation can be characterized briefly as follows: When
experiences are had and means are used with the direct intention
to achieve knowledge, then we call this work research. The
travelers on the important expeditions were doing research work.
But a youth group which wants to measure the territory of the
neighbouring forest is also doing research work. Means as well as
approaches are manifold. If research achieves any results, it
makes statements whose validity has to be proved. Presentation is
the attempt to redeem statements. The presentation reflects the
results of research in a series of argumentation steps in such a
manner that the directions for action contained in these
argumentation steps, if followed in the indicated sequence, will
surely lead to the established results. Reproduction is the
purpose and reproducibility the criterium of the presentation.

The order of the argumentation steps in such a presentation is
determined by two principles: it has to be methodical with respect
to the object, i.e., step by step and without going in circles,
and it has to be methodical with respect to any possible sceptic,
this means, it has to start from a common starting point and take
into account the doubts of the partner. At least the

understandability and accessability of knowledge is founded in a common practice of living and working. Reconstruction or going back to this common practice by doing something and redoing is therefore the last common starting point for methodological presentation.

This presentation can also be called "Lehre". The presentation and speaking practice of science is equated here with instruction. This equivalence has triple roots: (1) presentation is the scientific practice of speaking, it is of a dialogic nature; (2) the aim of argumentative speech is the general accessibility and communicability of the stated; (3) if the reproduction of the presented is to be separated from the conditions of the discoverers, the presentation must principally be comprehensible to everyone. The objectified relation between the dialogue partners (teacher, pupil) thus is nothing else than the order of presentation or the method. It is the objective form of teaching. It relates the order of the presented to the aim of the presentation. The linkage of both characterizes the idea of Pestalozzi's method and the "Faehigmachen der Geographie zur Lehre" (qualification of geography as a doctrine) by Ritter.

3. National Education and Physicotheology or the Purpose of Science

With the terminological differentiation between research and presentation, the dialogical aspect of science – its relation to teaching – becomes more distinct. This factor supplies the systematic foundation for German educational reform at the end of the 18th and the beginning of the 19th centuries. Whereas above the pressure of experience in the sciences was outlined, henceforth a readiness for education joins company. Both bestow significance to the problem of presentation in the sciences.

Both readiness and intention favoring education stand for a science ethos characteristic of the time as expressed programmatically in the works of Schelling, Humboldt and Fichte

concerning the unity of educational and scientific interest. Also
Carl Ritter's biography and his work are an expression of this
unity. [23] He was educated in Schnepfental in an educational
establishment of the so-called philanthropinists (Basedow, Campe,
Trapp) run by Salzmann. His teacher was Gutsmuths, also a
high-ranking educationist. Ritter practised his chosen profession,
that of being a private tutor, for almost 20 years. From this
period dates his geographic work which laid the foundation for his
fame. In 1804, his first geographic work appeared under a title
which already indicates his interest in didactics and pedagogy:
"Europa, ein geographisch-historisch-statistisches Gemaelde fuer
Freunde und Lehrer der Geographie". Especially the expression
"Gemaelde" (portrait) should be noted, by which the problem of
presentation emphasized in this paper is linked with its aesthetic
context. Ritter published in Gutsmuths educational journal
(between 1806 and 1811) a number of works on methodical
instruction in geography and on Pestalozzi's method.[24] He had met
Pestalozzi personally on three of his journeys to Switzerland
(1807, 1809, 1811) and visited in Pestalozzi's famous school in
Yverdon. He promised Pestalozzi a conception of geography on the
basis of his method: "My first intention when starting this work
was to keep a promise that I had given Pestalozzi to work on
geography for his institute in the spirit of his method; I
actually started my work, but when dealing with the geographic
material I found only patchy work and accidentalness, i.e.,
arbitrariness in the treatment of science. However, as I despised
any arbitrariness - in keeping with the spirit of method (because
methodologists themselves know nothing about geography) - and
looked for the necessary: so I was lucky in finding it, as I
believe, in the geographic chaos, and now that I had the end of
the thread the whole entangled ball unwinded itself and I found,
even in my geography - which, apart from the satisfaction of the
mind also pleases the heart by its high wisdom and regularity,
which revealed itself in everything - a not unimportant
contribution to physicotheology". [25] The mentioned relates to a
handbook on physical geography which was never published but the
drafts of which quite probably formed a basis for the manual
"Ueber die Methode beim geographischen Unterricht" (On the Methods
of Geography Instruction) written by Henning, a collaborator of
Pestalozzi. [26]

National education soon joins physicotheology: "The matter of
national education still remains the main subject of my activities
in spite of any obstacles there may be" he wrote to Pestalozzi in
1814.[27] In the introduction to his "Erdkunde", the first volume of
which is dedicated to his teachers Gutsmuths and Pestalozzi, he
connects Physicotheology with the idea of national education for
the purpose of science.[28]

With this physicotheology, Ritter places himself in the tradition
of the generally understandable books on physics of the 18th
century which - like one of the most successful works of this kind
"Le spectacle de la nature" by N.-A. Pluche in succession to this
trend - contain "the propaganda for ideologic and religious
ideas".[29] However, it is not possible to brush Ritter's
physicotheology aside as mere propaganda; on the contrary, this
conception forms an essential part of Ritter's attempt to achieve
a methodically necessary order in geography. It can be regarded as
the most important link to Pestalozzi, especially in Niederer's
mediation for Ritter's concept of method. In the diary of his
first stay in Yverdon in 1807 he wrote: "Also Niederer consents to
this communication of ideas about the absolute form of that which
is objective, which he believes to have found. It lies in the
history of creation as told by Moses (this is the highest form and
sole science of the universe)".[30] This still lingers in the
introduction to "Erdkunde", almost ten years later, and shows the
strong impression it made when he saw the goal science should
re-approach "in its whole dimension shining towards us from a dark
previous world only in the songs of the prophets with the
enthusiastic view into nature and into history"[31]. As will be
shown later, Ritter pinpointed here the weak point of Pestalozzi's
conception of method.

For Ritter, too, the idea of national education forms a rather
problematic bridge to Pestalozzi. This links him more closely to
the spirit of national consciousness - which was a decisive factor
for a publicly supported and promoted reception of Pestalozzi in
Germany - after the defeat of Prussia in 1806. However, Ritter
described this new wave of national education with certain reserve
in 1807: "Everything - so they believe - will be destroyed ...
since princes and counts and other aristocrats were also unable to

avert the disaster, and everything was blamed on the deplorable
education; since then my pupils are expected to educate themselves
properly. Before, all this was not necessary, but now, since the
battle of Ulm, they are told every day that now is the time to
educate one's mind".[32] It was especially Fichte, who in his "Reden
an die deutsche Nation" dealt with the specific connection of
romantic national education and enlightening revolutionary
education of people, and who also pointed the way towards
Pestalozzi.

Ritter received it emphatically: "Oh read what Fichte in his
speeches to the German nation, Jean Paul in his peace sermon,
Schleiermacher and Ch. Villers in their essays on German
universities and many other people say, and - I am convinced - not
say in vain, because it is but a loud echo of what was softly
heard in every soul".[33] Here also is reason to assume that the
future professor at the Prussian military academy in Berlin
emphasized the national aspect a bit more than the revolutionary
educationist, just as is shown above for the theological aspect.

Nevertheless, both aspects contain a historically contingent, but
further-reaching model of the conception of science. In the idea
on physicotheology, the purpose of science and its positive effect
are anchored in a guaranteed and perceptible order of the world;
in the link to national education, the universal nature of science
is concretized: scientific knowledge as principally accessible and
available to anyone.

4. The Method

To make knowledge available to everyone is Pestalozzi's concern.
He actually put the universality of science into practice: "He
wants to popularize science".[34] The instrument for this
popularization of science is the method. From the beginning, the
aim and means of Pestalozzi's work exhibit a peculiar
ambiguousness and vagueness. On the one hand, method seems to be
the way in which to bring available knowledge in a certain order
which can also be followed by the poorest of people. On the other

hand, this order is not only sought in the realms of meaning, but also in the human cognitive faculty as its natural laws: "According to these laws, I have tried to simplify the elements of all human knowledge and to arrange them into an order of presentation whose result should have the psychological effect of disseminating comprehensive knowledge of nature, bringing general brightness into the essential concepts and getting energetic practice in the essential skills − also to the lowest class of the people".[35] Niederer remarks in this connection that with this scheme Pestalozzi turns around his previous idea to popularize knowledge for the people and now wants to raise the people to science.[36]

Though Niederer sees this as a revolution, we may interpret it as a vacillation in Pestalozzi's concept of method which results from the undefined relation between presentation and research. If method is linked to the presentation aspect of science, it guarantees a successful reproduction of knowledge but principally differs from the real way on which research reached the discussed and, thus, the methodically founded results. It guarantees the reproduction of science for everyone, but not the production of new knowledge. The revolutionary impact of Pestalozzi's method, noted by Niederer, is to bridge over this hiatus. Pestalozzi himself never clarified his method with regard to this fundamental epistemological problem. How the logic of presentation is related to the production of new knowledge (research) remains open and uncertain. While presentation emphasizes the reasonable and logically consistent reproduction of knowledge,i.e. the rules for arranging the material, and asks for the elementary unities, the research aspect asks after the cognitive faculty, its power and its "natural progress". Here, a tension between the elementary (subject−oriented) and the formal educational principle (development of power) of Pestalozzi was observed. However, he did not only want both; his method was the attempt to connect them in a necessary and intrinsic way. He wanted "to subject the mechanic form of all instruction to the eternal laws according to which the human mind rises from sensual to distinct concepts".[37] These were identical to those "through which physical nature in general unfurls its potential".[38]

When Pestalozzi pleads in such a decisive and unmistakable way for
the self-acting individual, the pupil, for an unbroken faith in
the cognitive ability of children "which construct for themselves
the science they are to learn",[39] he does this on the background
of a pre-critical idea of the divine and perceptible order of the
world. He draws a parallel between the order of presentation and
the order of research. The idea of an existing "ordre de Dieu" is
a pre-condition for this parallel. The concept of "das
Naturgemaesse" (correspondance with nature) is the code with which
this pre-stabilized harmony is signed.

The harmony between the order of cognition and the order of the
recognized objects is the basis of method. The spontaneity of
human cognitive power leads from "vague notions to distinct
concepts".[40] In the still "vague notions" that "ordre de Dieu",
the entirety of the world, is already present. Method has only to
unfold it. In his intuition-concept, Pestalozzi largely remains on
a pre-critical standpoint. When, he counts on the cognitive power
and the "natural mechanism of teaching and learning", he always
does it with the mental reservation of the given. This is most
evident in his treatment of language in which the dictionary or
"Namenlehre" as a "sequence of names of the most important objects
from all fields of nature, the history for the description of
earth, the human professions and circumstances"[41] has the function
of securing the contents of the transition from vague notions to
distinct concepts.

The concept of intuition and the presupposition of given ´ordre de
Dieu´ are the two points of link to Ritter´s physicotheology which
was outlined above. The epistemological premise of his works -
which he has in common with Pestalozzi - lies for him "in the
sphere of faith", on an "intuition", "not in the truth of a
concept, but in the entire content of all truths".[42] That the
theological element in Ritter´s understanding of science is linked
with the idea of intuition emphasizes his Pestalozzian scheme of
science. Since Delekat´s analyses[43], there remains no more doubt
about the "semi-religious meaning"[44] of ´intuition´. This is also
the point which links Ritter, as well as Pestalozzi, to Herder.
Therefore it seems to me that a dispute about who was influenced
by whom to what extent is obsolete.

Different influences have been made responsible for the breaks and uncertainties in Pestalozzi's method: a Leibniz- Wolff-, a Herder-, and a Kant-direction.[45] But in spite of these difficult relations, the sense of the method will be found rather in a development of the epistemological position beyond Kant than in a demonstration of its pre-critical elements. In spite of all pre-critical and irrational moments in Pestalozzi's elementary method, the determination and resoluteness with which he made the rationality of cognition and learning the fundament of his educaton should not be concealed[46].

Thus, the epistemological sense of Pestalozzi's method of instruction cannot be doubted. That it has been developed most clearly in the teaching of forms and numbers is related to the fact that form and contents coincide in this subject and that the order of presentation and of the presented, respectively presentation and research, converge.

It is exactly this comprehension of the constructive and knowledge-generating sense of Pestalozzi's method which Ritter emphasizes when he writes: "all branches of science and of learning thus evolve from man, and every pure intuition is the principle of a science which is developed by the active idea in the child himself according to the law of an inner necessity. The principle of this science thus is a pure product of the child's soul, the regulative of one's own inner spiritual life"[47].

5. Genesis and Construction

But what is the epistemological content of Pestalozzi's method of instruction?

In this connection, "pressure of experience" - outlined in the beginning - should be recalled once more which around 1800 placed the problem of presentation of science into the foreground. "Temporalizing" was seen in relation to "pressure of experience".

It is a general procedure to set the increasing amount of
individual facts within a frame of historical development.
Lepenies[48] suggested establishing such a relation between the
origin of historical thinking and just this pressure of
experience. In Ritter, anyway, we have a prominent and
uncompromising advocate for "temporalizing" his subject: "The
earth, apart from its spatial presence, also has an existence
within time".[49] In his lecture "Ueber das historsche Element in
der geographischen Wissenschaft", he establishes a connection
between "temporalizing" and "presentation". He refers to the
enormous growth of knowledge through new investigation techniques
which puts every individual thing into a new light for man.
Scientific progress and "genuine doctrine" cannot be won for
geography neither from its anecdotical enrichment and compendious
expansion nor from the rigid retreat to an "entirely pure
exclusively physical" geography, but only from a study of the
whole. A systematization of his subject results for him "like for
all organisms" when "the part can only be understood in relation
to the living whole".[50] It is not just the close interrelation
between the history of man and the earth he lives on which
demanded a developmental theory for geography. Ritter goes even
further when he speaks of the "activity of nature" and by,
analogy, of "organism". He wants to grasp "the image and life of
nature in its context" and to follow "the progress of its simplest
and most widely spread geographic laws in static and dynamic
formations".[51] All new and long established facts could thus "be
organized into a clear whole".[52] The teleological outlines of his
anthropo-geographic design thus also have at least an
epistemological component.

To present the geographic material in an "unchangeable order which
is steered by nature itself"[53] was the intention of Henning, a
collaborator of Pestalozzi who was greatly influenced by Ritter.
"It would be entirely in opposition to method if the outward
appearance of things and their relations, the material, should
determine its progress" Ritter wrote about Pestalozzi's method.[54]
Method is allotted the character of an objective educational
course. The evolution of the object and the way of knowing an
object are parallelized.

Those who know the rules of formation and development also have the rules of construction. The idea of the topology of nature is linked with the idea of the construction of knowledge.

I want to further interpret this connection of "temporalizing" and "methodization" according to the "Konstruktive Wissenschaftstheorie" and especially its concepts of methodical presentation – outlined above – and "normative genesis". The term "normative genesis" is introduced at first by P. Lorenzen as a model to reconstruct concrete situations, in which moral decisions are to be set. The term normative means that – in contrast to historical and factual genesis – all steps of reconstruction have to be transsubjectively justified.[55] With reference to this model, P. Janich formulated and briefly explained the "Principle of the genetic organization of scientific instruction material".

He defines the term 'genetically' as "methodically under additional consideration (1) of the purpose of science, (2) the history of science".[56] Janich requires of such a methodical procedure that the beginning of the construction be named, and that in the construction itself no gaps and jumps or pragmatic or terminological circles should be permitted. The construction has to be done stepwise and without gaps. This also characterizes Pestalozzi's method, as we will show at the end. It is to be noted that the concept of genetic organization and its methodical interpretation differs from Pestalozzi's "natural progress" mainly by the fact that for him time is also a dimension of the subject while for Janich it is related to the history of science. This difference applies particularly to Ritter's reception.

6. Elementary Means and Sequence Without Gaps

As we have seen, methodical order mainly raises two questions: one regarding the starting point and given elements and one regarding the sequence. Pestalozzi proposed answers for both. Answering the second, he requires "a progress without gaps from the completed first to the mere beginning of the second and in the adherence to the second until it has been completed like the first". He recognized it as the "path of nature", its "mechanism".[57] He left no doubt about the "harmonious progress" of "physical mechanism" and "intellectual activity".[58] But what can this mean? I suggest seeing in this a statement about the relationship between the presentation and the presented. Then "harmonious progress" characterizes the demand that the sequence of the presented argumentation steps (methodical order) corresponds to the sequence of action steps (pragmatic order). The sequence of action steps has necessarily to be observed until the end of the action is reached. The methodical order is a symbolical representation of this sequence. The demand of a progress without gaps can then be understood as demand for the absence of circles in the argumentative presentation.[59] I believe this interpretation brings out the reasonable sense of Pestalozzi's vague ideas about method which is knowledge generating – despite his pre-critical position in other aspects. Argumentative presentation thus turns out to be the aim of Pestalozzi's methodology with regard to the individual sciences.

The question as to the sequence is accompanied by the question relating the starting points. For Pestalozzi, the question of the starting point was a question about elements of knowledge as well as the fundamental operations with which to begin. Here again we find the vagueness mentioned several times. His proposed starting points can neither be quite ascribed to Kant's a priori as forms of knowledge nor to Goethe's idea of the archetypes. If one adheres to such a cognitive dualism of form and contents, it cannot come as a surprise that Pestalozzi was not successful in developing his method equally in all fields (the cognitive and even the physical and ethic-religious ones as was his intention).

But the work was differently easy to manage for the different fields of knowledge. For mathematics, it was most simple and easy to realize "because it was the only consequent science – established in itself and one step conditioned by the last – which is based on the purely given".[60] In the doctrine of forms and numbers, the formal conception leads to corresponding distinct and clear development of method. But Pestalozzi does not remain on a static formal position; he connects the forms of knowledge with elementary operations. Thus, I want to suggest, let us speak of a constructive foundation of science. Pestalozzi introduces the numbers by elementary counting operations and for the doctrine of forms there exists a sequence from intuition to measuring and drawing and finally writing.[61]

While here the elementary means "form", "number", and "measure" are at the same time categories of the construction of knowledge, Ritter treats the same elements for geography mainly as "means of demonstrating spatial conditions in graphical presentations".[62] The geometric figures serve as demonstration forms for the basic formation of land areas, so the triangle for the western continents, the square for the Peloponnes and the Spanish peninsula Abundance and deficiency in the accomplishment of such "basic figures" show, according to Ritter, the peculiarities of these land areas. Their detailed definition could be acquired from the "implemented use of numbers by which the numerical conditions of these areas and figures can be summarized".[63] Ritter regards these figures - in contrast to the arbitrary departments of national borders - as "natural" forms of the areas.

Nevertheless, Ritter's idea of the "geographic individual" may be recognized in this form of presentation. It is the delayed answer to Pestalozzi's question: "The last day you are here, also tell us what to do. We do not know what books, what sciences we need. Tell us! In the perception lies the original image of everything, in the claws of the cat the claws of the tiger, in the cabbage leaf, all sorts of cabbage. How many original forms are in the trees, how many in the bushes, the blossoms, the animals etc.. Tell us - it does not matter if it takes years".[64]

References

1 Beck, H.: Geographie, Muenchen, Freiburg 1973, p. 228.
2 Plewe, E.: Untersuchungen ueber den Begriff der "vergleichenden" Erdkunde und seiner Anwendung in der neueren Geographie, Berlin 1932, p. 29.
3 "Meine ganze geographische Arbeit ist Darstellung der Pestalozzischen Methode". Extracts from letters and diaries kept

in Ritterarchiv Quedlinburg (further cited as 'Ritterarchiv')
are published by E. Plewe, in: Die Erde 90 (1959), pp. 98-166,
cit. 165. The author is responsible for the english version of
german originals as quoted in the text.

4 Natorp, P.: Gesammelte Abhandlungen zur Sozialpaedagogik,
Stuttgart 1922, 2d ed., p. 38.

5 I use the German word because it encompasses both the meaning
of "instruction" and "doctrine" which also are expressed
etymologically by the Latin "doctrina" and in a similar way by
"disciplina". This interrelation of "to teach something to
someone" and a well constructed system of propositions is focused
upon here.

6 "... das, was er sich als einzige wissenschaftliche Methode in
der Geographie denken konnte in dem Elementarkurs zu Yverdon
ausgefuehrt zu finden." "... er ist der unermuedliche Bearbeiter
dieses Zweiges der Methode, er hat nach meiner Ueberzeugung das
Verdienst, der Geographie die Basis der Wissenschaft gegeben zu
haben, eine Basis, die sie bisher nicht hatte". Cit. by
Schmitthenner, H.: Studien ueber Carl Ritter, in: Frankfurter
Geographische Hefte 25 (1951), pp. 47f.

7 "... die Kunst, die Erde mit Linien zu bezeichnen". Lindner,
F.W.: Beitraege zu einer besseren und zweckmaessigeren Methode
des geographischen Unterrichts, in: Gutsmuths Zeitschrift fuer
Paedagogik (1806), Aprilheft, pp. 270-279. C. Ritter published in
the same journal 'Einige Bemerkungen ueber den methodischen
Unterricht in der Geographie', pp. 198-219. In some critical
remarks he treats the contribution of Lindner.

8 Luedde, J.G.: Die Geschichte der Methodologie der Erdkunde,
Leipzig 1849.

9 "...die Grenzen zwischen beiden seien nicht leicht
aufzufinden". Luedde, Die Geschichte (ref. 8), p. IV.

10 Beck, H.: Entdeckungsgeschichte und geographische
Disziplinhistorie, in: Erdkunde IX (1955), pp. 197-204, cit. 198.

11 Lepenies, W.: Das Ende der Naturgeschichte, Muenchen, Wien
1976, p. 16.

12 Cf. Plewe, E.: Carl Ritter. Hinweise und Versuche zu einer
Deutung seiner Entwicklung, in: Die Erde 90 (1959), pp. 98-166,
cit. 99.

13 Cit. in Lange, G.: Varenius ueber die Grundfragen der
Geographie, in: Petermanns geographische Mitteilungen 105 (1961),

pp. 274-283.

14 Pfeifer, G.: Ritter, Humboldt und die moderne Geographie, in: Deutscher Geographentag Berlin 1959. Tagungsbericht und wissenschaftliche Abhandlungen, Wiesbaden 1960, pp. 69-83, cit. 76.

15 "...Diese Vernichtung des vielartigen und fast unuebersehbaren Stoffs durch die Form scheint das hoechste Beduerfnis der geographische Wissenschaft in ihrer Faehig- machung zur Lehre, welche von dieser Seite weit hinter ihren uebrigen Schwestern der naturbeschreibenden Wissenschaften zurueckgeblieben ist, und darum die unbehuelflichste Masse fuer den bildenden Schulunterricht wie fuer die Wissenschaft selbst bis heute bleibt, die durch keine noch so viele Anstrengung hat ueberwaeltigt werden koennen." Ritter, C.: Bemerkungen ueber Veranschaulichungsmittel raeumlicher Verhaeltnisse bei graphischen Darstellungen durch Form und Zahl, in: Ritter, C.: Einleitung zur allgemeinen vergleichenden Geographie und Abhandlungen zur Begruendung einer mehr wissenschaftlichen Behandlung der Erdkunde, Berlin 1852, pp. 129-151, cit. 133.

16 Ibid., p. 131.

17 Cf. Lepenies, Naturgeschichte (ref. 11), pp. 131-168.

18 In a letter to Gutsmuths from 29.7.1810. Ritterarchiv, p. 134.

19 Cf. Plewe, E.: Carl Ritters Stellung in der Geographie, in: Deutscher Geographentag. Tagungsberichte und wissenschaftliche Abhandlungen, Wiesbaden 1960, pp. 59-68, 63.

20 Plewe, Ritter (ref. 12), p. 106.

21 See ref. 13.

22 In my context the following texts are used: Lorenz, K.: The concept of science. Some remarks on the methodological issue 'construction' vs. 'description' in the philosophy of science, in: Bieri, P., Horstmann, R.-P. and Krueger, L. (eds.): Transcendental arguments and science, Dordrecht 1979, pp. 177-190; Volk, D.: Philosophie im Mathematikunterricht, in: Zeitschrift fuer Didaktik der Mathematik (1977), pp. 121-130; Wolrapp, H.: Analytischer versus konstruktiver Wissenschaftsbegriff, in: Zeitschrift fuer Allgemeine Wissenschaftstheorie VI (1975), pp. 252-275; Wolrapp, H.: Was ist ein methodischer Zirkel, in: Mittelstrass, J., Riedel, M. (eds.): Vernuenftiges Denken, Berlin, New York 1978, pp. 87-103.

23 Simon, K.: Carl Ritter als Erzieher, in: Die Neue Deutsche Schule (1929), pp. 607-614.

24 Ritter, C.: Schreiben eines Reisenden ueber Pestalozzi und seine Lehrart, in: Neue Bibliothek fuer Paedagogik, Schulwesen und die gesamte paedagogische Literatur Deutschlands IX (1808), pp. 17-33, 112-135; C. Ritter, 2. Brief an den Herausgeber ueber Pestalozzis Methode angewandt auf wissenschaftliche Bildung, in: Neue Bibliothek fuer Paedagogik, Schulwesen und die gesamte paedagogische Literatur Deutschlands IX (1808), pp. 193-214.

25 "Meine erste Absicht bei der Unternehmung dieser Arbeit war ein Versprechen zu erfuellen, das ich Pestalozzi gegeben hatte, fuer sein Institut im Geiste seiner Methode, die Geographie zu bearbeiten; wirklich begann ich meine Arbeit, fand aber in der Bearbeitung des geographischen Stoffes nur Stueckwerk und Zufaelligkeit, also in der Behandlung der Wissenschaft Willkuer. Da ich nun im Geiste der Methode (denn die Methodiker verstehen selbst nichts von Geographie) jede Willkuer verschmaehte und das Notwendige suchte: so fand ich es auch, glaube ich, gluecklich aus dem geographischen Chaos heraus und nun wickelte sich mir, da ich einmal den Faden hatte, der ganze verwirrte Knaeuel von selbst auf, und ich fand sogar in meiner Geographie, welche ausser der Befriedigung fuer den Verstand auch das Herz erhebt, durch die hohe Weisheit und Gesetzmaessigkeit, die sich in allem offenbarte, einen nicht unwichtigen Beitrag zur Physikotheologie." In a letter from 1809, cit. by Kramer, G.: Carl Ritter, ein Lebensbild nach seinem handschriftlichen Nachlass, vol. I, Halle 1864, p. 207.

26 Cf. the reconstruction and analysis of the sources by Plewe, Ritter (ref. 12), pp. 113-116.

27 "Die Sache der nationalen Erziehung soll der Hauptgegenstand meiner Taetigkeit bleiben, so viel sich mir auch in den Weg legt". In a letter from 1814, cit. in: Pestalozziblaetter 11 (1890), p. 16-19, cit. 19.

28 Ritter, C.: Die Erdkunde im Verhaeltnis zur Natur und zur Geschichte des Menschen oder allgemeine, vergleichende Geographie, als sichere Grundlage des Studiums und Unterrichts in physikalischen und historischen Wissenschaften, Berlin 1822, Einleitung, pp. 6f.

29 Kleinert, A.: Die allgemeinverstaendlichen Physikbuecher der franzoesischen Aufklaerung, Aarau 1974, p. 107.

30 "Auch Niederer ist einverstanden mit dieser Mitteilung der Ideen ueber die absolute Form des Objektiven, die er gefunden zu haben glaubt. Sie liegt in der mosaischen Schoepfungsgeschichte

(dies ist die hoechste Form und einzige Wissenschaft des Universums ...)." Ritterarchiv, p. 139.

31 "... in seiner ganzen Groesse nur in den Gesaengen der Propheten mit dem begeisterten Blick in die Natur und in die Geschichte aus einer dunklen Vorwelt zu uns herueber leuchten". Ritter, C.: Einleitung zu dem Versuch einer allgemeinen, vergleichenden Geographie, Berlin 1852, p. 8.

32 "Alles glauben sie nun, wird zerstoert werden ... seitdem auch Fuersten und Grafen und andere vornehmen Leute das Unglueck nicht abwenden konnten, und man alles der erbaermlichen Erziehung zuschrieb, seitdem sollen nun meine Zoeglinge sich selbst recht ausbilden. Vorher war das alles nicht noetig, aber jetzt ruft man ihnen alle Tage zu seit der Schlacht bei Ulm, jetzt muss man seinen Kopf bilden." In a letter from 1807 cit. by Schmitthenner, Studien (ref. 6), p. 15.

33 "Oh, lesen Sie, was in diesem Augenblick Fichte in seinen Reden an die deutsche Nation, Jean Paul in seiner Friedenspredigt, Schleiermacher und Ch. Villers in ihren Schriften ueber die deutschen Universitaeten und viele andere Leute und, wie ich ueberzeugt bin nicht vergeblich sagen, weil es nur lauter Widerhall dessen ist, was in jeder Seele leise anklang." In a letter from 1808 cit. by Kramer, Ritter (ref. 25), p. 181.

34 "Er will die Wissenschaften popularisieren." Pestalozzi, J.H.: Saemtliche Werke, vol. 13., Berlin, Leipzig 1932, p. 209.

35 Ibid., p. 103: "Nach diesen Gesetzen habe ich gesucht, die Elemente allen menschlichen Wissens zu vereinfachen und sie in einer Reihenfolge von Darstellungen zu bringen, deren Resultat psychologisch dahin wirken soll, umfassende Kenntnis der Natur, allgemeine Heiterkeit in wesentlichen Begriffen und kraftvolle Uebung in den wesentlichsten Fertigkeiten auch bei der niedersten Volksklasse zu verbreiten."

36 Ibid., p. 504, footnote to p. 104

37 Ibid., p. 242: "... die mechanische Form alles Unterrichts den ewigen Gesetzen unterwerfen, nach welchen der menschliche Geist sich von sinnlichen zu deutlichen Begriffen erhebt."

38 Ibid., p. 246: "... durch welche die physische Natur allgemein ihre Kraefte entfaltet."

39 Ibid., p. 208: "... die sich die Wissenschaft selber konstruieren, die sie lernen sollen."

40 Ibid., p. 235: "... von dunklen Anschauungen zu deutlichen Begriffen ..."

41 Ibid., p. 264: "... Reihenfolgen von Namen der bedeutendsten Gegenstaende aus allen Faechern des Naturbereiches, der Geschichte und der Erdbeschreibung, der menschlichen Berufe und Verhaeltnisse ..."

42 Ritter, Einleitung (ref. 15), p. 26: "... im Gebiet des Glaubens ..." "... inneren Anschauung ...", "... nicht in der Wahrheit eines Begriffs, sondern im Gesamtinhalt aller Wahrheiten ..."

43 Delekat, F.: Johann Heinrich Pestalozzi, Leipzig 1928, 2d ed.

44 Spranger, E.: Pestalozzis Denkformen, Heidelberg 1959, 2d ed., p. 52.

45 Ibid., p. 54.

46 Cf. Stein, A.: Pestalozzi und die Kantische Philosophie, Darmstadt 1969, 2d ed. (1st ed. 1927), pp. 205ff.

47 Ritter, Schreiben (ref. 24), p. 26: "Alle Zweige des Wissens und Lernens bilden sich daher vom Menschen aus, und jede reine Anschauung ist das Prinzip einer Wissenschaft, welche durch die taetige Idee im Kinde selbst aufgebaut wird, nach den Gesetzen der inneren Notwendigkeit. Das Prinzip dieser Wissenschaft ist also reines Erzeugnis der Kinderseele, das Regulativ eigenen inneren geistigen Lebens."

48 Lepenies, Naturgeschichte (ref. 11), p. 18.

49 Ritter, C.: Allgemeine Erdkunde, ed. by Daniel, cit. by Plewe, Untersuchungen (ref. 3), p. 40:. "Die Erde hat ausser dem raeumliche Dasein noch eine Existenz in der Zeit."

50 Ritter, C.: Ueber das historische Element in der geographischen Wissenschaft, in: Ritter, Einleitung (ref. 15), pp. 152-182, cit. 181: "... wie bei allen Organismen ...","... der Teil nur als dem lebendigen Ganzen begriffen werden kann ...".

51 Ritter, Einleitung (ref. 15), p. 7: "... das Bild und Leben der Natur in ihrem ganzen Zusammenhang ...","...den Gang ihrer einfachsten und am allgemeinsten verbreiteten geographischen Gesetze in den entstehenden und bewegten Bildungen ..."

52 Ibid., p. 6: "... zu einem ueberschaulichen Ganzen geordnet wird ..."

53 Henning, J.W.M.: Leitfaden beim methodische Unterricht in der Geographie, Ifferten 1812, cit. by Spranger, E.: Der Bildungswert der Heimatkunde, Stuttgart 1849, p. 37.

54 Ritter, Schreiben (ref. 24), p. 26: "Der Methode waere es ganz widerstrebend, wenn das aeussere Dasein der Dinge ihre Verbindung, das Materiale, ihren Gang bestimmen sollte."

55 Cf. Lorenzen, P.: Normative logic and ethics, Mannheim, Zuerich 1969, pp. 88ff.

56 Janich, P.: Die Integration der Naturwissenschaften auf der Grundlage ihrer theoriebildenden Methoden II: Die genetische Organisation naturwissenschaftlichen Lehrstoffes, in: Frey, K., Haeussler, P. (eds.): Integriertes Curriculum Naturwissenschaft. Theoretische Grundlagen und Ansaetze, Weinheim, Basel 1979, pp. 117–127, cit. 119.

57 Pestalozzi, J.H.: Saemtliche Werke, vol. 16, Berlin, Leipzig 1932, p. 57.

58 Pestalozzi, Saemtliche Werke, vol. 13 (ref. 34), p. 105.

59 Cf. Wohlrapp, Zirkel (ref. 22).

60 Ritter, Schreiben (ref. 24), p. 13: "... weil sie die einzige konsequente, in sich selbst gegruendete, von Schritt zu Schritt bedingte Wissenschaft war, deren Fundament das rein Gegebene ist ..."

61 Pestalozzi, Saemtliche Werke, vol. 13 (ref. 34), p. 121.

62 Ritter, Einleitung (ref. 15), p. 129.

63 Ibid., p. 136: "... durchgefuehrten Gebrauch der Zahl durch welche die numerischen Verhaeltnisse jener Raeume und Figuren zusammengefasst werden koennen ..."

64 Ritterarchiv, p. 138: "Den letzten Tag, wenn ihr hier seid, sagt auch, was wir machen sollen. Wir wissen nicht die Buecher, die Wissenschaft, die wir brauchen. Saget uns! In der Anschauung liegt das Ururbild von allem, in der Klaue der Katze die Klaue des Tigers, in dem Kohlblatt die Kohlarten alle. Wieviele Ururformen sind in den Baeumen, wieviele in den Straeuchern, in den Blueten, den Tieren etc. Saget uns — es macht nichts, wenn es Jahre dauert."

Detlef K. Mueller

POSSIBILITIES AND LIMITS OF THE PRUSSIAN SCHOOL REFORM AT THE
BEGINNING OF THE 19TH CENTURY

In Prussia, the first Government order referring to the majority
of the male population of school age is given in connection with
the reform of the army. In 1733 the mercenary army is replaced by
the introduction of a differentiated conscription for Prussian
subjects. The country is devided into strictly delimited military
areas (Kantone) in which the draftees are registered and called
up. The aristocracy, being landed proprietors, are officers born,
dependent peasants are common soldiers, free peasants are
non-commissioned officers. The aristocracy are subject only to the
king. Within the borders of their estates they can excercise
unlimited control over the dependent population. The majority of
subjects are under a life-long conscription which consists, after
a longer period of basic training, in annual reserve manoevres.[1]

The barracks have the function of vocational schools for the
double role of the subject. The period of military service means
the first realized compulsory education for the majority of the
population. Exempt from service are the aristocracy, citizens, and
free peasants with a capital of over 6000 talers, civil servants,
and certain professions in trade and commerce. Pupils of Latin
schools and students are not liable to military service,
regardless of their social extraction. With regards to the
educational system it can be maintained that those parts of the
population are exempt who take care of their children's education

H. N. Jahnke and M. Otte (eds.), Epistemological and Social Problems of the Sciences in the Early Nineteenth
Century, 183–206.

themselves without government compulsion. In order to avoid
conscription, the sons of peasants and non-exempt craftsmen and
provincials attend Latin schools.

The measures demanded by the government to protect conscription
coincide with the suggestions for a reform of the Prussian
education system which are discussed not much later by the supreme
education authority ('Oberschulkollegium'; in 1787 appointed to
the state's education authority). The chancellor of Halle
University, von Hoffmann, demands the introduction of entrance
examinations for universities in order to prevent a transformation
of the universities into professional training institutions and
also in order to control the Latin schools which prepare for
university. In 1787 the supreme education authority asks the
universities of Halle, Frankfurt/Oder, Koenigsberg, and seven
headmasters and grammar school teachers to deliver their expert's
opinion on the reform of schools and universities. The nine
statements delivered agree in a negative judgement on present
conditions. The majority criticized the uncertainty concerning
objectives of the schools and the ponderousness of authorities,
teachers, and parents when reforms are discussed.[2] The following
measures of change are suggested:

1. Attempt for an overall organization of the educational system.
   Decree for universal rules and regulations for the conduct of
   examinations.
2. General curriculum for schools and universities; precise
   stipulations of the limits and objectives of qualifications and
   examinations.
3. State regulations for the studies and exams of different groups
   of teachers; greater independence for teachers from schools
   fees, parents and private school committees.
4. State regulations for grants, abolishment of choristers.
5. Attempt to relate graduation, achievement in the final
   examinations and qualification for the public services.

An entrance examination at university is only demanded for a
transitory period in which the schools can be checked. In general,
judgement is to be left to the teachers of the schools which
prepare for university. In school, promotion and graduation are to

be regulated by exams. The qualifications thus achievable are to be taken as a basis with applications for the civil service or admission to university.

The present function of the Latin schools - catering especially for the education of the male pupils of school age in their respective areas - was accepted without criticism. Special intermediate exams are demanded in order to make it more difficult for these pupils, i.e. especially the children of not academically trained parents, to attend higher classes and pass on to university. The pupils must not be confronted with a fait accompli and, when rejected by the universities at the end of a long time at school, left to fend for themselves. They must prove their claim on further education at a time when they are not yet too old for an apprenticeship. A tripartial examination system is to control the various passages: 1. the passage from elementary to higher classes; 2. graduation from grammar school; 3. at the end of a professional training or a university course. According to Kant's vote - he was dean of the philosophical faculty in Koenigsberg - "among the very poor" students, "natural talents" and "urge to learn" must decide their school career, grant worthiness and exemption from conscription.[3] In one specialist's opinion only, examinations are detached from social objectives and seen as general certificates of performance. Uncapable pupils are to be excluded from the attendence of public schools and universities, even when their parents are capable of long-term financial support. The other specialists want to keep open all possible professions for lesser talented pupils as well, "only with the difference that these must always have an income of their own."[4]

The objectives of these suggestions can only be understood correctly when their being related to the then current education system is observed. The Latin schools are elementary, secondary, and grammar schools all in one. In order to render a university-related education possible in the senior grades and in order to give academically trained teachers the chance of a regular income, fee-paying pupils are to supplant scholarship holders and choristers. Extending the ability principle to children of fee-paying parents would at this point in time be

contrary to the reform strategy. Particularly these social classes
must be won for the public education system if the status of the
teachers and with that the standard of the institution is to be
improved.

Friedrich Gedike (entrusted with the preparation of laws for
schools and universities within the supreme education authority)
attempted – more determinedly from year to year – to find
practical solutions which involve the present independence of the
individual schools in only an immaterial way. Gedike sees no
chance for thorough reforms based on the ideas of enlightened
pedagogues, since Woellner (set over the supreme education
authority as Lord Chancellor since 1789) was fanatically opposed
to the Enlightenment. Gedike wants to protect the activities of
progressive teachers from bureaucratic interventions and at the
same time give them financial support. He therefore puts forward
those suggestions for alterations which do not demand decisions on
principle about structure and curriculum of the education system.
The problem of matriculation standard is reduced to examination
modalities in the discussion about the introduction of rules for
the 'Abitur'. Gedike thus initiates a Prussian tradition. Drafts
of regulations for the entire education system are permanently
sacrificed to individual regulations for particular fields and
interests.

In order to improve the senior classes in schools, Gedike shows
interest for those specialist opinions which suggest generally
obligatory passing exams and finals. The students-to-be should not
leave the grammar schools too early; university teachers should
not rival with senior class teachers. Grammar schools and
universities should be related to one another. The precondition of
a matriculation at university should be the attendance of the
senior classes of a grammar school for at least two years; it
should be concluded with a final exam, the 'Abitur'. Thus Gedike
wants to force the sons of the solvent and distinguished parts of
the population to go to the municipal schools with
university-orientated senior classes. Even pupils with private
tuition should obtain their qualification only through
participation in the 'Abitur' examinations of a state school.
"However, if the purpose of the exams to be ordered is not to be

that of either admitting to" or excluding from "university, depending on the success, then I fear that these public exams will rather increase than lessen the evil."[5] Under this condition Gedike interprets the introduction of the 'Abitur' exam firstly, as a revalorization of school and academic qualification certificates and secondly, as measures for regulating the excessive supply of qualified applicants for civil service posts which existed since the 1770ies. In an article in the 'Berlinische Monatsschrift' in 1788 it is explained that the chances of reform depend on the social status of the civil servants. The intensity of their education is to become the main criterion of eligibility; the exams shall not so much discriminate against talented children of the non-academic classes as prevent subjective preferences for applicants irrespective of their qualification and the dependence following from that. "The number of educated and uneducated young people who raise claims on civil service posts is ... so great that all councils are swamped with them. ... Only ask when one of the most unprofitable posts is to be awarded, what a host of applicants at once come forward, who offer themselves to the state for any, even the most trifling salary [;] ... such endeavours to get the start of each other can easily influence the morality of the educated for the worse."[6]

Gedike cannot prevail on the supreme education authority. In December 1788, the 'Abitur' exam is made law for the main reason of excluding poor pupils and students from scholarships. "We do, however ... not intend to restrict the citizen's freedom, as every father and guardian should now still be free to send even an immature and ignorant youth to university."[7] Thus the regulations for both 'scholarly schools' (Gelehrte Schulen) and universities attain conservative objectives. The first laws influencing the public education system in general start off with granting privileges to a minority of students.

Gedike tried to enforce the unlimited obligation of the 'Abitur' regulations by planning to introduce a special exam for pupils and applicants for scholarships who were subject to conscription at the end of their compulsory education (13 to 14 years of age). Despite the above described function of the 'Abitur' the government insists on the introduction of a special intermediate exam. In 1791, a cabinet issue again calls to mind the regulations about "the admittance of draftees to university".[8] In the same year, the supreme education authority puts forward suggestions for implementing statutes. The exams shall take place at a time when the children usually begin practical work. All boys liable to military service shall continue their school career only if they are extraordinarily talented. The law of 1792 provides for the social discrimination of those liable to military service. While the academic middle classes, the free peasants owning more than 12000 talers, the population of chosen cities, specially named craftsmen, and the aristocracy are free to send their sons to university even if their talents and capability are below average, the children of provincials and rurals are impeded in their attendence of intermediate and senior grades of fully developed schools. The execution of this law depends on its social and political interpretation by the civil servants and teachers concerned with it. Those who fight privileges of birth and rank protect their pupils from conscription under the shield of this law. The emphasis does then not lie on "extraordinary genius" for passing the exam but on the right of being exempt from conscription after passing. But the regulations for conscription award only technical precedence to the teachers' decision as against the claims of the military authorities. In the case of real conflicts the state only uses sanctions to enforce selection and not the protective function of the law.[9]

Until 1806 the supreme education authority discussed the structure of the curriculum, the exam system and the training of teachers. In 1810 the deputation for public tuition (wissenschaftliche Deputation) renews this discussion. The deputation is formed in 1810 as a substitute for the dissolved education authority. This happened in connection with the reform of the administration which was conducted in Prussia since 1808.[10]

In a report from 1809, Wilhelm von Humboldt also ascribes the function of a government-independent board of experts for school reforms to the deputation in Berlin which, with branches in Breslau and Koenigsberg, is intended as the examination board for secondary school teachers. Beside the department of culture and public tuition, which is confronted with questions of administratory technique and presided over by W. v. Humboldt, another gremium is formed which, freed from the pressure of making pragmatic daily decisions, is supposed to design objectives for the future in order to win standards for the present. The deputation is to proceed from a profound knowledge of the existing education system and judge the department's decisions according to their effect on the development of the whole organization, analyse curricular contents and methods of instruction, make suggestions of their own and develop new structures of organization.

The parallel activities of department and deputation are to prevent that financial-political and bureaucratic reservations against reforms on the part of the school administration taboo traditional methods of school practice. W. v. Humboldt wants to institutionalize a reformatory body in which independence from government, career, and class-political pressure groups on the one hand and a scientifically founded capability to stay detached from traditional forms of organization and didactic methods on the other hand guarantee that school-political activities of the state do not suppress the very innovations and reforms which progressive-humanistic pedagogues want to carry through with the help of the state.

Since March 1810 the deputation under the interim direction of Schleiermacher consists of five regular members, six associate members and two corresponding members. Beside the Berlin grammar school headmaster Bernhardi, three professors of Berlin grammar schools are among the five regular members. The former precedence of directors gives way in favour of teaching experts. The reform committee is no gremium of classical philologists. In the later discussion, the regular members represent the subjects German (Schleiermacher), foreign languages (Bernhardi), mathematics, natural history and natural science, history and geography; the associate members represent mineralogy, botanics, chemistry, cosmography, archaeology. Without excluding an "important subject of the sciences" from the conference, Humboldt wants to achieve – through a greater responsibility of the regular members – that "scientific education" is not split "... according to external purposes and conditions, individually", but that it is determined by the principal objective of the general education system.[11]

In 1810 the department commissions the deputation with the
development of a school developing scheme. After receiving and
discussing the subject-specific opinions Bernhardi designs a
scheme of structure to serve the department as a skeleton plan for
reforms. The points of Bernhardi's scheme which concern the
function of the deputation and the external and internal
organization of the education system are objectives which he - as
headmaster of the Friedrichs-Werdersches Gymnasium - discusses
extensively in the schoolprograms from 1808 to 1820 and which he
partially realizes in his school.[12]

To an education system to be institutionalized, Bernhardi assigns
the function of social selection for a society which is to be
modernized and in which, in long terms, traditional ranks of birth
are to be replaced by social classes whose social order shall
depend on their members' quality and quantity of knowledge and
whose patronization shall be regulated by means of school and
university qualifications. A political reform scheme comparable to
the principles of a "democratic achievement society" is placed in
front of the pedagogic objectives. The choice of profession is to
follow mainly the inclinations and talents of the student. The
education system shall provide possibilities for a majority of
students to get to know the special education objects of different
fields of activity and observe their own chances. Under the
condition of a relative minimum of education for all - dependent
on the standards of development of the society - this special
instruction can, according to Bernhardi, only refer to subjects
which can legitimately be made compulsory for all pupils, i.e.
which are of a formally educating nature. The term "formal
education" (formelle Bildung) signifies the attempt "to make life
as it is just now accessible to the pupil". For Bernhardi, "formal
education" comprises "education towards humanity" in a present
situation and not in a timeless perspective. "Every institute for
the people's education [must], if it is to be true to its purpose,
go with the time ..., which it wants to affect ... The least
possible, however, a sudden upheaval seems to be in a people's
education ..., because in this, so much depends on the voluntary
efforts of each individual; it should be met with love and not
rebuffed and puzzled by sudden ... alterations."[13]   General

education cannot be restricted to a canon of subjects, nor does it allow a concentration on one particular period within the historical development.

According to Bernhardi, public education institutes are not subject to the pressure of fee-paying parents whose wishes – which change like fashions – must be complied with in private schools. The mechanisms of control must be institutionalized within the education system itself. Curriculum research shall permanently accompany teaching practice. Seven principles for its objectives can be obtained from Bernhardi's argumentation:

1. The objectives of education must be based in contemporary society. School must contribute to the conscious perception of the respective present and open dimensions for the future. Education is general, but not timeless.

2. The curriculum must connect universal and national education, cosmopolitan and national citizenship, i.e. it must complement the imparting of the philosophic-anthropologic self-conception of man with a sociological-political analysis of his concrete situation.

3. A lack of knowledge is harmful when political reforms demand a greater ability for reflection from the citizen, or when more differentiated professional demands emerge in the course of social change and processes of learning anew become necessary.
   A "surplus value" of general education, on the other hand, has positive effects for individual and society.

4. No school subject or object of instruction must be chosen for purely pragmatical reasons.

5. No specific talent must be overrated to the disadvantage of other possibilities.

6. The canon of subjects must be limited according to scientific criteria, not according to bureaucratic arbitrariness, teachers' preferences or pressure group politics.

7. Knowledge and skills must not be imparted without a theoretical foundation.

According to Bernhardi, there exist within a nation qualitatively different levels of education which depend on the developmental stage of the nation and which idealtypically coincide with the social pyramid. Every social class takes it for granted that its members possess not only specific professional skills but also some knowledge which is agreed on within society; the intensity of this knowledge depends on the social class situation. In contrast to technical schools for certain professions, the public education system serves to teach this general knowledge. "The school must teach its pupils this minimum of knowledge which the state demands of its citizens according to its highest standard and must not be content to impart this knowledge as it is demanded by the state in reality ..." - "you will admit that he who is endeavouring this will not be content with the mass of knowledge and education which his nation can give him on the whole through the level of education it has reached; he will rather regard the knowledge gained from his nation as only part of the treasure which the nations have horded at all times and of which he can also partake. In this endeavour he breaks through ... the barriers of nationality [and so of social classes] and joins humanity in general, he no longer belongs to an individual state [and as little to a specific social class] but becomes naturalized in the whole. All educational institutions must have regard for this striving for scientific universality, not ... by making the objects ... teaching objects ... ["wretched multiplication of objects"] ... but by trying, in their narrower and prepared circles, to educate the pupil in certain objects only as a human being".[14] Berhardi considers his model of social strata, in which any position depends on "the emergence of intellectual ability", as a fundamental draft, not as a practice-related analysis. He sees a distinction between the exclusively "intellectually active" - the scholars -, those who are artistically productive, i.e. craftsmen capable of rational planning and design - the middle classes ["mittlere Staende" (1814); "Kuenstler" (artists) (1809)] -, and those who do mainly "physical" work, i.e. the lower middle classes who are restricted to material skills. The public education system must embrace all social strata. Efficiency and willingness to learn are the main factors to decide the school grade and the claim on a social position within society which is connected with it. Formally, i.e. by reason of the organization of the schools, every child shall have the chance to obtain any possible qualification. The education system is to be organized in a manner which allows grade-specific teaching objectives neither to make the passing into the next grade more difficult nor to prevent a graduation. "There are three kinds of classes ... the school must pay attention to ... [by] comprising three levels of education ... in which the preparatory knowledge of each class is laid down, so that the two lower classes constitute the elementary school ("Buergerschule"), the two middle classes the secondary school ("Kuenstlerschule"; Realgymnasium) ..., the two upper classes the grammar school ("gelehrte Schule"). These three schools shall be separate but still united in an organization. ... They are united internally by the idea of progress, externally by the general education which is common to all classes, and also by the procedure of starting a subject in every upper class of the educational grades as a hint towards the imperfection of the educaton; this subject is then continued in the higher grade, such as Latin in the second form[upper class of the lower grade] and Greek in the fifth form [upper class of the middle grade]."[15] Bernhardi interpretes his grade scheme with the help of concrete examples of a curriculum: Those who have command of elementary calculation at the end of the lower grade are equipped with the minimal knowledge of this subject which in contemporary society is demanded of the lower social class and at the same time fulfil the requirements for taking in the mathematical matter of the next grade of the education system.

The connection of general education and professional practice is, however, only applicable to part of the subjects in school. In real life, the lower social classes need knowledge neither of Greek nor of Latin. But for a successful passing on to the next grade some knowldege of Latin is required, for the grade above that, Greek. In order to adjust the principles to reality, Bernhardi, like Gedike, must emphasize the generally educating character and the transferring effect of the classical languages. He takes it for granted (without having tested it) that a pupil who leaves school in one of the lower classes equipped with some knowledge of vocabulary and grammar was encouraged as much as the later graduate. It seems necessary to make classical languages obligatory for all pupils, if the grammar schools are to attract the upper classes without driving out lower class children and early leavers. It is not the objective of "intellectual-aristocratic" education of the elite but the emphasis on equality of chances which supports the obligatory

Latin classes in grammar schools. Like Gedike and Wilhelm v. Humboldt, Bernhardi opts for the formal principle of educaton in order to avoid class-specific school types as well as to guarantee an optimum of encouragement for every individual pupil.

Bernhardi distinguishes "Buergerschule", "Kuenstlerschule", and "Gymnasium" as consecutive parts of the one system, not as independent elements of a column structure. But together with Gedike's definition of grades he takes over the ambiguity of its terms in contemporary discussion. For Bernhardi, the term "Buergerschule" (elementary school) signifies the education of the entire male population of school age. But this concept does not go with the later demand for a common elementary or general education (to be organized according to years); it rather signifies the imparting of a dynamic minimum of education. The cognitive faculties and the extent of knowledge to be attained on this level are principally a sine qua non for all future citizens. Only after having obtained a middle-class education can the pupil continue in the following grades. The amount of time needed for this further education depends solely on the achievement of the pupil and in this sense on class-specific factors. Pupils who have difficulties in achieving the teaching objective remain in the lower grade in order to study the matter thoroughly - at the most until the end of the legally prescribed compulsory education.

Bernhardi connects the grades functionally, not causatively, with the social classes of society. He suggests three possible qualifications; a public examination is to check the reachable level of education and to sanction it as a rightful claim. These qualifications he calls "Abitur I", II, and III. The "Abitur I" - its demands should equal the achievement of a passing from the third form (Quarta) to the forth form (Untertertia) - qualifies for apprenticeship in a handicraft; the "Abitur II" - in line with the achievements of a one-year attendence of the fifth form (Sekunda) - allows access to the more technically developed trades, a commercial apprenticeship and subordinate civil service posts; the "Abitur III" - identical with the final exams of the sixth form decreed by the supreme education authority and the department - allows university studies in all faculties. "Gymnasium" as a definition of type in its wider sense includes the institution as a comprehensive school; the narrower, and true, sense means the middle and senior grades. If Bernhardi names preparation for university as the ultimate objective of the grammar school and wants to charge it with the education of future craftsmen only with regard to the "situation of school organization", he makes use of the ambiguity of the concept which was usual and very obvious in contemporary discussion. He does not speak of a type but of two different school levels. Within the existing organization the grammar school as a special part of the education system is not yet separated in locality from the lower grades (as the university is from the grammar school). A grammar school comprises not only the forth, fifth and sixth forms (Tertia, Sekunda, Prima) but also the junior grades which, from first to third form, were usually accounted as "school" (Schule) not grammar school (Gymnasium). Contrary to Gedike's and W. v. Humboldt's conceptions, Bernhardi regards the deficient development of the education system as the only reason for a temporary integration of all grades in one building which must be abolished in favour of independent middle and senior grades in the course of further development. The grammar school would then acquire a kind of college character and would only admit pupils who after having successfully finished the second grade, want to prepare for university. Such an organization would be based on the selective and conclusive character of the previous grades. The permanent restriction of pupils of a class who go on would correlate to the continually decreasing quantitative offer of the grade schools of which the grammar schools would have to be established mainly in the bigger cities. Thus a grammar school would consist of several fifth and sixth forms which would have to be differentiated in themselves.

Bernhardi's theoretic model reaches gradual realization in the Friedrichs-Werdersches Gymnasium. At first the institute comprises six forms which Bernhardi divides into three educational stages; until 1814 he has enlarged these to three classes each. To each stage three successive classes are assigned which can be complemented by parallel classes. The lowest class of a stage serves for repetition and confirmation of the previously taught matter, the second for the teaching of an adjoining section, the third for the thorough command and application of this new matter.

In the lowest stage Latin is taken up as the first foreign language; Greek follows in the second stage; modern languages are offered as optional subjects from the first form onwards. Parallel classes in the lower and middle grades are necessary because the existing grammar schools must supplement the next higher grades from their own contingent of pupils. The senior grade can only exist if enough pupils stay on after the previous possibilities of leaving. The smaller number of senior grade pupils prevents the theoretically planned differentiation. According to the downward shift of the institute's main point of activity, the interests of the majority of pupils must come first at the distribution of limited staff and localities. In order to be able to adhere at least formally to the 3x3-principle (three grades of three classes each) Bernhardi adopts the practice – usual in other schools – of dividing the first form ("Sexta") into lower first and upper first and fixes the end of the first stage on the end of the second form. The senior grade is supplemented by the upper fourth (Obertertia) as a third class which is comparatively large as compared with the fifth form. In the middle stage – which now begins with the third form –, the lower fourth (Untertertia) is devided in two classes with different functions: "Untertertia I" and "Untertertia II". While all other classes are hierarchically ordered, the "Untertertia II" comes in between third form (Quarta) and "Untertertia I" but without obligation to attend it. A pupil can pass directly from "Quarta" to "Untertertia I". The function of "Unterterita II" can be deduced mainly from the contemporary school situation. A large part of the pupils from higher social classes at first attend private schools and only enter grammar school at the end of "Schule", i.e. of the third form. In "Untertertia II" their different levels of knowledge shall be brought up to school level. At the same time this form offers all pupils with particular difficulties in individual subjects the chance to close their gaps by attending specific remedial courses. At an entrance age for the first form of at least eight to twelve years at the most, the minimal length of time spent in the lower grade is one-and-a-half years, two to three years in the middle grade and four to five years in the senior grade. A pupil of average talent exceeds this time by one to two years. For the differentiation of the grades Bernhardi retains the system of 'streaming'. Pupils can take a subject in that class of a grade which corresponds to their standard (e.g. English in the upper fourth, mathematics in the lower sixth). This principle is cancelled with the passing from one grade to the next. The speciality and aspired unity of the grades, which - as shown above - is to lead to a separation as an independent institution in the case of grammar schools, is emphasized by admitting only pupils who have achieved the set objective of the previous grade in every compulsory subject. As Bernhardi more or less reduces the lower and middle grades to two superior classes, he unintentionally furthers the system of age group classes within his course system which is independent of age.

In the lower grade, the "thorough and appropriate preparation for the lower middle classes" is aspired as specific objective of the education, in the middle grade, the preparation of "the upper middle classes" and in the senior grade that of "future scholars". "Those pupils who ... enter civic life directly and leave from the higher classes to 'Quarta' [since 1814, after the new arrangement - see above - to 'Quinta'], and who indicate which trade they want to take up can demand an examination and a certificate [which show] whether their knowledge qualifies them for the chosen position. According to this exam a specific certificate shall be issued for them."[16] Under the generic term of grammar school the institution is an integrated comprehensive school which receives children of all social classes and offers various levels of qualificaton.

In 1821, C.G. Zimmermann, who succeeds Bernhardi as headmaster of the Friedrichs-Werdersches Gymnasium, in his first program confirms the "purpose of the scholarly schools" as comprehensive schools.[17] "Gedike and Bernhardi enlisted every boy who was 7/8 years old, knew the Latin alphabet, could read German tolerably well and could just about write both kinds of letters ... I [believe] ... that I may retain this arrangement all the more because from here the beginner is led through these various grades to middle class business circles or to an academic career. This our educational institution consists of two main departments for the purpose of instruction: 1. the school ("Schule") and 2. grammar school ... Inbetween the school and the grammar school the middle grades are stationed." This arrangement "renders it superfluous to set so-called "Buergerschulen" and other schools inbetween the scholarly and the elementary schools. ... The Greek and the Romans ... bore no anxious care for the details, for that which belonged to every trade or business; but they had the whole destiny of mankind at heart, the ability to think, the enlightenment of the intellect, the formal training of the mind and of physical strength."

Progressive and conservative pedagogues differ in objectives and method, not in the evaluation of classical studies. A third group of academic teachers questions the value of Greek and Latin instruction itself. Beside the usual theological and philological studies they mainly dealt with problems of mathematics and natural sciences. Inferior to their colleagues with classical philological preferences where languages are concerned, they try to revalorize their extra knowledge professionally and to better the position of mathematics and physics in the grammar school curriculum. At the beginning of the 19th century, teachers of mathematics were discriminated against in state schools with academic staff. The two or three jobs for life in an institution, which neutralize the transitory character of a teaching job through the height of the salary, are only then available to them when they distinguish themselves mainly as theologists and philologists, not as mathematicians.

The mathematician E.G. Fischer, professor at the Berlinisch-Koellnisches Gymnasium in Berlin, whose school organization plans I shall discuss in the following chapter as an example for the beginning emancipation of the natural sciences as against the Arts in the education system, takes the subjects of natural science out of the classical-philological schools. In treaties about school programs between 1801 and 1827, he designs a type of school for the majority of pupils of the Latin schools in which mathematics and physics, i.e. the mathematicians dominate.[18] The class-political background of his reform plans alone would have persuaded neither the government, nor the municiple council, nor the parents. The natural scientists therefore need reasons which can be proved to be scientific in order to break the dominance of the philologists. Fischer's theory emerges as a synthesis of three popular reservations against the existing Latin schools: 1. the overrating of classical philologic instruction for general education; 2. the unsatisfactory relation of the schools to practice, 3. the overtaxing of the pupils.

1. Modern civilization needs rational proceedings and pragmatic thinking. Modern science must free itself from traditional prejudices and utopian speculation. The connection established by the Enlightenment to classical antiquity furthers secularization, but not rationalization. In the beginning of the 19th century, not so much religious dogmas but natural-scientific prejudices are antagonistic to progress. The enlightening function of the humanism of the 15th century is not valid for its modern renaissance. According to Fischer, one can only laugh at Epicur's attempt to explain the origin of the world by the mere motion of colliding atoms. The present enthusiasm for the Greeks is basically a reaction to modern thinking of natural science. The modern age begins with Newton. Only through the findings of natural science and their social consequences the European peoples attained the "freedom of the mind".[19] Their contempt for the natural sciences shows the theological origin of the Arts. It works in favour of metaphysics against the changing of reality. According to Fischer, enlightenment means rationalization of the basis, i.e. modernizing of agricultural and economic production, trade, administration and the armed forces. Mathematics comprises what philology aspires: truth and acute judgement. It thus qualifies for the central subject of general education.

2. and 3. The pupils of the middle and senior grades of grammar schools are divided into two groups: those who will go to university and those who will not. The scientific orientation of practice and the increasing wealth enable a growing part of the young to intensify their general education and extending their time at school. The curriculum of the existing institutions favour the claims of the minority who wants to study traditional university subjects, against the needs of the early school leavers. The learning of the old languages has no effect on the ability to learn and think in other fields. The transferring effect claimed for them fails to set in. The connection of middle class education and scholarly preparation leads to an overtaxing of the pupils.

With the help of school leaver rates of the
Berlinisch-Koellnisches Gymnasium Fischer proves that Gedike's
curriculum does not do justice to the pupils but to the classical
scholars of the institute. Between 1795 and 1805 529 pupils left
the higher forms of the grammar school. The chosen profession of
416 of them is known. Apart from the unknown cases, out of the 164
who went to university 54 chose theology, 87 law, 4 medicine; the
early leavers of the individual classes turned to the following
professions:[20]

occupational group	form: 4th	5th	lower 6th	upper 6th	total
office work	33	15	12	7	67
acriculture	9	9	8	–	26
civil engineering	5	13	5	3	26
commerce, industry	41	14	5	2	62
handicrafts	10	2	1	–	13
art	5	–	1	–	6
pharmacy, surgery	5	6	1	–	12
armed forces	16	6	3	2	27
teaching posts (teachers at private or municipal schools	2	1	6	4	13
total	126	66	42	18	252

In this survey, Fischer doubts the efficiency of a curriculum
which is compulsory for all pupils and based on classical
philology. Because of 18 upper sixth pupils who did not go to
university, 164 future students were burdened with subject matter
they had no interest in. And in the reverse, 192 pupils who left
after the forth or fifth form had to learn classical vocabulary
and grammar without ever being able to use them in reading. "It
must be obvious from all this that collective instruction must be
of disadvantage for both future students and non-students."[21]
Fischer grants the teaching of classical languages a rightful
place in the curriculum only if it can be done so intensively and
over a long time that pupils have command of the language both in

speaking and writing. As this is only possible for a minority, he
designs a majority school type without obligatory Latin and Greek
classes: the "Realgymnasium" (secondary school with scientific
bias). In the curriculum of the old grammar schools - in Fischer's
terminology the "language grammar schools" (Sprachgymnasium) - the
classical philologies and their supplementory sciences are to
dominate, following the example of the English grammar schools.
Latin is "fundamental teaching matter". Geography, history,
natural history and physics are united to a subsidiary subject
with few lessons. Mathematical instruction, however,
counterbalances the onesidedness of classical studies. "Pure
mathematics" establishes the connection of intellectual education
and real life. Fischer gives it particular emphasis so that he
does not have to exclude mathematicians from the privileged
institute for the elite. According to Fischer, the sole objective
of the classical grammar school is preparation for university.
With the help of a special senior grade subject ("general
encyclopaedia") pupils shall get to know structure and working
methods of the university so that they can start their particular
courses of study without loss of time.

Fischer justifies his design for a "Realgymnasium" with the early
school leavers. For them, the main point of interest lies in the
first to fifth forms. The establishment of a school without senior
grades would suffice for the majority of pupils whom Fischer wants
to draw away from grammar school. But this would result in the
restriction of teachers interested in mathematics and natural
science to a less respected lower school type. Fischer wants to
achieve opposite. He enlarges the "Realgymnasium" to a seven-year
school and demands equal rights with the old grammar school. He
wants to prevent an inferior status of schools concentrating on
mathematics and natural sciences by differentiating the
curriculum. As "if a Lambert, a Franklin, a Mendelssohn ... stood
even one step below a scholar whose career led him through a
university."[22]

In order to achieve greater prestige for the teachers of a
"Realgymnasium" by means of their pupils' origin, Fischer includes
the preparatory training of the studied practicians. Linguistic
grammar schools shall only be established for future scholars.

Those who need science as a means only and do not study it for its own ends (e.g. the practical theologist) shall go to a "Realgymnasium". Fischer bases his organization plan on the structure of the Berlinisch-Koellnisches Gymnasium in Berlin. Linguistic grammar schools and "Realgymnasien" as coordinated institutions shall base on a common lower grade, the "Realschule". The "Realschule" shall be the proper school of the school-age population and besides preparing for grammar school it shall complete the general education of the lower social classes. It consists of the classes "Sexta" (first form) to "Quarta" (third form) and presupposes elementary education. The main subjects are German and mathematics. Latin only starts in the third form as a voluntary subject. Only 15% of the pupils who pass on to grammar school shall attend the classical branch of a comprehensive or, in bigger cities, the independent linguistic grammar school. With this ratio, Fischer attacks the substance of the existing grammar schools. In their majority they would be transformed into "Realgymnasien", i.e. the superior position of the classical scholars would be replaced by the dominance of school mathematicians. As a compensation, a grammar school revalorized as an institute for the elite would be left to some of the classical scholars. Like Gedike's grammar school, the "Realgymnasium" together with the "Realschule" preceding it remains an integrated comprehensive school. In the "Realgymnasium", mathematics occupies the status Latin has in grammar school; Latin, however, is not granted the importance of grammar school mathematics. By reading translations in German classes the pupils are to be introduced to Greek and Roman literature.

While the curriculum of the linguistic grammar school needs not pay attention to early school leavers, the "Realgymnasium" shall offer permanent intermediate qualifications. The mathematical subject matter, for instance, is partitioned in a way which forms foundations for each form which are self-contained units even if they are not continued in the next form. Mathematics is not only a formally educating subject because of its method but also practice-related because of its contents. According to Fischer it also proves to be the mobility-furthering centre of gravity of a comprehensive school curriculum. He maintains that mathematics also reduces teacher's social prejudices against children from

non-academic classes, because it has more objective possibilities
of evaluation than classical studies. In comparison with the
classical languages, the mastery of the mathematical subject
matter is nearly independent from the former language level of a
pupil. Mathematical instruction does not require additional
motivation by the parents; according to Fischer it solves problems
which are of interst to every human being "who is not completely
demoralized by nature".[23]

The "Realgymnasium" comprises "Tertia", "Sekunda" and "Prima"
(forth, fifth, and sixth form); the two higher forms are conceived
as parallel classes with different functions. The objectives of
the parallel classes are aligned to the respective occupational
group for which they specifically prepare, besides their internal
function. All pupils attend the lowest class, "Tertia".
Externally, its completion qualifies for subordinate civil service
posts (clerk), for an apprenticeship in small business and
specialized crafts (carpenter, mason). The subject matter of
"Sekunda" is meant for future manufacturers, businessmen, and
technicians. Pupils who aim at the higher scientific education
pass on to "Prima" (two years) immediately after "Tertia"; at the
end of "Prima" they shall obtain a subject-specific qualification
for university.

Fischer does not deduce his conception of the comprehensive school
- which shall include all children of school age apart from the
pupils of the "Studienschule" (school preparing for university) -
from pedagogic but from national-economic requirements.
Traditional thinking is to be replaced by modern methods of
natural science. The craftsmen's restriction to guilds shall be
radically erased to enable Germany to make good the advantage of
French and English industry. Craftsmen and tradesmen shall be
trained to "Sextro's industry-mindedness", i.e. to creative
independence. According to Fischer, the Prussian state will be
unable in the long run to protect itself from foreign competition
by means of tax and toll regulations. It must increase the
competitive chances of its manufactures with the help of
progressive school politics. This cannot be achieved by "Erwerbs-
oder Armenschulen" (schools for occupational groups or for the
poor), but only by a profound, scientifically founded education.

Epigonic imitation of the Englishmen shall be replaced by own inventions. Fischer attempts to prove that the conservative pedagogues endanger the very thing they want to protect: the stability of the political system. According to Fischer the investments for reforms omitted for fear of overstocking in academic professions at the same time restrict the field of activity for the academically educated. Science and education require economic growth. Economic advancement requires new manners of thinking and behaviour which can only be achieved by institutionalized education processes and which must not exclude any part of the population; "a good brain must be enabled to become what Mother Nature has intended him to".[24]

References

1 Cf. Mueller, D.K.: Sozialstruktur und Schulsystem. Aspekte zum Strukturwandel des Schulwesens im 19. Jahrhundert, Goettingen 1977; Buesch, P.: Militaersystem und Sozialleben im alten Preussen 1713 - 1807. Die Anfaenge der sozialen Militarisierung der preussisch-deutschen Gesellschaft, Berlin 1962, esp. pp. 11-20, 21-50.

2 Cf. Merleker: Wie sind die preussischen Gymnasien zu ihrer gegenwaertigen Einrichtung gelangt, in: Zeitschrift fuer das Gymnasialwesen 2 (1848), pp. 681-709; Schwartz, P.: Die Gelehrtenschulen Preussens unter dem Oberschulkollegium (1787 - 1806) und das Abiturientenexamen, vol. 1, Berlin 1910; Schwartz, P.: Die Gelehrtenschulen Preussens unter dem Oberschulkollegium (1787 - 1806) und das Abiturientenexamen, vol. 3, Berlin 1912, pp. 531-532.

3 Cf. Gutachten der philosophischen Fakultaet der Universitaet Koenigsberg, quoted in: Schwartz, Die Gelehrtenschulen Preussens ..., vol. 1 (ref. 2), p. 74.

4 Gutachten Noebling, quoted in: Schwartz, Die Gelehrtenschulen Preussens ..., vol. 1 (ref. 2), p. 95.

5 Gedike: Entwurf fuer ein Pruefungsreglement, in: Schwartz, Die Gelehrtenschulen Preussens ..., vol. 1, (ref. 2), p. 103.

6 Article: Ueber die zu grosse Anzahl der Studierenden, in: Berlinische Monatsschrift XII (1788), p. 251.

7 Reglement fuer die Pruefung an den Gelehrten Schulen, in:

Schwartz, Die Gelehrtenschulen Preussens ..., vol. 1 (ref. 2), pp. 122-128.

8 Kabinettsorder an das Oberkriegskollegium und das Generaldirektorium ueber die Zulassung der Kantonpflichtigen zum Studium, Potsdam, 31. Oktober 1791, in: Schwartz, Die Gelehrtenschulen Preussens ..., vol. 3 (ref. 2), pp. 532-533.

9 About the examinations of pupils liable to military service cf. Schwartz, Die Gelehrtenschulen Preussens ..., vol. 3 (ref. 2), esp. pp. 545-556, about the conflict between military and school administration cf. pp. 557-560.

10 Cf. Schwartz, P.: Die Gruendung der Unversitaet Berlin und der Anfang der Reform der hoeheren Schulen im Jahre 1810, in: Mitteilungen der Gesellschaft fuer deutsche Erziehungs- und Schulgeschichte 20 (1910), pp. 151-208; Wienecke,F.: Die Begruendung der Berliner Schulkommission am 1. September 1811, in: Brandenburgia. Monatsblatt der Gesellschaft fuer Heimatkunde der Provinz Brandenburg in Berlin XX (1911).

11 Humboldt, W.v.: Ideen zu einer Instruktion fuer die wissenschaftliche Deputation bei der Sektion des oeffentlichen Unterrichts, in: Gebhardt, B.: W. v. Humboldts Politische Denkschriften, vol. 1 (1802-1810), Berlin 1903, p. 180.

12 Cf. Bernhardi, A.F.: Ueber Zahl, Bedeutung und Verhaeltnis der Lehrobjecte eines Gymnasiums, Berlin 1809; Bernhardi, A.F.: Ueber die ersten Grundsaetze der Methodik fuer die Lehrobjecte eines Gymnasiums, in: Oeffentliche Pruefung. April 1810. Friedrichs-Gymnasium, Berlin 1810, pp. 3-71; Bernhardi, A.F.: Ueber die ersten Grundsaetze der Disciplin in einem Gymnasium, in: Oeffentliche Pruefung. Maerz 1811. Friedrichs-Gymnasium, Berlin 1811, pp. 1-94; Bernhardi, A.F.: Schulordnung des Friedrichs-Gymnasiums, in: Oeffentliche Pruefung. Oktober 1812. Friedrichs-Gymnasium, Berlin 1812, pp. 1-152; Bernhardi, A.F.: Ansichten ueber die Organisation der gelehrten Schulen, Jena 1818; Mueller, A.C.: Geschichte des Friedrichs-Werderschen Gymnasiums zu Berlin, Berlin 1881, pp. 92-107.

13 Bernhardi, Ueber Zahl, Bedeutung und Verhaeltnis ... (ref. 12), p. 8.

14 Ibid., first quotation p. 25, second quotation p. 12.

15 Ibid., p. 30; cf. Bernhardi, Schulordnung des Friedrichs-Gymnasiums ... (ref. 12), esp. pp. 31-32.

16 Cf. Bernhardi, A.F.: Schulordnung des Friedrichs-Gymnasiums

... (ref. 12), esp. pp. 33–34 and 32.

17 Cf. Zimmermann, C.G.:   Einige Bemerkungen ueber die
Gegenstaende des oeffentlichen Unterrichts mit Ruecksicht auf das
Friedrichs-Werdersche Gymnasium, in: Oeffentliche Pruefung. April
1821. Friedrichs-Werdersches Gymnasium, Berlin 1821, pp. 1–27,
quotation pp. 4–5; Zimmermann, C.G.: Einige Gedanken ueber die
nach den Zwecken des gesellschaftlichen Lebens eingerichteten
Schulen, in: Oeffentliche Pruefung. 1822, Berlin 1822; Zimmermann,
C.G.: Kurze Auseinandersetzungen der Lehrgegenstaende, welche in
den Plan fuer Buergerschulen oder Realgymnasien aufgenommen werden
koennen, in: Oeffentliche Pruefung. 1824. Friedrichs-Werdersches
Gymnasium, Berlin 1824.

18 Cf. Fischer, E.G.: Ueber die Naturkenntnis und ihren Einfluss
auf die Ausbildung des Menschen (Speech of 23. Dez. 1799 at the
foundation festival), in: Gedike (ed.): Rede bei der vorjaehrigen
Gedaechtnisfeier der Wohltaeter des Berlinisch-Koellnischen
Gymnasiums. Einladung zur Feier. 19. Januar 1801, Berlin 1801, pp.
4–13; Fischer,E.G.: Ueber die zweckmaessigste Einrichtung der
Lehranstalten fuer die gebildeten Staende. Versuch einer neuen
Ansicht dieses Gegenstandes mit besonderer Ruecksicht auf Berlin,
Berlin 1806; Fischer, E.G.: Ueber die Englischen Lehranstalten in
Vergleichung mit den unsrigen, in: Oeffentliche Pruefung. April
1827. Berliner Gymnasium zum grauen Kloster, Berlin 1827, pp.
1–18; also Heussi, J.: Die Mathematik als Bildungsmittel, Berlin
1836; also Snell, K.CH.: Ueber Zweck und Einrichtung eines
Realgymnasiums, in: Oeffentliche Pruefungen. Bissthumsches
Geschlechtsgymnasium und Blochmannsche Erziehungs-Anstalt, Dresden
und Leipzig 1834, pp. 1–80, esp. pp. 79–80; Kloeden, K.V. in:
Kloeden, K.F. and Schmidt, V.H., (ed.) Die aeltere Geschichte des
Koellnisches Gymnasiums, bis zu seiner Vereinigung mit dem
Berlinischen Gymnasium, nebst einigen Worten ueber dessen jetzige
Bestimmung, in: Oeffentliche Pruefung. Maerz 1825, Berlin 1825.

19 Cf. Fischer, Ueber die Naturkenntnis und ihren Einfluss ...
(ref. 18), p. 10.

20 Cf. Fischer, Ueber die zweckmaessigste Einrichtung der
Lehranstalten ... (ref. 18), pp. 14, 19, 72.

21 Ibid., p. 18.

22 Ibid., p. 34.

23 Ibid., pp. 59–60.

24 Ibid., p. 97.

Brita Rang-Dudzik

QUALITATIVE AND QUANTITATIVE ASPECTS OF CURRICULA IN PRUSSIAN
GRAMMAR SCHOOLS DURING THE LATE 18TH AND EARLY 19TH CENTURIES AND
THEIR RELATION TO THE DEVELOPMENT OF THE SCIENCES

1. Preliminary Remarks to the Development of State and Society in
Prussia During the Period Under Study

The period under study covers, on the one hand, that pre-reform
era of the absolutist Prussian State in which the economic
activity of the state was expanded due to the interest - augmented
by the results of the Seven-Years-War - in increasing state
revenues. In this connection - that is, in order to increase the
effectiveness of economic policy - the State made organizational
efforts which also aimed at a rationalization of the
administration. In comparison to the development in England and
France, Prussia obviously was, and despite these efforts still
remained backward in economy. By the end of the 18th century
there were only just the beginnings of a "departure from the
pre-industrial mode of production". (Henning 1976)

My study also covers that phase of the Prussian-German development
in which, initiated or at least accompanied by reforms (from 1806
- after the defeats at Jena and Auerstaedt -: the liberation of
the peasants, the introduction of a general trade tax, the
abolition of compulsory guilds, limited equality for Jews, school
reforms), Industrial Revolution is being intensively prepared and
which in the thirties begins to assert itself in a way different
from that of the 'industrialized' countries of Europe (termed the

207

H. N. Jahnke and M. Otte (eds.), Epistemological and Social Problems of the Sciences in the Early Nineteenth
Century, 207–233.

"Prussian way to capitalism"). In spite of its increasing economic
power the bourgeoisie in this stage did not succeed in
emancipating itself politically from the feudal powers - even
though the Prussian reforms - due to the military weakness of the
feudal absolutist state - were primarily demanded by the
bourgeoisie and granted by the ´englightened´ state - because of
its very weakness. The pre-reform stage and the period after 1806
are linked by obvious efforts of the Prussian State to further the
increasingly necessary socialization (Vergesellschaftung, i.e.
generalization of industrial production and of the knowledge and
competence in the citizens required for the latter) by public
measures taken, among other things, in education.

Socialization (Vergesellschaftung) in France and England received
its impetus by the bourgeoisie, i.e. from below. In these
countries it was promoted together with, parallel to, and against
the feudal-absolutist state - beginning in pre-industrial and
industrial production, later expanding from this stronghold to
other areas of social life (politics, law, education). In Prussia,
however, this process of generalization was mainly attempted as a
´socialization from above´.
In so far, the Prussian state, in a phase of radical social
changes brought about by the Industrial Revolution and its
antecedents, manufactory and cottage industry, grew to a social
power over society. The Prussian State, under obvious pressure
from below, initiated and promoted changes which tended to make
bourgeois principles and interests prevail. But this public
action - because and in so far as it was bound up with feudal
interests or refracted by them - was taken in a contradictory way:
it did not only express direct rule, but was also pervaded with
ideological forms.

2. On the Actual Grammar School System of Education During the
Second Half of the 18th Century

The entire development of the Prussian school system can be traced
in the context of these public measures: according to a rough
classification of the whole period, we may speak of a first stage
up to the actual reform period (up to 1806), and of a second

stage, which began with the reforms themselves and under the banner of the emancipatory aims of the bourgeoisie. The second stage, however, is not only characterized by bourgeois trends for social progress but also by the counter movement emerging as a consequence of the restorative development in Europe.

In view of the obvious state activity in education, especially in the grammar schools, it is not surprising that other studies on the development of subject-matter in schools have hitherto traced the decrees and prescriptions issued by the state, and, using these as a starting point, have tried to define the respective stages of development. (cf. Paulsen 1897)

With regard to the period up to 1806, however, any study including the curricula of individual schools is confronted with a situation Schwartz not inappropriately compared to that of the Dutch Republic: "each form with its teacher an independent state with its governor." (Schwartz 1912: VII) These contingencies which, however, (as will have to be proved) are not historically accidental, raise the following questions:
- Which was the internal link keeping these manifold phenomena together?
- How are the state's actions taken with regard to these conditions to be judged? Which were the effects of these actions?
- What is the historical quality of grammar school education? Which new tendencies do emerge?

The number of schools preparing for admission to the university in the second half of the 18th century can only be roughly reconstructed - mainly for the reason that many schools were short-lived. If we take the 91 schools recognized as grammar schools after the efforts at reorganization in Prussia 1815-1818 as a basis, the number of schools "dismissing" students to universities before 1810 was disproportionately greater. Meierotto in his 1793 inspection report on the East Prussian schools, lists 60 schools just for this region "which prepare for the university". (Meierotto in: Schwartz 1910, p. 223) After 1818, there are only 12 schools left. Most of the schools in the pre-reform stage Meierotto inspected (Lateinschulen, Gymnasien, Gelehrtenschulen, Paedagogien, Ritterakademien), had only between one and three teachers. This situation was, however, not only typical for remote and under-developed East Prussia, but was also widely true for the western regions of Prussia. Snethlage's 1790 report to the "Oberschul-Collegium" (the central school authority established in Berlin in 1787) on the schools in the county of Mark and the dukedom of Cleve depicts a similar situation. He speaks of "some 20 small towns ... in each of which there is a Latin school, most of which having only one teacher, but very few two teachers. All these schools are still aligned to the old way. Only the Latin language is taught there ... . The teachers at these schools are for the most part ignorant... . It is easy to understand how inept and ignorant young people are when they leave these schools for the university." (Snethlage, quoted from Schwartz 1912, p. 221)

In these schools, there is not only an unusual structural variety with regard to the different number of teachers and 'classes' (of the latter there were often only two in the Lateinschulen; three to five in the better developed Gymnasien, assuming that a class will simply be denoted here as stage; the schools most developed under the influence of philanthropism had 8 stages resp. classes to show). Above all, the curricular situation differs. If we disregard the Lateinschulen which, as a rule, mainly taught what their name implies, and consider the range of subjects organized in three to five stages at the Gymnasien, we find that the latter is rather diverse. The reason for this diversity was that the traditional range of subjects aligned to the former functions of the Gymnasium was extended - a result of the demand for better qualitication raised by trade and industry - to those contents valued by the pre-industrial bourgeoisie. The functions of the Gymnasien during the second half of the 18th century were thus, as a rule, no longer confined to merely preparing future clergymen, lawyers, and physicians (i.e. of scholars) for the university, but extended as well to educating those strata of the urban bourgeoisie which had no desire to attend the latter. Owing to these conditions, lessons were divided among the following subjects (as shown by the 1788 syllabus of the Kolberg Gymnasium):

	I	II	III	
Latin	10	12	14	36
Greek	2	3		5
Hebrew	2			2
German	2	2		4
Scripture	4	4	8	16
History	2	1		3
Geography	2			2
Mathematics	2			2
Arithmetic			10	10
Physics		1		1
Natural History		3	2	5
Writing			8	8
Singing/				
French	private lessons			

A large part of the lessons listed here were administered privately. Things taught in the classroom did hardly adhere to any uniform concept. Scope and specific content of lessons depended on the teacher's education (even here, standard qualifications lacked: teachers, as a rule, were theology graduates still without a parish, and for the non-classical subjects often autodidacts), but also of the respective students, their different levels of previous knowledge, and their various educational goals. Tables on school leavers and school entrants reveal a large fluctuation and show that only a small proportion of the students wanted to go on to the university.

One of the results of the great fluctuation and the different levels of the pupils' previous education was that a system of classes divided according to age-group could hardly be introduced; rather, the student's way through school was structured by a system of classes according to subjects. For example, a student might already have reached the top level in Latin, but still be at the lowest level in arithmetic and perhaps even drop mathematics altogether (e.g. because it was not required for his theological studies at the university) On the other hand a prospective artisan or merchant could completely leave aside Greek and, of course, Hebrew, acquire only basic Latin, attend instead both classes in German (in which – as here in Kolberg – primarily spelling and writing was learnt) and do arithmetic, physics, natural history, writing, and perhaps French, too.

In spite of directions from the authorities to the contrary this system of classes arranged according to subjects in many places in Prussia lasted into the thirties. For different reasons, its abolition has been much regretted in the literature on the history of education (e.g. by Paulsen, by Furck, by D.K. Mueller), so that I should like to point out the conditions of this system and its historical backwardness. I consider this necessary particularly for seeing educational and scientific developments in connexion to each other.

The "classes according to subjects", in my opinion, represent a contemporary response to the different levels of previous knowledge the students have when they enter school. If we consider, besides, that a standardized elementary school system was still lacking, it may be said that "subject-specific classes" are the historical and organizational expression of the yet very low degree of generalization, or rather socialization (Vergesellschaftung), of school attendance and education. This situation, at the same time, corresponds to the contemporary stock of knowledge, or, more precisely, to the rudimentary development of the sciences. As long as a deliberate and wide-spread accumulation and integration of knowledge were yet lacking in most fields of science, school could only occasionally pick out elements from the stock of knowledge. The same was true for the various fields of knowledge or subjects which had not yet been integrated. Without going further into the complex relationship between language and mathematics, linguistic and mathematical mental processes, I should like to stress the historically heterogenous level of development in these fields: the marginal development of linguistic skills in German did not correspond to the level mathematics, for example, had already attained in France.

Hence, no impulses for a systematization of knowledge could come from the schools thus organized. The 'Abitur' examinations (graduation) in Prussian Gymnasien and Stadtschulen, which have been documented since 1788, show the fragmentary and accidental character of the knowledge acquired in school, and list, as a rule, a mere string of facts unrelated by any scientific understanding.

The focus of the school curriculum of that period is on Latin everywhere. Scripture, Greek, and German follow at a large distance. Mathematics covers a very small range and is usually done in two stages, i.e. taught for two years. Arithmetic is more extensive (but only under the condition that the school is not only preparing for university courses, but also for the activities of merchants artisans, and lower civil servants).

This situation is overlaid by a new understanding of school education encouraged by the interests of the (petty) bourgeoisie. This novel understanding - inspired. on one hand, by developments in manufacture, and by scientific developments on the other - attempts to align the organization and curricula of schools to the newly emerging diversity of knowledge, and to the increasing division of labour in society and production. One of these schools was, for example, the Lutheran Stadtgymnasium (Municipal Grammar School) in Halle. Content and structure of its teaching were the following: In 1788 and in subsequent years, there were 55 'subject-specific classes' sharing 6 to 7 classrooms. The curriculum consisted of a total of 21 subjects. There were 8 classes for Latin, 4 for Greek, 2 for Hebrew, 4 for French, 2 for Italian, 4 for theology, 1 for philosophy, 1 for mathematics, 3 for arithmetic, 4 for history, 1 for history of philosophy, 1 for the "history of Scholars", 7 for geography, 3 for natural history, 1 for physics, 1 for calligraphy, 1 for spelling, 1 for drawing, 2 for prosody, 1 for reciting, 2 for reading exercises.

The pedagogical theory of this development, known as "Philanthropism", emphasizes, in terms of methodology, sensualistic and empiristic principles. The sensual notion (Anschauung) of concrete objects is the immediate starting point

for any abstraction. In view of this premise, mathematicians will
not be surprised that teaching in these schools, according to
contemporaries, satisfied only "bare necessities".

The historical events in this development were first of all that
the bourgeoisie made its interests prevail: to assimilate and
generalize the existing school stock of knowledge. This
generalization, however, was still attempted in a quasi-artisan
way, based on experience and convention. There is as yet no
attempt to capture the differentiation of knowledge and of the
division of labour for basic education, through seeking general
principles as a basis for rational comprehension and use of
empirical phenomena and problems. The process of generalization
consists as yet of mere addition. This corresponds, to a large
extent, to social activity in this period of
proto-industrialization: The discoveries in nature, and productive
use of the natural environment and its laws are still more or less
left to chance. True, this use receives a decisive impulse from
expansion of the new bourgeois mode of production, which tends to
prevail in general, but it is not yet scientific, systematical in
the modern sense. Rather, this use is still made in a
pre-scientific way, that is relatively accidental and by mere
juxtaposition of elements of knowledge considered heterogenous. To
sum up: The few modern schools influenced by philanthropism of the
second half of the 18th century tend to become preparatory
institutions for the further development of the sciences and of
technology insofar as they make allowance for real life, i.e.
contemporary developments (quite unlike the traditionalist
Lateinschulen and Gelehrtenschulen). In fact, however, they
fulfill this propaedeutic task only to a limited extent, as the
power of synthesis of scientific abstraction, or of analytic
comprehension still plays no part, or only a minor one. The
enormous variety of newly-introduced subjects in some of these
schools is an indicator for the "faceabout towards real life"
occurring in education at that time, yet simultaneously for the
inability to classify and summarize the variety, heterogenity and
disparity of empirical phenomena and scientific insights in a way
suitable for the development of schools and science by means of
rational recourse to underlying general structures, causal

relationships, and laws. Hence, we are faced by schools and subjects of teaching belonging to the period of transition to industrial-capitalist society on one hand, and to the old society on the other. In terms of social and economic history this means: the curricular principles applied in these schools still correspond to pre-industrial and traditional forms of the division of labour.

3. Some Propositions Concerning the Importance of Neo-Humanism for the Introduction of Science into Gymnasium Curricula

The reorganization of Prussian Gymnasien, for which the influence of Neo-Humanism had paved the way, went, in its intentions, against the direction taken by the developments characterized above, and is thus not only the expression of a qualitatively new relationship between school and the development of science, but of a new stage of bourgeois development in Germany as well. In 1811 for example Jachmann voiced his criticism of the diversity of philanthropist schools reflected in the 'subject-specific classes'. "A natural consequence was that they organized their system of classes according to subjects, so that everyone might choose his lessons as he preferred, and make progress according to his talent and inclination... . Such schools resemble a haberdashery which stocks all kinds of fancy articles from all over the world to meet random demand... . This is why they parallel their classes so that everyone can pick and choose according to his whims... . Their forces are scattered, and diverge in various directions, instead of concentrating effectively on one generally accepted aim." (Jachmann, in: Joerden 1962, p. 94)

It was this concentration which the bourgeois reformers sought to attain in the Neo-Humanist way, by ascribing to the individual an active ability to structurize the cognitive material. In doing so, they emphasized the ability of the mind to achieve synthesis in the face of the diversity of the natural and cultural phenomena. The curriculum for the Neo-Humanist Gymnasium Wilhelm von Humboldt

proposed for Prussia is, in its intentional focus on a few fields
of   knowledge (languages,   history,   mathematics) itself an
expression of this capacity to achieve synthesis:
Language, as an indicator for linguistic ability, at the same time
presented as a medium giving access to the Greek world, and
experienced in literature as a framework for potential human
totality and harmony; history, conceived as a process of man's
self-fulfillment and perfection; mathematics, understood, on one
hand, as 'pure' cognition, and as a medium for critical-bourgeois
reasoning on the other.
These main elements of the new curriculum were not to lead away
from real life (as late bourgeois criticism has maintained almost
without exception), but contribute to the ability to conceive of
the immediacy of real life, from a distance, so to speak, in a
conscious way. In the history of philosophy, this development
corresponds to the transition from sensualism and empiricism to
dialectical idealism initiated by Kant in his "Kritik der reinen
Vernunft".

The enormous impact of German idealism on the promotion of a new
approach to problems of language and to the study of history is a
well known fact. We should now ask which consequences this new
mode of philosophical thinking may have had on the rapid
development of mathematics and the sciences, for there seems to be
a rather close correspondence between philosophy on one hand, as
far as it was inclined to detach itself from immediate empirical
reality, incorporating speculative aspects and oriented towards
the discovery of fundamental structures and principles, – and the
emerging new forms of mathematics and sciences on the other.

Incidentally, the effectiveness of Neo-Humanist education assumed
here is also conditioned by intentions, which are directed at the
same time at building up formal strength: not "just learning
anything, but training memory, sharpening the mind, correcting
judgement, refining morals by learning". (Humboldt IV, p. 217)

This educational objective is based historically, on real life
which becomes differentiated and extended, by means of increasing
division of labour, expanded exchange of commodities,
differentiations within society, growth of knowledge about

individual facts, discoveries and inventions. Neo-Humanist theory of education may thus be interpreted as the historical form of a scientific response to these very changes.

Nevertheless, we can easily recognize, in retrospect, the historically limited opportunities of the bourgeoisie, free only in its thinking, in this bourgeois concept of education which was advanced for its time. To achieve synthesis of the diversity of empirical reality is conceived of as a skill displayed by the separate, isolated individual. There is an abstract, idealistic neglect of the division of labour in that. This concept imagines that the tension between increasing universalization, and specialization as its historical counterpart, can be dissolved or cancelled by the single individual. Every teacher in the newly conceived Prussian grammar school is to be, simultaneously, a scholar of the classical and German philology, a historian and mathematician, and has to show not only these skills, but additional ones in the 'Examen pro facultate docendi'.

This is where the chinks appear in the assumed relationship between neo-humanist education and the development of sciences. Whereas science is progressing by means of increasing specialization, the Neo-Humanists neglect the dialectic of division of labour and co-operation, of specialization and universalization. During the period of Neo-Humanism the scientifically educated teacher is still conceived of as quasi pre-bourgeois universal scholar. The range of knowledge expected of him intentionally includes the totality of subjects taught in grammar schools on a scientific level.

4. Digression: The Significance and Sequence of the State's Measures in Grammar School Education

The effect and significance of the trend to uniformity that resulted from this Neo-Humanist understanding of reality cannot be fully understood without considering the attempts at socialization (Vergesellschaftung) made by the state. Hence, before describing the situation of the various schools and curricula, the activity of the state in secondary education in this historic period must be presented first. Of importance for the general enforcement of changes in Prussian grammar schools was the establishment of a central educational authority which, under professional instead of Church supervision, was to introduce a reorganization "according to the same proven principles" for "the entire school system" (Nov. Corp. Const. 1787, no. 25). The "Oberschulkollegium", which was to take over these responsibilities, was formed in 1787, under the Secretary of State and Minister of Justice, von Zedlitz. By means of a circular, the Oberschulkollegium (faced by the universities' critism of the student's level of knowledge) attempted, in 1788, to issue directives concerning the graduation examination ("Abitur") at the "Gelehrtenschulen". At the same time, inspections began in the various provinces in order to gain insight into the material and curricular conditions of secondary education.

In the context of the administrative reforms of 1808, the Oberschulkollegium was dissolved. In its stead, a 'Section for Culture and Public Education' was attached to the ministry of the interior. Humboldt was appointed director of this section in 1810. In 1817, finally the section became an independent ministry, the 'Ministry for Clerical and Educational Affairs' under the direction of v. Altenstein, who held this office until 1840.

This process of organization and reorganization of a central governing body for education was paralleled by the establishment of provincial authorities. The initial diversity of these regional authorities was not eliminated before 1808, and a 'Deputation for Culture and Public Instruction' was attached to each Prussian provincial government. In 1809, an additional step was made in the reorganization of secondary education at the regional level. In Berlin, Koenigsberg, and Breslau, 'Scientific Deputations' ("Wissenschaftliche Deputationen") were established, which were to control not only candidates for teaching posts in secondary education, in the various provinces, but also the curricula, text-books, teaching methods, and results of the graduation examinations. With the new administrative reforms starting in 1815, the 'Deputations for Culture and Instruction' were replaced by the 'Consistories for Church- and School-Affairs'

("Consistorien fuer Kirchen- und Schulwesen"). The three 'scientific deputations' also lost their significance and gave way to scientific examining boards, which were established in each of the ten (later eight) Prussian provinces. In 1825, finally, Altenstein's Ministry divided each of the consistories into two sections, one of which was exclusively responsible for secondary education in its province. This section was the 'Provinzial-Schulcollegium'. The seats of these 'provincial school councils' were Koenigsberg, Berlin, Stettin, Posen, Breslau, Magdeburg and Muenster. The scientific examining boards founded in 1816 for examining candidates for teaching posts and for the inspection of the graduation examinations remained as institutions of their own.

The local administration of the schools continued, however, to be organized in very different ways depending on the patronage of the school. There were municipal, ecclesiastical, Royal, charitable and private patronages, also co-patronages (i.e. several patrons for one school). Since these patronages were locally different, diverse school forms continued to exist side by side despite central attempts at standardization of curricula and organization of schools. Comprehensive standardization was not introduced until the late fifties of the last century when the 'Realschulen' (non-classical secondary schools), which had been partially attached to the Gymnasien before, were organized independently, and special regulations for teaching and examinations were issued for these schools.

Nevertheless we may speak of marked tendencies toward standardization during the time subsequent to the Prussian reforms, as compared to the second half of the 18th century. The educational constitution of 1816 initiated by Humboldt and drafted under Suevern fixed, even though it could not be made obligatory, the new structure of what was understood by "Gymnasialbildung" (grammar school education) in the reform period, and made organizational suggestions for the internal structure of a grammar school. According to these statutes, a Gymnasium was to have six consecutive forms within three stages. Sexta (VI), Quinta (V), and Quarta (IV) took one year each for the nine year old pupil coming

from compulsory elementary school, Tertia (III) and Sekunda (II)
took two years each, and Prima (I) three years, so that a student
left grammar school after ten years and went on to the university
at the age of nineteen. The following rule was proposed for the
syllabi and for the range of subjects:

Latin   VI and V   6 lessons a week
                         IV to   I   8 "   " "

Greek   IV and III   5 "   " "
                         II and I   7 "   " "

German   VI and V   6 "   " "
                         IV to   I   4 "   " "

Mathematics   VI to   -I   6 "   " "

Science
(Physics and
Natural History)   VI to   -I   2 "   " "

Hist./Geog.   VI to   -I   3 "   " "

Scripture   VI to   -I   2 "   " "

(Hebrew, Singing and Gymnastics were optional)

In order to attain systematic structurization of the learning
processes and integration of the individual fields of knowledge,
Johannes Schulze, on of Hegel's disciples, and civil engineer
(Technischer Rat) for secondary education, initiated the abolition
of the 'subject-specific classes'. The system of 'year classes'
was widely established in the twenties. In view of the lasting
differences as to content and structure between the various
grammar schools the Ministry under Altenstein, in 1837, attempted
once more to introduce an additional standardization by fixing the
number of subjects and the time allotted to them in a 'normal
syllabus':

	VI	V	IV	III	II	I	
Latin	10	10	10	10	10	10	lessons a week
Greek			6	6	6	6	" " "
German	4	4	2	2	2	2	" " "
French			2	2	2		" " "
Scripture	2	2	2	2	2	2	" " "
Mathematics			3	3	4	4	" " "
Arithmetic & Geometry	4	4					" " "
Physics					1	2	" " "
Philos. Propaedeutics						2	" " "
History/ Geography	3	3	3	3	3	2	" " "
Natural History	2	2	2	2			" " "
Drawing	2	2	2				" " "
Calligraphy	3	3	1				" " "
Singing	2	2	2	2			" " "

Even if we can only partly speak of a real standardization in
secondary education in view of the teaching provided in the
various schools (which can be seen from the syllabi) this
syllabus, and additional regulations, did take effect towards
creating similar situations in Prussian grammar schools.
On of these additional regulations was the obligatory examination
for candidates applying for teaching posts in secondary education,
which was introduced by the edict of July 12th 1810 (In: Roenne,
vol. II, p. 22ff.). Article 4 of this edict prescribed that every
candidate had to pass a special examination in philology (Greek,
Latin, German), and in mathematics and history, the so-called
'examen pro facultate docendi', unless he had already taken his
Master's degree or Doctorate at a faculty of philosophy. In 1831
the Ministry under Altenstein extended the compulsory range of
examination subjects to the science subjects of physics and
natural history, and stressed once more that a university
'Triennium", i.e. three-year university studies, must precede this
examination. At the same time, it emphasized that every

prospective teacher, no matter to which patronage the school belonged, had to pass this state examination. The fact that in 1838 a re-print and an obligatory acknowledgement of all the decrees concerning teacher education was sent to all the Provinzial-Schulcollegien shows, for such seemingly straight-forward regulations, how little impression of real life decrees will convey.

The development of grammar school contents was additionally structured from above by the regulations issued for a maturity examination. The first of these instructions issued in 1788 prescribed to examine a student's knowledge of languages (Latin, French, Greek, German) and sciences, especially of history. The documentation on the graduation examination (records from 1788-1804) presented by Schwartz from the files of the Oberschulcollegium shows how differently this directive was handled. The examinations in Greek and German frequently were not held - at the request of the candidates - , in many cases mathematics did not appear as an examination subject, neither. Physics was seldom examined. Up to 1812 only a small proportion of schools - and usually the more developed, larger schools - met the requirements of the graduation examination. Even the examinations held at these schools still differed greatly, because each student, owing to the system of 'subject-specific classes' appeared before the examining body with his individual educational background and could also be exempted from those parts of the examination which, because of his specific plans for his university studies, were of no significance to him for the future. For prospective theologians, physicians, and lawyers, mathematics, as a rule, was irrelevant. In order to control this situation and do justice to the new social requirements, the instruction of 1812, issued under Humboldt, stipulated the range of written and oral exams. It said that a written exam was to be held in German (essay), Latin, French, mathematics and Greek. These subjects, as well as history, geography and physics, were also to be tested orally. The examination results were marked in the following way:

"Absolute efficiency"   (I)
"Limited efficiency"   (II)
"Inefficiency"   (III)

Whoever received marks I or II could study at a university; with
mark III this was only possible within limits, in any case, there
was to be an additional examination at the university. As the
universities had maintained the right to regulate the entry
examinations,   and   as these examinations were easier, more
students-to-be, particularly the privately educated ones, seized
this opportunity, and could thus evade the graduation examination
regulations. It was not until 1834 that this situation was finally
remedied by issuing a decree which did not only reserve the right
to hold maturity examinations exclusively to grammar schools, but
also once more fixed the range of examination subjects: German,
Latin, Greek, French, scripture, history/geography, mathematics,
physics,   natural history and philosophical propaedeutics (a
subject introduced into schools at Hegel's suggestion) were to be
examined on the background of a well-defined level of knowledge.

The central authority and the Provinzialschulcollegien also tried
to influence the contents of the various subjects, and the use of
textbooks. The interests apparent in these issues cannot always be
clearly classified and differ in character from subject to
subject. In mathematics, for example, it is evident that the
authorities insisted on a certain range and proof of knowledge, on
a   certain   system, and on textbooks containing the latest
developments in science (Roenne II, 1855, p. 224ff, Regelungen und
Verordnungen ueber den Mathematikunterricht). In the science
subjects, however, the regulations are vague. Teaching is seen as
irrelevant and not as the place where scientific treatment of
object should occur. This was to be left to special schools and
universities (Roenne I, 1855, p. 685, II, 1855, p. 141). That
these intentions of the ministry cannot be simply considered as
part of the reactionary trends in Prussian politics may be seen
from the regulations for the humanities, which are rather more
exposed to ideological efforts. The ministry under Eichhorn (after
1840) recommended, for example, a German reader (conspiled by
Wackernagel) which try to maintain the literary tradition of
classical enlightenment.

An additional impulse, aimed at maintaining a certain scientific
level by means of standardization, can be seen in the instructions
concerning the "Schulschriften" (school year books). From 1824 on,

each Gymnasium was obliged to annually publish a yearbook not only containing the syllabi, and statistical information about the situation of the school, but also a new scientific publication emanating from the staff. The multitude of mathematical essays published in these yearbooks surely is evidence of the dissemination of mathematical knowledge in society.

5. Some Remarks Concerning the Curricular Reality in the Prussian Gymnasien During the Reform Period and the Post-Reform Period (1810-1850)

If we examine the syllabi of the Prussian Gymnasien after 1816 (when the teaching statutes were published for the Gymnasien and Stadtschulen), bearing in mind the state's efforts and the pedagogical curriculum debate of that time (Herder, Gesner, Ernesti, Herbart, Niethammer, Humboldt, Thiersch), we are at first surprised by the consistent formal similarity between pre-reform and reform grammar school syllabi - but also surprised at the lasting considerable differences between the various schools. At least formally, the range of subjects in the newer schools confirmed as Gymnasien during the reform period, seems at first - despite the concentrated efforts of Neo-Humanism - to be more or less congruent with that of the more developed grammar schools of the second half of the 18th century. This superficial similarity is obviously connected with the responsibility maintained by many grammar schools during the first half of the 19th century of dismissing students not only for the university, but also of dissmissing a large number of them into vocational life with an intermediate grammar school examination (cf. this and for the proposition on the 'comprehensive school function' of the grammar schools at that time: A. Rang 1968, W. Schoeler 1970, D.K. Mueller 1977).

Only if we bear these conditions in mind it will be understood why a syllabus like the following may still be found in 1833/34, in spite of the repeated efforts of the state to standardize grammar schools, and despite the reasons presented by the bourgeoisie for a concentration of the syllabus according to scientific principles:

Gymnasium in Stettin (1833/34):

	I	II	III	IV	V	VI
Scipture	2	2	2	2	2	2
Hebrew	2	2	2			
Greek	5	6	6	5		
Latin	9	9	10	8	8	6
German	2	2	2	2	4	5
French	2	2	2	2	2	
Greek Classics		1				
Metrics	1					
Philosoph.						
Propaedeutics	1					
Mathematics	4	4	4	4		
Physics	2	2	1			
History	2	2	3	2	2	2
Geography				2	2	2
Natural History					2	2
Geometry					2	2
Arithmetic					3	4
Calligraphy				2	2	4
Drawing				2	2	2
Singing				1	1	1

This traditional structure maintained in the Stettin syllabus has been more or less overcome at many other grammar schools - and that, upon closer look, is even true for Stettin, because here just as at the other grammar schools, the system of 'year classes' has been introduced, subjects like German and mathematics belong to the obligatory subjects, and can no longer be simply skipped like in the days of the 'subject specific class' system. Taking the "standard teaching plan" ("Normalplan") of 1837, we can show how, despite the organizational structure of schools which was still not completely standardized by the beginning of the fifties (the number of classes between Sexta and Prima for example varied despite attempts of regulation), a standardization of the grammar schools' range of subjects and the number of hours allocated to each subject nevertheless began to prevail. Although a

considerable number of schools are still teaching students who
leave school after Tertia, the specific content initially included
because of these early leavers is disappearing from the syllabus.
This means: the grammar school attains its special status within
the educational institutions earlier with regard to curriculum
than with regard to users.

What was offered in the various subjects, however, differs from
school to school. With regard to the syllabi, it is unfortunately
impossible to find out whether the length of time a student
remained in one class decisively determined and structured the
method and the depth of knowledge taught. In 1850 the Koeslin
grammar school, for example, which had nine classes (!), only
offered, in mathematics for the Oberprima, 'stereometry and
planimetry', whereas thirty years earlier the Bonn grammar school,
with only six classes, treated quadratic and cubic equations,
spherical trigonometry, and series. Nevertheless grammar school
mathematics, despite its unequal developments has become a
relatively standardized subject in 1840 already.

On the other hand, the science subjects of physics and natural
history are characterized, up to the beginning of the fifties, by
distinct differences (especially with respect to quality or
level). Since physics was limited to the last two stages Prima and
Sekunda and because of the lack of time this implied, it did not
offer the opportunity to put the scientific knowledge of the day
into a compulsory catalogue, as in mathematics. Besides,
mathematics apparently requires a more hierarchical structure of
knowledge, whereas physics may rather be seen in a horizontal
structure. This may also help to explain the immensely random
results and inequalities in the curricula for the science
subjects. In 1849 the Bonn grammar school for instance in Prima
and Sekunda offers magnetism and optics as part of physics; in
Essen, "acoustics and the cosmic system", heat and the
"equilibrium of solid, liquid and gaseous bodies" is taught at the
same level; in 1848, in the Putbus Prima it taught "on light", and
in Sekunda "Electricity and magnetism"; in Koeslin this is the
topic for Prima as well, as in this class a repetition of some of
natural history takes place (i.e. knowledge of biology). Subject
matter in history and German are even more diverse, and even in
Greek and Latin there are distinct differences from school to
school. This allows us to draw certain conclusions (bearing in

mind that some of the authors treated in school are more difficult
than others) about the different standards. Moreover, in the
so-called humanities more than in the science subjects, the
respective degree of bourgeois liberalism emerges, and together
with it adherence to or abandonment of bourgeois-enlightened and
revolutionary claims. In history, for instance, French
Enlightenment and Revolution may be a topic, but also the
genealogical history of the Hohenzollern. In languages, especially
in German, there are contrary positions such as emphasizing
classical literature and its interpretation (e.g especially
obvious at the Elberfeld grammar school), or offering grammar and
rhetorics as in the 18th century while teaching literature, if at
all, in compendium form (e.g. Koberstein's widely-used history of
literature).

The quality of the subject matter taught in Prussian grammar
schools has , however, clearly changed by the first half of the
19th century as compared to the 18th century, despite this
diversity of structure and curriculum. Even though some formal
similarities may still be found with regard to the number of
lessons and the importance attached to some subjects as compared
to conditions of the pre-reform period - a closer examination of
the contents taught shows the historical leap. This will be made
clear in one example:
In 1788, the Anklam municipal grammar school, in five classes,
offered a range of arithmetic and mathematics with numerous
lessons. It might, therefore, be formally compared to a grammar
school of the first half of the 19th century. If we look, however,
at what was actually taught in arithmetic and mathematics at this
school, the historical change in quality of the post-reform period
is immediately obvious. In 1788, both the mathematics and geometry
teachers of Anklam school report on their mathematics "course" to
the Oberschulcollegium in Berlin as follows:" In Ima (i.e. Prima,
B.R.) Jakobis Geometry for children and common life. Too
extensive, however, for two lessons a week, and too difficult for
the present situation of the school. In fact, a repetition of what
was done in IIda (i.e. Sekunda, B.R.), but more demonstratively.
Here and there additional material to arouse attention and
reflection. On the whole, as essential is scopus eruditionis can
only consist of reasonable application of the intellectual

faculties - here and there some remarks which do not fall under
the particular philosophy of quantities. Every § applied at once
by means of drawing set and paper. Is completed annually... . In
IIda. 1. Jakobis Geometry pp. Same method. Is completed every
year." (Schwartz 1911, p. 250) The geometry teacher writes in a
similar way about his lessons: in "geometry the method of teaching
is mathematical, where the ability of the students permits, and
catechetic, where their weakness demands...". (loc. cit., p. 252)
If we compare to this the mathematics curriculum of the Bonn
grammar school for 1819/1820, which was influenced in its theory
of education by Neo-Humanism, and in its content by the sciences
(both impulses being linked by means of the Neo-Humanist
understanding of the relation between perception, experience,
generalization, abstraction and idea), the difference is not only
a gradual, but also a substantial one. Mathematics lessons were
systematically organized in the six classes of the Bonn grammar
school in 1819/1820 and offered from Sexta to Prima as follows:

VI. The 4 fundamental rules of arithmetic in whole numbers and
     decimal numbers. Explanation of other number systems.

 V. Arithmetic, quantities.

IV. The basics of algebra; geometry as far as the teaching of
     similar triangles.

III. a) General arithmetic in squares, cubes and roots. Simple
     and quadratic equations. Progressions and logarithms.
     b) Proportions of rectilinear figures and of the circle.
     Stereometry.

 II. Progressions, logarithms, permutations, combinations and
     variations. The binomial theorem. Plane trigonometry.

  I. Spherical trigonometry. The Appolonian conic sections.
     Teaching series and higher equations.

The change in content of the grammar school curriculum noticeable
in these examples has many causes which can not only be immanently
explained in the context of academic development conditions.
Obviously, school is not merely a responding institution, but
initiates development itself, causes dynamic processes, supports
or hinders development. The attempt to sum up the essential
characteristics of the curricular situation in the new Prussian
grammar schools as compared to those of the pre-reform period,
will yield the following elements:

1) Because of the general introduction of 'year classes' instead of "subject-specific" classes each grammar school was forced to systematize the knowledge that was to be imparted in a certain way, and then to reflect on the experience made with the systematizations.

2) Because of the preliminary qualification demanded of them in sciences the teachers in each grammar school had to relate the scientific knowledge to the knowledge that was to be imparted in school.

3) As a result of the increasing state activity in education – understood as contradictory socialization (Vergesellschaftung) from above – each grammar school was forced to assert itself within the framework of general trends, and to account for deviations from the normal range of subjects. This resulted in an additional pressure to justify the activity of each teacher and the school programme as a whole.

4) In view of the process of differentiation within the universities according to the development of the sciences, grammar school inevitably had to change from an institution preparing for a few university courses (theology, law, medicine) to an instituion preparing for a scientific university education in a more general manner.

5) The compulsion to change content and methods of grammar schools was also obviously initiated by the developments in sciences. The 19th century grammar school clearly reflects the linguistic and literary (also, to a limited extent, the scientific) developments of this period. Even if the grammar school did not give in to the development of sciences in the same way, colloquial classifications are increasingly disappearing from the curriculum in favour of scientific ones. In natural history anthropomorphisms ("useful domestic animals", "vermin", "curious animals") give way to the classification established by Linné. Moreover, the grammar schools, particularly by the stress on "linguistic ability", functionally support scientific developments, and are therefore an instrument for the standardization of scientific knowledge.

6) The grammar schools, however, just as the sciences, were obviously subject to compulsions which were set in motion by the capitalistic mode of production. The increasing differentiation and structurization in the organization and curriculum of schools as a whole (just as of the subjects as particular fields)

corresponds, in capitalist production, to the division of the
process of production into particular components, and to the
technological organization of these processes on the basis of
applied scientific knowledge. Thus, the socialization
(Vergesellschaftung) of school carried out by the state, i.e.
'from above', is the expression of a process in society at large.
That school responds to that not only passively, but also
actively, is proved by the anticipatory principles of Neo-Humanism
named above, which provided an additional incentive. The fact that
this process was and remained bound up with the process of the
basic division of labour between manual and intellectual labour (a
division which signified, at the same time, a class division of
bourgeois society) may be criticized after the fact as the
expression of a narrow-minded bourgeois interest and awareness.
Historically, however, it is an expression of the most advanced
level of contemporary social and scientific development.

Annotation

It would be wrong to give the impression that there were mostly
curricula like those of the Stettin Grammar School among the
motley landscape of schools and curricula during the first third
of the 19th century. The extent of deviations in this period may
be shown by a curriculum placed at the other extreme as compared
to the Stettin conception of grammar school education, i.e. by one
clearly inspired by Neo-Humanist thought. The curriculum of the
Bonn grammar school (1819/1820) shows the following structure:

	I	II	III	IV	V	VI
Scripture	2		2		2	2
Latin	9	9	8	8	6	6
Greek	7	7	5	5		
German	4	4	4	4	8	8
Mathematics	5	5	5	5	6	6
Natural Philosophy/						
Natural History	2		2	2	2	2
History/						
Geography	3	3	4	4	3	3

What we see here is the new conception of grammar school education
which documented a conception of content completely novel in
historical terms. Above in this essay the range of mathematics at
the Bonn Grammar School is given; in German the classical poets
and "prose writers" were read. Nevertheless, neither this
curriculum nor the Stettin one ever had the status of a 'model'
for the development of curricula at the end of the thirties and
forties. The trend followed by this development, which became more
and more standardized, is hinted at in the 1849 syllabus of the
Bonn Royal Grammar School:

	I	II	III	IV	V	VI
Latin	8	10	10	10	10	10
Greek	6	6	6	6		
German	2	2	2	2	4	4
French	2	2	2			
Hebrew	2	2				
Scripture	2	2	2	2	2	2
Mathematics	4	4	3	3	4	4
Physics	2	1	2	2		
Natural History					2	2
History/						
Geography	2	3	2		2	2
Philosophical						
Propaedeutics	2					

The range of subjects (in 1849) has been extended as compared to
the earlier Bonn curriculum and clearly focussed as compared to
the Stettin curriculum. Mathematics has lost the importance it
still had in Bonn in 1819/1820 (probably under the influence of
France); German, too, has been reduced. French, which the
Neo-Humanists had removed from the range of subjects in an
antifeudalist impulse, has again taken its place in grammar
school.
With regard to the developments and changes in content we see that
the reduction of the number of lessons in Bonn also had
consequences for content, i.e. that problems in modern
mathematics, for instance the theory of combinations and series

(cf. p. 228 of this essay) disappeared from the curriculum. Higher
mathematics areas like spherical trigonometry and conic sections
remained, however.
The development of the curricula in Bonn grammar school at the
period under study which at first seemed so obviously influenced
by Neo-Humanist intentions, gives evidence to the consequences of
the 'Prussification' of Neo-Humanism, i.e. to its curtailment and
loss of stringency.

Literature quoted in the text

The sources used in this essay for the period before 1806 is the
material of P. Schwartz 1910 seq., taken from the files of the
"Oberschulcollegium" (1787-1806) and published in three volumes
(76. Repositorium des Geheimen Staatsarchivs in Berlin). The
material includes data on the situation of the 'Gelehrtenschulen'
in the Prussian provinces taken from inspection reports, excerpts
from teaching visits, data on graduation examinations and the
range of subjects taught, reports from the teachers on their
teaching activity in the various subjects, and on the various
books used. For the period after 1815, the school yearbooks of
three Prussian provinces were evaluated: from the Rhine province
and the provinces of Prussia and Pomerania. In view of the immense
stock of school yearbooks preserved from all Prussian provinces,
which were formerly collected by the Koenigliche Bibliothek Berlin
(each school was obliged to send in its annual yearbook) and
which are now stored - no longer catalogued - at the
"Staatsbibliothek-Stiftung   Preussischer   Kulturbesitz"   in
West-Berlin, it was necessary to select. In order to examine
schools from a politically and economically progressive Prussian
province, I have chosen the Rhine province, and, lest I omit the
historically existing backwardness, I analysed, as a contrast, the
yearbooks of the schools in Pomerania, East Prussia, and West
Prussia. (The situation of the schools cannot, however, be
schematically classified as progressive here, backward there.)
Another important source is "Das Unterrichtswesen des preussischen
Staates", a collection of statutory regulations concerning the
educational system by L.v. Roenne from 1855.

References

Furck, C.-L.:   Das unzeitgemaesse Gymnasium. Studien zur
                     Gymnasialpaedagogik, Weinheim 1965
Humboldt, W.v.:   Werke in fuenf Baenden, ed. by A. Flitner and K.
                     Giel, Darmstadt 1960ff.
Henning, F.-W.:   Die Industrialisierung in Deutschland 1800 bis
                     1914, Paderborn 1976, 3d ed.
Jachmann, R.B.:   Ueber das Verhaeltnis der Schule zur Welt,
                     Berlin 1811, Repr. in: Joerden, R. (ed.):
                     Dokumente des Neuhumanismus I, Weinheim 1962, 2d
                     ed., pp. 88ff.
Paulsen, F.:   Geschichte des gelehrten Unterrichts, 2 vols.,
                     Leipzig 1896ff., 2d ed.
Rang, A.:   Historische und gesellschaftliche Aspekte der
                     Gesamtschule, in: Zeitschrift fuer Paedagogik
                     14 (1968), pp. 1-20
Roenne, L.v.:   Das Unterrichtswesen des preussischen Staates.
                     Eine systematische Sammlung aller auf dasselbe
                     Bezug habenden gesetzlichen Bestimmungen,
                     2 vols., Berlin 1855
Schoeler, W.:   Geschichte des naturwissenschaftlichen
                     Unterrichts im 17. bis 19. Jahrhundert, Berlin
                     1970
Schwartz, P.:   Die Gelehrtenschulen Preussens unter dem
                     Oberschulkollegium (1787-1806) und das
                     Abiturientenexamen, 3 vols., Berlin 1910ff.
Wiese, L.:   Das hoehere Schulwesen in Preussen.
                     Historisch-statistische Darstellung, Berlin 1864
Wiese, L.:   Sammlungen der Verordnungen und Gesetze fuer die
                     hoeheren Schulen in Preussen, 2 vols., Berlin
                     1888, 3d ed.

Walter Langhammer

SOME ASPECTS OF THE DEVELOPMENT OF MATHEMATICS AT THE UNIVERSITY
OF HALLE-WITTENBERG IN THE EARLY 19TH CENTURY

The "Seminar fuer Mathematik und die gesamten Naturwissenschaften"
at the University of Halle-Wittenberg was one of the first to
include mathematics at a Prussian university. The following
article discusses some aspects of the early history of this
Seminar. Its interest is not in the development of mathematics
itself, but rather in understanding the concrete-historical
social, political and intellectual conditions under which
mathematicians subjectively approached the urgent issues of the
reform of the world of learning. The guiding consideration of our
discussion will be the advancement of new developments in the
institutional structure of university life. Since there is the
academic and political desire in the GDR to make use of the
history of learning as an important factor in the attempt to
attach greater relevance to integrated scholarly dialogue, such
issues are important to the level of knowledge in pertinent fields
of research.[1]

We start from the assumption that the history of institutional
structures, as one aspect of the complex phenomenon of the history
of science, will show in a particularly striking fashion how
indissoluble academic life is involved with its wider context of
socio-historical conditions. In the early nineteenth century these
conditions were characterized for the Prussian state as the most
serious enemy of bourgeois revolution and of the democratic

235

*H. N. Jahnke and M. Otte (eds.), Epistemological and Social Problems of the Sciences in the Early Nineteenth
Century, 235–254.*
Copyright © 1981 by D. Reidel Publishing Company.

unification of Germany, by a very contradictionary process of
transition from absolutism to capitalism.[2] From abroad, the
influence of the French bourgeois revolution resulted in
ideological, political and economic competition – and finally in
military confrontation. At home, the "quiet work" of the masses of
the people was not only creating demands for radical
socio-economic change. The activities of progressive political
forces, which had evolved in Prussian history as opposed to the
nobility and land-owning classes, also included socio-political
movements directed towards promoting a bourgeois social
revolution.

Although the pressure of anti-absolutist opinion after the defeat
of 1806 was insufficient to precipitate the feudal clan onto a
revolutionary course, it created sufficient scope for liberal
aristocrats and bourgeois opposition to induce an upheaval of
national dimensions.[3]

In this process, the great-power interests of Prussia concurred
partially (not excluding serious conflicts) with certain
requirements of social progress – as often before in history.
Prussia underwent rapid industrial development, owning not least
to its efficient state machinery. Economic, cultural, and
intellectual potentials were realized, and these achievements
contained the germs of future social progress. Although the
restoration of aristocracy retarded the development of capitalism,
it did not preclude the establishment of capitalist economic
relations, or the preconditions for their development. Relevant to
our purpose is the public education system, and the world of
learning, as well as the influence these had upon one another. The
world of education does not exist independent of society, it
participates in realizing conditions of production.[4] The level of
learning reflects the degree of development in the productive
sector of society, and the economic relations within which men
work, in a specifically analogous fashion, and hence also reflects
the conflicts between these two fields.[5] The world of learning,
as an element in society's intellectual culture, and as a
political means and end, is thus deeply involved in the movement
of social forces.

These correlations are apparent in long-term, fundamental processes. For our purposes, it is important to note that the absolutist university lost its importance, and that certain ideas and principles characteristic for the bourgeois university began to prevail, which simultaneously expressed intellectual needs and a changed socio-economic and political situation. Of particular relevance here were the influences of a new philosophy and theology founded on rationalism which - like "Neuhumanismus" later - had great importance for the evolution of the self-confident world-view of bourgeois society. Just as vital were the study of education, the increasing importance of mathematics and the physical sciences, and finally the implementation of all these new factors in the principles of intellectual freedom and of the primacy of research.[6]

The Friedericiana in Halle had a great influence throughout Prussia in shaping and popularising these ideas as an ideological prerequisite for the transition to the bourgeois type of university. Names such as Thomasius and Wolff are inseparably linked to the increased importance and newly-defined function of faculties of philosophy. In Halle, the foundation statutes had granted equal rights to this faculty at an early stage

These long-term developments were the basis for the change of organisation and direction of academic studies in the nineteenth century. Halle became the "first modern university", the first to be founded on the principle of "libertas philosophandum".[7] This principle of intellectual freedom was inevitably associated with a changed conception of the function of university education. This change reflected the interests of the bourgeoisie; renouncing the dogmatic tendencies of absolutist education, it grew from the belief that, "we must seek the truth; the task of education is to enable men to do that."[8]

Thus the university was to become a cradle of research, and research was to bring together teacher and student. New, co-operative relations in the process of learning were developed. These new relations were confirmed by the foundation of new Seminars, and are thus easily traceable as visible developments. Halle also took the lead in establishing these "real social structures, and in the co-operation which shaped this development".[9] F.A.Wolf, the founder of neo-humanism, created the first Seminar for (philological) science, inspired by the theological Seminar of 1769; the later Seminar for education grew from it. Its function was to train, for grammar schools, a staff of teachers freed from the tutelage of theology, and to train antiquarians for their scientific work. It is interesting that C.G.J. Jacobi, the founder of the first mathematical Seminar at Koenigsberg, had been a member of the "philologisches Seminar" at Berlin during Wolf's presence there. Jacobi owed the idea of applying his experience to the field of mathematics to his stimulating encounter with Wolf. Halle's provisions for the establishment of valuable collections, clinics, etc., permit us the assert that the modern conceptions of the university and university life has had its origin at the University of Halle at the turn to the nineteenth century.[10]

But historical events severely disturbed the life of the university before Halle could, even at home, realize its new ideas. The Napoleonic Wars and their after-effects dramatized the entire historical dimension of the conflict between two socio-economic systems, especially with regard to the role of Prussia. Among other symptoms of the lingering illness of the old order, this conflict brought the absolutist universities to their crisis and dissolution. Scope was now available for progressive forces to initiate social changes by means of reforms. Pertinent here is the foundation of the university of Berlin as a "universitas litterarum".

The university of Halle, as a testing-ground for the men and ideas which had proved themselves in the struggle against Napoleonic foreign domination, was closed in 1806, owing to the efforts of some of the professors, it was re-opened, and led a shadow existence until 1813, when Jerome ordered the final closure of the university, then in the kingdom of Westphalia. Jerome's order was, however, superseded by events.

Although Halle drew new life from the closure of other universities (J.H. Pfaff, for instance, came from Helmstedt in 1810), and was finally united with Wittenberg in 1817, these years

were a considerable setback in the consolidation of the first
stage of university reform. There were also important losses of
staff. Because of the difficult situation, Wolf, Schleiermacher,
and Schmalz went to Berlin, where they found new scope for
activity at the new foundation, and where, ultimately, resources
were concentrated. Some time elapsed before Halle could resume and
further its development.

Thus far we have discussed the general historical conditions which
were reflected in the advance of mathematics as a discipline
within the faculty of philosophy. Let us proceed to consider the
personalities who created mathematical knowledge, but also new
organisational principles during this period. Let us begin with
Georg Simon Kluegel, who was called to Halle from Helmstedt as the
successor to Christian Wolff (1695-1723 and 1740-1753) and to
Andreas Segner (1755-1777). He taught here from 1787 to 1812 and
was succeeded, as he had happened before in Helmstedt, by Johann
Heinrich Pfaff. Pfaff taught in Halle until 1825 and, along with
Gauss, was considered one of the most important German
mathematicians of this time.

Wittenberg belonged to that part of Saxony which was given to
Prussia by the Congress of Vienna. It was therefore Prussia which
united the universities of Halle and Wittenberg. This union meant
the absorption of Wittenberg by Halle. For Wittenberg this was a
result of the crisis of the absolutist unversity; for Halle, the
union performed the transition to a bourgeois university. After
1817, Halle was the first university with two tenures for
mathematics - held by Pfaff and the Wittenberg ordinary professor
Steinhaeuser. An extraordinary professorship was given to J.C.
Gartz in 1823, and two more were created for H.F. Scherk and A.
Rosenberger in 1825, after Steinhaeuser and Pfaff had died. Scherk
came from Koenigsberg, was professor from 1832 to 1835, and
continued his career at Kiel. Rosenberger was professor from 1831
to 1879. Scherk's successor, Pluecker, was succeeded as early as
1835 by Ludwig Adolf Sohnke, who had been one of Jacobi's
disciples and colleagues at Koenigsberg. He taught at Halle until
1853. Among those students who later achieved academic or
administrative distinction were E.E. Kummer (whom Scherk had drawn
to mathematics), Moebius, Grunert, Gerling, Mollweide, Dirksen and

Carl   Neumann. Furthermore Kaemtz and Gartz, who became professors
at   Halle   and Schellbach, who later became well known because of
his   work in creating the 'Physikalisch-technische Reichsanstalt'
and his efforts to create a 'Lehrerseminar'.

In   the   following the aforementioned developmental trends will be
examined in order to study the effectiveness of the Halle
mathematicians. Special consideration will be given to changes in
the   organisational structure of their department, and to changes
in   the   content of its discipline, as far as they are documented
and   accessible. The objective is to understand which social and
intellectual conditions were subjectively considered important
enough to lead the mathematicians of the day to a new evaluation
of   the role of the university and to initiate relevant changes in
its structure, and to study the social and intellectual conditions
which influenced the results of their activities.

Let us begin with some aspects of the work of Pfaff, the most
eminent Halle mathematician of that time. In contrast to his
disciple Gauss, Pfaff can be considered, in Felix Klein's words,
as "typical of the nineteenth century". Pfaff combined teaching
with research, thus himself exemplifying a transformation in the
character of university teaching. He often lectured before large
audiences, clearly, without prepared text or regard for obsolete
conventions. His academic work was of high calibre. But Pfaff
shows that the struggle for a new kind of academic education was
not yet over, although his work prepared for its resolution. His
correspondence shows him involved in the contemporary intellectual
debate over the liberalization of traditional teaching work and
methods. His friend Bredow confided to him some reservations with
respect ·to the realization of libertas philosophandi in a
sceptical account of the teaching at the new Berlin university:
"Some talk like a book - very learnedly, full of new opinions and
general ideas. But is this, by itself, what university lectures
are for?"[11] Mathematics expressed this radical change in a
specific fashion, visible in the growth of "pure mathematics" - a
pattern of thought and academic orientation appropriate to the
time. Pfaff's disciple Gerling reported from Goettingen, clearly
describing a diametrical opposite to the more modern form of
discourse, saying that Thibaut "speaks from the rostrum, almost as

Goethe writes, and demonstrates proofs by forms of reasoning, which might better be described as prose periods." He declared that this "could do more harm than good to a clear survey and illuminating understanding of his subject."[12] But different ideals were striven for not only with regard to the form of lectures. Pfaff also had to argue against some very different opinions about the possibility of teaching modern analysis. Kaestner wrote to him: "France is famed, in the pages of the Journal, for the learned institution where LaGrange teaches; it is said that the students arrive there with such knowledge that they start where students at German universities leave off. Now that is a stiff breeze of French republicanism, more disturbing than their royalism. French teaching in the rudiments of mathematics is much poorer than at any German university, and certainly produces nobody who could listen to LaGrange with profit. It is particularly ridiculous to listen to someone one ought to read – and that is what those Germans who have learnt the rudiments do by themselves, if they have the time and inclination."[13]
Kaestner went as far as to spurn "Mécanique analytique", now appreciated as a "triumph of pure analysis"[14]:"The useful in it has long been known – but here it is incomprehensibly dressed up in mere abstract expressions."[15]

Pfaff seemed to disagree. Even though the Halle lecture lists indicate the use of traditional literature where his teaching is concerned, he nonetheless attempted to bring the results of new research into discussion by other means. He organized an academic reading circle to follow contemporary scholarly literature in the company of his colleagues. He saw to it that the university library was made more accessible to students. Bearing in mind the restrictions of the time, these are no mean achievements.

From his own experience, Pfaff knew and deplored the gulf between staff and students which so inhibited the academic development of the young. He was interested in ways of teaching which would permit this gap to be reduced. He questioned Gerling closely about the practice at Goettingen, and asked, "what happens in the practice-lessons which Thibaut advertises? Does he sometimes hold a mathematical Disputatorium, and what is it like?"[16]

Pfaff, however, never achieved a solution. The time of innovation, of attempts at reform, began with Pfaff and Steinhaeuser's successors. Gartz had printed textbook-like explanations to his lectures, not only "to be rid of the nuisance of dictation", but also to give "clear and modern explanations suitable to the spirit of the new mathematics."[17] In fact, these textbooks meant a step forward in the evolution of "pure mathematics", as compared to the books Pfaff was still using; they also signal an advance of the principle of intellectual freedom. Gartz' contributions to the Halle Encyclopedia show that he quickly had appropriated Cauchy's new findings on the foundation of infinitesimal calculus, and certainly introduced these into his teaching too.

Scherk, the only Halle mathematician to publish in the first issues of Crelle's Journal (Vols. 3, 4, 9, 10, 11), was also important in another way. He achieved greater renown for his teaching than Gartz, and was able, from 1826, to announce a "mathematical society" in the lecture list and successfully organize its activities for many years. This society had the status of a private tuition group (or Seminar), and was run with the collaboration of Rosenberger, so that this "society" can be described as an immediate precursor of the later 'Mathematisches Seminar'.

Schweigger, too, alluded to the substantial tradition of the group's academic work, writing on this matter to the Dean of the faculty of philosophy in 1838: "I am quite certain that much thorough work has been done in Professor Scherk's mathematics tuition group."[18] Towards the end of the twenties such groups arose in almost every subject of the sciences. Particular mention may be made of Schweigger's society for physics and chemistry, about whose work ample evidence has survived.[19] Among its participants were, for instance, Wilhelm Weber, and H. Hankel, who was later to be Professor at Halle.

Along with such substantial social development in the intellectual process, the need for appropriate materials and apparatus grew. But no less important was the need for a recognized status for such new forms of teaching and research activity. These needs were finally met by the foundation of the "Seminar fuer die Mathematik und die gesamten Naturwissenschaften". The real impulse for this

foundation came from outside, from L.A. Sohnke, who had drafted
the statutes of the Seminar at Koenigsberg together with Jacobi,
and who shortly afterwards accepted a call to Halle.

The circumstances of the foundation of this Seminar merit more
detailed considerations, when we bear in mind the social
conditions of the development of learning in early nineteenth
century Prussia, and the interrelationships between school,
university, and the requirements of education at that time. Among
the conditions of the early nineteenth century, whose gradually
growing awareness prompted academics to found Seminars for
mathematics and for the physical sciences, two groups of factors
seem to be of particular importance:
a) There was a growth of professional specialization, and with it
a growing internal differentiation in the disciplinary
organization of faculties of philosophy. The growth corresponded
to the scope of academic work in this area, to the accumulation of
the results of research, and the maturation of specialized
processes which had to be mastered in order to ensure success in
the ever deeper and more complicated learning process. This
development demanded new kinds of cooperation in research, a new
step forward in the socialization of education, and also new
viewpoints on the transmission of knowledge. The training of
academically competent students who could participate in the
completion of ever more complex programmes of work demanded that
their training in methodology starts earlier, and continues
longer, and also that students contribute to the initiation of
research. As it is demonstrated by our example, this cognitive
aspect of the growth of institutional structures in academic
life[20] is also very important as it shows a fundamental desire to
create new opportunities of achieving academic distinction (or of
securing a certain standing).
b) The dominance of the self-generating technology of the
Industrial Revolution - the new aspect of constructive work -
demanded more widely scientifically and mathematically trained
specialists. From this need grew requirements asked of the entire
educational system, first of all of the grammar schools whose
task was understood to be "the education of the leading classes of
the people by means of a preparatory scientific education which
will be oriented towards the academic teaching of higher

education."[21] In accordance with this demand, not only scientifically but also pedagogically competent teachers were required.
This double requirement made the desires which grew from intellectual conditions socially relevant, and thus justifiable. At this point men's subjective desire can be reconciled with objective intellectual and socio-political necessities; as the reformers attacked the Prussian state, the state replied with selective political measures.

The resulting demands did express the interest of the forces bound up with industrial development, as is shown by A. v. Humboldt's earlier remarks to his teacher Pfaff.[22]

In Halle there were, at the beginning of the nineteenth century, constant efforts to achieve progress in the study of education. Here again it is worth to recall the Seminar for theology and pedagogy and the department of education which grew from it. Later a "training school for teachers" was planned under the leadership of Niemeyer in connection with this department and with the extensive establishments of the Francke'sche Stiftungen, where about seventy teachers were permanently employed. Surviving study plans show that an orientation towards the study of education may be seen as an aspect of the 'Zeitgeist', for which the idea of the Seminar played a leading part. The Seminar was to be "partly a means of education and preparatory practice for that which students, matured at the university, will be doing in their professions immediately after leaving university, and partly the means to accustom them to working and thinking of their own – a thing from which simply listening to university lectures so easily distracts."[23]

The faculty of philosophy did have the idea and experience which were in favour of a reform of study courses appropriate to the time. Sohnke, however, who had just published a study on elliptical functions (Crelle-Journal, vol. 16, 1837), was the first, together with the physicist Kaemtz, to advance the proposal to institutionalize substantial reforms by means of establishing a Seminar for mathematics and physics They presented draft statutes to Kurator Delbrueck for the first time on October 29th, 1836.

Their   reasons   for this step, and the draft itself, were oriented
towards the requirements of the "Hoeheres Lehramt". As compared to
the new regulations authorized for Koenigsberg in 1834[24], which
mentioned no specific new pedagogical goals, they represent a
change of emphasis. Kaemtz and Sohnke had observed that many
candidates for teaching posts in mathematics and physics applied
without having completed adequate studies, in the hope of
obtaining an early appointment. Others had completed their
studies, but had never expressed their ideas and knowledge orally
or in written form. Both these facts were leading to widespread
incompetence, with detrimental effects on students and on the
discipline. The goal according to Sohnke and Kaemtz, was that
tasks be not only solved, but solved elegantly, that digressions,
long-windedness and incompetence in teaching be eliminated. The
Seminar was to give poor students practice in mathematical
precision as well as in physics experiments, and at the same time
to encourage better students in productive work.

Thus, the claims raised for the Seminar were the following: "The
Seminar's objective is twofold: 1) to train the students in free
discourse on matters of mathematics and physics, 2) to stimulate
their own activity [Selbsttaetigkeit] concerning private studies
and experiments."[25]
Kaemtz' and Sohnke's draft statutes went so far as to require that
none of those who had studied for some time in Halle be admitted
to examinations without having been a member of the Seminar. But
they also expected the proposal to arouse opposition: they were
the only staff members provided for in the proposal, despite the
fact that other professors of mathematics and physics taught in
Halle as well. Kaemtz and Sohnke defended their position for a
considerable time with some obstinacy, with favorable consequences
for posterity, as their contemporaries, as scholars, were
compelled to state their own views. In investigating their
opinions we come a little nearer to a "history of everyday
life"[26] . The ministry's first response was in favor of the
foundation of the Seminar. The proposal, however, met with further
opposition before reaching a form acceptable to all parties. Here
Schweigger played the most important part. He was the first to
propose a Seminar for mathematics and all physical sciences to
include every professor. This Seminar was then to be devided into

appropriate departments. Schweigger evolved his conception of the
Seminar's work from the experiences of his journeys to England,
and from comparisons with other German universities. His principal
idea concerned the introduction of reform, with consideration for
the traditions of intellectual life. At German universities, he
missed "a connecting link between professors and students", while
in Oxford or Cambridge, "where the old system still holds sway",
and "is said to be satisfactory", with the institution of the
tutorial assistent, "who goes through those classical works with a
student, which this one has read in the course of the day".[27]
Schweigger desired to revive the system of tutorial assistents
("Repetenten"), with the intention that "young trainee
schoolteachers who have passed their exams in mathematical or
scientific subjects should join the Seminar as tutors, while
carrying out their year of probation at one of the local
schools [28] - but without pay. This inclusion of trainee teachers
was defended by Schweigger for reasons of sociology of science:
the increase in student numbers made the few professors unable to
pay sufficient attention to the private work of the students.
Finally, he also argued to those in power that an expansion of the
sciences, of academic life, would strike a blow against
"unscientific circles". This politically conceived notion should
have appealed to the taste of the ministry, which indeed, as
Koch's "Sammlung von Verordnungen ..." shows, was meticulously
bent on bearing upon progressive movements in favor of the 'raison
d'etat'.
Schweigger's plan obtained the support of the Seminar, and was
passed on with the additional comment that other institutions,
such as Bonn, already possessed Seminars for the physical
sciences, and were, for this reason, held high in public esteem,
so that grammar schools recommended their university candidates in
the sciences to study there.[29]

Here it is evident that, during Altenstein's time, educational
policy (in the sense as one can speak of such a thing at this
stage) largely consisted of realizing the narrow political
interests of the state, and not (as was evident earlier in France,
and had to be accepted as a challenge by Prussia) in planning and
inplementing changes "from above" in a general and uniform
fashion. The consequences of a general development of progressive

doctrines continually endangered the balance of political powers in Prussia. This also brought about an ambivalence in Prussian policy with regard to the development of learning. During the time in question, the universities were to a large degree treated as autonomous entities as far as their academic development was concerned, but their life was controlled by criteria of political interest, and their activities were selected according to similar standards. Here inspiration, interests and efforts displayed by the immediate representatives of the movement "from below" were brought into play and used, provided they were acceptable to the state of Prussia. These interests obviously did not originate purely in intellectual conditions, but were stimulated by feelings of rivalry. This did not only occur in the debate about the role of the university. Kaemtz and Sohnke had to appear willing to compromise, if only where their desires as regards teacher training were concerned. We may suppose that both expected improvements from the Seminar in their own area of work. It is apparent that Sohnke, influenced by Jacobi (like Jacobi, he had given his work on elliptical functions as the first "modern lecture" in Halle) pleaded strongly for the concept of specialized "pure mathematics", and wanted to distinguish himself from some conservative trends of thought among his colleagues. To reach an agreement, the Halle scientists proposed statutes similar to those of the Koenigsberg Seminar of Science, with the result that mechanics and their mathematical basis were not sufficiently represented in the training of teachers for the grammar schools and the "Buergerschulen" - as Schweigger commented.[30]

Finally an agreement was reached in which Kaemtz and Sohnke saw a guarantee of their independence. On the strength of this, the faculty applied to the Ministry with the hope that a university institute would supplant the private institutions which then dealt with practical and theoretical training. They added that "sufficient justification of this desire is provided by the growing requirements which the progress and broadening of the physical sciences are now placing upon the universities, and by the advantages for the study of the sciences which can be expected from a formal unification of the means and staff which are available here."[31] The proposal was endorsed by von Altenstein, with miner alterations, as a "provisional regulation", in the form quoted by Koch.[32] This regulation exhibits many characteristics of contemporary progressive thought: §1) Firstly, it is explicitly designed for the training of teachers. 1 mentions: "The purpose of the Seminar ... is to offer an introduction to private study, and to lectures in the sciences mentioned, with special regard to the training of teachers for grammar schools and higher Buergerschulen. Teachers should be able to contribute not only to the dissemination of knowldge, but also to its growth."[33] Finally, in §6, teachers already working in schools were admitted as members of the Seminar, or as tutors. §13 attempted to further the interests of the Seminar by means of granting certain material privileges, which were to have a direct effect upon studies. These concerned a relaxation of the regulations concerning the use of the library, and the inclusion of extensive work in the Seminar (including practical teaching) in a year of probation for student teachers.

2) Nonetheless the regulation expressed a tendency typical of nineteenth century Prussia in emphasizing the requirement of competence for indepedent scientific work asked of teachers qualified for secondary education. (cf. §1, but also §§8-10, where there is less emphasis on the practice of teaching than upon academic achievement).

3) The Seminar created an institutional status of equal rank for the substantially independent sub-seminars, corresponding to the tendency towards, and the need for, specialization which was accomplished in the early nineteenth century.

4) According §6.2 admittance to the Seminar is to be granted to "all those who are simply registered at the faculty of philosphy for the study of a special mathematical or scientific subject, all those who have graduated from Realgymnasien or Gewerbeschulen with good results belonging among them."[34] This measure conforms closely with the interests of the bourgeoisie.

Unfortunately, the "registers of the participants of the Seminar" have not yet been discovered. This volume was to provide a survey of their progress according to the reports of their supervisors. Only the annual reports of the directors of the Seminar offer material by which the work of the Seminar may be evaluated. These reports, however, show that the plans executed up to then were one thing, and reality another. And it is reality which must be examined as far as possible, if we are to escape a distorted picture of the developmental problems of this later successful institution.

The reports of the Seminar directors show a significant contradiction between the plans of the faculty and the real social situation. They clarify the real problems of institutional change in relation to the social and intellectual conditions necessary for success. These difficulties are differnt from the matters discussed in the surviving correspondence of those concerned with the foundation of the Seminar.

Rosenbergers report of 1843 shows that the number of participants in the Seminar was unsatisfactory - and even decreasing. In the fourth and fifth semester of the Seminar's existence, the mathematicians had participants for the first time (Sohnke 16, Rosenberger 13). In the physical sciences the situation was a little better.

The then directors found themselves forced to study ways to clarify and improve the situation, and relevant proposals were addressed to the Ministry. In his first report already (1840), Schweigger had elaborated interesting ideas. He stated that a "Buerger-Institut fuer angewandte Naturwissenschaften", a "Technischer Lesezirkel" and a "Polytechnische Buergergesell-schaft" under the supervision of school-teachers were working in Halle under quite unsatisfactory external conditions.[35] These societies aimed to disseminate practical, technical, and scientific knowledge. Schweigger proposed to unite the facilities of the Seminar with the efforts of these societies, and, for instance, to have members of the Seminar offer lectures. He drew his ideas from a discussion of Liebig's paper "On the Study of Science and the State of Chemistry in Prussia". He demanded "the dissemination of the sciences among the people", and the creation of something similar "to the Royal Institutions", institutes of applied science which he recognized as "intellectual centres of trade and industry in England".[36]

Schweigger's general conclusion was that it was up to mathematics and science teachers, and to secondary and vocational schools, to start and supervise such institutions everywhere. Membership of the Seminar was also ment to be preparation for this task. Parallel to this, it was proposed that the Seminar would also accept secondary school graduates in order to provide these with a formal qualification. This proposal was declined by Berlin, with referral to examination regulations. The Ministry, writing to the Kurator on the 29th of September, 1841, decreed that "lectures by members of the Seminar in front of mixed audiences were to be discontinued, because they were not provided for in the regulations."[37] This decree was certainly no chance expression of Prussian bureaucratic logic, but prompted by the political intention of preventing students from associating with the organized bourgeoisie. It is seen that Prussian policy could not infinitely promote the progressive forces of science.

Rosenberger's 1843 report also described other restrictions, which stress the social conditions necessary for the successful reorganization of academic life. It mentions, statistically, that a total of thirty-three students had enrolled with the Seminar between 1839 and 1843 and a total of one hundred and eleven with the individual sub-Seminars. Other students had certainly taken part in the work of the Seminar without formal enrolment. In 1843, six students, and among them one mathematician, had successfully passed the teacher's exam. The number of registered students, however, exceeded the numer of submitted papers and research reports.

Rosenbergers report mentions more problems then results, and attempts to analyse the reasons for the doubtlessly disappointing performance of the Seminar. Rosenberger alleges that a gulf had widened between teaching staff and students, and that the lectures of even popular teachers could not be begun because of the lack of audience. Indeed he goes on to say that the students assiduously avoided all exertion, but he tries to give reasons for this, too. Many Halle students, and especially those in the faculty of philosophy who were studying to become teachers, suffered from severe lack of funds. They were forced, at an early stage, to give badly paid additional lessons, privately or in schools, and were thus kept from their studies. This was the source of the Seminar's low reputation, which contributed to the lamentable situation. "Nothing discourages enrolment more than the inability of this institute to offer its students much material encouragement, while every comparison [this remark relates to the financial support given to the Seminars of theology and education] shows that certain expectations are associated with the name of Seminar."

These expectations doubtless arose in the first terms and contributed to a lively participation in the Seminar's work, which has since then noticeably declined, because the hope that the institute could offer material advantages of any kind had to be given up. In the course of the years 1840, 1841, and 1842, seventeen, thirteen, and three regular students were enrolled, respectively, but there has not been a single student since November 1842.[38] Rosenberger applied to the Ministry to grant free board solely to enrolled students, and to have a subsidy-fund of 100 thalers placed at his disposal. Only the latter request was conceded - after much correspondence. So altogether it must be said that little was done for this aspect of the social welfare of the growth of learning. This is the reverse side of the Prussian state setting aside two thirds of its revenue for military expenditures.

So Rosenberger's report did not meet with sympathetic readers. The recently appointed reactionary Kurator Pernice sent it to Eichhorn in Berlin, together with a commentary, doubting Rosenberger's powers of judgement, and discrediting his comments as a regrettable expression of the "materialism of the age".[39] Obviously, it must be noted that there were other reasons, apart from these social causes, for the unsatisfactory results of these efforts on behalf of the Seminar. The success of Jacobi's Koenigsberg Seminar, which worked under certain comparable conditions, is an indication for that. Here, the role of intellecutal conditions emerges, and that of the context of solutions to problems of institutional organisation.

Jacobi's Seminar, as we have said, was not devoted specifically to the training of teachers. Moreover, it was founded to encourage the work of talented people. As described by Lorey[40], the complete teaching programme in Koenigsberg was designed with Jacobi in mind. The first terms were run as a preparation for work under him, for his modern lectures which expounded the most recent results of research, and for work in the seminar. The chance to work in the Seminar was a distinction which could be won by achievement. Jacobi's concept of academic life was certainly broad, strong, and attractive enough to permit team-work with adequately prepared students. The situaton in Halle can scarcely be compared with this. Sohnke stood virtually alone. His academic reputation in the context of his environment was perhaps insufficiently distinguished to encourage an atmosphere similar to that in Koenigsberg. The transplantation of organisational structure alone thus will not reproduce their specific intellectual conditions.

Obviously, the following years produced an ever better understanding as to how the existing institution could be used in appropriate ways. The work of the Seminar stabilized towards the middle of the nineteenth century. Sohnke, in his 1849 report, was able to state that fifty-four students had enrolled in the past four years. The majority had participated actively, and trainee teachers had studied in the Seminar every discipline of practical value - and among these, mathematics.

So far the example of the Halle Seminar (which later became famous for the activities of Georg Cantor) at least shows, that a "history of events" is inadequate to describe Prussian policy of science or to understand the complicated process of mediation of social and cognitive aspects of institutional structures within the learning process.

References

1 Cf. Mocek, R.: Aktuelle Probleme der Wissenschaftsgeschichte, Wiss. Beitr. d. Martin-Luther-Universitaet Halle-Wittenberg, (A 48), Halle 1979, p. 1.

2 Cf. Engels, F.: Marx und die 'Neue Rheinische Zeitung' 1848-1849, in: Marx/Engels: Werke, Vol. 21, p. 20.

3 Cf. Bartel, H., Mittenzwei, I., Schmidt, W.: Preussen und die deutsche Geschichte, in: Einheit 6 (1979), pp. 637ff.

4 Cf. Mocek, R.: Thesen zu einer Theorie der Wissenschaftsgeschichte, in: Arbeitsblaetter zur Wissenschaftsgeschichte, N. 1, Martin-Luther-Universitaet Halle-Wittenberg 1977, pp. 24ff.

5 Bykov, V.V.: Der konkret-historische Charakter der Verbindung der Wissenschaft mit der Produktion, in: Wissenschaft als Produktivkraft, Berlin 1974, pp. 78ff.

6 Very interestingly elaborated material in: Geschichte der Martin-Luther-Universitaet Halle-Wittenberg 1502 - 1977;

Abriss.   Wiss.   Beitr.   d.   Martin-Luther-Universitaet
Halle-Wittenberg, 3 (Pt 13), Halle 1977, Chap. 5, 6.

7 Paulsen, F.: Die deutschen Universitaeten und das
Universitaetsstudium, Berlin 1902, p. 55.

8 Ibid, p. 56.

9 Boos, B., Franke, B., Otte, M.: Gesetzmaessigkeit in der
Entwicklung mathematischer Taetigkeit, in: Hegel-Jahrbuch 1972,
Meisenheim a. Glan 1972, p. 50.

10 Geschichte der Martin-Luther-Universitaet (ref. 6), p. 52.

11 Pfaff, C. (ed.): Sammlung von Briefen, gewechselt zwischen
Johann Friedrich Pfaff und Herzog Carl v. Wuerttemberg,
F. Bouterwek, A.v. Humboldt, A.G. Kaestner und anderen, Leipzig
1853, p. 263, Bredow to Pfaff, 15.4.1809.

12 Ibid., p. 275, Gerling to Pfaff, 21.10.1810.

13 Ibid., p. 218, Kaestner to Pfaff, 28.04.1797.

14 Struik, D.J.: Abriss der Geschichte der Mathematik, Berlin
1972, p. 142.

15 Pfaff, Sammlung (ref. 11), p. 222, Kaestner to Pfaff,
30.09.1798.

16 Ibid., p. 270, Pfaff to Gerling, 24.09.1810.

17 Gartz, J.C.: Allgemeine Groessenlehre, Halle 1820, preface,
p. iii.

18 Zentrales Staatsarchiv, Dienststelle Merseburg, Ministerium
der geistlichen-, Unterrichts- und Medizinalangelegenheiten.
Geistliche und Unterrichts-Abteilung, Rep. 76 V a, Sekt 8, Tit. X,
36, Vol. 1, p. 53.

19 Cf. ibid., pp. 55-57, report by Schweigger for the year 1838.

20 Cf. also Jachiel who states: "Moreover, the
institutionalization of intellectual activities is primary, in
that individual social or professional institutionalization is
only one condition (though a necessary one) for the realization of
the process of academic recognition, and therefore also for
intellectual institutionalization in knowledge itself". Jachiel,
N.: Soziologie und Wissenschaft, Koeln 1978, p. 214.

21 Paulsen, Universitaeten (ref. 7), p. 545.

22 Pfaff, Sammlung (ref. 11) p. 232f., A. v. Humboldt to Pfaff,
11.05.1789.

23 Zentrales Staatsarchiv, Dienststelle Merseburg
Rep. 76 V a, Sekt. 8, Tit. VII, 4., Anleitung fuer angehende
Theologen ..., Halle 1825.

24 Koch, J.F.W.: Die Preussischen Universitaeten. Eine Sammlung
von Verordnungen ..., vol. II, pp. 858f.

25 Zentrales Staatsarchiv, Dienststelle Merseburg, Rep. 76 V a,
Sekt. 8, Tit. X, 36. Vol. I, p. 74.

26 Cf. the ideas of J. Kuczynski in: Prolegomena zu einer
Geschichte des Alltags des deutschen Volkes, in: Spectrum (1980),
no. 1, pp. 6-10.

27 Zentrales Staatsarchiv (ref. 18), pp. 43f.

28 Ibid., p. 45.

29 Ibid., p. 35, letter from the faculty of philosophy to the
ministry, 16.02.1838.

30 Ibid., pp. 50f.

31 Ibid., p. 30, letter to the ministry, 30.07.1839.

32 Koch, Universitaeten (ref. 24), pp. 839f

33 Ibid.

34 Ibid.

35 Zentrales Staatsarchiv, Dienststelle Merseburg, Rep. 76 V a,
Sekt. 8, Tit. X, 36, Vol. I, p. 97f.

36 Ibid., p. 101.

37 Ibid., p. 120.

38 Ibid., p. 136.

39 Ibid., p. 150ff.

40 Cf. Lorey, W.: Das Studium der Mathematik an den deutschen
Universitaeten seit Anfang des 19. Jahrhunderts, in: Klein, F.
(ed.): Abhandlungen ueber den mathematischen Unterricht, vol. II,
no. 9., Berlin, Leipzig 1916, pp. 68ff.

41 Zentrales Staatsarchiv (ref. 18), pp. 175ff.

Albert C. Lewis

JUSTUS GRASSMANN'S SCHOOL PROGRAMS AS MATHEMATICAL ANTECEDENTS OF
HERMANN GRASSMANN'S 1844 'AUSDEHNUNGSLEHRE'

The following three examples show the growth of certain
mathematical ideas from one mathematical generation to the next
(in this case, literally from father to son) as they were
published first in the school texts and programs of Justus
Grassmann between 1817 and 1829 and then, beginning in 1839, in
the books and journal papers of Hermann Grassmann.

Justus Grassmann (1779–1852) taught at the Stettin gymnasium from
1806 until 1852 when his son, Hermann (1809–1877), succeeded him
as head of mathematics. In spite of efforts to achieve a
university position Hermann remained, like his father, a
school-teacher. Nevertheless, Hermann's work, in particular the
Ausdehnungslehre of 1844 [1844] and its rewriting of 1861, has had
a substantial influence in mathematics and has continued to
interest mathematicians. On the one hand, the Ausdehnungslehre
appears to have been far in advance of its time in a number of
respects, but, on the other, many of its basic ideas had already
appeared in the rather obscure school writings of his father.

1. Hermann's notion of nth-step extension of linear vector space,
including the notions of linear independence and basis, correspond
to Justus' geometrical combinatorics used in his crystallographic
representation scheme.

H. N. Jahnke and M. Otte (eds.), Epistemological and Social Problems of the Sciences in the Early Nineteenth
Century, 255–267.

2. Outer multiplication in Hermann's [1844] corresponds to Justus'
geometric multiplication with the seminal difference that Hermann
introduces anti-commutativity.

3. Hermann implies in [1844] that the presentation of mathematics
- whether in its teaching or in presenting new mathematical
creations - is an intimate part of the development of mathematics
itself and, thus, that part of the justification for mathematics
as scientific comes from attention to its method of presentation.
From this it follows that mathematics depends on personal,
particular, communication whereby the reader (or learner) is
allowed to have the same vantage point over the mathematical
development as the author (or teacher). Such ideas, in a less
well-developed form, can be found in Justus' writings. Following
are some of the texts upon which these comparisons are founded.

1. The Linear Vector-Space Idea

Justus' 184-page Geometrische Combinationslehre [1829] is the
first and only part published of a periodical intended to provide
greater clarity and better arrangement of the elements of
elementary mathematics, including educational methodology only to
the extent that it is related to this goal. This first part seeks
to investigate how such a treatment of mathematics could affect
the sciences ("Naturkunde"). Justus admits his pedagogical style
of presentation is not the best to make scientists aware of the
work and later he published in a scientific journal a version,
[1836], consisting only of the essential elements which,
presumably, would stand the most chance of appealing to
crystallographers.

In [1829] we consider three mutually perpendicular lines, called
axes, intersecting at a point O in space. Each line determines the
family of parallel planes perpendicular to the line, and the six
planes, two on each line, equidistant from O determine a cube.
Thus, from O, the point of symmetry of the cube, emanate six
normals to the faces of the cube called rays; let b, c, d, denote
three mutually perpendicular rays normal to three faces and b',
c', d' the rays normal to the opposite faces respectively. Figure
1 shows the plane section containing the two rays b and c.

A combination of two rays is defined to be the diagonal of the parallelogram formed by them; three rays give the diagonal of the parallelepiped. Opposite rays, such as b and b', are not allowed in a combination. If all permissible combinations in pairs without repetition of the six rays are made there are then 12 diagonals – one perpendicular to each of the 12 edges of the cube. These are then regarded as rays normal to 12 new planes at their endpoints. These planes determine a rhombic dodecahedron each face of which contains an edge of the cube (see Figure 2). This crystal form therefore corresponds to the results of binary combination without repetition. Ternary combinations without repetition, bcd, b'cd, b'c'd, ... give the eight rays to the vertices of the cube and determine an octahedron.

If repetition of letters is allowed, e.g., bb written as b^2, this coressponds to an integral multiple of – in the case of b^2, double – the length of the ray and if this is introduced into combinations, as in b^2cd^3m the exponents then show the multiples of each component that go to make up the resulting ray. Given a regular pattern for generating all the unary, binay, and ternary combinations, $b^\beta c^\gamma d^\delta$, of b, c, d, b', c', d', these letters can be dropped and the exponents $\beta\gamma\delta$ considered on their own as the determining factor in creating combinations. The exponents together with the accents denoting the negative, then become, in effect, coordinates (Justus calls them "Coefficienten") based on the rays b, c, d.

Hermann in [1839] rewrote Justus' [1829] and gave more succinctly and clearly the vector space aspect of this use of exponents. He pointed out that b, c, d, expressed in terms of the exponents in the combination b c d become 100, 010, 001 respectively, and that in this representation each other ray is thus a combination of integral multiples of these three original rays if exponents on b', c', d' are accented and treated as negative numbers. Hermann illustrates the manner of joining combinations by stating that the "mean" ray "between" 531 and 42'1 is 912 since 9 = 5+4, 1 = 3+2', and 2 = 1 + 1. In one section he points out without proof that three and only three independent rays are required to determine a crystal form; also, that any three mutually independent rays can be used to determine a crystal form since each of the three

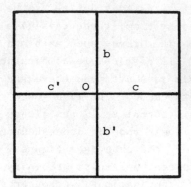

FIGURE   1

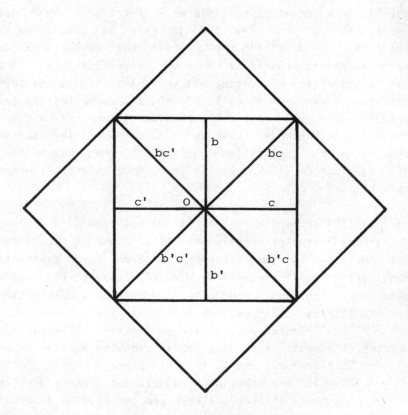

FIGURE   2

original rays can be expressed as a linear combination of them.
Though here in lattice form, these are basic linear algebraic
notions which appear again in his [1844] and [1861].

2. Outer Multiplicaton

By analogy with arithmetic Justus in a footnote to his Raumlehre
[1824, p. 194-5] defines a geometric multiplication:
"Das Rechteck ist eigentlich selbst das wahre geometrische
Produkt, und die Construktion desselben, wie sie §53 gezeigt ist,
die eigentlich geometrische Multiplikation. Nimmt man den Begriff
des Produkts naemlich in seiner reinsten und allgemeinsten
Bedeutung, so bezeichnet er das Ergebniss einer Construktion,
welches aus einem schon Erzeugten (Construirten) auf gleiche Weise
hervorgeht, als dieses Erzeugte aus dem urspruenglich Erzeugenden,
und die Multiplikation ist so nur eine Construktion in einer
hoehern Potenz In der Geometrie ist der Punkt das urspruenglich
Erzeugende; aus ihm geht durch jene Construktion die Linie hervor.
Machen wir die begrenzte Linie (als das durch die erste
Construktion Erzeugte) zur Grundlage einer neuen Construction,
indem wir sie auf gleiche Weise behandeln, wie vorher den Punkt,
so entsteht das Rechteck. Das Rechteck entsteht also aus der Linie
eben so, wie die Linie aus dem Punkte entstand.
So verhaelt es sich nun auch in der Zahlenlehre. Hier ist das
urspruenglich Erzeugende die Einheit, welche in Hinsicht auf die
Zahl als schlechthin gegeben angesehen werden muss. Aus dieser
geht durch das Zaehlen (die arithmetische Construktion) die Zahl
hervor. Macht man diese nunmehr gebildete Zahl zur Grundlage eines
neuen Zaehlens, indem man sie an die Stelle der Einheit setzt, so
erhaelt man die arithmetische Verbindung zur Multiplikation,
welche also nichts anders ist, als eine Zahl auf hoeherer Stufe,
eine Zahl, deren Einheit auch eine Zahl ist. So koennte man etwa
sagen, das Rechteck sei eine (begr.) Linie, bei der an die Stelle
des erzeugende Punkts auch eine (begr.) Linie getreten sei."

["It is essentially the rectangle itself that is the true
geometric product and its construction, as given in §53, the true
geometric multiplication. In its purest and most general meaning
the concept of product refers to a result of a construction, which

comes in the same way from something already generated or constructed, as the latter was generated from the original generator; thus multiplication is only a construction of a higher power. In geometry the point is the original generator, from it by means of that construction comes the line. If we make the bounded line (as that which is generated by the first construction) the basis of a new construction, which we perform in the same way as before for the point, then the rectangle is formed. The rectangle is therefore formed from the line in the same way as the line was formed from the point.

The same relation holds in arithmetic. Here the original generator is the unit which for the number must be regarded simply as given. From this through counting (the arithmetic construction) the number results. If the number thus produced is made the basis for a new counting by putting it in place of the unit then the arithmetic contact to multiplication is made, which is therefore nothing other than a number of higher step, a number whose unit is also a number. It could thus perhaps be said that the rectangle is a (bounded) line in which the place of the generating point is taken by a (bounded) line."]

This passage can be compared with the following from [1844, p. 80–81]:
"Die Art dieser Erzeugung ergiebt sich sogleich analog der Art, wie aus dem Elemente die Ausdehnung erste Stufe erzeugt wurde, indem man nun auf gleiche Weise die saemtlichen Elemente einer Strecke wiederum einer andern Erzeugung unterwerfen kann; und zwar fordert die Einfachheit der neu zur erzeugenden Groesse die Gleichheit der Erzeugungsweise fuer alle Elemente, das heisst dass alle Elemente jener Strecke a eine gleiche Strecke b beschreiben. Die eine Strecke a erscheint hier als die erzeugende, die andere b als das Mass der Erzeugung. Und das Ergebnis der Erzeugung ist, wenn a und b ungleichartig sind, ein Theil des durch a und b bestimmten Systemes zweiter Stufe, muss also als Ausdehnung zweiter Stufe aufgefasst werden."

["The mode of generation is immediately provided analogously to the way the extension of first step was produced from the element since in the same way the totality of elements of a stroke can be subjected again to another generation. Furthermore, the simplicity

of the newly to be generated magnitudes requires the equality of
the mode of generation for all elements; i.e., that all elements
of that stroke a describe an equal stroke b. The one stroke a
appears here as the generator, the other b as the measure of
generation, and the result, if a and b are inhomogeneous, is a
part of the system of second step determined by a and b, and
therefore must be conceived as an extension of second step."]

In [1835] Justus expresses the same idea. The similarity between
Hermann's and Justus' expressions is clear if in Hermann's account
a is pictured as the line which is moved parallel to itself
"through" line b (assumd not parallel to a). Though the kernel of
Hermann's idea is evident in Justus', the differences are great.
Hermann discusses multiplication on three levels: in the general
theory of forms ("allgemeine Formenlehre"), in the calculus of
extension itself, and in "applications" in geometry. And, at each
level, it is possible for multiplication to be non-commutative.

3. Method of Presentation.

Justus' ideas are expressed in the Raumlehre [1817, p. viii], a
guide to teachers of young school children:
"Nur dadurch koennen sie dauernden Werth erhalten, dass sie die
ersten Anfangspuncte, welche dieses sowohl fuer die Wissenschaft
als fuer den Unterricht sind, aussuchen, diese in ihrem
natuerlichen Zusammenhange mit Klarheit verfolgen, und den
Schueler dadurch jedesmal in die Mitte der Untersuchung stellen,
so dass er nicht nur den Weg, wie er bis dahin gekommen, deutlich
uebersieht, sondern auch im Stande ist, vorwaerts zu blicken, und
schon im Voraus zu bestimmen, was nun folgen muesse."

["Only in this way can they [the students] obtain enduring
benefit, that they seek out the initial starting points, which are
the same for the science as for [its] instruction, follow these
clearly in their natural interrelationship, and thereby place the
pupil each time in the midst of the investigation, so that he not
only clearly sees over the way which he has come, but is also in
the position of looking forwards and determining at the outset
what must next follow."]

In the Raumlehre this statement can be easily regarded as a rather
trivial expression of pedagogical concerns. The statement is not
precise enough to determine one method as better than another. In
the Raumlehre, at least, this method appears to consist of
intensive training of physical-geometrical intuition in the first
part, i.e., concepts of length, width, breadth, volume, and
direction are linked to physical exercises involving motion of
body and arms.

Hermann Grassmann has a long passage in [1844] on the method of
presentation comparing mathematics with philosophy, and the
Euclidean method with more preferable ones. Excerpts from this
follow:
"Es kommen oft Beweise vor, bei denen man zuerst, wenn nicht der
Satz obenan staende, gar nicht wissen koennte, wohin sie fuehren
sollen, und durch die man dann, nachdem man eine ganze Zeitlang
blind und aufs Gerathewohl hin jeden Schritt nachgemacht hat,
endlich, ehe man sich versieht, ploetzlich zu der zu erweisenden
Wahrheit gelangt. Ein solcher Beweis kann vielleicht an Strenge
nichts zu wuenschen uebrig lassen, aber wissenschaftlich ist er
nicht; es fehlt ihm das zweite Erforderniss, die
Uebersichtlichkeit.
Ist hingegen der Leser in jedem Punkt der Entwicklung in den Stand
gesetzt, zu sehen, wohin er geht, so bleibt er Herrscher ueber den
Stoff, er ist an die besondere Form der Darstellung nicht mehr
gebunden, und die Aneignung wird eine wahre Reproduktion."

["Proofs often occur, in which at first, if it were not for the
statement [of the theorem] standing above, one would not know at
all where it is supposed to lead. Consequently, after one has
haphazardly and blindly followed each step for quite some time,
finally, before you expect it, that truth which was to be proved
is suddenly obtained. Such a proof can perhaps leave nothing to be
desired in rigor, but it is not scientific; the second requirement
is lacking, the provision of an overview.
If, on the other hand the reader is put in the position, at each
point of the development, of seeing where he is going, then he

remains in command of the material, he is no longer bound to the particular form of presentation and the incorporation becomes a true reproduction."]

More details on Hermann's philosophy is given in my [1977].

Though these comparisons between father and son, given here in a very brief fashion, are interesting in themselves, the next step should, I believe, include a comparison of Justus' work with contemporaneous school texts. He has, for example, contrasted his fundamental approach with the Pestalozzian school and it should be interesting to determine just what this contrast is.

A Note on Justus Grassmann's Philosophy of Mathematics

The main purpose of this paper is to point out some of the direct links between the works of the Grassmanns, father and son; some presentation of Justus' philosophy of mathematics may help, however, to place his ideas in a broader context. One can only speculate what direct influence these ideas had on Hermann.

On the verso of the title page of the Geometrische Combinationslehre [1829], as an epigraph preceding the Foreword, is an epigram by Schiller:
"Wo du auch wandelst im Raum, es knuepft dein Zenith und Nadir
    An den Himmel dich an, dich an die Axe der Welt.
 Wie du auch handelst in dir, es beruehre den Himmel der Wille,
    Durch die Axe der Welt gehe die Richtung der That."

["Wheresoever thou wanderest in space,
                    thy zenith and nadir
  Unto the heavens knit thee. unto
                    the axis of the earth.
  Howsoever thou actest, let heaven be
                    moved by thy purpose,
  Let the aims of thy deeds traverse
                    the axis of the earth!"]

Another epigraph by Justus Grassmann, opposite the first page of text, helps to make the connection between Schiller's epigram and the work itself:

"Es giebt eine Methode Linien und Flaechen so miteinander in Verbindung treten zu lassen, dass sich daraus von selbst eine Menge der einfachsten und regelmaessigsten Gestalten entwickeln, welche, wie aus einer Zauberlaterne hervorgeholt, vor dem Blicke des Geistes auftauchen, mit ihren klaren Augen gegen den Himmel schau'n, und die finstern Tiefen der Erde mit ihrem Lichte erhellen und durchsichtig machen."

["There is a method allowing lines and surfaces to be connected with each other so that from them a collection of the simplest and most regular forms is developed, which, as if produced from a magic lantern, emerges before the mind's eye, shining against the heavens with its clear view and brightening the dark depths of the earth with its light, making it transparent."]

There are, thus, two levels of meaning for the first epigraph by Schiller which J. Grassmann provides in this work on crystallography: the mathematical and the metaphysical.

The principal distinctive feature of J. Grassmann's mathematical system is the choice of a point in the interior of the crystal as origin. By imagining oneself at this point one can think of being in the center of a room with the walls, floor, and ceiling oriented analogously to the faces of the cube with respect to the origin 0, using the above notation. This analogy is first used on p. 9 and helps in understanding the astronomical - zenith and nadir - analogy on p. 6f:

"Diese Bezeichnungsart setzt uns jedesmal selbst in die Mitte der zu beschreibenden Gestalt, also in dieselbe Lage, in welcher sich der Astronom in Beziehung auf den Himmel befindet, - oder in Ruecksicht auf das Planetensystem auf den heliocentrischen Standpunkt. Die Krystallographen sind gewohnt, von Aussen zu beschreiben, welches ich fuer weniger vortheilhaft halte. Ihre Ansicht verhaelt sich zu der unsrigen, wie die eines kuenstlichen Himmelsglobus zur Ansicht des Himmels unmittelbar, - oder in jener andern Ruecksicht, wie das Ptolomaeische Weltsystem zum Copernikanischen."

["This notation puts us in the middle of the form being described and thus is like the position the astronomer has to the heavens - or, in the solar system, the heliocentric viewpoint. Crystallographers are used to describing from the outside, but I believe this is less advantageous. Their view is related to ours as the study of a man-made astronomical globe is to the direct view of the heavens - or as the Ptolemaic system is to the Copernican."]

The astronomical analogy is particularly evident in this use of stereographic projection [1829, pp. 37, 77] where 0 is regarded as the center of a sphere and each ray corresponds to the point of intersection of the ray, extended if necessary, with the sphere. Orientation with respect to the human body is remindful of Justus' technique in [1817] and [1824] of using exercises involving bodily motions for developing geometric and spatial intuition in children.

Justus Grassmann describes the geometrical, or spatial, combinatorial analysis as the best means of applying pure mathematical concepts - combinatorial analysis - to the forms in which nature presents crystals [1829, p. v.]; it opens a new field of intellectual development whose goal is "to produce simple and compound forms, to indicate their connection, and to include all crystal forms under a single type of problem." [1829, p. 7] In Schiller's epigram the position of man between heaven and earth with the capability of affecting each is reflected in J. Grassmann's geometrical combinatorial analysis which ideally is to provide "the connecting link in the galvanic chain [voltaic cell] whose extremes are mathematics and natural science [Naturkunde] ..." [1829, pp. 171-2]. The totality of the theory of magnitudes ("Groessenlehre"), combinatorial analysis, and natural science in this ideal state would be comparable to language which is similarly positioned between nature and intellect according to Justus. As in the case of language, it would be product of human instinct, arising from submersion of the intellect in nature - the intellect as not yet separated from nature - a mirror of the world; it would provide the representation of the correspondence of nature and intellect, the reconciliation and uniting of these separate spheres, and deliver human intellect from the torture of

empty   abstractions   and   rough   empiricism.   "It   would   thereby
directly   assume   a religious character since it points inevitably
to   the highest and ultimate ground of this unity   and thus enters
into   the   most   intimate   connection   with   the highest estate of
mankind   in   which alone each thing can obtain value and meaning."
[1829, p. 172]

The   appendix where these remarks occur elaborates further on this
idea   by   pointing out the combinatorial quality – the combination
in   integral   multiples   –   of   tones   in   a   musical scale and of
elements   in   chemical   composition   [1829,   p.   178–83].   In the
stereographic   analogy: the   essence   of   the   material   earth is
thereby   projected   in   such a manner as to make it as visible and
orderly   as   the heavens. J. Grassmann believes these applications
are   revealed   by a recovery of the true nature of mathematics and
of   this   particular   branch,   for   it   is   the   proper   place of
mathematics,   which   it once had in ancient times, to be the inner
expression   of the outer world as far as it may be revealed to us.
Thus the need for considering the first principles of mathematics;
if   these   can   be   recovered   and mathematics developed along the
lines   started   by   J.   Grassmann,   the   link will have been found
giving nature and human intellect the ideal unity described above.
As evidence that this state of affairs can actually come about, or
at   least   be   more closely approximated, an example is given of a
construction   or synthesis of the intellect, conic sections, which
only   after a thousand years entered into a synthesis of nature in
the paths of the planets; Apollonius could have had no idea of the
use   Kepler   would   make   of   conic   sections.   Similarly   it is
constructions of the intellect, materialized, which we note in the
crystal   forms. Where, Justus Grassmann asks, were there any truly
great   intellectual   constructions   which   have   not been realized
through constructions of nature?

Admittedly as long as nature is external to us, we can essentially
never   understand   it,   but can delineate and control it and watch
includes with   a   plea   for   a philosophy which supports a balance
beteen speculation and observation.

References

Grassmann, H.:   Ableitung   der   Krystallgestalten   aus   dem
                   allgemeinen Gesetze der Krystallbildung, in:
                   Programme der Stettiner Ottoschule 1839

Grassmann, H.:   Die   Lineale   Ausdehnungslehre, ein neuer Zweig
                   der   Mathematik   dargestellt   und   durch
                   Anwendungen auf die uebrigen Zweige der
                   Mathematik, wie auch auf die Statistik,
                   Mechanik, Lehre vom Magnetismus und die
                   Kristallonomie, Leipzig 1844

Grassmann, H.:   Die Ausdehnungslehre, Berlin 1861

Grassmann, J.:   Raumlehre fuer Volksschulen, 1st pt. (Ebene
                   raeumliche Verbindungslehre), Berlin 1817

Grassmann, J.:   Raumlehre fuer die untern Klassen der Gymnasien,
                   und   fuer   Volksschulen,   2nd   pt.   (Ebene
                   raeumliche Groessenlehre), Berlin 1824

Grassmann, J.:   Zur physischen Krystallonomie und geometrische
                   Combinationslehre, 1st vol., Stettin 1829

Grassmann, J.:   Lehrbuch   der   ebenen   und   sphaerischen
                   Trigonometrie, Berlin 1835

Grassmann, J.:   Combinatorische   Entwicklung   der
                   Krystallgestalten, in: Annalen der Physik und
                   Chemie 30 (1836), "Ergaenzungsband", pp. 1-43

Lewis, A.C.:   H. Grassmann's   1844   'Ausdehnungslehre'   and
                   Schleiermacher's 'Dialektik', in: Annals of
                   Science, 34 (1977), pp. 103-162

Gert Schubring

ON EDUCATION AS A MEDIATING ELEMENT BETWEEN DEVELOPMENT AND APPLICATION: THE PLANS FOR THE BERLIN POLYTECHNICAL INSTITUTE (1817 - 1850)

Traditionally, the Ecole Polytechnique in Paris appears as the model of the new, close relationship between science and social applicaton, which marks the beginning of the 19th century. Especially in the framework of the history of technology it is understood as the "prototype of all technical educational establishments" (Manegold 1966, 183). In fact, a series of higher technical educational establishments were founded according to this model: Madrid (1802), Prague (1806), St. Petersburg (1809), Vienna (1815), Karlsruhe (1825), Copenhagen (1829), etc.

Between 1817 and 1850, plans for a polytechnical institute were often debated in Prussia, occasionally with great intensity. These were not oriented towards applicaton, such as the training engineers, but were concerned with the education of teachers, who in turn were to teach in schools in various fields of application. Whereas this orientation in the plans had been played down until then, or merely interpreted as a later deviation from the original plans in the Paris Model, it is the conception of teacher education which provides us with a deeper understanding of the relations between development and the application of knowledge and the social conditions required. The plans for the Berlin Polytechnical Institute proved to be an instrument for integrating mathematics into the new essentially social process of scientific activity: the professionalization and institutionalization of

H. N. Jahnke and M. Otte (eds.), Epistemological and Social Problems of the Sciences in the Early Nineteenth Century, 269–284.

mathematics. At the same time, mathematics became the starting
point for attaining a new level in this process: the
professionalization and institutionalization of the natural
sciences. The driving force in this historical process was
education (in its broadest sense), especially in the institutional
form of teacher education. In the various stages of the plans,
orientation towards teacher-education was increasingly stressed,
together with the latter's relationship to the meta-theoretical
conception of "pure mathematics" (cf. Schubring 1979) as a basis.
As far as their immediate objectives are concerned, the plans
failed; such an institute was never founded.

1. Plans for a Mathematical-Technical College

This failure is not so much due to the attitude of the Prussian
Military, whose resistance has hitherto been considered decisive
in the literature, but rather to the resistance of the Ministry of
Commerce.

The mistaken view which assigns a decisive role for the
implementation or non-implementation of the plans to the Prussian
Military is too narrowly oriented on the Paris Model and
disregards the fact that social conditions in France and Prussia
were different. After the bourgeois French revolution (1789/1794),
professional careers were determined, in France, by individual
achievement. In Prussia, however, the King's edict of 1808
stipulating that officer's promotion was to be contingent only on
knowledge and achievement, did not prevail against the vested
rights and privileges of the aristocracy. Thus there were only few
officers in the Prussian Military during the first half of the
19th century who stood up for knowledge and its dissemination.

Due to this situation it turned out to be fatal for the plans that
there was no agreement within the Bourgeoisie with regard to the
desired level of technical and scientific education and to an
adequate professionalization of teachers. In the first half of the
19th century for a great part of the schools run by it, the
Ministry of Commerce did not want to have full-time teachers, but

requested, as in the case of the provincial trade schools, that the teachers' main vocation be a trade (Schiersmann 1979).

The differences between the Handelsdepartement (resp. -Ministe-rium[1]) and the Kultusministerium can be particularly well illustrated by the earliest phase of the plans for a Polytechnical Institute. A study by P. Lundgreen has shown that, prior to the three known stages in the plans for the institute, there was a plan under discussion by which an already existing institution, the Bau-Akademie, was to be reformed according to polytechnical principles: the courses were to be founded on mathematics, the education was to be oriented towards practical application.

On the grounds of "decline of teaching" at the Bau-Akademie, Tralles, professor of mathematics, had been charged by the Sektion fuer Kultus und Unterricht to develop plans for a reorganization of the academy, as well as an "academic plan" (Lundgreen 1975, 33). In 1817, Tralles submitted a memorandum "Ueber eine Mathematisch-Technische Lehranstalt". The objective of the new institute was to train "architects and engineers". This training was separated from university studies, as the latter were considered unsuitable for the acquisition of the necessary "positive knowledge", whereas a Bau-Akademie expanded to a "mathematical-technical college" was considered to provide an adequate training. Tralles understood mathematics as necessary general education for technical applicaton: "Das mathematisch Technische loeset sich aber nicht in die genannten Zweige, besonderer Thaetigkeit einzelner Techniker als in so viele von einander gesonderte Theile auf. Sie sind vielmehr so in einander verschlungen, dass keiner ohne den anderen vollstaendig erlernt und ausgeuebt werden kann" (ZStA III, sheet 14)[2].

The Bureau of Commerce objected to the new objectives which would have included the training of free-lance architects. It insisted on the training of low-level, civil engineers and correspondingly lower theoretical standards. The department was also willing to dispense with an obligatory systematical education and to reduce the establishment's activity to the holding of examinations, by permitting external preparation for these as well (l.c., sheet 25).

In addition to that, the Bureau of Commerce had to cope with the opposition of the General-Verwaltung responsible for mining and smelting, which was strictly against including the training of the so-called ´Bergwerkseleven´ - the future civil servants in key position in the mining and smelting industry - among the responsibilities of the establishment. As the future place of work of these civil servants was determined at an early stage - as opposed to surveyors and civil servants in public construction - each of them had to receive special training, so the authorities argued. Hence, "a single educational establishment was out of the question". The argumentation shows that the authorities saw the contracts concluded with individual teachers as menaced by the establishment of a central institute of technology (op. cit., p. 33).

The Bureau of Commerce under Beuth´s direction did reject the 18th century guild-based training and regarded technical education as general vocational education (cf. Schiersmann 1979), but it had in mind, as far as engineers were concerned, only the department´s immediate demand for civil engineers. Therefore in 1820 the Kultusminister had to give up its plan of combining "the scientific and technical at the same time" (ZStA III, sheet 63). The only thing attained was a reform of the Bau-Akademie in its now limited objectives.

Upon comparing Prussia to France one sees, however, despite these differences, an essential systematic moment, common to both ministries. As T. Shinn has demonstrated, the French state attempted to keep the engineers, educated at the Ecole Polytechnique from applying their knowledge in private industry. This is why private schools had to be founded in order to train engineers for work in Industry (see Shinn 1978).

As opposed to this reluctance to promote economic development, there was, in Prussia, a common orientation in the Kultusministerium and in the Handelsdepartement, which may, in economic terms, be called "liberalism" and which was expressed in the joint strategy of using education - but for the enhancement of "industriousness" ("Gewerbefleiss") and industry. Hence, it was a matter of promoting industry by means of the education of the citizens. This policy was intended to facilitate the transition from the primarily state-organized economic activity, as it prevailed in mercantilism, to a mobilization of citizen's own activity ("Selbsttaetigkeit"), a prerequisite for the bourgeois mode of production.

The great emphasis placed on education is due to the fact, that there were, up to the second half of the 19th century, only very few immediate links between scientific development and industrial production or application. As Basalla puts the separation of scientific and industrial revolution: "Great Britain did not achieve industrial eminence because of these rather casual contacts (of eighteenth-century scientists with inventors and industrialists). The close rapport between science and technology, which has strengthened many modern industries, is a product of the late nineteenth and the early twentieth centuries" (Basalla 1970:15).

One can speak of a proper industrial development both for France and Prussia only after 1850. As industrial groth can thus not be considered its cause, the rapid professionalization in Prussia – as opposed to England (Basalla 1970:9) and France (see Schubring 1980) – must be seen as due to other conditions. Indeed, they can be found in the Prussian state policy of using education as a means for promoting growth. The high social value of knowledge and its dissemination resulted from this.

2. The Call to C.F. Gauss

The first main stage of the Institute Plans (1823/24) is linked to the failure of the attempt to call Gauss to Berlin. This failure has always been seen as due to Gauss' financial demands and the Ministry of Education's too reluctant efforts to provide the necessary funds. Gauss' refusal seems to be the result of the unreasonable demands associated with the funds offered. It is important to see that at this stage there already was a conception within the Ministry of Education to transmit the development and the application of science by means of teacher education. The call to Gauss was seen as an appropriate means for establishing a new

polytechnical institution. Because of its neo-humanist conception
of science the Ministry of Education interpreted Gauss'
well-known refusal to teach at the university as his willingness
to realize the unity of teacher and scientist education implicitly
contained in the seminar conception in training skilled
mathematicians.

In his memorandum for the King, the Minister of Education,
Altenstein considered special institutions necessary for the
training of scientists, and for "the very personal contact" and
"the conduct of scientific projects of their own" required for the
latter.

"Higher education and training of mathematicians cannot be done
just and exclusively by the universities." Altenstein points to
the "long period of time" necessary for the "completion" of
scientists' training: "Nicht sowohl Vorlesungen als die Leitung
eigener Arbeiten und Studien junge Maenner bewirkt solches und
daher sind die Akademiker ohne Nebenaemter[3] allein geeignet und
deshalb auch so sehr noethig" (ZStA I, sheet 74).[4]

Hence, he suggested founding for mathematics a school to train
skilled teachers. His proposals did not exclude the idea that the
institute might serve as a central institute for subsequent
special schools providing for the various branches of civil
administration.

The consultations about the plan initiated by the King between the
Ministry of Education, the Ministry of War, the Ministry of the
Interior and the Bureau of Commerce were ended by Gauss' refusal
(Manegold 1966, 186).

3. Teacher and Scientists Education and Pure Mathematics

The second main stage of the plans dates between 1828 and 1835.
After A. v. Humboldt's return from Paris, the plans for a
polytecnical institute were taken up again and put on a new basis
with respect to the development of science in France: mathematics
and chemistry were to become the fundamental fields for this

training. At the same time, the conception of teacher education as a means for orientation towards practical application was fully developed. In his request for an expert opinion concerning the chemical and mathematical departments of the Institute addressed to Mitscherlich and Crelle resp., Altenstein wrote in 1828 that his intention was not "Specialschulen fuer die Bildung der Gewerbe oder der einzelnen technischen Fertigkeiten zu gruenden, sondern blos Lehrer fuer solche Specialschulen heranzuziehen." (ZStA II, sheet 4)[5]

Besides Gymnasiums and Buergerschulen he named the following: schools for the arts, for trades, for construction, for mining, and for the military (ZStA II, sheet 6).

Johannes Schulze's (Ministry of Education, responsible for higher education) statutes of 1832 for a polytechnical institute integrated Mitscherlich's and Crelle's drafts, and limited the number of non-teacher students to a quarter at the utmost. "The main purpose" of the institution, "to educate teachers of mathematics, physics and chemistry for the entire needs of secondary public education in its various stages", is explicitly justified with the task of mediating between the development and the applications, for "the pursuit of this main propose will both secure a decidedly scientific approach for the seminar and at the same time meet a real practical demand" (ZStA II, sheet 146). It was provided in the statutes, that professors for universities and teachers for schools were to be educated simultaneously and in the same manner: This is proved, for example, when the common entrance requirements speak of those, who "intend to qualify themselves for a teaching position in mathematics, physics, and chemistry at a university, a Gymnasium or a hoehere Buergerschule" (ibid., sheet 147). Thus scientist education is here organized along the lines of the future teaching function.

This particular form of unity of teacher and scientist education is explicable in light of the high social value of knowledge and its dissemination which it was to realize and by the strong position granted to mathematics within the neohumanist reform of the school and university system: in order to make the acquisition of knowledge appear a desirable goal to all citizens, teachers in

the 19th century were soon freed of the degrading part-time duties
they formely had to fulfill. Gymnasium teachers were oriented away
from the former "pedagogue" image discredited by philanthropinism,
and towards the scholar as a model. It was thus only consistent if
Johannes Schulze's main criterion for judging applicants for the
position of head of a Gymnasium were the applicant's
publications [6]. The fact that the title of "professor" could be
conferred on Gymnasium teachers points in the same direction This
applied in the first place to "distinguished teachers of
mathematics and science (...) who have made themselves known by
important scientific achievements and ... who have taught with
particularly outstanding success" (decree of 1838; in: Roenne,
107). From its very beginning, professionalization of Gymnasium
teachers was not opposed to the specialization of teachers with
respect to subjects but integrated their specific activity into
the general conception of education and science. Within this
specialization, room for mathematics was explicitly provided.

Neo-Humanism, or the 'scientific-world-view' of the aspiring
bourgeoisie, which was opposed to the traditional education
aligned to the guilds and corporations of the 18th century,
implied, to begin with, a homogenous conception of knowledge:
languages and mathematics became the essential elements of the
Gymnasium curriculum. This is how the responsibility for training
mathematics teachers for secondary education was placed with
mathematicians within the Faculty of Arts and Humanities. The
close connection between languages and mathematics was not only a
factual relationship, but also an explicitly intentional
complementary unity of grammar and mathematics to further the
education of the mind as formulated by Bernhardi in his famous
programme: "Mathematics and Languages. Contrast and Complement".
The so-called "General Examination" made sure that all teachers
possessed basic knowledge in all principal subjects [7].

It was not only the central position of mathematics within the
educational system which was essential to the development of
mathematics (and of the plans for the Institute, in particular),
but also its justification in philosophy and in educational theory
as 'pure mathematics'. On the basis of Kant's concept of pure
science, the educational debate on pure mathematics in Germany

from the end of the 18th century and into the first third of the 19th century acquired a salience well beyond the traditional distinction based on systematics of science between pure and applied (or "mixed") mathematics.

This eventually enabled Fries to elaborate the programme and the methodology of ´pure´ mathematics (see Schubring 1979). The separation of pure from applied mathematics, however, did not place pure mathematics in opposition to its application; rather pure mathematics was considered a prerequisite for the latter: as meta-knowledge setting up the rules for applications. This is quite clear from the attitude taken by representatives of applied mathematics, technicians who strongly favored calculusization: A.J. Hecker [8] requested that students of the Realschulen study "pure mathematics" as well: "Wenn daher auch mancher Schueler in Hinsicht seiner kuenftigen Bestimmung vielleicht bloss mit den praktischen Wahrheiten der reinen Mathematik bekanntgemacht werden duerfte: so wird er doch diese, wenn ihm alle theoretischen Vorkenntnisse mangeln, unfehlbar groessten Theils schwer, unverstaendlich und raetselhaft finden. Bei gruendlicher Kenntnis der Theorie werden sie ihm dagegen leicht zu verstehen seyn." [9]

Therefore he requested that Euclid´s first four books be used at the Realschulen as well.

Crelle, who had been educated as a constructional engineer (Baumeister) and had been active as an engineer in road construction and who later, in addition to his functions as a consultant to the Ministry of Education, was active in the construction of railway lines as well, wrote textbooks on the algebraization of differential and integral calculus which were based on Lagrange´s books. The mathematics of the combinatorical school, which was the prevailing form of "pure" mathematics in Germany in the first decades of the 19th century do, in fact, appear as the specific expression of an "educational mathematics" aimed at mediation of the development and the applications. Evidence on this point may be seen in the fact that this school made the sign function of mathemtical terms its starting-point (for the sign concept see: Jahnke 1978). Thus, Eytelwein – the Prussian dyke inspector and later director of public construction and head of the Bauakademie from 1824 to 1830 - was doing work on the systematization and simplification of combinatorics.[10] To Dirichlet, he wrote: "Wie geht es wohl zu, dass die von uns Deutschen bearbeitete combinatorische Analysis so wenig Eingang in Frankreich findet, da doch durch sie die schwierigsten analytischen Probleme einfach geloest und dargestellt werden koennen. Es ist freilich nicht zu verkennen, dass die hoechst verwickelte und schwierige Hindenburgsche Bezeichnung Schrecken verursacht und selbst Deutsche hierin Anstoss finden. Ich habe es daher versucht in meiner im vorigen Jahr herausgegebenen Analysis, eine einfache Bezeichnung einzufuehren, und zugleich die wichtigsten Lehren der combinatorischen Analysis zusammen zu stellen"[11].

Crelle used Altenstein's request to furnish an expert opinion for the mathematical part of the Institute to create the prerequisites for the professionalization of mathematics on the basis of the conception of pure mathematics. By means of a strict separation, pure mathematics, as the prerequisite of any application, was to become the focus of teaching. Crelle's plan was no longer focussed on the director of the institute as was the plan of 1823/24, but required the preparation of a sufficient number of posts for young scientists able to work in research on the basis of their teaching salaries. That nothing was done to implement this plan after Crelle's report for the polytechnical institute, or seminar, had been submitted towards the end of 1828 could be due to the fact that no eminent mathematicians were available for full-time employment. On the other hand it can be shown that the failure of the institute plans during this stage in 1835 is connected to the fear that the relatively great number of teachers trained at the Institute would eventually be in competition to those teaching part-time at special schools, and enjoying a sinecure there.

4. Plans for a Mathematical Institute 1844 - 1850

A last stage (1844-1850) actually prepared the breakthrough of the subject-specific research character of the scientist's activity at the universities. The plan was now directly linked with the conflicts due to clashing social forces between Realschulen and

Gymnasien. In the last instance, the failure of the plan in attaining its immediate objectives goes back to these contradictions. The strongest partisan of the plans was the Gymnasium teacher K.H. Schellbach.

The plan had been aligned to the person of C.G.J. Jacobi, who, with the "mathematisches Institut", as it was now planned, would have come a step nearer to his goal of institutionalizing scientists education and disseminating of mathematical knowledge as well as enhancing the influence of his scientific school. Together with Schellbach he had obviously been under consideration as one of the two directors. Shortly after his temporary transferral to Berlin the plan was introduced, and shortly after his final appointment to the Academy in 1850, it was filed away. Jacobi had, however, taken an active part in the consultations.

This plan was again based on the idea that both "Docenten der Universitaet" (University lecturers) and school teachers should be educated for the different secondary educational establishments as well as for the special schools. Schellbach assumed that teacher education alone was not sufficient for the social dissemination of knowledge owing to the reduction of opportunities for teaching and learning mathematics brought about by the structure of the educational system, which had meanwhile evolved. Therefore "scientific practitioners" were to be educated in order to "introduce mathematics in real life" (ZStA II, sheet 236).

Schellbach and Jacobi had to struggle against ministerial attempts to define the Institute as a continuation of the Realschulen. They considered the scientific orientation of the institute endangered by an orientation towards Realschulen graduates, as these students would have depended on the education provided by the institute as their vocational training, and thus would have lowered the Institute's standards to an immediating application-orientated level.

As opposed to that, Schellbach and Jacobi wanted to educate scientific practitioners, besides teachers. The formers' social basis was to be found, owing to the still not very numerous posts for scientists, only among the more prosperous classes. This is why the orientation towards Gymnasium graduates had to remain: "Es laesst sich erwarten, dass bemittelte Eltern ihre Soehne diesem Institut anvertrauen werden, um sie dort zu wissenschaftlichen Praktikern ausbilden zu lassen." (ibid.)[12] Hence, Greek as a teaching subject at the institute was essential to Jacobi.

After, however, the responsible administrators had abolished Greek and insisted on their defining proportional equation stating that the relation between the Institute and Realschulen was to be similar to the relation between universities and Gymnasien, Jacobi and Schellbach made no further efforts to implement the plans.

While the institute plans, in their prior stage, had resulted, among other things in an extraordinary professorship being established for Steiner at the Berlin University, Jacobi's main interest, even after he had received and accepted his definite call to the Berlin Academy, was still to achieve the institutionalization of mathematics by means of establishing, at each university, a minimum of one full tenure and one extraordinary professorship for mathematics, and by separating existent joint tenures for mathematics and physics. His sudden death prevented him from pursuing these plans himself. These plans, however, were gradually realized later, as can be seen from the increasing foundations of mathematical seminars.

Notes

1 The Department fuer Handel und Gewerbe (Bureau of Commerce) with P.C.W. Beuth as head (1818–1845) has been the only 'fixpoint" in the permanent organizational and competence changements of the commercial affairs between 1810 and 1850. This administrational field has been temporarily independent as an Handelsministerium, but otherwise it has been divided in the competencies of several ministries.
2 "The mathematical-technical, however, cannot be dissolved into the branches of special activity of the individual engineers

mentioned, or into as many separate components. Rather, these are so intricately interwoven that none can be fully learned and exercised without the other."

3 Thus implicitly criticizing the mathematicians at the Academy, who had held several positions at the same time, this shows the awareness for the problems of professionalization.

4 "Not just lectures but the conduct of studies and of scientific projects of their own on the part of young men leads to this effect; and, therefore, academicians without supplementary duties are solely qualified and therefore so urgently needed."

5 "to found special schools to train in the crafts or individual technological skills, but only to qualify and develop teachers for such special schools".

6 Later, when the prevailing conception of education changed, this criterion was often ridiculed. Its effect, however, was twofold: it encouraged the development and acquisition of knowledge and helped to establish the social position of Gymnasium teachers. This was ensured by the Prussian decree of 1824 which obliged each Gymnasium to publish a paper within the so-called school-programmes "on a scientific subject not alien to the teacher's profession and apt to call the general attention of at least the educated classes to matters of public education in general, or to a topic of interest to Gymnasium in particular. The objective was to encourage the heads and senior teachers of Gymnasiums to continue their studies without interruption." (Roenne, 158). The obligation to annually publish a scientific treaty was rescined in 1875.

7 Even in the Gymnasiums, the position of mathematics was at first not bad as compared to the classical languages, as can be seen from the school-programmes. A rough survey yields the following relations between mathematical topics and classical language topics: for 1825 to 1840 the relationships was 1 : 3.9, for 1841 to 1850 it was even higher 1 : 2.3; whereas the classical language programmes increased in absolute and relative terms after 1850: for 1851 to 1860 the relationship was 1 : 4.9.

8 For his conception for schools see D.K. Mueller 1977, pp. 177ff.

9 "If it should thus happen that some student with regard to his future vocation, be made familiar with the practical truths of pure mathematics only, he will inevitably find the latter, if he

lacks all previous theoretical knowledge, for the most part difficult, unintelligible, and puzzling. If, on the other hand, he has been provided with a thorough understanding of theory, he will readily understand these practical truths." (A.J. Hecker 1797)

10 Obviously, there is a close relationship between the combinatorical theory and the development of pure mathematics, the "freedom to construct new ideas and connections in mathematics" (Dauben 1972, 133). J. Grassmann wrote enthusiastically on combinatorical theory and demanded its development to a pure discipline: "Combinatorical theory is yet in its infancy, just as if mathematics, by way of comparison, had not progressed beyond addition. — Unfortunately, this theory has immediately been made the handmaid of analysis; this early servitude has hampered its growth and development and even now, the era is biased against it to the extent that this servitude will enable it to live. There will, however, be the time when this child of the gods will emerge in its full beauty, and as nothing will be required of it, as it will not be destined to serve; its harmless presence will cast its light on all branches of science" (J. Grassmann 1827, 7).

11 "How does it come that the combinatorical analysis developed by us Germans meets with so little reception in France, despite the fact that it will serve to solve and represent the most difficult analytical problems in a single way. It can not be overlooked, however, that Hindenburg's most complicated and difficult term has a discouraging effect, even Germans taking offense. This is why I have attempted, in my Analysis published last year, to introduce a simple term, at the same time offering a summary of the most important rules of combinatoric analysis." (Letter dated July 7, 1826 from the estate of Dirichlet, Staatsbibliothek Preussischer Kulturbesitz Berlin).

12 "It may be expected that parents of ample means will entrust their sons to this institute in order to have them educated as scientific practitioners there."

References

Primary Sources

a) Zentrales Staatsarchiv der DDR, Dienststelle Merseburg: Files
   of the former Prussian Ministerium der geistlichen-,
   Unterrichts- und Medizinalangelegenheiten:
   1. Rep. 76 Vc, Sekt. 2, Tit. 23, Lit. F, Nr. 2, Bd. 2 Bl. 72–82
   (ZStA I),
   2. Rep. 76 Vc, Sekt. 2, Tit. 23, Lit. A, Nr. 17 (ZStA II).
   Files of the former Prussian General-Verwaltung resp.
   Ministerium fuer den Handel und die Gewerbe:
   3. Rep. 93 B, Nr. 60, Bd. 1, Bl. 10–106 (ZStA III).

b) From the Handschriftenabteilung der Staatsbibliothek
   Preussischer Kulturbesitz: letter from Eytelwein to Dirichlet,
   7.7.1826, in: Nachlass P.G. Lejeune-Dirichlet

Secondary Sources

Basalla, G. (ed.):   Victorian Science, Garden City (N.Y.) 1970
Bernhardi, A.F.:   Ansichten ueber die Organisation der gelehrten
                     Schulen, Jena 1818
Dauben, J.W.:   Georg Cantor, Cambridge (Mass.) 1979
Eccarius, W.:   Der Techniker und Mathematiker A.L. Crelle und
                     sein Beitrag zur Foerderung und Entwicklung
                     der Mathematik im Deutschland des 19.
                     Jahrhunderts, Leipzig 1974 (Diss.)
Fries, J.F.:   System der Logik, Heidelberg 1837, 2d ed. (1st
                     ed. 1811)
Fries, J.F.:   Die mathematische Naturphilosophie nach philo-
                     sophischer Methode bearbeitet, Heidelberg 1822
Grassmann, J.G.:   Ueber den Begriff und Umfang der reinen
                     Zahlenlehre. Programm des Gymnasiums, Stettin
                     1827

Hecker, A.J.:   Einige Gedanken ueber verschiedene Unter-
                        richtsmethoden in den mathematischen
                        Wissenschaften auf Gelehrten- und auf Kunst-
                        und Buergerschulen. Programm des
                        Fr.-Wilhelm-Gymnasiums und der Realschule,
                        Berlin 1797

Jahnke, H.N.:   Zum Verhaeltnis von Wissensentwicklung und
                        Begruendung in der Mathematik - Beweisen als
                        didaktisches Problem, Bielefeld 1978 (Materia-
                        lien und Studien, vol. 10) (Diss.)

Lundgreen, P.:   Techniker in Preussen waehrend der fruehen
                        Industrialisieung, Berlin 1975

Manegold, K.H.:   Eine Ecole Polytechnique in Berlin, in:
                        Technikgeschichte, 33 (1966), pp. 182-196

Mueller, D.K.:   Sozialstruktur und Schulsystem, Goettingen
                        1978

Neuerer, K.:   Das hoehere Lehramt in Bayern, Berlin 1978

Roenne, L.v.:   Die hoeheren Schulen und die Universitaeten
                        des Preussischen Staates, Berlin 1855

Ruf, W.:   Der Neuhumanismus in Baden und seine
                        Auswirkungen auf die Gelehrtenschulen,
                        Muenchen 1960 (Diss.)

Schiersmann, C.:   Zur Sozialgeschichte der preussischen
                        Provinzial-Gewerbeschulen im 19. Jahrhundert,
                        Weinheim 1979

Schubring, G.:   On the relation of professionalization and
                        institutionalization of teacher educaton. A
                        re-analysis of the plans for a polytechnical
                        school in Berlin, forthcoming in: Historical
                        Studies in the Physical Sciences

Schubring, G.:   Bedingungen der Professionalisierung von
                        Wissenschaft. Eine vergleichende Uebersicht,
                        forthcoming in: Lendemains 19 (1980)

Shinn, T.:   Des Corps d'Etat au secteur industriel. Genese
                        de la profession d'ingenieur, 1750-1920, in:
                        Revue française de Sociologie, 19 (1978), pp.
                        39-71

III

MATHEMATICS IN THE EARLY
19TH CENTURY

Lorraine J. Daston

MATHEMATICS AND THE MORAL SCIENCES: THE RISE AND FALL OF THE
PROBABILITY OF JUDGMENTS, 1785 - 1840

All attempts to apply mathematics to the phenomena of experience
presume some degree of analogy between the subject matter and the
mathematical formalism employed. For eighteenth-century
practitioners of "mixed" mathematics, the requisite degree of
analogy bordered on congruence: mathematical models were conceived
not merely as analogues which shared certain key features with the
real phenomena they described, but rather as mathematical
"portraits" - highly schematic ones, to be sure - of the phenomena
and/or the underlying mechanisms which produced them. In the
physical sciences, a neo-pythagorean outlook sanctioned this
assumption of pre-arranged harmony between, for example, conic
sections and planetary orbits for seventeenth- and
eighteenth-century mixed mathematicians. Similarly, mathematicians
intent on modeling psychological and social phenomena invoked
assumptions which likened human thought and conduct to
mathematical techniques. These assumptions were colored by the
political climate of the moment, by the reigning theoretical
orientation of the moral sciences, and by the available
mathematical tools. This paper examines the rise and fall of the
probability of judgments, one of the earliest attempts to apply
mathematics to the social realm, against this shifting background
of mathematical, philosophical, and political elements. The ways
in which the mathematical probabilists - notably Condorcet,
Laplace, and Poisson - sought to accommodate their theory to the

287

H. N. Jahnke and M. Otte (eds.), Epistemological and Social Problems of the Sciences in the Early Nineteenth
Century, 287–309.

volatile French political milieu during the period 1785-1840 in order to achieve a match between moral phenomena and mathematical treatment, and to rally the prestige of mathematics behind specific articles of judicial reform shed light on the interaction of mathematics and society at several levels.

Although the probability of judgments emerged only in the last quarter of the eighteenth century, mathematical probability had been closely linked with jurisprudence from its inception. The legal doctrine of aleatory contracts - i.e. all those agreements involving an element of chance, such as games of chance, annuities, etc. - had shaped the earliest expositions of mathematical probability by Pascal, Fermat, and Huygens, who took the legal notion of equal expectation, rather than probability per se, as their point of departure.[1] Classical probabilists also adopted the legal interpretation of probability as a "degree of certainty" apportioned to the probative force of various types of evidence. Roman and canon jurists had developed an elaborate hierarchy of so-called "legal" proofs which assigned the evidence procured from both witnesses and things a fixed fractional value.[2] These fractional "probabilities" corresponded to degrees of assent in the mind of the judge, and were summed to obtain the complete or "full" proof required for conviction. Many of the classical probabilists, including Jacques and Nicholas Bernoulli, Condorcet, and Laplace, attempted to convert these legal "probabilities" into a mathematical probability of testimony and conjecture.[3]

Hence jurisprudence provided classical probabilists with a natural field of applications; in fact, almost all of the typical problems addressed in the eighteenth-century literature of classical probability originated in one or another legal context, although they assumed an independent interest and broader focus in later treatises.[4] Therefore, there would have been no a priori objections to the probability of judgments, which computed the probability that a tribunal or jury composed of a given number of members would arrive at a correct decision by a certain majority, as an inappropriate application of mathematical probability. Despite the later criticisms of the probability of judgments as the "scandal of mathematics", classical probabilists viewed the theory as reasonable and useful. In order to understand their optimism, and the later antipathy of their critics, several elements of the intellectual and political milieu in late eighteenth-century France must be taken into account: the methodology of the moral sciences; their perceived relationship to mathematical probability; and the urgent interest in judicial reform.

The eighteenth-century moral sciences correspond only approximately to the latter day social sciences, although the disciplines share many common concerns and are of course historically continuous. For the purposes of this discussion, the two salient points of contrast concern objectives and units of analysis. The moral sciences not only sought to formulate theories which would describe (and ideally predict) psychological and social phenomena; they also undertook to establish standards for rational thought and conduct. Descriptive and prescriptive elements were so closely intertwined as to be inseparable. Even the Physiocrats, who professed to seek the "natural laws" which governed the social realm, understood these laws in a very different way than that in which, for example, a physicist might. Obedience to physical laws was not a matter of choice, but submission to the laws of the moral realm was voluntary, although in the best interests of the individual and of society.[5] For Comte, Quetelet, and other nineteenth-century social theorists, however, the laws of psychology, sociology and economics were as inexorable as those of physics. The eighteenth-century moral sciences studied the deliberations and behavior of a select group of individuals designated as "rational" in the hopes of deriving a set of explicit rules to guide the less astute majority. Their perspective was psychological and individualistic. Societies figured in these theories only as aggregates of individuals, with properties inferred from the sum of their parts. In contrast, nineteenth-century social theorists investigated societies as coherent units (Comte went so far as to deny psychology the status of an independent science), and expected to discover law-like regularities only at the macroscopic level. The rational individual gave way to Quetelet's fictitious homme moyen, an average of all physical, intellectual, and moral features rather than an exemplar of a small elite of hommes éclairés.

To its eighteenth-century practitioners, classical probability
theory seemed to be the uniquely appropriate mathematical tool for
the analysis of the thought processes of the rational individual
investigated by the moral sciences. This was because mathematical
probabilists subscribed to psychological theories which described
mental operations in terms congenial to their theory. According to
Locke, Hartley, and Hume, the mind reasoned by implicit
computation and comparison of probabilities. The association of
ideas in principle mirrored the regularity and frequency of events
culled from experience: in an unbiased mind, associations of ideas
corresponded to real connections between the events and objects
represented by the ideas. The very workings of the human
understanding, when undistorted by strong emotion or uncritical
custom, imitated Bernoulli's theorem, which Hartley claimed was
"evident to attentive Persons, in a gross general way, from the
Common Methods of Reasoning."[6] Associationism also emphasized the
analytic, combinatorial operations of the mind. All intellectual
novelty owed to the mental combination and recombination of simple
ideas. In Condillac's influential psychology, analysis revealed
ideas "under all sorts of aspects, and daily creates new
combinations from them" by "a kind of calculus."[7] Condorcet
affirmed Condillac's claim that the best intellects were those
which excelled in analysis and in "uniting more ideas in memory
and in multiplying these combinations."[8] If the mental operation
of analysis was "a kind of calculus", the combinatorial calculus
of probabilities could be viewed as the mathematical expression
and extension of the psychological processes that constituted
right reasoning.

This parallelism between natural reasoning and mathematical
probability led classical probabilists to identify their theory
with common sense. In Laplace's famous phrase: "the theory of
probability is at bottom nothing more than good sense reduced to a
calculus which evaluates that which good minds know by a sort of
instinct, without being able to explain how with precision."[9] By
codifying the principles which guided an elite of reasonable men,
the probabilists hoped to make rationality accessible to all, for
common sense was not all that common. Unruly passions, prejudices,
self-interest, and over-wrought imagination had corrupted the
ability of all but a select few to estimate probabilities and to

form combinations of the right sort. When the results of
mathematical probability contradicted the judgments of these
hommes éclairés, mathematicians anxiously re-examined the premises
of their theory in order to realign the mathematical consequences
with enlightened opinion.[10] It was in this spirit that the
mathematicians addressed the probability of judgments.

Probabilists insisted that the mathematical theory only described
and systematized, rather than dictated, reasonableness. Condorcet
often repeatet his claim that his calculations on judicial
tribunals concurred with what "the simplest reason would have
dictated", and justified his lengthy computations on the grounds
that human reason was occasionally perplexed by "sophistry" and
"vain subtleties" which mathematical demonstration and calculation
alone could dispel.[11] He assured his Lycée audience that the
calculus of probabilities as applied to tribunal judgments would
lead them "by a sure route, considering only the common interest
and justice, to the same human maxims and magnanimity that you
find in your hearts, and teach you that the first cry of nature
did not lead you astray."[12]

Condorcet and the other probabilists who grappled with the
probability of judgments constructed a model of human behavior, or
at least that part of human behavior which concerned rational
decisionmaking. Not surprisingly, this model reflected
contemporary assumptions concerning human nature — for example,
that every individual possessed a certain endowment of lumières
which determined the accuracy of his judgment on each and every
occasion. The available mathematical techniques, in particular the
theorems of Bernoulli and Bayes, and the extant domain of
applications to natural phenomena also shaped the partial model of
human behavior to which the probabilists subscribed. The
mathematicians conceived the probability of judgments to be only a
branch, albeit a particularly important branch, of the probability
of causes. Moral and physical causes were to some extent
susceptible to the same mathematical treatment, if the latter were
complex enough. Condorcet believed that the moral (like the
physical) sciences were founded upon the "observation of facts"
and should therefore "follow the same method" in order to attain
the "precision" which distinguished scientific truths from the

intuitions of good sense.[13] Laplace predicted that the same combination of observation and mathematics which had served the physical sciences so well would produce comparable successes in the moral sciences, and even suggested that the causes which regulated moral phenomena were precisely analogous to those responsible for physical effects. For example, sudden changes in the moral order, "as in the physical order, never operate without a great loss of force vitale."[14] Poisson considered his law of large numbers to be a universal truth, demonstrating the general applicability of the probability of causes to both physical and moral phenomena.[15]

The probabilists justified their mathematical forays into the moral sciences on both methodological and metaphysical grounds. The obstacles which nature's opacity and daunting complexity posed to imperfect human understanding were an order of magnitude more formidable in the moral sciences. If meteorology and human mortality stymied attempts to discern causal links, the study of human action dealt with, in Laplace's words, "so many unforeseen or hidden or inappreciable causes... that it is impossible to judge their results a priori."[16] Bernoulli's model of a sealed urn, the unknown causes represented by its unknown contents, fit the methodological predicament of the would-be moral scientists in that it permitted only a posteriori knowledge of effects.

Condorcet, Laplace, and Poisson adopted both the mathematical format of the probability of causes based on Bernoulli's and Bayes' theorems and the concomitant assumptions concerning the uniformity and independence of trials in their treatments of the probability of judgments. Each judge was likened to an urn containing so many balls marked "true", corresponding to a correct decision, and the rest marked "false" to denote an incorrect decision. The proportion of "true" to total balls was the probability v that the judge would decide correctly on any given occasion. For $n = r + s$ urns, all of identical composition – corresponding, to n judges with identical individual probabilities v, whose decisions were further assumed to be absolutely independent of one another – Condorcet posited that the probability of a correct decision rendered by a majority of r, $r>s$, would be:

$$\frac{\binom{r+s}{s} v^r (1-v)^s}{\binom{r+s}{s} v^s (1-v)^r + \binom{r+s}{s} v^r (1-v)^s} = \frac{v^r (1-v)^s}{v^r (1-v)^s + v^s (1-v)^r} \qquad 17.$$

Since v could not be ascertained a priori, the probabilists resorted to the use of inverse probabilities. Laplace amended Condorcet's treatment to permit v to vary over the interval (1,0), so that the probability of a correct decision rendered by a given majority r of n judges, computed by Bayes' theorem, would be:

$$\frac{\int_{1/2}^{1} v^r (1-v)^s \, dv}{\int_{0}^{1} v^r (1-v)^s \, dv} \qquad 18.$$

Poisson assimilated the probability of judgments to a more statistical approach by assuming that the guilt or innocence of the accused operated as an unknown cause subject to his law of large numbers.[19]

With the aid of certain assumptions concerning the prior probability of the defendant's quilt k and also of the annual statistics on the number of convictions and acquittals compiled by the French Ministry of Justice from 1825 on,[20] Poisson was able to derive the probability that r out of n judges would render a correct decision:

$$\binom{n}{r} [kx^r (1-x)^{n-r} + x^{n-r} (1-k) (1-x)^r] \qquad 21.$$

Although these mathematicians differed in the details of their treatments and, as will be seen below, in the political tenor of their results, they all accepted the versimilitude of the political tenor of their results, they all accepted the versimilitude of the probabilistic model for judgment. Later critics of the probability of judgments such as John Stuart Mill and Louis Poinsot found it all but incomprehensible that thinkers of Laplace's stature could have compared judges "to so many dice, each of which has several sides, some for error, others for truth."[22] Joseph Bertrand objected that decisionmaking was intrinsically particular, governed by determinate but fluctuating factors: if a judge erred, it was for a specific reason, not because he had "put his hand in an urn" and made an unlucky draw.[23] Yet for the classical probabilists, primed as they were by associationist psychology to view thought processes as essentially combinatorial and probabilistic, these assumptions did not appear so outlandish. Condorcet and Laplace admitted that the conditions of independence, equality, and constancy for individual probabilities were simplifications, but argued that all mixed mathematics involved idealizations, and further maintained that such approximations "founded on the data indicated by good sense" were preferable to nonmathematical "specious reasoning."[24] However, the "good sense" confirmed by such calculations varied widely with political circumstances.

Rousseau's 'Le contrat social' (1762) stimulated interest in a related branch of inquiry, the mathematical theory of elections and committees.[25] In his treatise, Rousseau stipulated the practical maxims by which to set the required plurality for assembly: the more important the issue, the closer to unanimity the required plurality; and the more urgent the decision, the smaller the required plurality. Circumstances dictated the proper balance of the two constraints, for "it is by a combination of the two maxims that we can determine the right size for the majority that is to decide on any question."[26] Condorcet recast these two competing principles of unanimity and expediency in judicial terms in his mathematical treatment of tribunal decisions. Grave issues, such as a decision to abrogate natural rights or to inflict punishment, demanded a very high plurality; pressing matters could be dispatched with a simple plurality.[27]

Condorcet, like many other prominent intellectuals during the 1770's and '80's, enlisted in the philosophes' ardently waged campaign for judicial reform. Fueled by Voltaire's tracts on notorious miscarriages of justice in the cases of the Calas family and the Chevalier de la Barre,[28] and by the Abbe Morellet's widely read translation of Beccaria's 'Dei Delitti e delle Pene' (1764;

trans. 1766), the controversy centered on the provisions for torture, pre-trial detention, secret testimony, capital punishment, and other criminal procedures codified in the French Ordinance of 1670. Condorcet intended his 'Essai sur la probabilité des décisions' as a mathematical apology for liberal reforms, and took pains to summarize his principal conclusions and their policy implications in an long preface addressed to lay readers,[29] and in a similarly pointed and de-mathematicized correspondence with Frederick II of Prussia.[30]

Condorcet did not claim any novelty for his conclusions, which simply affixed the imprimatur of mathematical demonstration to the views dictated by "the simplest reason."[31] Instead, he regarded the Essai as an opportunity to harness the calculus of probabilities to the ends of political and social reform endorsed by all rightthinking people. Starting with the premise, which he described as "rigorously true", that "all possibility of an error in judgment is a true injustice",[32] Condorcet mathematically examined the means of minimizing that injustice. In doing so, he relied on a number of assumptions and techniques borrowed from earlier applications of the calculus of probabilities: Buffon's attempt to quantify the psychological impact of probabilities;[33] the constant causes and independent trials posited by Bernoulli's theorem; the classical probabilists' maxim that their results merely translated good sense into precise terms. Condorcet combined these assumptions with more political precepts such as the sanctity of natural rights, the social need for expediting legal procedures, and the inherent tension between individual and social interests implied by a contractual view of society. Condorcet's analysis attempted to determine the level of "sufficient assurance" that justice would be done in any individual case, given the inevitable injustice enacted in the long run by fallible ($v<1$) judges.[34]

In order to evaluate this critical level of sufficient assurance – i.e., the probability that any individual would be correctly judged – Condorcet proposed that citizens in a just society should run no greater risk of being wrongly convicted and punished for a crime than that to which they would "voluntarily expose themselves without any preformed habit, for an interest so slight that it

could not be compared to one's life, and without requiring any
courage":[35] for example, the difference between the probabilities
of dying suddenly within a week for two different age groups,
which Condorcet computed from the mortality tables to be
1/144,768. In essence, this was the fraction of individual liberty
traded for the benefits of community, as well as the acceptable
probability of an unjust conviction.[36] Condorcet conceived of
justice as a kind of contract in which risks to social order and
to individual liberty were balanced in the same way that risks and
potential gain were balanced in a fair game. However, Condorcet
recognized that this analogy was flawed:

"Society, if you will, would play a fair game, because it plays an
indefinite number of times; but it would not be the same for an
individual who, relative to the small risk he runs from freed
criminals, can only play a number of rounds too small for equality
to obtain for him."[37] Hence the need for an extremely high level
of sufficient assurance to safeguard individual liberties in the
game of justice. Voltaire's ringing denunciations of judicial
blundering in the case of the Calas family made Condorcet
sensitive to the possibilities of wrongful conviction. Because of
the inevitable, if miniscule, possibility of judicial error,
Condorcet argued against the death penalty as the only
irreversible punishment. Condorcet's other recommendations derived
from his mathematical treatment of the problem. Increasing the
number of judges n, the required majority r, and/or the individual
probability v all raised the overall probability of an correct
decision, but the last factor was the decisive one. If v was
greater than 1/2, the probability of a correct decision increased
with n. Condorcet interpreted his calculations as a mathematical
mandate for the rule of an enlightened elite:

"Thus the form of assemblies which decide the lot of men is far
less important for their happiness than the enlightenment
[lumières] of those who compose it: and the progress of reason
will contribute more to the good of the People than the form of
political constitutions."[38]

While Laplace seconded Condorcet's claim that the probability of
judgments produced "general results dictated by simple good
sense", the years of political upheaval which separated
Condorcet's Essai from Laplace's 'Théorie analytique des

probabilités' (1812) prompted Laplace to dilute Condorcet's optimism with repeated disclaimers that the mathematical treatment could not take account of all the relevant factors, due to the interference of "so many passions and special interests."[39] Recent history explained much of Laplace's caution. The Revolution, Directory, Consulate, and Empire had witnessed a succession of judiciary reforms which kept pace with the shifting locus of power. Among the most striking innovations were the institution of juries and the transformation of the system of "legal" proof. Whereas the hierarchy of proofs had spelled out the "probability" accruing to each type of evidence, effectively minimizing the personal discretion of the judge, the post-Revolutionary codes instructed juries to decide according to their "intimate conviction", explicitly prohibiting formal rules "according to which the completeness and sufficiency of a proof must depend" in favor of an appeal to intuition and conscience.[40] Although these reforms were aimed at the legal system of arbitrary "probabilities", the mathematical applications to jurisprudence appear to have been tainted by association. The probability of judgments smacked of the arid arithmetic of proofs decried by reformers as morally bankrupt.[41]

Yet despite this increasingly hostile climate of opinion, Laplace continued Condorcet's investigations on the probability of judgments, albeit with the caveats cited above. The prospect of practical applications may well have attracted Laplace to the subject. Under Napoleon, a new criminal code had been enacted at the end of 1808, effective as of January, 1811. Although many of the liberal reforms of the Revolution were superseded by regulations revived from the Old Regime, the comparatively new system of juries was retained over the Emperor's objections.[42] In his discussions of the probability of judgments, Laplace undertook to evaluate the probable accuracy of the jury system. Laplace pronounced the probability of a wrong decision under the extant system to be a "terrifyingly" high 65/256, and suggested corrective measures.[43]

Like Condorcet, Laplace found good sense to be vindicated by calculation: "Analysis confirms what good sense tells us, namely, that the correctness of judgments is as probable as the judges are numerous and enlightened." However, the prescriptions of good sense seemed to require a more subtle exegesis, for Laplace felt obliged to revise his treatment of the probability of judgments in the First Supplement of the 'Théorie analytique'. In this discussion, Laplace broached the difficulty of how the circumstances surrounding a legal case might legitimately influence the decision of the judges or jurors. In Laplace's opinion, this problem bore directly on the probability of a correct decision, or rather, upon the definition of what it meant for a decision to be correct:

"If I am not mistaken, this judgment reduces to the solution to the following question: does the proof that the accused committed the crime possess the necessary high degree of probability so that citizens have less to fear from the errors of the tribunal if the accused is innocent and convicted, than from his new attempts at crime, and those of the wretches emboldened by his impunity, if he is guilty and absolved?"[44]

In contrast to Condorcet's attempt to balance the contractual obligations of the individual and society to protect the rights of the individual being tried, Laplace's treatment considered all factors with regard to societal dangers. Each judge must assess not only the immediate probability that the accused was guilty or innocent, but also the probability that overriding social interests would be served by a particular verdict in a specific case. Both the gravity of the crime and the severity of the punishment must also be taken into account in order to render a "just" decision.

Poisson also wrote his "Recherches sur la probabilité des jugements" (1837) with the aim of evaluating existing judicial procedures. He benefited from the annual compilation of legal statistics begun in 1825. Several observers, including Quetelet and Guerry, had noted the striking constancy of certain figures from year to year: the national proportion of convictions to acquittals varied surprisingly little. Predisposed to interpret such statistical regularities in terms of the probability of causes from Laplace's demographic research, Poisson regarded the guilt or innocence of defendants as the "unknown cause" of the judgment pronounced. Influenced by the more macroscopic

perspective of the new social theorists, Poisson translated
rational decisionmaking into statistical terms. Like Condorcet and
Laplace, Poisson marched under the banner of "good sense"; in
fact, Poisson presumed to correct Laplace only in the spirit of
the master's own adage that probability theory was simply "good
sense reduced to a calculus." Laplace's computation of the
probability of an erroneous conviction under the French system
struck Poisson as "exorbitant, and counter to ideas generally
held."[45] Writing as a conservative official of a cautious regime,
Poisson tailored good sense to fit the interests of the state, as
Condorcet had matched mathematical results to liberal opinion.
Poisson for example rejected the assumption that there existed no
prior presumption of guilt against the accused, objecting that
criminal investigation procedures preliminary to the trial created
an a priori probability of guilt of at least 1/2: "certainly no
one would hesitate to wager in an equal game on his quilt over his
innocence."[46]

Like his predecessors, Poisson reflected upon the criteria for a
tolerable margin of error in criminal proceedings. Condorcet had
appraised the risk in terms meaningful to the individual citizen,
setting the level as low as possible so as to allow maximum
individual liberty. Poisson dismissed this approach as "much too
subtle for such serious issues", and although he considered
Laplace's balance of societal risks to be more suitable, Poisson
asserted the perogatives of societal security over individual
liberty even more emphatically. In Poisson's opinion, the jury did
not decide upon the actual guilt or innoncence of the accused, but
rather upon whether public security was better served by
conviction or an acquittal. With this criterion in mind, Poisson
substituted the word "convictable" (condamnable) for "guilty"
(coubable). Hence, the probability of an incorrect judgment
measured "the proportion of convictions which had too low
probability, not to establish guilt over innoncence, but rather to
establish that conviction was necessary for public security."[47]
The acceptable probability for conviction varied with
circumstances, depending on the judges, the nature of the crime,
and the details of the case. For example, a military tribunal
trying an espionage charge in the presence of the enemy would

require a far lower probability to convict than was customary in civilian trials.[48]

Poisson admitted that it would be impossible to determine this probability for any individual case, but insisted that such values were in any case irrelevant. Because the probability of error concerned only societal risks, only longterm results mattered. Condorcet had rejected the use of average probabilities and expectations reckoned thereupon because individual defendants would not have the opportunity to "break even" by playing many rounds of the game of justice. By eliminating all but societal concerns from his "convictable" probability, Poisson cleared the way for a statistical treatment of the probability of judgments. Judicial proceedings, like mortality rates, followed the universal law of large numbers if considered en masse. The perturbations caused by the effects of individual caprice, self-interest, or ignorance were no more erratic than those affecting human lifespan.[49] As long as the specific details of individual cases could be safely ignored, the law of large numbers applied equally well to all phenomena, moral and physical. By redefining the probability of judicial error solely in terms of public security, Poisson was able to extend the law of large numbers to the probability of judgments. Poisson underscored the importance of his analysis for judicial legislation, then in a state of flux, claiming that "nothing can replace the analytic formulas which express these various probabilities."[50]

The heated debate prompted by Poisson's papers on the probability of judgments in the Académie des Sciences bears witness to the controversial nature of the topic by the 1830's. Poisson's colleague Poinsot attacked the probability of judgments as "a false application" of mathematics, marred by ludicrous assumptions about the nature of decisionmaking. At bottom, Poinsot suspected any application of mathematics to situations involving human "passions and ignorance": reason had no truck with unreason, and the pretensions of a calculus of such irrationality could give rise to a "dangerous illusion" of precision in such incorrigibly inexact matters.[51] Charles Dupin, also a mathematician and a member of the newly reconstituted Académie des Sciences Morales et Politiques, faulted the probability of judgments for its oversimplifications, arguing that the causes which bore on judicial decisions were so complex and variable that any attempt to assign fixed probabilities was destined to failure. Dupin doubted that data subject to such fluctuating influences would approach stable limits defined by average terms, and moreover questioned the utility of averages which differed significantly from individual elements in the series.[52]

The mathematician and mechanician Navier came to Poisson's defense, and ,more generally to the defense of the universal applicability of mathematical models. Poinsot and Dupin agreed that applications of probability theory in the moral sciences mismatched analytic tools with the intended subject matter, albeit for different reasons: Poinsot feared that human affairs were to irrational to submit to mathematical description; Dupin maintained that they were too complex for the simplistic hypotheses posited by such abstract treatments. For his part, Navier decried the schism between the natural realm governed by invariable laws, and the moral realm where all was assumed to be "fortuitous and accidental". He championed the homogeneity of facts, even political and judicial facts in which passions and interests interfered.[53] Navier admitted that the mathematical model could not encompass every detail, but protested that this was as true in the physical sciences as it was in the biological and social sciences: "the art of the mathematician consists above all in distinguishing the principal elements, and in formulating an abstract problem which resembles the natural problem as much as possible, and to which analytic methods may be applied."[54]

The conservative tendencies of Poisson's statistical approach may well have piqued the more liberal sensibilities of Poinsot and Dupin; they outraged John Stuart Mill, who charged the probability of judgments with responsibility for making the calculus of probabilities "the real opprobrium of mathematics." To Mill, common sense rightly rejected any attempt to assess average probabilities of correct decisions as an abridgement of the rights of individuals and an absurdity to boot. A libertarian of Mill's persuasion would have found Poisson's "convictability" solution to the disparity between individual and average values untenable.[55] Joseph Bertrand echoed Mill in ridiculing the probability of judgments as a caricature of real decisionmaking, in which individual circumstances were of paramount importance and judges' decisions were anything but independent.[56] Bertrand branded all such speculations the "scandal of mathematics", ironically quoting Condorcet's appeal for "truly enlightened men."[57]

By 1840, the theory once advertised by its most prominent practitioners as a mathematical affirmation of "the primary insights of good sense"[58] struck mathematicians and philosphers alike as an "aberration of the intellect." In order to describe phenomena such as decisionmaking in mathematical terms, probabilists had made assumptions of both omission and commission concerning the salient features of the problem. Like all mathematical models, this one was valid on two conditions: first, that the assumptions accurately described certain features of decisionmaking; and second, that they omitted no essential aspects of that process. Two strains of eighteenth-century thought lent credence to the probabilistic model. First, theories of associationist psychology implied that reasonable judgments were formed on the basis of implicit mental calculations based upon individual acumen and past experience. Even intuitive judgments were intrinsically probabilistic. For reasonable men at least, the level of sagacity could be presumed fairly constant and uniform: hence the importance of hommes éclairés in the probability of judgments. Second, the Roman-canonical hierarchy of proofs had treated legal reasoning in a quasi-quantitative manner. Although the applicatons of mathematical probability to legal problems was by no means equivalent to this "legal" system of proofs, there existed shared assumptions concerning the possibility and desirability of reducing legal procedures to formal rules.

Both psychology and jurisprudence had considerably changed by 1835. Although associationist theories were still influential, they emphasized the pathologies of reason created by habit, prejudice, self-interest, and ignorance rather than the smoothly functioning mental calculus of Hartley. Good sense was no longer so clearly identified with computation and comparison of probabilities. The deliberately anti-formal, anti-analytic system of "free" proofs had replaced that of legal proofs, substituting an intuitive appeal to "intimate conviction" for any formal reckoning. The links between mathematical probability and the discarded arithmetic of proof rendered the probability of judgments suspect in the eyes of many, including the literary historian La Harpe and the Idéologue Destutt de Tracy, who dismissed the theory as "learned nonsense."[59] Poinsot's objections to the probabilistic model for the moral sciences reveal how far the notion of good sense had diverged from the mental calculus of the associationists, and how completely the free system of proofs had severed the older connection between legal and mathematical probabilities:

"It is the application of this calculus [of probabilities] to things of the moral order which offends the intellect. It is, for example, to represent by a number the truth of a witness; to thus assimilate men to so many dice, each of which has several sides, some for error, others for truth; to treat other moral qualities in the same way, and to convert them into so many numerical fractions... to dare, at the end of such calculations in which the numbers derive only from such hypotheses, to draw conclusions, which purport to guide a sensible man in his judgment of a criminal case... this is what seems to me a sort of aberration of the intellect, a false application of science, which it is only proper to discredit."[60]

Several of the most prominent spokesmen for ascendant moral sciences, including Auguste Comte, recommended judicious borrowing from the natural sciences and affirmed the existence of determinate (if not deterministic) social laws, but repudiated the reductionist model propounded by the probabilists as a kind of physico-mathematical imperialism. In their opinion, the "social mathematics" of Condorcet and his school abounded in ill-chosen problems, unjustified or even bizarre assumptions, vastly oversimplified hypotheses, and a pernicious tendency to obscure the characteristic complexity of the social realm by taking averages. Although there was little consensus regarding alternative methods or models, the moral scientists were generally united in rejecting both the problems and the assumptions of the probabilistic model. Comte strongly endorsed the study of mathematics (as well as the natural sciences which logically and historically preceded sociology in his classificaton of the sciences), but warned that the complexity of biological and a

fortiori sociological phenomena precluded the application of
mathematical methods to such subjects. Comte singled out attempts
to apply probability theory to the moral realm as particulary
misguided, and rebuked Condorcet, Laplace, and their followers for
"repeating the fancy, in heavy algebraic language, without adding
anything new, abusing the credit which justly belongs to the true
mathematical spirit."[61] Mill cautioned against the same misplaced
abstraction in his discussion of the relation of the "geometrical
or abstract" method to the moral sciences. The geometrical method
deduced conclusions from a "suppositious set of circumstances",
and was valid only to the extent that those suppositions were both
true and comprehensive.[62]

Although jurists for the most part pointedly ignored the
mathematical incursions of the probabilists into their domain, a
few rallied to the defense of traditional non-mathematical
procedures. Perhaps the most interesting of these "conservatives"
was the philosophical radical Jeremy Bentham, whose multi-volume
treatise on evidence was originally published in a shorter French
edition, Traité des preuves judiciaires (1823). Bentham objected
primarily to the false aura of certainty surrounding mathematical
treatments of legal matters. The greatest strength of traditional
legal methods consisted in the case-by-case orientation which
allowed full scope to individuating circumstances. The
oversimplified hypotheses of the probabilists yielded results
which were the "inverse of common sense" in any particular case.[63]
His disciple John Stuart Mill also upheld conventional legal
reasoning against the "rude standard" offered by the probability
of testimony and judgments.

Nor did the remarkable political plasticity of the probability of
judgments win for it the legislative approval sought by the
mathematicians. Comte, Poinsot, and Mill were especially anxious
that the arrogant claims of the probabilists to have
"demonstrated" their solutions might tarnish the reputation of
mathematics for irrefragable certainty. Their fears seem to have
been partially justified. Bertrand relates an anecdote about the
physicist and statesman Arago, a protégé of Laplace and co-editor
of Condorcet's works, who reportedly upheld Laplace's views on the
required majority of jurors for an acceptably low probability of

an erroneous conviction in a legislative debate over judicial reform. When a fellow Deputy expressed his reservations, Arago curtly replied that "when he spoke in the name of science, it was not for ignoramuses to contradict him."[64] The probabilists' mathematical hubris gained few friends for their policy recommendations.

Between 1785 and 1840 the peculiar constellation of intellectual and political factors which had created the probability of judgments dissolved. The transformation of associationist psychology, jurisprudence, the moral sciences, and good sense itself during this period destroyed the "pre-arranged harmony" which classical probabilists had assumed to exist between the mathematical theory and its subject matter. The mathematical techniques remained the same, but the context which had defined the analogy and therefore motivated the application had been drastically altered. Although probability theory retained a foothold in the social sciences, the focus of the model shifted from the psychology of the rational individual to statistical compilations and the distribution of traits in a large population. Poisson's treatment of the probability of judgments straddled the two approaches, repeating the format and assumptions of the classical analysis, but with the addition of statistical information. With Quetelet, who discussed judicial statistics but not the probability of judgments, the transition was complete. Condemned by the enlightened opinion its proponents had hoped to codify, the probability of judgments ceased to be a plausible description of the moral realm.

References

1 See Coumet, E.,: La théorie du hasard est-elle née par hasard? in: Annales: économies, sociétés, civilisations 25 (1970), pp. 574–98; also Daston, L. J.: The Reasonable Calculus. Classical Probability Theory, 1650–1840, Harvard University 1979, ch 1. (Unpublished Ph. D.).
2 See Villers, R.: Les preuves dans l'ancien droit francais, du XVIe au XVIIIe siècles, in: Recueils de la Société Jean Bodin pour l'Histoire Comparative des Institutions 17 (1965), pp. 345–56.

3 Bernoulli, J.:   Ars conjectandi, Basel 1713), Part IV, Ch. 3;
Bernoulli, N.: De usu artis conjectandi in jure, Basel 1709, Ch.
9;   Condorcet, M.-J.-A.-N.:   Sur la probabilité des faits
extraordinaires, in: Mémoires de l'Académie royale des Sciences
1783 (1786), pp. 553-59; Laplace, P. S.: Théorie analytique des
probabilités Paris 1812. (3rd ed. Paris 1820), Oeuvres complètes,
vol. 7, Paris: 1886, Ch. 11,. See also Daston, The Calculus
(ref. 1), Ch. 4.

4 Calculations on games of chance and annuities lost their
earlier associations with contract law and equal expectations; the
probability of testimony was expanded to treat the credibility of
historical reporters as well as courtroom witnesses; the
probability of legal conjectures inferred from the "nature of
things" became the probability of causes.

5 Quesnay, F.: Despotisme de la Chine (1776), Oeuvres économiques
et philosophiques de Quesnay, Oncken, A. (ed.): Paris 1888, p.
645.

6 Hartley, D.: Observations on Man, His Frame, His Duty and His
Expectations, vol 1, London 1749, p. 331.

7 Condillac, E.B. de: Essai sur l'origine des connaissances
humaines (1746), Oeuvres de Condillac, vol.1, Paris An VI (1798),
pp. 100; 109.

8 Condorcet: Vie de Turgot (1786), in: Oeuvres de Condorcet F.
Arago, F. and Condorcet-O'Connor, A., (eds.): vol. 1, Paris
1847-49, p. 222.

9 Laplace, Essai philosophique sur les probabilités (1814),
Paris 1825, 5th ed., p. 275.

10 Such a case arose with the St. Petersburg problem and
mathematical expectation. See Daston, L. J.: Prudence and Equity.
Expectation in Classical Probability Theory, forthcoming in:
Historia Mathematica.

11 Condorcet: Essai sur l'application de l'analyse à la
probabilité des décisions rendues à la pluralité des voix, Paris
1785, p. ii.

12 Condorcet: Discours sur l'astronomie et le calcul des
probabilités, lu au Lycee (1781), in: Oeuvres, vol. 1 (ref. 8), p.
502

13 Condorcet: Discours prononcé dans l'Académie Française (1782),
in: Oeuvres, vol. 1, (ref. 8), pp. 392-93.

14 Laplace, Oeuvres, vol. 7, p. lxxviii.

15 Poisson, S. D.: Recherches sur la probabilité des jugements en matière criminelle et en matière civile, Paris 1837, pp. 80–81.

16 Laplace, Oeuvres, vol. 7, p. lxxviii.

17 Condorcet, Essai (ref. 11), pp. 10–11.

18 Laplace, Oeuvres, vol. t. 7, pp. 522–26.

19 Poisson, Recherches (ref. 15), p. 12.

20 Garde des Sceaux, Ministère de la Justice, Compte général de l'administration de la justice criminelle en France, Paris 1827.

21 Poisson, Recherches (ref. 15), pp. 386–87.

22 Poinsot, quoted in: Comptes rendus hebdomadaires des séances de l'Académie des Sciences 2 (1836), p. 399.

23 Bertrand, J.: Calcul des probabilités, Paris 1889, p. 326.

24 Laplace, Essai (ref. 9), p. 268.

25 See Black, D.: The Theory of Committees and Elections, Cambridge 1958, ch. 18.

26 Rousseau, J. J.: The Social Contract, Maurice Cranston trans., 1968, p. 154.

27 Condorcet, Essai (ref. 11), pp. xv–xvi. Condorcet broached similar questions with respect to the deliberations of assemblies, in: Essai sur la constitution et es fonctions des assemblées provincales (1788), Oeuvres, vol. 8, pp. 115–659; and in: Sur la forme des élections (1789), Oeuvres, vol. 9, pp. 285–330.

28 See Imbert, J. (ed.): Quelques procès criminels des XVIIe et XVIIIe siècles, Paris 1964, for detailed accounts of both cases.

29 Condorcet, Essai (ref. 11), p. ii.

30 See Condorcet to Frederick II, 2 May 1785, in: Condorcet, Oeuvres, vol.1, p. 305.

31 Condorcet, Essai, p. ii.

32 Condorcet to Frederick II. 2 May 1785, in: Concorcet, Oeuvres, vol. 1, p. 305.

33 Buffon, G. L.: Essai d'arithmétique morale, in: Supplement de l'histoire naturelle, vol. 4, Paris 1777, pp. 56–8.

34 Condorcet, Essai (ref. 11), p.xxxix.

35 Ibid., p.cix.

36 Ibid., p. cxiii–cxiv.

37 Ibid., p. lxxix.

38 Ibid., p. lxx.

39 Laplace, Essai (ref. 9), p. 268.

40 From the Instructon of 21 October 1791, quoted in Gilissen, J.: La preuve en Europe du XVIe au début du XIXe siècle, in:

Recueils de la Société Jean Bodin pour l'Histoire Comparative des Institutions 17 (1965), pp. 831-32. These instructions were reprinted in the Code of 1808.

41 Bar, C. L. v.: A History of Continental Criminal Law, Boston 1916, pp. 337ff.

42 For eighteenth-century criticisms of the legal system of proofs see Beccaria: Traité des délits et des peines, Abbe Morellet trans., Lausanne 1766, p.42; Voltaire: Essai sur les probabilites en fait de justice, Oeuvres de Voltaire, vol. 30, Paris 1785, p. 462.

43 Laplace evidently intended his results to be taken seriously as policy recommendations, for he appended a passage (Article 351) from the most recent Code de l'Instruction Criminelle to the section of the Supplement of the Théorie analytique dealing with the probability of judgments in order to criticize its provisions from the standpoint of his mathematical results.These observations were published in a pamphlet entitled "Sur une disposition du code de l'instruction criminelle" (15 November 1816) and aired in the Chambre des Pairs debate of 30 March 1821. See Archives parlementaires, 2e série, XXX, pp. 531-32.

44 Laplace, Oeuvres, vol. 7, p. 521.

45 Poisson, Recherches (ref. 15), p. 7.

46 Ibid., p. 4.

47 Ibid., p. 6.

48 Poisson reassured his readers that although his calculations did not concern the number of innocent people wrongly convicted, he did not believe there were many such victims except in political trials. Ibid., p. 6.

49 Ibid., p. 12.

50 Poisson, S.D.: Recherches sur la probabilité..., Comptes rendus 1 (1835), p. 485.

51 Poinsot, quoted in: Comptes rendus, 2 (1836), p. 380.

52 Dupin, quoted in: ibid., p. 381.

53 Navier, quoted in: ibid., p. 382.

54 Comptes rendus 1 (1835), p. 249.

55 Mill, J. S.: A System of Logic (1843), New York 1881, 8th ed., p. 382.

56 Bertrand, Calcul (ref. 23), pp. 319-26.

57 Ibid., p. 327. Emphasis added by Bertrand.

58 Poisson, S. D.: Note sur la loi des grand nombres, in: Comptes

rendus 2 (1936), p. 399.

59 La Harpe,   J.-F.: Lycée, ou Cours de littérature ancienne et
moderne, vol. 14, Paris: 1813, p. 9; Destutt de Tracy, A.L.C.:
Eléments d'idéologie, vol. 4, Paris 1818, 2nd ed., pp. 37-38.

60 Poinsot,   in: Comptes rendus, 2 (1836), p. 399. I am indebted
to   Dr. Ivor Grattan-Guinness for the information that the
manuscript draft of Poinsot's remarks is preserved in the D. E.
Smith Collection at Columbia University.

61 Comte, A.:   The Positive Philosophy, vol. 2, London 1875, p.
100.

62 Mill, Logic (ref. 55), p. 371.

63 Bentham, J.:   Traité des preuves judiciaires, ed by Etienne
Dumont, vol. 2, Paris 1823, pp. 53-55.

64 Bertrand, Calcul (ref. 23), p. 371.

Judith V. Grabiner

CHANGING ATTITUDES TOWARD MATHEMATICAL RIGOR: LAGRANGE AND ANALYSIS IN THE EIGHTEENTH AND NINETEENTH CENTURIES

Introduction

To say "scientific developments have social and epistemological causes" is to state a generality to prove it requires an empirical base of specific examples. I wish to focus on one example from the history of mathematics: the foundations of the calculus between the late eighteenth and early nineteenth centuries. We will see, in some detail, the ways external factors can influence the choice of problems in mathematical research. And, because of the particular subject chosen – the foundations of the calculus – we will see the mechanisms by which external factors worked to increase the rigor of a branch of mathematics.

Eighteenth-century calculus was characterized by powerful techniques and novel results, nineteenth-century calculus by clear definitions and rigorous proofs. Throughout the nineteenth century, men like Cauchy, Bolzano, Abel, Weierstrass, and Dedekind advocated increased rigor in analysis. They also helped provide it, to the point that Henri Poincaré, looking back on the work of the nineteenth century, could claim that "absolute rigor" had been attained.[1]

Eighteenth-century mathematicians, by contrast, are not noted for great contributions tho the foundations of the calculus. The

H. N. Jahnke and M. Otte (eds.), Epistemological and Social Problems of the Sciences in the Early Nineteenth Century, 311–330.

problems of most importance to eighteenth-century analysts were those which could be treated without paying much attention to the foundations of the calculus.

These men drew no strict line between the calculus and its applications, between mathematics and mathematical physics. Though not indifferent to foundations, they preferred to concentrate on results, exploiting the heuristically powerful notation of Leibniz rather than the more certain, but apparently less fruitful, theorem-and-proof procedure characteristic of Greek geometry. The century was dominated by a few enormously productive mathematicians - the Bernoullis, d'Alembert, Euler, Laplace, Lagrange - whose work, except in part for Lagrange's, generally exemplifies the tendencies just described.

In the present paper, we will take these observations, which could be documented at length, as our point of departure. It was not until the end of the eighteenth century that the foundations of the calculus came to be recognized by leading mathematicians as a mathematical problem of central importance. Our question will be: how, and why did this recognition occur? The history of technical changes in the foundations of the calculus is, of course, part of the answer, but it is one which we have treated elsewhere.[2] In this paper, we focus not on technique, but on the change in mathematicians' attitudes toward the foundations of the calculus.

Believing rigorous foundations to be important was a necessary condition for producing them. After all, the existence of an unsolved problem does not mean that people will even attempt to solve it, let alone succeed in doing so. Though mathematical ideas have a life of their own, conditions external to mathematics frequently influence the choise of problems - as they did in the present case. Thus this paper will be a case study of one complex of external influences on the way mathematicians choose problems.

We will first explain why eighteenth-century mathematicians discussed foundations on the particular occasions they did. We will then look closely at the period when attitudes toward foundations changed. Our principal conclusion is that J.-L. Lagrange played a decisive role in bringing about this change. Accordingly, we will show what led him to consider, again and again, the question of foundations of calculus. The example of Lagrange will help us see how an individual mathematician, responding to outside influences, can catalyze an important development in the history of mathematics.

Eighteenth-Century Discussions of Foundations: When and Why?

In the eighteenth century, explanations of the basic concepts of calculus by leading mathematicians were usually found in four places: in the introductions to expository works on calculus; in popular expositions of mathematics for the non-mathematical reader; in replies to attacks on the logical soundness of the calculus; and in calculus classes. The "foundations" given in expository works are generally part of the introductory material. In contrast to nineteenth-century practice, rigorous foundations were seldom used to justify the full complement of results of the calculus. On the other hand, one place where contributions to foundations are conspicuous by their absence is in papers published in scientific journals. All of this means that foundations were not a topic of serious research, merely a prerequisite to explaining what really mattered.

The need to begin the exposition of a subject with definitions of its basic concepts is both psychological and logical. And since the calculus was a new subject, even a non-elementary treatise like Newton's "Method of Fluxions" would have to conclude introductory sections explaining the basic concepts. With the growing eighteenth-century community of scientists, the potential audience for such expository works was larger than it had ever been, and many mathematicians wrote such works, which included foundations.[3]

There was also a large non-professional audience for books about science in the eigtheenth century. Great popular interest had been aroused by the success of Newton's physics in understanding the laws of the universe, and both the mathematicians and the philosophers of the Enlightenment were involved in explaining the new science to laymen. For instance, the French "philosophes" produced the great 'Encyclopédie', intended to systematize the knowledge of the Age of Reason. In d'Alembert's articles for this Encyclopédie, we find his often-quoted explanations of the foundations of the calculus, which are presented without any accompanying exposition of the chief results of the subject.[4]

Philososophical disputes also contributed to discussions of foundations. For instance, one offshoot of the Newton-Leibniz controversy was the argument for the superiority of Newton's calculus over Leibniz's because of the claimed superior rigor of geometry when compared to algebra.[5] Even more important, the rigor of all versions of the calculus was sometimes attacked by philosophers, and mathematicians then moved to defend it. The most influential and best-known attack came in 1734 from George Berkeley, the Bishop of Cloyne;[6] it was undertaken partly in the service of Berkeley's idealist opposition to the ruling philosophical opinions of the Enlightenment, though its claimed motivation was to reply to an attack on religion from an unnamed "infidel mathematician." Berkeley ridiculed higher-order fluxions as "ghosts of departed quantities", and gave a tongue-in-cheek "defense" of the calculus by asserting that it got the right answers by "the compensation of errors". Several eighteenth-century discussions of foundations were stimulated by Berkeley's attack, most notably that given in Maclaurin's monumental "Treatise of Fluxions" of 1742. Moreover, Berkeley's criticisms of specific arguments in the calculus pointed out real deficiencies. Berkeley's theologically and philosophically motivated attack thus not only kept the question of foundations alive and under discussion, it pointed to questions that had to be answered by any successful foundation. For instance, d'Alembert implicitly answered some of Berkeley's arguments in his articles in the Encyclopédie;[7] Lazare Carnot based his book on foundations on his supposed proof that Berkeley's "errors" were always compensated;[8] and Lagrange used Berkeley's criticisms as part of his own critique of all earlier foundations.[9]

Another factor helping direct attention to the task of shoring up foundations was a feeling on the part of some eighteenth-century mathematicians — which has been labelled "fin de siecle pessimism"10 - that their subject was nearly a completed whole. The philosopher Denis Didérot reflected this feeling when he said that men like the Bernoullis, Euler, and d'Alembert "auront pose les colonnes d'Hercule" beyond which later ages could not pass.11

Lagrange apparently shared this view since he once characterized higher mathematics as "decadent."   I think it no coincidence that Lagrange said this in the same year that he published the first version of his new foundation for the calculus, defining the derivative by its position in the Taylor series;   if the structure was almost complete,it was surely time to attend to the final details of its foundations. This late-eighteenth-century feeling of great accomplishments virtually completed also produced synthetic textbooks like S.-F. Lacroix's three-volume "Traite du calcul differentiel et integral" of 1797, intended to bring together the mathematical work of the century. Lacroix's Traite, though it drew on a variety of mathematical works for its results, used Lagrange's foundation for the calculus - one mark of the influence we shall claim for Lagrange.

Last but not least, explanations of the calculus grew out of actual classroom teaching, particularly by around 1800. Earlier in the century, many scientists had depended upon royal or aristocratic patronage, or on personal wealth, for financial support, and there had been relatively few teaching positions. But as the scientific community grew and more men of the middle class entered science, both more teachers and more paying jobs were needed.   Also, there was a growing awareness that scientists could aid a nation's industrial and military progress. In response to these developments, new schools, and new positions teaching science in older schools, were established. The most important such new school was the Ecole polytechnique of Paris, founded in 1795 by the Revolutionary government of France. Other nations followed the French example. By the end of the eighteenth century, most active mathematicians were also teachers. And teaching the calculus, perhaps even more than writing textbooks, stimulated mathematicians to consider the foundations of their subject. Having students actually present helps make the teacher expound the first principles of the subject clearly, and encourages him to think them through once more. These observations help explain the fact that the major work on the foundations of the calculus by Lagrange and by Cauchy originated in their courses of lectures at the Ecole polytechnique.[16]

All this explains when and why foundations were discussed troughout the eighteenth century. But none of what has been said ist enough to explain why the foundations of the calculus became considered an important unsolved problem precisely near the end of the eighteenth century on the Continent. The chief agent of this change was Lagrange. Responding to many of the factors we have just discussed, Lagrange repeatedly investigated foundations. Not only does his career exemplify the way the causes we have listed spurred mathematicians to treat foundations, his work, stimulated by these causes, also influenced others to intensify their interest in foundations. In particular, as we shall describe, Lagrange moved others to contribute to foundations by at least three important actions. First, Lagrange published a paper in 1772 which dealt in part with Taylor series; this paper gave rise to a memoir by L. F. A. Arbogast which in turn contributed to Lagrange's own later efforts.[17] Second, Lagrange proposed, for the Berlin Academy's prize competition of 1784, the topic of finding a foundation for the calculus; this competition led to the publication of two major books on foundations, each growing out of entries to the competition, one by Simon L'Huilier, one by Lazare Carnot.[18] Last, and most important, Lagrange published two books: "Théorie des fonctions analytiques" (1797) [hereinafter called FA], and its immediate successor, "Leçons sur le calcul des fonctions" (1799–1801) [hereinafter called CF], both based on his lectures at the Ecole polytechnique. Lagrange's "foundations" in these works produced many others in the same tradition.[19] Moreover, his program of rigorizing calculus through abandoning appeals to geometry in favor of algebraic arguments was an important influence on both Bolzano and Cauchy.[20] Another measure of FA's influence is that journal articles on foundations, owing much to Lagrange's ideas, began to appear.[21] The most important such article is that in which A.-M. Ampère tried to establish an inequality-based foundation for the calculus, independent of Taylor series and still using Lagrange's proof techniques; as we have recently shown,[22] Lagrange's proofs about derivatives in FA and CF, mediated by this 1806 article by Ampère, helped form the basis of Cauchy's successful theory of the derivative.

In the light of Lagrange's influence in general, and the influence of FA in particular, it is important both to explain why Lagrange was concerned with foundations and to explain why his conclusions ultimately took the form they did. Part of the reason is not external, but is to be found in Lagrange's approach to mathematics. Lagrange's feeling for the general shines out in his papers: a particular result, whether the unsolvability of the quintic, the equation of motion for a physical system, or a theorem in number theory, is seen as a special case of some more general principle.

This feeling for general, rather than just specific, results made Lagrange more receptive to discussing foundations, when the occasion arose, than were his contemporaries. And Lagrange returned on many occasions to the problem of foundations. The fact that he returned so often matters, because Lagrange's views about the nature of the concepts of the calculus changed considerably over the course of his career. His mature work on foundations was the product of a lifetime of reflection on a relatively unfashionable subject. Since it was his repeated consideration of the question of foundations that eventually produced his FA, it is important for us to show both why he first took up this question and why he went back to it so often.

Lagrange's Early Ideas On Rigorous Calculus

Lagrange began his work on foundations for the usual eighteenth-century reasons. His first mention of the foundations of the calculus stemmed from teaching. In a letter to Euler dated 24 November 1759, Lagrange said he had worked out the elements of the differential and integral calculus for the use of his students at the military school in Turin.[23] He even said that he had "developed the true metaphysic of their principles, insofar as this is possible." It has been claimed that his phrase "insofar as this is possible" meant that he felt he had completely solved the problem, and that he had done it with the Taylor-series definition of f′(x) that he published some years later.[24] But I think it more likely that Lagrange in 1759 meant only that his presentation was the best possible, given the difficulty of the task. We do not know for sure, because Lagrange at this time seems still to have shared the general eighteenth-century view of the lack of mathematical importance of foundations, to the point that he did not even give any of the details of his own foundation to Euler. In the absence of a set of notes from Lagrange′s course at Turin, we cannot be sure what he thought the "true metaphysic" was in 1759. But we can make a good guess, since we do know what he thought in 176o: he accepted the Newtonian theory of first and last ratios.

Lagrange′s 1760 foray into the subject of foundations was a response to views expressed by a philosopher, the Barnabite friar Hyacinth Sigismund Gerdil, about the calculus. Gerdil held, in opposition to Fontenelle, that there was no actual infinite, and denied that the infinite was essential even in mathematical arguments which, like L′Hospital′s determination of the asymptotes to the hyperbola, explicitly used actual infinites or infinitesimals.[25] Lagrange added a footnote to Gerdil′s paper, in order to show not only that the calculus could reach conclusions without the actual infinite, but that it could do so rigorously. Lagrange wrote that the method of infinitesimals could indeed produce correct conclusions, but that it could do so only by a compensation of errors.[26] He did not, as is sometimes said, intend the compensation of errors to serve as his foundation for the calculus;[27] he simply used it to explain why infinitesimals work. As for justifying the results of calculus. Lagrange said that Newton′s method of first and last ratios – presumably as elaborated by d′Alembert, whose work Gerdil had mentioned, or by Euler – was "entirely rigorous, in the assumptions and in the procedures of computation; for [Newton] conceives that a secant becomes a tangent only when the two points of intersection come to fall on each other, and then he rejects from his formulas all the quantities which this condition makes actually zero". That is, Newton′s method requires that "the quantities whose first or last ratio we seek be regarded as evanescent, that is as zero."[28] In 1760, Lagrange hat not yet begun to criticize the eighteenth-century locutions "secant becomes a tangent," "points come to fall on each other," or "evanescent," all of which, as he was to point out in 1797, carry with them the idea of motion, which is foreign to analysis.[29]

Sometime between 1760 and 1772, however, Lagrange changed his views about the validity of the Newtonian basis for the calculus. In 1772, Lagrange published a paper - largely devoted to another subject, an operational calculus for the operators d and d/dx - which required some use of the Taylor series. And using Taylor series in this paper led Lagrange to make some remarks about these series and their relationship to the foundation of the calculus. Since these remarks are only incidental to the subject of his paper, it is clear that the foundations of calculus were on his mind and that he welcomed the occasion to discuss them. It is clear also that he no longer thought the concepts of the calculus were best explained by the method of first and last ratios. He declared instead that the concepts of the calculus could be made rigorous only if they were defined in terms of algebraic concepts, and we will see below that by "algebraic" he meant the algebra of infinite series.[30] Lagrange did not say why he rejected his earlier views, but I think he became dissatisfied with the Newtonian foundations by reflecting on Berkeley's criticisms of them.[31] In any case, while he no longer believed that the old foundations measured up to the standards of reasoning expected in mathematics, he did think that algebra provided an acceptable standard. Why might he have thought this?

First, an algebraic foundation for calculus is consistent with what we have said about Lagrange's general mathematical style: reducing a special or complicated topic to a more general or simple one. Second, by 1772, Lagrange seems to have believed that there was a wholly algebraic "theory of series" which gave any function a power-series expansion (except possibly at some finite set of isolated points). The origin of his belief was probably Euler's "Introductio in analysin infinitorum" (1748), which derived infinite series expansions for many functions, including transcendental ones, without ever appearing to need the concepts of the calculus. As Lagrange later acknowledged,[32] John Landen had defined the concepts of the calculus in terms of series in his

"Residual Analysis" (1764), though we may point out that Landen, unlike Euler and Lagrange, neither identified his series with Taylor's nor derived series for transcendental functions.

Out of this background, Lagrange developed his new idea for an algebraic foundation for the calculus. He said that "the known theory of series" gives u(x+h) as a power series in h:

$$u(x+h) = u(x) + ph + p'h + p''h + ...,$$

where p, p', p'', ... are new functions of x, "derived" in a certain way from the function u. "The differential calculus, considered in all its generality", Lagrange declared, " consists in finding directly, and by easy and simple procedures, the derived functions p, p', p'', ..."[33] Then, defining the functions u', u'', u''', ..., by

$$p = u', (u')' = u'', (u'')' = u''', ...,$$

Lagrange proved that

$$u(x+h) = u + h u'(x) + h /2 u''(x) + ...$$

He then asserted that the functions u', u'', u''', ..., so defined, could be seen to be equivalent to the well-known differential quotients du/dx, d u/dx ,... Lagrange said that his new view of the calculus was "the clearest and simplest yet given." Thus, he broke, both consciously and explicitly, with most earlier traditions about foundations. His self-proclaimed new view was intended to reduce the calculus to algebra, thus making it "independent of all metaphysics and all theory of infinitely small and evanescent quantities."[34]

With the phrase just quoted, Lagrange in 1772 became the first leading mathematician to grant the validity of the criticisms which had been levelled against the old foundations of the calculus, and to reply by proposing a new foundation instead of insisting indignantly that all was well. Yet in 1772 Lagrange still had not parted company with the eighteenth-century assessment of foundations as relatively unimportant. By this I mean: he stated no explicit, detailed criticisms of existing foundations; nor did he deduce even the basic algorithmic rules of the differential calculus from his foundation, let alone use that foundation to prove more advanced results. Though he thought the foundations of the calculus should be algebraic, in 1772 it was for him a goal hoped for, but not fulfilled. We know he was not yet satisfied with what he had done, because, by means of the prize competition of the Berlin Academy of Sciences in 1784, he (and his colleagues) appealed to the whole mathematical world to solve the problem of finding a rigorous foundation for the calculus.

The Berlin Prize of 1784

Scientific academies, born in the seventeenth century, were a social concomitant of the scientific revolution. In the eighteenth century, such academies often offered prizes for the solution of outstanding problems, to attract the attention of scientists to a major question and get it answered. In 1784 the Berlin Academy, at Lagrange's suggestion,[35] proposed the question of the foundations of the calculus as its prize problem. Thus in 1784 Lagrange publicly acknowledged not only that the existing foundations were unsatisfactory, but that rectifying this situation posed a major problem. Even more important, the wording of this proposal, for almost the first time, shows an awareness that solving the problem would be more than just a matter of finding plausible-sounding definitions for the basic concepts; a key point would be to justify the power of the methods of the calculus and its wealth of results.[36]

Lagrange and his Berlin colleagues did not get what they wanted. Though the prize was awarded to Simon l'Huilier, the Academy was not satisfied with any of the entries it got. The committee reported that the various contributions all were deficient in "clarity, simplicity, and especially rigor." They also complained that the contributors had not explained the past success of the calculus in deriving so many correct results. The tone of the committee's report shows that L'Huilier's paper was regarded as the best of a bad lot; the prize question, they concluded, "had received no complete answer."[37] Lagrange must have become even more dissatisfied with the state of the foundations of the calculus after reading so many weak papers by people who claimed they had solved the problem.

But dissatisfaction with old theories is not in itself enough to make a person produce a new one. Lagrange still did not convert his dissatisfaction into a new attack on the problem.[38] In the 1780's, he was completing his "Méchanique analytique", not working out foundations for the calculus. However, his "Méchanique analytique" may well have given Lagrange one more reason to want to make the calculus rigorous; having, as he thought, reduced all of mechanics to the calculus, he could make mechanics rigorous by showing the calculus to be so.[39] However this may be, when Lagrange, with the decline of Frederick the Great's court, moved from Berlin to Paris, he fell into a long depression during which he did no work at all.

Still, the Berlin episode had borne fruit in the work of others. Two full-scale books by mathematicians, intended not to teach the calculus but to expound the foundations and to derive the existing structure of results from those foundations, were based on essays submitted to this contest: L'Huilier's "Exposition élémentaire des principes des calculs supérieurs" (1787), and Lazare Carnot's "Réfléxions sur la métaphysique du calcul infinitésimal" (1797). Since these, and Lagrange's own FA, were the only major books with these goals published on the continent in the eighteenth century, Lagrange was directly responsible for the chief eighteenth-century continental manifestations of the new interest in foundations as a respectable mathematical problem.

The Making of Lagrange's Theory of Analytic Functions

If it had not been for the French Revolution, which resulted in Lagrange's being required to teach analysis at the Ecole polytechnique, he might never have written his FA. However, as he acknowledged, he had been "engaged by particular circumstances to develop the general principles of analysis."[40] For the task of teaching the calculus again after so many years, it no longer sufficed for him just to recognize the inadequacy of older foundations - even though he prefaced his book with arguments for their inadequacy. He needed, as well, a positive doctrine; so, as he put it, he recalled his "old ideas" on the principles of the differential calculus and worked them out further. These old ideas were the Taylor-series definitions first expounded in his Paper of 1772.

But FA contained much more than Lagrange had done in 1772. He now actually carried out the full program of deriving all results of the caculus from his definitions. In this task, he was aided by the fact that in 1789, at a meeting of the Paris Academy, he had heard L. F. A. Arbogast read an "Essai sur de nouveaux principes du calcul..." - still unpublished now. Lagrange was apparently quite impressed, since he said in 1797 that Arbogast's "beau mémoire" left nothing to be desired, except that it had not been published.[41] Lagrange's debt to Arbogast's memoir provides us another example of the influence of scientific academies on the development of scientific thought: here, in promoting the dissemination of yet-unpublished knowledge to their own members.

Arbogast said that the purpose of his "Essai" was "to bring to the higher calculus the same evident quality that reigns in ordinary algebra." Like Lagrange in 1772, Arbogast did this by defining the differential quotient by its occurrence as the coefficient of the linear term in the power-series expansion of the function, arguing that the differential calculus thus became "nothing but a particular case...[of] the general method of series."[42] Arbogast deduced the rules for finding differentials of some particular functions, of the product of functions, and so on, from his definition of dy/dx, something Lagrange had not done in the 1772 paper. Of course deriving these rules is easy, but it is still the necessary first step in working out the consequences of definitions, and thus a requirement for any serious work on foundations.

Arbogast also pointed out that an infinite series, when one took finitely many terms, had a remainder, which always needed to be taken into account.[43] In particular, Arbogast stated: "In the development of $\phi(x+\Delta x)$, one can always take for Δx a value finite and assignable, small enough so one of the terms of the series will be greater than the sum of all those which follow." Though Arbogast gave no reference, this principle can be found in Euler's "Institutiones calculi differentialis" (1755). In a recent

paper, I have called this principle "Euler's criterion," and have
shown it to be an essential part of Lagrange's inequality-based
proofs about derivatives, proofs later adopted - though
differently justified - by Ampère and Cauchy.[45] Arbogast seems to
have been the first to use that property to deduce, from
power-series definitions, the received results of the differential
calculus, including the important examples of the necessary
conditions for relative maxima and minima, and the analytic
treatment of orders of contact between curves. Later, Lagrange did
these same things in a fairly similar way. Examining the
manuscript shows that Arbogast's contribution, then, was to
reproduce for Lagrange Euler's work on inequalities involving
Taylor series, in the context of a Taylor-series definition of the
derivative. Thus wen the call came to teach in 1797, Lagrange had
at his disposal not only his Taylor-series definition of $f'(x)$,
but some indication of the techniques and direction he would use
in his theory of analytic functions.

Of course Lagrange went far beyond Arbogast. FA was a treatment of
foundations unprecedented both in scale and in quality. It began
with a full critique of all earlier foundations for the
calculus;[46] any new foundation, like Cauchy's, would have to meet
those criticisms. Moreover, FA demonstrated by example that a
foundation for calculus required exhibiting the received results -
and new ones like the Lagrange remainder of the Taylor series - as
parts of a logical structure resting on the definitions. In
particular, Lagrange derived from his Taylor-series foundation and
from Euler's criterion what I have called the Lagrange property of
the derivative:
"For any given D, h can be found small enough so that
$[f(x+h)-f(x)]/h$ lies between $f'(x)+D$ and $f'(x)-D$."
He exploited this property in his inequality-proofs about the
derivative, proofs which - given Cauchy's definition of the
derivative as a limit - could be adapted and justified by Cauchy
and his successors. So, when Cauchy taught calculus at the Ecole
polytechnique, he could build his course using many materials
provided by Lagrange.

For our purposes, it is important that Lagrange's book provided
his successors - especially Bolzano and Cauchy - not only with

techniques, but also with the example of a thoroughly worked-out foundation. Further, though Lagrange's Taylor-series definition of the derivative is logically inadequate, his view that the calculus should be rigorized by being reduced to algebra ultimately prevailed. Another measure of his influence is the near-universal adoption of his term "fonction derivee" (our "derivative") and the notation $f'(x)$ he introduced for it. The high priority Lagrange accorded foundations was essential to the nineteenth-century establishment of the rigorous basis for the calculus. Of course, since much of the technical content of his FA and CF could be used in Cauchy's foundation for the calculus, technical developments in Lagrange's books had as much to do with their influence as the new attitude toward foundations that the books proclaimed. But that is another story, which we will tell at another time.[48]

Conclusion

In this paper, we have stressed the social and epistemological causes of the change in attitude about foundations: the requirements of an expanding scientific community, philosophical questions, the need to teach. In fact, even after foundations had been firmly established by the work of Cauchy and Weierstrass as an essential — just pedagogical or philosophical — part of calculus, teaching and philosophy continued to stimulate contributions to the subject. Thus, for instance, Cauchy, Weierstrass, and Dedekind had pedagogical motivations; Bolzano and Cantor, philosophical.[49] Indeed, the rigorization of analysis in the nineteenth century can be seen as one more example of a phenomenon common to many of the sciences in the nineteenth century, and thus — presumably — at least in part externally caused: establishing the legitimacy and autonomy of newly systematized individual disciplines.[50] Mathematical ideas certainly have a life of their own, and the influence of external forces on mathematics is at best subtle and occasionally negligible. But, as the case of the foundations of the calculus between the eighteenth and nineteenth centuries demonstrates, even the technical history of mathematics cannot be fully understood without attention to non-mathematical conditions.

References

1 Poincaré, H.: in: Compte rendu du 2me Congrès internationale des mathématiciens. 1900, Paris 1902, pp. 120–122.

2 Grabiner, J.V.: The Origins of Cauchy's Rigorous Calculus, forthcoming; compare Grabiner, J.V.: Cauchy and Bolzano. Tradition and Transformation in the History of Mathematics, in Mendelsohn, E. (ed.): Transformation and Tradition in the Sciences, forthcoming.

3 E.g. Newton, Euler, Maclaurin, l'Hospital, Lacroix, etc. See the bibliographies in: Boyer, C.: History of the Calculus, New York 1959, and in: Cajori, F.: History of the Conceptions of Limits and Fluxions in Great Britain from Newton to Woodhouse, Chicago and London 1919.

4 Especially the articles 'Limité' and 'Différentiel'.

5 See Cajori (ref. 3).

6 Berkeley, G.: The Analyst, or a discourse addressed to an infidel mathematician (1734).

7 'Limité' and 'Différentiel'; though he did not cite Berkeley, both the similarities in language and the coincidence of problems support this conclusion.

8 Carnot, L.N.M.: Réflexions sur la métaphysique du calcul infinitesimal, Paris 1797.

9 Lagrange, J.-L.: Théorie des fonctions analytiques, Paris, 1797, preface, repr. in: Oeuvres de Lagrange, vol. IX, pp. 16–20. Compare Lagrange, J.-L.: Discours sur l'object de la théorie des fonctions analytiques, in: J. Ecole poly. (1799); repr. in: Oeuvres de Lagrange, vol. VII, p. 325.

10 Struik, D.J.: Concise History of Mathematics, New York 1967, p. 137. Compare the assessment by J. Dieudonné that mathematics in 1797 had just entered "a period of stagnation": Abrégé d'histoire des mathématiques, Paris 1978, p. 337.

11 Didérot, D.: De l'interprétation de la nature, Section IV, in: Vernière, P. (ed.): Oeuvres philosophiques de Didérot, Paris 1961, pp. 180–181.

12 Lagrange, letter to d'Alembert, 24 February 1772; in: Oeuvres de Lagrange, vol. XIII, p. 229.

13 Sur une nouvelle éspèce du calcul rélatif à la differentiation et à l'intégration des quantités variables, in: Nouv. Mem. Berl. (1772), pp. 185–221; Oeuvres de Lagrange, vol. III, pp. 329–476.

14 Lacroix, S.-F.: Traité du calcul différentiel et intégral, Paris 1797, Ch. 1.

15 See, e.g., Struik, History (ref. 10); Ovaert, J.-L. et al.: Philosophie et calcul de l'infini, Paris 1976; and Mendelsohn, E.: The Emergence of Science as a Profession in: Hill, K. (ed.): The Management of Scientists, Boston 1964, pp. 3-48.

16 Lagrange, J.-L.: Theorie des fonctions analytiques (1797) (2d ed. 1813); Leçons sur le calcul des fonctions (1799-1801); Cauchy, A.-L.: Cours d'analyse, Paris 1821; Resumé des leçons... sur le calcul infinitesimal, Paris 1823.

17 Arbogast, L.F.A.: Essai sur de nouveaux principes de calcul differéntiel et intégral, independants de la théorie des infiniment-petits et celle des limites, Biblioteca Medicea-Laurenziana, Florence, MS Codex Ashburnham Appendix Sign. 1840. I thank the Laurentian Library for providing me a copy of this manuscript. Grattan-Guinness, I.: Development of the Foundations of Mathematical Analysis from Euler to Riemann (Cambridge, Mass., 1970), cites another manuscript version, p. 155 of his bibliography, which I have not seen: MS 2089, Ecole des ponts et chaussées, Paris. Arbogast's manuscript "Essai" will be discussed below.

18 Carnot, op. cit.; l'Huilier, S.: Exposition élémentaire des principes des calculs supérieurs, Berlin 1787.

19 See Dickstein, S.: Zur Geschichte der Prinzipien der Infinitesimal-Rechnung. Die Kritiker der 'théorie des fonctions analytiques' von Lagrange, in: Abh. z. Geschichte der Math. 9 (1899) (= Z. fuer Math. u. Phys., Supplement to 44(1899)), pp. 65-79.

20 Grabiner, Cauchy and Bolzano, (ref. 2).

21 Dickstein, op. cit.

22 Grabiner, J. V.: The Origins of Cauchy's Theory of the Derivative, in: Hist. Math. (1978), pp. 379-409. Compare Dugac, P. in: Histoire du theorème des accroissements finis, Paris 1979, which includes extensive citations from the primary sources with a connecting narrative.

23 The letter is reprinted in: Oeuvres de Lagrange, vol. XIV, p. 173.

24 As claimed by Jourdain, P.E.B.: The idea of the 'Fonctions analytiques' in Lagrange's early work, in: Proc. Int. Cong. Math. II (1912), pp. 540-1; Jourdan's reasons are: (1) Lagrange had

introduced the prime-notation for the coefficients in the Taylor series in 1761, and (2) in 1772 Lagrange did define the derivative as the coefficient of h in the Taylor-series expansion for f(x+h). However, (1) does not support Jourdain's conclusion, since the "reform" in the 1761 paper is merely one of notation; for our explanation of (2), see our text.

25 Gerdil, H.S.: De l'infini absolu, in: Misc. Taur. (1760-61), pp. 1-45.

26 Lagrange, J.-L.: Note sur la métaphysique du calcul infinitésimal, in: Misc. Taur. (1760-61), pp. 17-18; repr. in: Oeuvres de Lagrange, vol. VII, pp. 597-9.

27 As Boyer seems to imply, op. cit., pp. 257-8, and as Carnot apparently believed, op. cit.

28 Lagrange, op. cit., p. 598.

29 FA, preface, p. 4, in: Oeuvres de Lagrange IX, p. 17.

30 Grabiner, J.V.: Is Mathematical Truth Time-Dependent?, in: Am. Math. Monthly 1974, pp. 354-365; see pp. 356-7.

31 Lagrange certainly was acquainted with some of Berkeley's ideas, since he uses the concept and the term "compensation of errors." There is no direct evidence about when, if ever, Lagrange read the Analyst itself; Lagrange did read English, as his citations of Landen and Maclaurin show. And Lagrange does use Berkeleyan arguments in his critique of older foundations; see FA, preface, in: Oeuvres de Lagrange, vol. IX, pp. 16-20.

32 In the preface to his FA; see: Oeuvres de Lagrange, vol. IX, p. 18.

33 Sur une nouvelle espece du calcul, in: Nouv. Mem. Berl.(1772), pp. 185-221; repr. in: Oeuvres de Lagrange, vol. III, pp. 439-476, p. 443. The notation here is confusing, since it is not the prime-notation for derivatives which he introduces later in the same paper; but it is his notation nevertheless.

34 Loc. cit.

35 The prize competition was set by the "Classe de mathématiques" of the Academy, which in 1784 included Lagrange, Johann (II) Bernoulli, and Johann Karl Gottlieb Schulze. Lagrange was the leading light, and had long been concerned with this problem. That it was his idea is supported by Hofmann, J.E.: Geschichte der Mathematik, vol. III, Berlin 1957, p. 68, and by Youschkevitch, A.P.: Lazare Carnot and the Competition of the Berlin Academy in 1787 on the Mathematical Theory of the Infinite, in which he drew

on the manuscript collection of the Berlin Academy; the article is to be found in: Gillispie, C.C.: Lazare Carnot Savant, Princeton 1971, pp. 149-168; see p. 155.

36 Since the whole idea of "infinite magnitude" seemed to be inherently contradictory, the Academicians asked "that it can be explained how so many true theorems have been deduced" from such a problematic concept. See Hist. Acad. Royale, Berlin 1784, pp. 12-13.

37 Hist. Acad. Royale, Berlin 1786, p. 8.

38 Vivanti, G.: Infinitesimalrechnung, in: Cantor, M.: Vorlesungen ueber Geschichte der Mathematik, vol. IV, Leipzig 1908, p. 645, has claimed this; however, the time lag is simply too great.

39 As he said explicitly in the preface to the second edition of that work, the "Mechanique analytique" uses infinitesimals, but these can be given a rigorous basis by using the theory of analytic functions; Oeuvres de Lagrange, vol. XI, p. xiv.

40 FA (1797), preface, p. 5; Oeuvres de Lagrange, vol. IX, p. 19.

41 Loc. cit.

42 Quoted from the MS by Zimmermann, K.: Arbogast als Mathematiker und Historiker der Mathematik (Heidelberg, 1934), p. 45.

43 Arbogast: Calcul des dérivations, Paris 1800, p. xiii, in his own account of this manuscript.

44 Loc. cit. Cp. Zimmermann, Arbogast (ref. 42), pp. 47-48.

45 Grabiner, Cauchy's Theory of the Derivative, (ref. 22), p. 385.

46 See ref. 29.

47 Grabiner, Cauchy's Theory of the Derivative (ref. 22), p. 384; see CF, 2d ed., in: Oeuvres de Lagrange, vol. X, p. 87; the notation is his, exept that I have substituted the more usual h for his i.

48 See ref. 2.

49 For Weierstrass, see Klein, F.: Entwicklung der Mathematik im 19ten Jahrhundert, vol. I, Berlin 1926, p. 283ff.; compare Dieudonné, Abrégé d'histoire (ref. 10), pp. 370-3. For Dedekind, see his own introduction to: Continuity and Irrational Numbers [1872], New York 1963, p. 1. For Bolzano, see. e. g., his: Paradoxes of the Infinite; on Cantor, see first Dauben, J. W.: Georg Cantor, Cambridge (Mass.) 1979.

50 I owe this observation to the remarks at the Bielefeld
conference of L. J. Daston and E. Mendelsohn. And, as I. Tòth
pointed out at the conference, within mathematics itself the
development of non-Euclidean geometry provides an instructive
example of the definition of a new - and autonomous -
subdiscipline, and of the intercation between mathematics and
philosophy.

Winfried Scharlau

THE ORIGINS OF PURE MATHEMATICS

0. Timetable

L. Euler	1707–1783	J. L. Lagrange	1736–1813
G. Monge	1746–1818	P. S. Laplace	1749–1827
A.-M. Legendre	1752–1833	J. Fourier	1768–1830
C. F. Gauss	1777–1855	V. Poncelet	1788–1867
A. L. Cauchy	1789–1857	A. F. Moebius	1790–1868
J. Steiner	1796–1863	J. Pluecker	1801–1868
N. H. Abel	1802–1829	C. G. J. Jacobi	1804–1851
G. P. L. Dirichlet	1805–1859	W. R. Hamilton	1805–1865
E. E. Kummer	1810–1893	E. Galois	1811–1832

1. From the 18th to the 19th Century

In this lecture I would like to address the question when, how, and under which historical conditions modern mathematics originated as a science. My viewpoint on this matter is one of a mathematician who is interested in the history of the development of his own field.[1] I must stress from the outset, however, that I can only contribute an informal discussion to this vast area of study, and that many important historical points which would be appropriate for a detailed presentation of the subject will only be fleetingly touched upon.

H. N. Jahnke and M. Otte (eds.), Epistemological and Social Problems of the Sciences in the Early Nineteenth Century, 331–347.

The most important books on the history of mathematics largely
agree that pure mathematics had its origins in the time span from
the 18th to the 19th century. To give a survey of the subject, so
that particular questions can be more clearly addressed later, I
will first quickly sketch this development and verify it with a
few quotations.

In comparison to the preceeding as well as the following century,
the 18th century is characterized by a remarkable continuity and
uniformity: In the foreground stands analysis and its application
to mechanics, and in particular to celestial mechanics.[2] In this
sense, the mathematics of the 18th century is applied mathematics,
i.e. primarily aligned with the natural sciences and subordinate
to the description of physical phenomena. "Far more than in any
other century the mathematical work of the eigteenth was directly
inspired by physical problems. In fact, one can say that the goal
of the work was not mathematics, but rather the solution of
physical problems; mathematics was a mean to physical ends."[3] What
we understand today as pure mathematics, namely theoretical
mathematics in which mathematical theories are developed for their
own sake and then applied to particular mathematical problems for
their solution, first existed around the beginning of the 19th
century.[4] Struik says the following: "The new mathematical
research gradually emancipated itself from the ancient tendency to
see in mechanics and astronomy the final goal of the exact
sciences... A division between 'pure' and 'applied' mathematics
accompanied the growth of specialization."[5]

Felix Klein saw this development in a similar light: "That earlier
epoch held as most important the development of differential and
integral calculus begun in 1700, which furnished new possibilities
for mastering mechanics and astronomy. It reached its climax in
the works of two french mathematicians... Lagrange... and
Laplace... The 19th century now displayed a completely different
character... Pure mathematics stepped boldly and significantly
forward in two ways: Completely new areas were created... the
traditional legacy of science was scrutinized..."[6]

The long dominating position of applied mathematics is perhaps
most convincingly illustrated in the themes of the

prize-competitions of the prominent academies of science, especially the Paris academy. These range from the optimum arrangement of ship masts (1727), the movement of the moon (1764/68), the movement of the satellites of Jupiter (1766), the three-body problem (1770/72), the secular perturbations of the moon (1774), the perturbations of comet orbits (1776/78/80), the perturbation of the orbit of Pallas (in the beginning of the 19th century), to the question of heat conduction (1810/12), or the propagation of sound waves in liquids (1816). It was only with a certain reluctance that questions of pure mathematics would occasionally be posed, for example the theory of polyhedrons (1810) or the Fermat problem (1816).

Before we close this section, I should perhaps clear up a possible misunderstanding: Pure mathematics certainly existed much earlier, e.g. in classical antiquity or with Fermat. Nevertheless, we are interested here in the process of the evolution of mathematics. And this process, in the sense of a continuous development, begins approximately with Newton and Leibniz. Previously, developments which had begun pointing towards the future had time and again been abruptly cut off; the number theory of Fermat, to cite an important example, stood still for one hundred years.

Now that we have an overview of the time sequence, we should examine under which politico-sociological, philosophical, and intra-mathematical circumstances and influences pure mathematics arose, and which effect, if any, these had.

Before we begin, however, a still more general restriction must be made. Certainly in the evolution of every science over a long perod of time one can always detect the lines of development and perhaps also a certain rigidity and conformity. In addition, one can usually identify those external forces which have a more or less noticeable effect. In our case, however, one should keep in mind that the mathematics of the period under discussion consisted to a large degree of the work of only a very few mathematicians, and their individual interests - perhaps not in the long run but definitely for half a century - had a fundamental influence on the development of mathematics. The example of elliptic functions -

which more than any other area played a central role in the
mathematics of the first half of the 19th century - should make
this clear.

This theory, as is well-known, was created by Abel and Jacobi.
Abel came upon it partly by accident through a suggestion of the
no longer mathematically prominent but learned mathematician F.
Degen.[7] His suggestion showed quite clearly that the theory was to
a certain extent up in the air. The enormous development that then
followed, however, was the personal work of Abel and Jacobi, and
was largely due to their ambition at the time to beat the other to
the discovery and proof of new theorems. The development was
pushed so far ahead that afterwards a long period of relative
stagnation set in and only quite recently a deeper understanding
of many results has become possible.

2. After the French Revolution

The decisive sociological and political event of the period under
discussion was the French Revolution. It is not necessary to give
a detailed account here of its effect on the natural sciences and
on mathematics in particular. An accurate summary was given by
Struik:
"The French Revolution and the Napoleonic period created extremely
favorable conditions for the further growth of mathematics. The
way was open for the Industrial Revolution on the continent of
Europe. It stimulated the cultivation of the physical sciences; it
created new social classes with a new outlook on life interested
in science and in technical education. The democratic ideas
invaded academic life; criticism rose against antiquated forms of
thinking; schools and universities had to be reformed and
rejuvenated.
The new and turbulent mathematical productivity was not primarily
due to the technical problems raised by the new industries.
England, the heart of the Industrial Revolution, remained
mathematically sterile for several decades."[8]

The crucial point is expressed in the last two sentences. It is
quite clear that the social development made possible a great

upswing in the sciences. But there is no evidence here of anything in particular which would have promoted the growth of pure mathematics. While it is plausible that applied mathematics would have acquired a certain impetus, in order to understand or even to explain why pure mathematics sprung up at this time - and indeed an especially unapplied area like number theory - in terms of the political situation and the necessities of society, one must look further.

A glance at the lives of a few of the most important mathematicians of the time gives us a clue: Beginning about this time it was possible for the dependents of the poor and the unskilled ranks of society to obtain enough elementary education and material necessities so that a step up to the level of a scientist was possible for the very first time. Neither the career of Gauss who rose out of small town circumstances, nor that of the farmer's son Steiner who still could not read or write at the age of sixteen, nor that of the pastor's son Abel who grew up under the poorest conditions in isolated Norway, would have been possible a hundred years earlier. There simply would not have been anyone who would have recognized and encouraged their genius. Now, through this minimum of general education and social security, a large reservoir of gifted people had been opened up. It is significant, but also easily understandable, that this reservoir was predominantly of benefit to theoretical mathematics. In the beginning these self-taught people had no chance to educate themselves sufficiently in the complicated and technically advanced disciplines of applied mathematics and theoretical physics to be able to work successfully in these fields. They had to rely on what they found within themselves, such as number theory (Gauss), synthetic geometry (Steiner), or abstract algebra (Abel).

3. The Rejection of Idealism

On the whole, the mathematics of the 18th century fit smoothly into the various though related philosophical systems of the French and the English during the Age of Enlightenment (encyclopedianism and mechanical materialism, empiricism and

utilitarianism). With the more rationalistic and eventually
idealistic German philosophies, at least a peaceful coexistence
was possible for some time. The eminent significance of mechanics,
celestial mechanics, and mathematical physics is a direct and
consumate expression of the philosophy of this century which
believed in progress, and was perhaps most clearly formulated in
Laplace's introduction to his great work on probability theory:
"An intelligence which, for a given instant, knew all the forces
by which nature is animated and the respective position of the
beings which compose it, and which besides was large enough to
submit these data to analysis, would embrace in the same formula
the motions of the largest bodies of the universe and those of the
lightest atom: nothing would be uncertain to it, and the future as
well as the past would be present to its eyes."[9]

This harmony of development came to an abrupt halt with the
beginning of the new century. The new idealistic philosphy of
Fichte, Schelling, Hegel and "their kind"[10] was (and is)
decisively rejected by most mathematicians. This may seem
surprising at first, since who if not the pure mathematician deals
so much with ideal objects. G.H. Hardy - a mathematician pure as
the purest water, utterly convinced of the beauty, depth, and
eternity of mathematics - nevertheless convincingly delineated why
mathematics and idealistic philosophy could not tolerate one
another. In comparing physical and mathematical objects, he comes
to this conclusion:
"At any rate (and this was my main point) this realistic view is
much more plausible of mathematical than of physical reality,
because mathematical objects are so much more what they seem. A
chair or a star is not in the least what it seems to be; the more
we think of it, the fuzzier its outlines become in the haze of
sensation which surrounds it; but '2' or '317' has nothing to do
with sensation, and its properties stand out the more clearly the
more closely we scrutinize it. It may be that modern physics fits
best into some framework of idealistic philosophy - I do not
believe it, but there are eminent physicists who say so. Pure
mathematics, on the other hand, seems to me a rock on which all
idealism founders: 317 is a prime, not because we think so, or
because our minds are shaped in one way or another, but because it
is so, because mathematical reality is built that way."[11]

An apparent exception perhaps was C.G.J. Jacobi, in whose often
quoted sentences an idealistic viewpoint can actually be
discerned: "Anyone who carries the idea of a science within
himself can do nothing more than evaluate things according as his
human intellect reveals them to him ..." "- because only in the
movement of thoughts man is free and by himself -", and lastly the
famous reply to Fourier: "... le but unique de la science, c'est
l'honneur de l'esprit humain ..."[12]

I believe, however, that one must view these sentences not only as
a conscious expression of idealistic philosophy but in equal
measure as the expression of the basic ideals of neohumanism of
which the philosphically and historically well-educated Jacobi was
an eminent representative.

For the purposes of this lecture it is not necessary to pursue the
connections between philosophy and mathematics any further. One
should only keep in mind that during the critical transition
period, mathematics received no real stimulus from philosphy.
Looking ahead, it can be added that since this time the
relationship between both disciplines appears to be deeply
disturbed. "Our principal intellectual doctrines and outlook were
fashioned then, and we still live in the shadow of the Age of
Reason."[13] "... more than any other philosophy, Hegel's system has
contributed to the division between scientists and philosophers".[14]

4. Misconceptions about Rigor

An essential difference in the mathematics of the 18th and 19th
century, as we have already noted in the quote of F. Klein, was
the appearance of a steadily growing need for "rigor" and exact
foundations. The situation is often depicted as if the building
erected by Newton, Leibniz, Euler, and Lagrange was about to
collapse and in the direst need of rescue by Gauss, Bolzano,
Cauchy, and Abel. That of course is simply not the case; in
reality, even the essentially new theories of the 19th century
(such as elliptic functions, (algebraic) number theory, complex
analysis) in all important respects could have been built up with

the traditional mathematical notions (indeed, because of them),
since they utilize the unproblematical analytic functions.

Nevertheless, the question is of some interest, particularly for
the philosophy of mathematics, since the need for rigor is
obviously not a purely intra-mathematical one. I would like to
briefly explain how this need came about and which effect it had.
As far as the cause is concerned, the most important viewpoint is
found in a paper of J. Grabiner, which incidentally also contains
some debatable points: "In bringing about the change, there is one
other factor which, though seldom mentioned in this connection,
was important: the mathematician's need to teach... Teaching
always makes the teacher think carefully about the basis for the
subject. A mathematician could understand enough about a concept
to use it, and could rely on the insight he had gained through his
experience. But this does not work with freshmen, ... Beginners
will not accept being told, 'After you have worked with this
concept for three years, you'll understand it.'"[15]

This argument can be elaborated somewhat: Not only for teaching
rigor is useful and requisite, but also for the increasing
communication between mathematicians. As the first important
textbooks were being written, it appeared necessary - as Grabiner
has also stressed - to lay down the foundations clearly and
carefully. Yet, a consequence of this development was that new,
difficult and mathematically interesting problems emerged - and
this alone made the whole affair interesting to mathematicians.
Perhaps the most important of these questions was which functions
could be represented by their Fourier series. No problem
contributed more to working out the notion of a function or of
convergence - and also a good deal of set theory - than this.

I might add that in the entire philosophical and historical
discussion of foundations of this century the same above mentioned
mistake has been repeated. The great upswing of mathematical logic
and proof theory, as well as related areas (set theory, model
theory) had very little to do with an intensified need of
mathematicians for an "exact foundation" of their subject. These
areas were undertaken because they presented many difficult and
interrelated unsolved problems.

5. The Growing Together of Mathematical Areas

We have seen in the first four sections that external influences had only a very indirect and almost imperceptible effect on the origins of pure mathematics. They can be understood - and there is much agreement to this - only in terms of intra-mathematical developments. Struik, as we have already quoted, views the origins of pure mathematics in connection with an increasing specialization. Felix Klein sees the matter similarly, even though he does not formulate it so explicitly. A generally accepted view is expressed by Alexandrov in the following way: "The new development of mathematics at the beginning of the 19th century was primarily brought about by the necessity to solve its own problems which had assumed the character, so to speak, of puzzles." As examples he then cites non-Euclidian geometry, complex numbers, the theory of algebraic equations, and the precise foundation of analysis.[16]

Being somewhat in agreement and somewhat opposed to this view, I would like to advance the thesis that the decisive condition for the origin of pure mathematics was the fact that for the first time in the history of mathematics a large number of connections were discovered between seemingly different problem areas and results.

Until well into the 18th century, mathematics was comprised of many isolated areas of study into which some order was slowly introduced with the help of partially developed methods - for example differential equations and the calculus of variations in analysis. The range of application of these methods was easily grasped and apparently somewhat limited. Then connections between the most distant branches of mathematics suddenly appeared. It is obvious that this must have led to a completely new intensity of development and that this development rose to a new level. To that extent I maintain rather the opposite of Struik: Pure mathematics originated in the transcending of special viewpoints.

It seems to me that the theses of Struik and Alexandrov (which were selected somewhat at random but are nevertheless typical) are not well-suited for elucidating the reasons why pure mathematics originated. The ideas they express are indeed correct, yet they basically explain little: Every theoretical science is responsible for solving its own problems which are always somewhat puzzling, and in every science the constantly increasing specialization is the inevitable result of further development. This does not explain any essentially qualitative changes in the development of a science. On the other hand, if one sees formerly separated and independent branches in a science starting to come together and influencing one another, then one would expect that the development of this science would be fundamentally changed. This can also be seen for example in the history of physics.

I believe that the asserted thesis can be conclusively proven, but of course this would require a detailed account of the historical and mathematical development of many difficult mathematical problems. Since, on the other hand, I do not want to simply refer to the collected works of Gauss, Fourier, Abel, Jacobi, and Dirichlet, I will content myself here as a compromise with a few detailed indications and examples, which perhaps will lend my thesis some credence.

1. One of the most famous and well-known results from the foundational period of analysis is Leibniz's series

$$1 - \frac{1}{3} + \frac{1}{5} - \frac{1}{7} \pm \ldots = \frac{\pi}{4}$$

Gauss discovered that one could derive this result from a purely number theoretic fact, namely that the Unique Factorization Theorem holds for complex integers $a+ib$, $a,b \in Z$. This connection would later be recognized by Dirichlet as one of the key points of a whole theory.[17]

2. One of the greatest results of Euler was the calculation of the series

$$1 + \frac{1}{4} + \frac{1}{9} + \frac{1}{16} + \ldots = \frac{\pi^2}{6}$$

Fourier obtained this calculaton - as well as the Leibniz series and many others - as a consequence of his theory of Fourier series which he had developed to solve problems of heat conduction in solids.[18]

3. One of the most interesting number theoretic problems left behind by Fermat was the question of how many different ways can a number n be expressed as the sum of four squares,

$$n = a^2 + b^2 + c^2 + d^2 .$$

Euler had an ingenious idea: If one develops the function

$$f(z) = (1 + z + z^4 + z^9 + \ldots)^4$$

in a power series

$$f(z) = 1 + a_1 z + a_2 z^2 + \ldots ,$$

then a_n is exactly the desired number. Jacobi was the first to succeed in computing the a_n within the framework of the theory of elliptic functions. And this, in the final analysis, comes down to problems of integral calculus, namely finding the integral of functions like

$$(x^4 + ax^2 + b)^{-\frac{1}{2}}$$

These elliptic functions are involved with many other areas; they are used in theoretical physics, and Gauss encountered them again in his calculations on the perturbations of planets.

4. A comprehensive topic which is connected with the first example should now be somewhat elaborated. Gauss began his mathematical career with the solution of a question thousands of years old, namely the construction of a regular polygon with 17 sides. I have already mentioned how typical it is for a self-taught person to get involved with such "pure" problems. As is well known, the question of constructibility amounts to the problem of whether the irreducible algebraic equation

$$x^{16} + x^{15} + \ldots + x + 1 = 0$$

can be reduced to a system of quadratic equations. Gauss was able to answer this algebraic question affirmatively. In his solution, it turned out that the first necessary step could be carried out for an arbitrary prime p instead of 17. That is, the expression

$$S = \sum_{k=1}^{p-1} \left(\frac{k}{p}\right) \exp\left(\frac{2\pi ik}{p}\right)$$

satisfies the equation $S^2 = \pm p$, as can be easily verified.
Furthermore, Galois' theory shows that this first step is
essentially necessary. So, in his solution, Gauss must have
arrived at the Gaussian sum in some form or another. Indeed, he
was able to guess this expression and thus solve his algebraic
problem, only because he had been previously involved with
quadratic residues, that is, the Legendre symbols $\left(\frac{k}{p}\right)$. The
fundamental theorem concerning the Legendre symbols is the
Reciprocity Law, which Gauss (re-)discovered because of numerical
evidence and was first to prove,

$$\left(\frac{p}{q}\right)\left(\frac{q}{p}\right) = (-1)^{\frac{p-1}{2}\frac{q-1}{2}}$$

This proof was his second outstanding achievement. Because of the
great significance of this formula for number theory, Gauss was
involved with it again and again, and later discovered two
particularly elegant proofs which are based on the calculation of
the above sum.[19] He certainly would not have been able to find
these proofs if he had not already been involved with partitions
of the circle.

The story, however, did not end for a long time after this:
Dirichlet solved the difficult problem of calculating S exactly
through a most ingenious and elegant application of the theory of
Fourier series (whose origins we have already noted). In addition,
he encountered the Gaussian sums in a completely different
connection, namely in his famous proof of the Prime Number Theorem
where they play a central role in the calculation of $L(1,X)$. For
this purely number theoretic theorem (if a,b are relatively prime,
then there exist infinitely many prime numbers of the form a+kb),
he had to invent a completely new analytic theory, the theory of
Dirichlet series, whose first origins in turn can be traced to
Euler. At the latest, it was from this point on in the development
that there was no more holding back: In every direction new
connections to Pell's equation, to quadratic forms, to the
ζ-function, etc. became clear.

5. As a last and somewhat different example (since it is not
derived from an individual problem), I should mention the calculus

of residues in complex analysis which, as is well known, made possible to a great extent the calculation of difficult real integrals (and also the Gaussian sum S!).

6. Fourier and the Analytic Theory of Heat

With regard to the already established though not yet explicitly stated thesis that history of mathematics is essentially the history of mathematicians and their individual interests, I would like to close our discussion by considering one of the masterpieces of the transition period to modern mathematics. This is Fourier's principal work, "Théorie Analytique de la Chaleur", which appeared in 1822 but which had already been drafted in the previous two decades. This book can be looked upon as a key work of the transition period because it is
- the clarified result of careful, years-long, and strenuous research
- presented in a finished and polished form
- written by a non-mathematician (namely, a politician) who could view his work to a certain degree from the outside and who was in a position and of the inclination to clearly and convincingly bare his philosophical position
- originated from the analysis of basic physical problems for whose solution a new mathematical theory was developed which transcended the original physical questions, provided a deeper insight into numerous earlier individual mathematical results, and has had an impact on pure mathematics even up to this day
- and finally - as was already briefly pointed out - gave impetus to the first foundation crisis in so far as a more exact establishment of the most important notions of analysis became imperative.
There is scarcely another work in the mathematical literature of the world for which a similar description would be true!

If one now looks at this book in the light of the questions being discussed in this lecture, then the persistent impression remains of the inevitable consistency with which the development leads to pure mathematics. This corresponds in no way to Fourier's original intentions; in the foreword and introduction he refutes again and again the value of pure mathematics:"... [these methods] lead to the last numerical calculations, and that one must demand of every investigation if one does not want to merely obtain useless transformations"." "The truth which we want to uncover lies no less hidden in the analytical formulas than in the physical problem itself."[20] Things go quite differently in the book, however: Numerical calculations are completely missing, "useless transformations" abound. As an example, one needs only to inspect the important Articles 163–181 in which one can follow how the Fourier series – which today are one of the most important mathematical resources of every physicist and electrical engineer – are generated. The problem concerns the stationary temperature distribution in the infinite half plate with certain boundary conditions, and is described by the Laplace equation $\Delta v = 0$. Through a separation of variables one finds particular solutions and then the general solutions as linear combinations. These have the form of trigonometric series and the boundary conditions lead to an infinite system of equations for the coefficients. In the calculation of these coefficients Wallis' product for $\frac{\pi}{4}$ appears, and somewhat later there is finally the "derivation of new expressions for π" which concerns series similar to those in section 5 above. Here one is in the middle of the purest mathematics, and it is high time for Fourier to say that all of this is of "no interest". Yet, here is exactly one of the points where relationships to other questions can be created and further development – e.g. with Dirichlet – resumed.

With his utilitarian convictions which he is quick to repeat at every opportunity, Fourier is completely shipwrecked. In the whole book he makes only one attempt at a "useful" application (Art. 86), and this attempt could really not have ended more deplorably: "In reality, our results will be modified... by the many incidental circumstances which have not been considered. Strictly speaking, our formulas are likely to find no practical applicatons. Nevertheless, they have an inner value since they are based on the true principles of heat theory..." With this reference to inner value we are not very far from his antithesis, from Jacobi.

If one looks for an explanation for these constant, unintentional turns to questions of pure mathematics, then one is led to a completely new viewpoint. To a certain extent, the path to physics was blocked for Fourier: More than almost any other phenomenon, the search for the physical nature of heat posed unsolvable problems in his days. On the one hand, heat behaves in a solid body like a material substance, similar to a spreading and thinning gas; on the other hand, it can penetrate empty space like the heat radiation of the sun and be reflected like light. Actually, the only thing that was clear was that a purely mechanistic interpretation – in the sense of the above quotation of Laplace – would cause the greatest difficulties.

This explains also the phenomenalistic assessment of Fourier which made him one of the foremost proponents of positivism. In reality, this positivistic position ÷ his principal work begins with the famous sentence: Les causes primordiales ne nous sont point connues ... – was a kind of retreating position in which he had to swallow his pride because the purely mechanistic-materialistic world view had come under question, to say the least. Thus, he placed value in building his theory only upon foundations "which are well accepted by all physicists whatever their view in regard to the inner nature of heat might otherwise be". If one considers now that he was a careful man by nature, that he like every scientist had gone down countless wrong paths in the course of decades of effort in his work, that in his life as a politician he had more than his share of the "changes and errors of the human intellect", then one can understand why he only wanted to go as far as he could really be sure of his subject.

This led him, after he had established once and for all the differential equations of heat conduction based on physical evidence, to questions of pure mathematics from which he never escaped.

And in the introduction he also described this science with moving and penetrating words: "Such a science can only slowly cultivate itself, what it has but once obtained on fundamental principles, it will retain forever; it grows and increases without stopping amidst so many changes and errors of the human intellect. Its main

W. SCHARLAU

characteristic is clarity; it possesses no symbols for
representing muddled ideas. It brings all of the most diverse
phenomena together and discovers the hidden similarities which
connect them."

References

1 A. Weil has repeatedly pointed out that this is the only
possible viewpoint from which the history of mathematics can be
meaningfully undertaken. See e.g. Helsinki Lecture 1978, Coll
Works, vol. III.
2 Cf. Struik, D.J.: A Concise History of Mathematics, New York
1948, 2d ed., p. 163.
3 Kline, M.: Mathematical Thought from Ancient to Modern Times,
Oxford 1972, p. 616.
4 No attempt should be made here to define a precise boundary
between pure and applied mathematics, nor to dogmatically separate
them.
5 Struik, History (ref. 2), pp. 2olf.
6 Klein, F.: Vorlesungen ueber die Entwicklung der Mathematik im
19. Jahrhundert, pt. I, Berlin 1926, Einleitung, pp. 2f.
7 Cf. Ore, O.: Niels Hendrik Abel. Mathematician Extraordinary,
New York 1974 (Repr. of 1957), p. 35.
8 Struik, History (ref. 2), p. 201.
9 Laplace, quoted from ibid., p. 196.
10 Gauss used the term "Konsorten".
11 Hardy, G.H.: A Mathematician's Apology, Cambridge 1969,
art. 24.
12 Qoted from Koenigsberger, L.: Carl Gustav Jacob Jacobi.
Festschrift zur Feier der hundertsten Wiederkehr seines
Geburtstages, Stuttgart 1904, pp. 11, 13.
13 Kline, M: Mathematics, a Cultural Approach, Reading (Mass.)
1962, p. 23.
14 Reichenbach, H.: The Rise of Scientific Philosophy, 1951,
p. 72.
15 Grabiner, J.: Is Mathematical Truth Time-Dependent?, in: Am.
Math. Monthly (1974).

16 Quoted   from: Otte, M. (ed.):   Mathematiker ueber die
Mathematik, Berlin 1974.

17 The historical situation is unfortunately not completely
clear, since sources as to whether, how, and when this result of
Gauss became known to Dirichlet are missing.

18 Cf. the following section on Fourier.

19 The problem is to determine the sign of S.

20 If one reads the introduction to his less significant book
'Analyse des Equations Determinées' one would be inclined to doubt
that he was in a position to really understand a question of pure
mathematics at all.

Ivor Grattan-Guinness

MATHEMATICAL PHYSICS IN FRANCE, 1800 - 1835

[Lagrange's foundations of the calculus] est
assurement une très-intéressante partie de ce qu'on
pourrait appeler l'étude purement philosophique; mais
quand il s'agit de faire de l'analyse transcendante
un instrument d'exploration pour les questions que
présentent l'astronomie, la marine, la géodésie et
les différentes branches de la sciences de
l'ingénieur, la considération des infiniment petits
conduit au but d'une manière plus facile, plus
prompt, plus immédiatement adaptée à la nature de ces
questions, et voilà pourquoi la méthode leibnitienne
a, en général, prévalu dans les écoles françaises.

(de Prony 1843, p .11)

1. Introduction

Around 1800, the branches of physics which had received
substantial mathematical treatment were terrestrial and celestial
mechanics, and some aspects of optics. The physics was based on

H. N. Jahnke and M. Otte (eds.), Epistemological and Social Problems of the Sciences in the Early Nineteenth
Century, 349–370.

Newtonian principles (optics was then usually regarded as a particlate phenomenon), together with various additions and refinements. The mathematics involved was centred largely on the solution of differential equations: it comprised the differential and integral calculus, and some aspects of the calculus of variations, the summation of series and the theory of equations. The calculus was based on Lagrange's assumption that every finite-valued function f(x+h) could be expanded as a convergent power series in h, whose coefficients supplied the derived functions of f at x.

During the next quarter of a century both the physics and the mathematics expanded greatly. Heat diffusion, electricity and magnetism received substantial mathematical as well as physical treatment, and the realm of optics was considerably extended. Similarly, the calculus was broadened by the accretion of new theories of the convergence of infinite series, complex variable and Fourier analysis, and greatly increased knowledge of some special functions and the theory of equations. For the rest of the century much work in both physics and mathematics was devoted to the extension and consolidation of the innovations made during these twenty-five years. For the next decade up to 1835 almost all the major contributions were French.[1]

2. Principal Events in France, 1800 - 1825

The first major innovation was Fourier's work on heat diffusion. Initially presented to the Institut de France in 1807, it was the first substantial mathematical treatment of a physical phenomenon which did not fall within Newton's laws of mechanics. In it Fourier re-introduced, and greatly extended, the discredited method of solving differential equations by trigonomentric series. Furthermore, he had a busy, and surely full-time, job as a provincial French préfet. For such reasons his work caused considerable controversy; and even though Fourier and his supporters secured a prize problem for heat diffusion in 1812, which he won with a paper in which he introduced the Fourier integral, his work did not secure major publication until his 'Théorie analytique de la chaleur' of 1822 (see my and Ravetz's 1972).

Meanwhile, optics was greatly advanced by the work of Malus, Biot and Arago on polarisation and double refraction around 1810, and a few years later entered a controversial period with Fresnel's proposal of a wave theory of light to replace the prevailing, and Newtonian, particulate interpretation (see Frankel 1976). Fresnel's theory included a significant mathematical component.

By the early 1820s, when Fresnel's 'victory' was becoming generally rezognised, there was great excitement in scientific circles concerning electromagnetism and electrodynamics; for it was clearly quite a shock that there could be close connections between these two classes of phenomena. Among the French, Ampère's work is best remembered; but there were also contributions to the mathematical side of the theory from Biot and Savart, and both before and after this time Poisson wrote important papers on electrostatics and magnetism.

In this way apparently non-Newtonian physical theories were introduced and published by 1825; together with the Newtonian mechanics, they formed 'mathematical physics'. There were many connections between the traditional and new areas, not merely on physical grounds but also because of the versatility of application of the mathematics. Differential equations and their solution were the principal study (see Burkhardt 1901–08), and Fourier's methods offered strong but controversial competition to the traditional power-series and functional solutions. Cauchy came to Fourier integrals independently of Fourier, and he and Fourier showed their superiority for linear equations over the traditional methods (of which Poisson was the chief defender) in the late 1810s. Cauchy made various other major contributions, especially the beginnings of his theory of complex variable functions and their residue integrals; and it was also he, with his 'Cours d'analyse' (1821) and other books of the time, who showed the way to the 'new' mathematical analysis, in which the calculus, the convergence of series and the theory of functions were unified under the definition and theory of limits (see my

1970 and 1980b).[2] Mathematical analysis quickly became established, and Fourier's and related methods of solving differential equations gained the support of the new generation of mathematicians.

3. Physics and Mathematics: A Similarity of Structural Change

The changes in physics and mathematics over this period are remarkably similar, for in each case we see a body of 1800 knowledge becoming part of a broader range of theories. Further, in each subject the 'traditional', 18th-century, areas received substantial extension of their own. Within mechanics, sound, elasticity, hydrodynamics, pendulum theory, capillary action, attractions, and perturbations of planetary orbits were especially popular. Within the calculus, the 'derived function' of Lagrange's power-series was replaced in Cauchy's theory by the derivative, defined as the limiting value (if it exists) of the difference quotient; while the integral, defined in Lagrange's theory as the converse of the 'derived function', became an area regarded as the limiting value (if it exists) of a sequence of partition-sums.

In one important respect the similarity between physics and mathematics does not apply. While there was a hope in the early 19th century that Newtonian theories would be able to explain the expanding realm of physical phenomena, by the late 1810s the hope was becoming forlorn (see Fox 1974), and no alternative concept was to emerge until consideration of energy and its convertants in the middle of the century. Thus there was then no concept in mathematical physics to play the unifying role that was fulfilled by limits for mathematical analysis. Instead, there were discussions of analogies between branches, which were not normally regarded as epistemological reductions. For example, one could regard heat as like optics if one supported a wave theory of each, without claiming that either was reducible to the other, or that each was a special case of a more general third category.

One source of analogies was the aether, which continued to receive widespread support (see Whittaker 1951); there was much discussion of the properties it might have, especially as to whether it was elastic like an elastic fluid or stretchable membrane. Another similarity with mathematics arises here; for mathematicians continued to make extensive use of infinitesimals (as de Prony noted at the head of this article), although doubts concerning their legitimacy — which had in part motivated Lagrange's own view — were still raised.

I mentioned above a respect in which mathematics and physics were not similar. This respect is an example of the general question of the extent to which the structure of a piece of mathematics can, or cannot, be interpreted as structure in the physical theory also. Take, for example, a Fourier series, which was an important new mathematical technique of the period. Mathematically it has the structure of a (hopefully convergent) infinite series of periodic functions. Can it also be interpreted this way in a physical context? For acoustics, such an interpretation seems natural: the first term gives the harmonic, and the coefficients determine the super-harmonics. But for heat diffusion, which was Fourier's initial context, he was careful not to insist that temperature be interpreted as a sum of a series of heat states to which the individual terms might refer, nor to support the wave theory of heat just because of the presence of periodic functions. Similarly, he could without contradiction claim the autonomy of heat diffusion from Newtonian mechanics (on the issue of irreversibility) while aware of the interpretability of Fourier series in both areas: for the autonomy concerns the physical theory while the versatility of interpretation occurs in the mathematical theory.

The point made here concerns any use of mathematics in physics; indeed, it is a philosophical point, not only an historiographical one. Its importance is provided not only by its ubiquity but also by the perplexing variety of degrees to which the similarity of structure between mathematics and physics may occur in a given situation. It was also a source of controversy about the mathematicisation of science. More is the pity, then, that historians of physics pay so little attention to the mathematics that is often involved in physics, and rarely regard mathematics as a source of historical and historiographical questions.

4. People and Place

I have named various people in the earlier sections, so it would
be meet now to list the principal French figures. Although I have
been discussing the period 1800–1825, I shall extend the period in
this section to 1830, to accommodate the emergence of some younger
important figures.

Paris was, of course, the dominant centre, and all the major
figures were there for at least a substantial part of their
careers. The main centre for the presentation of results was the
Institut de France, and the principal stimulus to the important
educational aspects was the Ecole polytechnique. But there were
many other societies, journals and schools where important work
was done and presented (see Crosland 1967). Indeed, the Institut
was notoriously slow at publishing papers presented by members
(and even slower with the accepted works of savants étrangers), so
that publication of results was usually first made in summary
papers in the satellite journals. And the establishment of
'property' was certainly well-advised; for many of these men were
extraordinarily ambitious and competitive, and the literature
contains many polemics. Some are merely priority disputes or
accusation of plagiarism, but many raise substantial points of
disagreement over theoretical conceptions of the physical
phenomena , or the legitimacy of mathematical methods.

The competitiveness of French science has often been noted before;
but the kind of competition needs specifying in more detail. I
make a distinction between 'internal' and 'external' competition.
Internal competition occurs within, or concerning, a community or
one of its institutions; for example, in entry to the Ecole
polytechnique and achievement of high results while there, or in
rivalries between members of the Institut over some scientific
issue.[3] External competition occurs between communities and their
institutions; for example, whether a student goes to the Ecole
polytechnique or some other school. Now the French are strongly
competitive in the internal sense of the term, but not
particularly so in the external aspects. For example, an aspiring

roads engineer will want to go to the Ecole polytechnique and then the Ecole nationale des ponts et chaussées; other alternatives are without doubt inferior. Again, the career scientist places membership to the appropriate class of the Institut far higher than any other possible membership (the Société philomathique, say). And for everybody at all times, there is the desire to be in Paris rather than anywhere else: 'people and place', as I titled this section.

The most interesting feature of the community is that in terms of its intellectual interests, especially research, it divides into two groups. One group usually worked in the more traditional areas, mechanics and calculus, even when the new areas were emerging. They were also very active in engineering (on which I shall comment in section 7-8), and some were quite good, or at least diligent, experimenters. Members of the other group usually worked in both the traditional and the new areas. By and large they were the better creative mathematicians of the community, but were less competent at the experimental work and sometimes even ignorant of the physical situations to which their mathematics was purportedly relevant. Both groups worked in mechanics and calculus, but even then they tended to reveal the different kinds of interest; for example, Navier seems to have studied elasticity because of its bearing on the flexure of timbers, while Cauchy may have been chiefly attracted by the differential equation involved.

In Table 1 I present the principal figures in each group. They are divided into three generations: those who were active and prominent by 1800, those who achieved prominence between 1800 and 1815, and those who came to prominence between 1815 and 1830. I have excluded physicists such as Arago and S. Carnot, whose mathematical contributions were very slight.

After 1830, and especially after 1840, we see France decline somewhat in prominence as scientific centre – although I am inclined to regard the decline much as the rise of other countries (compare my 1980a, sections 10-11). I suspect that the rise in importance of France at the beginning of the century was caused in part by the intensity of internal competition (to use my terminology of a few paragraphs ago), and the decline as a result

Table 1

Principal members of the French community in
mathematical physics, 1800 - 1830

Prominent	Mathematical physics/ mathematical analysis		Mechanics/calculus/ engineering	
By 1800	Lagrange Legendre	Laplace	L. Carnot de Prony	Monge
1800–1815	Ampère Biot Fourier Poinsot	Binet Cauchy Malus Poisson	Dupin Girard Navier	Francoeur Hachette Poncelet
1815–183o	Duhamel Lamé Sturm	Fresnel Liouville	Coriolis Puissant	Poncelet

of the lack of external competition to provoke response to
changing problems and interests. However, I regard the degree of
decline after 1830, suggested in influential papers such as
Ben-David 1970 and Kuhn 1976, as greatly exaggerated. I give some
evidence of health (and also of a rise in external competition) in
connection with engineering in section 8 below). I may also note
here the considerable rise in importance after the 1830 revolution
of the Ecole normale as a scientific centre, in which the
philosopher and administrator Cousin played an important role (see
Dupuy 1884 and Zwerling 1976). From the mid 1830s onwards, French
mathematical physics was graced by the presence of normaliens.
Their contributions were largely on the 'pure' side, which is not
surprising, since from its beginnings in 1808 the Ecole was
primarily concerned with humanities subjects.

5. Two Philosophical Issues

In addition to the technical developments of the various branches
of physics and mathematics, there were several philosophical
issues which were discussed. I shall briefly describe two: one
concerned with physics, and one with mathematics.

One can take two views about the foundations of a physical theory:
either they are secure, or they are not secure. At this time those
who claimed that foundations were secure usually asserted that
they were established by induction from primordial facts: the
development of the theory upon these foundations was to be
understood as articulation. But the view that the foundations of a
physical theory are hypothetical, and that the development of the
theory is for the purposes of prediction, gained considerable
acceptance during the early 19th century, both in France and
elsewhere. In fact, the chronological character of the change is
its principal feature: it does not seem to correlate with
intellectual interests, for example. All the members of the first
generation in Table 1 appear to follow the inductive view, but
many members of the later generations adoped the hypotheticist
position. Poisson seemed to adhere to the traditional view; Biot,
for one, vacillated between one position and the other; while
Poinsot may be an example of someone who did not discuss the
matter. But the change is quite noticeable, and constitutes a
major historiographical problem for the period. It is particularly
notable in Fresnel, who replaced the inductive 'truth' about the
corpuscalarity of light with an hypothesis concerning its waval
character (see Silliman 1975). It may also be the source of
another similarity between physics and mathematics; for one source
of superiority which Cauchy claimed for mathematical analysis (in
the introduction to his 'Cours d'analyse' (1821)) was its
avoidance of relying on mathematical inductions as used in algebra
at that time.

This change of view by generation also has considerable interest
for the history of education; for the members of the first
generation (except L. Carnot) were principal teachers and/or
examiners of the Ecole polytechnique during its early years, while

those in the later generations were initially either minor teachers or students there. We may have here an unusual example of 'student revolt'.

The mathematical issue of philosophical character which I wish to raise concerns whether one basically works or thinks in geometrical, algebraic or analytical terms. The difference manifests itself, for example, in thinking of the integral as an area, as the value of the converse differential operator, or as the limiting value of a sequence of partition-sums. It is a rather subtle distinction, for it is not that between geometry, algebra and analysis themselves; for example, one may do geometry rather algebraically, or express oneself geometrically without necessarily drawing diagrams. I stress the distinction because a) many of the figures named in section 5 show one or other style quite markedly; b) it seems to be a significant mode of influence: the geometrically inclined, for example, will respond to the work of geometrical predecessors – and not only to its geometrical component – because of that commonality of thought; and c) it crosses the boundaries of intellectual interest, since it is concerned with how one works rather than what one works on.

As an example of all three factors I consider Lagrange and de Prony, and Monge and Fourier. Lagrange was strongly algebraic in both mathematics and mechanics, to the extent of emphasizing the absence of diagrams in his works. De Prony was also highly algebraic, even though he was largely concerned with engineering problems. By contrast, Monge was entirely geometrical in style, and not only in his descriptive geometry; his interpretation of differential equations and their solutions was geometric in form (see Taton 1951). Fourier followed Monge entirely in this view of differential equations, even down to details of notation, although he did not research in engineering or descriptive geometry. Thus, in terms of interests Fourier belongs with Lagrange and de Prony with Monge, but relative to this aspect of methods Fourier followed Monge and de Prony followed Lagrange.

As an example of the scale of the difference that is involved here, I may contrast Monge's and de Prony's treatment of the foundations of statics. In his textbook Monge relied constantly on diagrams; in the sixth edition 1826, which is basically the 1810 edition edited by Hachette, 215 octavo pages of text are accompanied by 100 diagrams. By contrast, de Prony's 'Mécanique philosophique' (1799) algebraically presents the foundations of statics, dynamics, hydrostatics and hydrodynamics in 486 quarto pages and no diagrams at all. Now both these works were used as text-books at the Ecole polytechnique at the same time, and the contrast in style is so marked that alert students must at least have been puzzled. Perhaps this was a source of their disaffection from the view that the foundations of a physical theory are secure!

The variety of published treatments of the same topics suggests that there was no ruling orthodoxy about styles of thinking. In other words, I think that a man presents his work in a particular style because he really wants to think it out and present it that way; we do not seem to have a case here of men working privately one way and writing it up for publication in another, 'approved', style. On the occasions when I have seen manuscripts of one of these men, for example, they usually reveal the same style as is manifest in their publications.

It follows that a man does seem to intend the style that he has adopted. But this makes especially difficult (and also important) the question of why he adopts one style rather than another, a process which usually seems to occur during his education or soon afterwards. Maybe the type of problem he prefers to study is a factor. For example, a cause of the decline of the algebraic style is that Lagrange's formulation of mechanics makes much use of variational principles, which provides general principles and methods independent of geometrical configurations but is thereby rendered intractable when the solutions to the problems are not known. Hence a man like Poisson, anxious to work within established problem areas, will respond to the algebraic style (especially as this type itself was dominant at the beginning of his career), while path-breakers like Fourier and Fresnel find the intuitive geometric style more fitting.[4] But I would not wish to rest an explanation solely on such factors, since the causal relationship is unclear. (For example, does Poisson adopt an algebraic style because he wants to work within established

problem areas, or does he work in these areas because he works
algebraically?) I cannot help feeling that in part we are involved
here in the psychology of mathematical thought and creation, but I
do not know how to handle this topic beyond pointing to parallels
– such as the fact that Lagrange, who was entirely algebraist in
style and discouraged the geometrical, also liked music but not
the theatre.

The brief history of the fortunes of all three styles in France is
as follows. Around 1800 the algebraic style was dominant: it was
inspired by Lagrange, and exhibited also by Ampère, L. Carnot,
Laplace and Poisson. It was challenged by the geometrical style
(of which Euler was the chief 18th-century exponent), which was
maintained by Fourier, Hachette and Monge and continued later by
Dupin, Fresnel, Lamé and Navier. Then in the 1820s the analytical
style used by Cauchy gained converts among the new generation
(Duhamel, Liouville and Sturm) and became perhaps the dominant
style by the 1840s. The distinction between these styles is
evident also in other countries.

6. Some Remarks on Foundational Aspects of the Mathematics

I may comment here on some absences from the developments in
mathematics. The reasons why a problem is not discussed are
various, and do not necessarily indicate uninterest. A problem may
not be discussed because (rightly or wrongly) it has become
regarded as unimportant; or because it is very interesting but too
difficult; or because it is just overlooked; or because it is
(quite) interesting but seems to be (basically) solved. I suspect
that this last cause, rather than uninterest, explains the rather
perfunctory treatment of the foundations of the calculus by most
18th-century mathematicians. One could appeal to Lagrange's
treatment, or else to Euler's theory of differential coefficients
which was its parent; and live with the conceptual problems of
infinitesimals, or perhaps appeal to Berkeley's solution by
compensating errors (not that it is a solution: see my 1969).
Cauchy definitely refuted Lagrange's view in his paper 1822 with
the counter-example of $\exp(-1/x2)$, which does not take a
power-series expansion around   . Now this result was not

particularly important for Cauchy's reforms, for they were already well under way; but had this counter-example been noticed in 1800, say, when Lagrange's view was still prominent, then I am sure that the apparently non-problematic nature of foundational questions would have been exposed, and studies rapidly undertaken. I can point to an exactly analogous situation (structure-similarity once more!) in Lagrange's foundations of mechanics, as furnished in part by the 'principle of virtual velocities' in his 1788 'Méchanique analytique'. The difficulty here was that Lagrange supplied no proof of the principle, and this lacuna led to an extensive range of researches for a proof, discussion of the nature of a legitimate proof, and alternative equivalent foundations to mechanics (see Lindt 1904).

I am not certain that Lagrange's formulation of the calculus was widely accepted at the time of the 18th and 19th centuries; for while he can produce forms of all his basic definitions and theorems of the calculus, it is not at all obvious how one finds a power-series expansion in h of f(x+h) around x for any function, and especially whether one can avoid limits and infinitesimals in the process. His books produce the 'derived functions' of only the most elementary functions (by the use of standard known series and simple functional equations). A need to fill this partial gap may have been a motivation for Arbogast's 'Calcul des dérivations' (1800), where general algebraic procedures are provided for converting wide classes of algebraic expressions into the form of a power series.

7. Some Remarks on Descriptive Geometry

It is a characteristic of the French that many of them were very active in the engineering component of mathematical physics. One reason was its military value, which was heavily stressed in the early years of the Republic. For various reasons (discussed in my 1980a, section 10) the emphasis on engineering decreased after about 1840, and the new generations of mathematicians and physicists tended more to the theoretical rather than the practical sides of mathematical physics (as Table 1 in section 4 hints). But the engineering component remained of considerable

significance, and needs special consideration. I shall confine
myself to two topics: descriptive geometry in this section, and
the concept of work and related matters in the next section.

Descriptive geometry was raised to prominence in mathematics by
Monge (see Loria 1921). It was extensively taught at the Ecole
polytechnique and elsewhere - indeed, it was the New Mathematics
of its day, and because of its military uses it was classified for
a time. On looking at Monge's and others' text-books on the
subject I am not sure if the secret was worth keeping. It is a
theory of projecting a three-dimensional configuration into
two-dimensional sections, and carrying out the analysis of the
configuration on these sections. Its value for canon design,
fortifications, and engineering and architectural structures of
various kinds, is quite clear (see Booker 1963, chs. 9-10). But
Monge's text-book is largely taken up with rather non-military
problems such as finding a sphere to touch three given spheres:
indeed, in his edition 1811 of Monge's lectures Hachette added a
supplement which began with a list of the uses to which this
mathematics could be put.

I am also puzzled by the proofs, which often involve conoids and
conical surfaces of various kinds. They occur even in the
occasional practical studies; for example, the engineer, out in
the hills with his plan of the area, has to imagine conic surfaces
rising through the wind and the rain in order to determine his
altitude from the altitudes of points given on his plan (1811, pp.
119-124). I am sure that in this case one could obtain the desired
result from triangulation alone; and to speak more generally, I
suspect that much of the mathematical sophistication in which
Monge dressed his subject could be removed without loss of
mathematical content. Thus his descriptive geometry falls between
the two stools of cook-book mathematics for engineers and research
mathematics for mathematicians; the practical value was muddled
rather than enhanced by the mathematical trappings, while the
theoretical quality was limited by the kinds of practical
application to which it was related. I am not surprised that
interest in it fell off in the 1820s: without the military
imperative, the mathematics alone could not overcome the
intellectual competition of other areas of mathematical physics.

It was also rather slow in adoption in other countries; in particular, the historian should note that the term 'descriptive geometry' in 19th-century Britain often refers to the family of geometries based on projections and orthography, not necessarily to the Mongean form. For much orthographic drawing proceeds by making apparent planar projections (not necessarily two) of the three-dimensional configuration, while Monge's descriptive geometry leads to 'true' planar projections and leaves the configuration as an appearence, or an abstraction.

Probably the most significant mathematical development related to descriptive geometry was the projective geometry of Poncelet (see his 1822). Today we remember Poncelet for his contributions to projective geometry; but in his own day he was known for his extensive teaching of engineering mathematics, at the 'Ecole d'application' de l'artillerie et du génie at Metz for a decade from 1825 and then at the Ecole polytechnique. Indeed, his treatises were so well known that pirate editions of them were published. Now one feature of those books is the small component of descriptive and projective geometry in them.[5] They are chiefly of interest for their stress on concepts such as work.

8. 'Work For the Workers': Engineering and Its Education in Paris, 1825 – 1835.

The concept of work emerged from a lengthy and confused discussion of force, action, energy, work and momentum in the 18th and 19th centuries. L. Carnot deserves some credit for his contributions around the turn of the century (see Gillispie 1971), but the definitive treatments, with applications, are due to Coriolis, Dupin, Navier, Poncelet and de Prony around the mid 1820s (see Kuhn 1959 and Scott 1970). The applications were widespread – with Navier 1832 they even included the action of the wings of birds in flight, and with Coriolis 1835 they also involved the (re)introduction of the 'Coriolis force' into dynamics – but were mainly concentrated on the performance of machines. Furthermore, the teaching of the theory was given to the working and industrial classes as well as to the elitist schools such as the Ecole polytechnique. Thus one might speak of 'work for the workers'. The

idea is more than a pun; for example, Dupin was particularly
concerned with the social applications of engineering (a research
interest of his was in ship-building, and for a time he was
Ministre de la marine), and he wrote extensively on the 'work of
children' in industry (see especially his 1840-47).

There were some political and philosophical associations of this
movement with Saint-Simonism and Comtism; an interesting example
is the 'Journal du génie civil', an engineering journal of
positivist inclinations, which began in 1828. Comte was one of the
collaborators, who also included Clapeyron, Dupin, Girard and
Lamé. In fact, Lamé and Clapeyron were in Russia in the 1820s as
Lieutenant colonels in the Russian 'Corps des voies des
communications' (see Bradley 1980), and the 'Journal du génie
civil' reprinted several articles by them and others on
engineering projects which were first published in the St.
Petersburg 'Journal des voies de communications' (1826).

Comte and positivism were also prominent in the 'Association
polytechnique', an association of old students from the Ecole
polytechnique which was founded shortly after the 1830 revolution
to provide education and instruction for the 'labouring classes'
in Paris (see Association polytechnique 1880). Its teaching
included descriptive geometry and the theory of machines, and
under Comte's influence it put across a strongly positivist view
of science. Poncelet's teaching at Metz was one of the
inspirations for the foundation of the Association, as it
recognized in 1877 by inaugurating a Poncelet medal.

One of Poncelet's colleagues for a short while in 1828 was
Olivier, the most fervent advocate of Monge's descriptive
geometry, freshly back from some years teaching in Sweden. He was
anxious for the Paris life, and seized his chance with the
opening there in 1829 of the 'Ecole centrale des arts et
manufactures'. This new school was designed to provide 'médecins
des fabriques et des usines', as its founders put it; to provide
three-year courses in science with special reference to the needs
of industry (see Comberousse 1879).

Olivier was one of the four principal founders of the Ecole, and organised the teaching of descriptive geometry. The other three founders were Dumas, who covered chemistry; Péclet, recently deprived of his chair at the Lycée at Marseilles for his liberal views, who was responsible for physics; and the notary Lavallée, who dealt with the administration and was the first director. There were many early difficulties: the departure of Benoit, who helped organize mechanics teaching; 'évenements' after the 1830 revolution; and the 1832 cholera epidemic. But later in the decade it built up its student numbers to around 300 and recruited new staff. Belanger was a prominent teacher of mechanics, publishing several text-books for use at the school and becoming director of studies after Olivier's initial occupancy of the post. Coriolis taught mechanics after Benoit's departure, Volladon steam engines, and Liouville mechanics. There was plenty of 'work' for the industrial workers, then, although in these early years the amount of mathematics taught was very small.

One interesting social feature of these institutions described in the last paragraphs is that they brought into Paris an element of external competition, in the sense of the term introduced in section 4. The training at the Ecole, although of primary concern with industrial contexts, certainly overlapped with the training provided by the other major Paris 'écoles', while the 'Journal du génie civil' carried articles which might have been seen in the journals of those écoles. Similarly, the inauguration of the 'Association polytechnique' was a comment on the inadequacy of the education of the 'labouring classes'. But the structure of French science was not fundamentally affected by these innovations: the degree of external competition was small; and so was the response to the rise in importance of mathematical physics in other countries. But that is another story.

Notes

1 I have confined the references to some primary items, and secondary literature where further references to both primary and secondary writings may be found. For more details of all aspects of this paper see my lengthy paper 1980a.

2 Yet there is a strange feature of 'Cauchy's Cours' and his other text-books of the 1820s. Since there is no doubt of the extent of their intellectual influence, the amount of their sales seems surprisingly low. As far as I know, they were never reprinted, although similar, later, volumes by others (especially Navier and Sturm) went through many editions during the 19th century. Cauchy's ideas were helped in diffusion abroad by translations (the 'Cours' was translated into German twice and Russian once, for example), and his acolyte Moigno published several text-books from the 1840s which were apparently based on Cauchy's teaching.

3 There seems to have been little competition even between journals, which tended to be segregated with regard to content or level, or both. Indeed, such competition as there might have been was resolved by a paper being published in several journals within a short time! This situation makes the literature more complicated than it was both before and afterwards. No secondary literature that I have seen has begun to cope with these complications.

4 The small degree of intuition in the algebraic mathematical physics of this period can cause a practitioner to lose contact with the physical interpretation and so produce very notional results, where the formulae calculate an effect which cannot be calculated numerically or tested experimentally to the required degree of accuracy, or where mathematical procedures are followed which make no physical sense. A significant proportion of Poisson's work in mathematical physics falls into this 'notional' category, I fear (and so does Cauchy's sometimes, for the analytical style is subject to this pitfall to some extent), while the geometrically thinking Fourier almost entirely avoids it.

5 Poncelet's writings provide several interesting examples of manifestations of a style of thinking, in his case the geometrical. For example, as Scott shows (in 1970, p. 176), he illustrated the work function geometrically, as the area under a curve. (The algebraic de Prony would rely on the appropriate formula.) Again in his 1822 on projective geometry he advocated a 'principle of continuity', a rather vague claim that figures

retain their projective properties while suffering continuous transformations 'within certain limits'. Cauchy objected to the unclear and apparently inductive character of this principle in his report 1820 to the Academie on Poncelet's book; for Cauchy, the analyst par excellence, continuity must be understood in terms of limits (the continuity of a function, for example, in the 'Cours d'analyse').

Some curious connections can be seen between the interests of Poncelet and of L. Carnot (see Gillispie 1971). As mentioned in the text, Carnot is of importance for the clarification of the concept of work. He also had a principle of continuity, but this one concerned maximising efficiency in a hydraulic machine by eliminating percussion or turbulence (it is sometimes called 'Carnot's principle'). Finally, in his work on geometry he followed a principle similar to Poncelet's later 'principle of continuity' concerning the transformation of figures! The curious nature of the connections may partly be explained by Carnot's algebraic style of working, in contrast with Poncelet's geometrical style: the contrast is noticeable even in their common interests in (proto-)projective geometry (Carnot 1803 and Poncelet 1822).

References

Arbogast, L.F.A.:	Calcul des dérivations, Strasbourg 1800
Association poly-	Histoire de l'Association technique, Paris 1830–1880
Ben-David, J.:	This rise and decline of France as a scientific centre, in: Minerva 8, pp. 160–179
Booker, P.J.:	A history of engineering drawing, 1980 London 1963, (repr. 1979)
Bradley, M.:	Russo-French scientific links and the careers of Lamé and Clapeyron (in preparation)

Burkhardt, H.F.K.:   Entwicklungen nach oscillierenden Funktionen und Integration der Differentialgleichungen der mathematischen Physik, in: Jber. Dtsch. Math.-Ver. lo (1901-08), pt. 2

Carnot, L.:   Géométrie de position, 1803

Cauchy, A.-L.:   [Report to Académie des sciences on Poncelet 1822], in: Ann. math. pures appl. 11 (1820), pp. 69-83; also with comments by J-D. Gergonne in: Poncelet 1822, pp. vii-xvi; also in: Cauchy: Oeuvres, ser. 2, vol. 2, pp. 329-342; also in: Proces-verbaux... de l'Académie ..., vol. 7, pp. 55-60 [report only]; also in: Poncelet, Application d' analyse ..., vol. 2, Paris 1864, pp. 555-563

Cauchy, A.-L.:   Cours d'analyse..., Paris 1821; also in: Oeuvres, ser. 2, vol. 3

Cauchy, A.-L.:   Sur le développement des fonctions en série..., in: Bull. sci. Soc. Philom., Paris 1822, pp. 49-54; also in: Oeuvres, ser. 2, vol. 2, pp. 283-299

Comberousse, C. de: Histoire de l'Ecole centrale des arts et manufactures depuis sa fondation jusqu'a ce jour, Paris 1879

Coriolis, G.G.:   Sur les équations du mouvement relatifs des systèmes de corps, in: J. Ecole Polyt. (1835), cah. 24, pp. 142-154

Crosland, M.P.:   The Society of Arcueil, London 1967

Dupin, F.P.C.:   Du travail des enfants qu'emploient les ateliers, les usines et les manufactures..., 2 pts., Paris 1840-47; Summary in C. r. Acad. Roy. Sci. 10 (1848), pp. 607-612

Dupuy, P.:   Notice historique in: Ecole Normale (1810-1883), Paris 1884, pp. 1-79

Fox, R.:   The rise and fall of Laplacian physics, in: Hist. stud. phys. sci. 4 (1974), pp. 81-136

Frankel, E.: Corpuscular optics and the wave theory of light:..., in: Soc. stud. sci. 6 (1976), pp. 141–184

Gillispie, C.C. (ed.): Lazare Carnot. Savant, Princeton 1971

Grattan-Guinness, I.: Berkeley's criticism of the calculus as a study in the theory of limits, in: Janus 56 (1969), pp. 215–227

Grattan-Guinness, I.: The development of foundations of mathematical analysis from Euler to Riemann, Cambridge (Mass) 1970

Grattan-Guinness, I.: Mathematical physics in France, 1800–1840. Knowledge, activity and historiography, in: Papers in honor of K.-R. Biermann, New York 1980a

Grattan-Guinness, I.: The emergence of mathematical analysis and its foundational progress, 1780–1880, in: Grattan-Guinness (ed.): From the calculus to set theory, 1630–1910. An introductory history, London 1980b, pp. 94–148

Grattan-Guinness, I. and Ravetz, J.R.: Joseph Fourier 1768–1830..., Cambridge (Mass.) 1972

Kuhn, Th.S.: Energy conservation as an example of simultaneous discovery, in: M. Clagett (ed.): Critical problems in the history of science, Madison 1959, pp. 321–326 (1977), pp. 66–1o4

Kuhn, Th.S.: Mathematical vs. experimental traditions in the development of physical science, in: J. interdisc. hist. 7 (1976), pp. 1–31, and (1977), pp. 31–65

Kuhn, Th.S.: The essential tension..., Chicago 1977

Lindt, R.: Das Princip der virtuellen Geschwindigkeit..., in: Abh. Gesch. Math. 18 (1904), pp. 145–195

Loria, G.: Storia della geometria descrittiva..., Milan 1921

Monge, G. : Géométrie descriptive, Hachette, J.N.P.' (ed.), Paris 1811

Monge, G.:   Traité élémentaire de statique...,
                              Hachette, J.N.P. (ed.), Paris 1826

Navier, C.L.M.H.:   Rapport sur un mémoire de M. Chabrier...
                              [followed by] Note sur l'évaluation
                              approximative de la quantité d'action
                              necessaire pour le vol des
                              oiseaux..., in: Hist. Acad. Roy. Sci.,
                              11 (1832), pp. lxi-cxviii

Poncelet, J.V.:   Traité des propriétés projectives des
                              figures, vol. 1, Paris 1822

Prony, G.C.F.M.
    Riche de: Mécanique philosophique..., in: J.
                              Ecole Polyt. 3 (1799), cah. 8a; also
                              published separately: Paris 18o7

Prony, G.C.F.M.
    Riche de: Brunacci, in: Biog. univ. anc. mod.
                              6 (1843), pp. 10-12

Scott, W.L.:   The conflict between atomism and
                              conservation theory 1644 to 1860, London,
                              New York 1970

Silliman, R.H.:   Fresnel and the emergence of physics as a
                              discipline, in: Hist. stud. phys. sci.
                              4 (1975), pp. 137-162

Taton, R.:   L'oeuvre scientifique de Monge, Paris
                              1951

Whittaker, E.:   History of the theories of aether and
                              electricity, in: The classical theories,
                              London 1951

Zwerling, C.S.:   The emergence of the Ecole Normale
                              Supérieure as a center of scientific
                              education in nineteenth century France,
                              Harvard 1976 (Ph. D.)

Joseph W. Dauben

MATHEMATICS IN GERMANY AND FRANCE IN THE EARLY 19TH CENTURY:
TRANSMISSION AND TRANSFORMATION

George Sarton once lamented that the principal problem with the
history of science is that it is far too big a subject. Even so
specific a topic as the transmission of mathematics from France to
Germany and its subsequent transformation in the hands of German
mathematicians in the first half of the 19th century cannot be
treated simply or succinctly. This paper, however, represents a
preliminary attempt to sketch some of the major aspect of the
changes German mathematics experienced early in the 19th century
as Berlin emerged to challenge Paris as the leading center for
teaching and research in mathematics. This is not to suggest that
mathematics ever left Paris, but as Berlin established itself as a
major European capital, growing as the political, cultural and
intellectual center of Prussia, the status and stature of
mathematics in Berlin underwent a concomitant, progressive
transformation.

German mathematicians were greatly indebted, in fact, to what they
borrowed or even copied directly from the French model of
scientific enterprise. This paper, however, will not attempt to
compare differences in the content, style or nature of mathematics
in France and Germany during the 19th century. Instead, it will
concentrate on institutional and social factors involved in

*H. N. Jahnke and M. Otte (eds.), Epistemological and Social Problems of the Sciences in the Early Nineteenth
Century, 371–399.*

establishing mathematics in Prussia. To avoid drawing too broad a picture, in the limited space available here, focus is narrowed almost entirely to the specific example of mathematics in Berlin.[1]

This restriction is made possible, at least in connection with these Proceedings of the Bielefeld Conference, "Epistemological and Social Problems of the Sciences in the Early 19th century", by virtue of a number of contributions which were concerned specifically with institutional factors affecting science generally in both France and Germany during the 19th century. Significant new research by Ivor Grattan-Guinness on the subject of mathematical physics in France and its development in Germany between 1800 and 1835 describes well the milieu in which scientific activity developed in post-revolutionary France.[2] As he notes, Paris was the dominant creative center, particularly for presentation of results at the 'Institut de France' and for institutional innovations in research and teaching associated with new establishments like the 'Ecole Polytechnique'.[3] Other papers presented during the conference at Bielefeld also consider institutional as well as theoretical factors underlying the advance of French science after the French Revolution. Here the contributions of Maurice Crosland, Lorraine Daston, Judith Grabiner and Terry Shinn are especially useful.[4] Similarly, the general historical context of the post-Napoleonic era in Germany is significant for understanding the progress of the sciences generally in 19th-century Germany. This is made clear in Brita Rang's paper, and her remarks suffice to indicate the character of the relevant socio-economic context, particularly for Prussia.[5] Likewise, the intellectual background of German Idealism and Naturphilosophie for German science in the early 19th century is covered by Dietrich v. Engelhardt, Michael Heidelberger, Volker Lenhart and Imre Toth.[6] Finally, while the major focus of this paper is Berlin and the development of mathematics there during the first half of the 19th century, several other contributions to the Bielefeld conference offer studies of other institutions in Germany which make it possible, at least tentatively, to consider some preliminary comparisons with Berlin. Here Walter Langhammer's study of mathematics at Halle, and that by Herbert Mehrtens for Kiel are especially noteworthy.[7] With all of these diverse factors in mind, let us now turn to consider the status of mathematics in Berlin, particularly at the University, as the 19th century was just getting underway.

The University of Berlin, founded in 1810, was relatively new when compared with older German universities, which traced their origins back to the Middle Ages.[8] The first professor of mathematics (and physics) at Berlin was a rather colorless and uninspiring individual, Johann Georg Tralles, who had studied in Goettingen. Although Tralles had been elected to the Berlin Academy of Sciences in 1804, his work (largely in applied mathematics) was apparently dry and less than stimulating – certainly reason enough for the apparent lack of enthusiasm for mathematics and physics among the earlist students at Berlin.[9] Franz Neumann, who attended some of Tralles' early lectures, never forgot one experience in particular. At the first meeting of a lecture course Tralles was scheduled to offer, he wrote formulae on the blackbord for an hour, then bowed stiffly, and left the room. Five students were present at the time, and one cannot help but wonder that any would have chosen to continue the course. In fact, at the second meeting, only three students appeared, then two, and finally Tralles announced that there were not enough auditors to continue, and so the course was cancelled.[10]

In addition to Tralles, whose official position was that of Ordinarius, there were several members of the staff who held the position of Extraordinarius. One of these, Abel Burja, was so incensed at the minimal respect paid to mathematics at Berlin, that in 1811 he sought to transfer to the section of the Academy of Sciences devoted to history and philosophy, rather than remain in the section for mathematics.[11] Unfortunately Burja, like others even as late as Dirichlet, Kummer and Weierstrass, had to supplement his teaching at the University with income from other positions, at first at the Ritter-Akademie and later by teaching at the Franzoesisches Gymnasium. Others would regularly supplement their income through positions at the War College or at local scondary schools.

It was also possible to teach at the University by virtue of membership in the Academy of Sciences, a privilege that was often

exercised by members in the section for mathematics. One of these
was Johann Gruson, although from 1816 to 1850 he also held the
university position of Extraordinarius.[12] Gruson is best known
for his translations of Euler and Lagrange into German. Such
translations were essential in facilitating the introduction of
advanced mathematics from a scientifically sophisticated country
like France to a mathematically underdeveloped country like
Germany at the onset of the 19th century. As a translator, Gruson
was helping to transmit basic knowledge to German students. He
also claimed the distinction of being the longest-lived fellow of
the Academy, having been a member for over 60 years. But his fate
at the hands of the French is instructive, for during the
Napoleonic occupation of Berlin he lost all of his belongings, and
in order to earn more money, aimed his university courses at those
who might be most inclined to take them − namely at future
teachers and jurists. His large. public lectures were consequently
taught at a very elementary level. On the other hand, his courses
in pure mathematics were only offered "privatissimus", on a
correspondingly limited scale.

Other mathematicians at Berlin in various capacities during its
first decade included Johann Eytelwein, Ernst Fischer and Ludwig
Ideler.[13] Of these, Ideler is perhaps the most relevant for
understanding the initial reaction to mathematics at the
University, for until the arrival of Dirichlet in Berlin, it was
Ideler who taught the elementary mathematics courses. These, it
turns out, were based mostly on the writings of Lacroix. Moreover,
Ideler was not ashamed to admit that he was unfamiliar with most
recent advances in mathematics. This, too, indicates that the
faculty at the University of Berlin did not pretend − and it
certainly did not regard itself − as working on the frontiers of
mathematics at the time.

Thus, as Felix Klein has noted, with the exception of Gauss in
Goettingen, the level of mathematics in German universities during
the first quarter of the 19th century, including Berlin, remained
at an unfortunately low level.[14] The first student to apply for
Habilitation at Berlin, in fact, Christian Zimmermann, was so
unsatisfactory that he was never approved.[15] The second aspirant
was only slightly better. Although Daniel Lehmus did receive his

Habilitation (on the subject of inequalities, suggested by Tralles), he went on to teach at an artillery and engineering school.[16] The first successful student in mathematics at the University of Berlin, and the first Privatdozent to remain in Berlin, was Samuel Lubbe, who taught from 1819-1846 at the Friedrich-Wilhelms Gymnasium. His dissertation, however, was unimpressive, and even his advisor, Tralles, was obliged to write that his work was "unclear, sometimes wrong".[17] The best indication of the regrettably low level of mathematics at Berlin during its early years is the fact that for the defense of Lubbe's dissertation, no opponent could be found. There simply were no students to take on the public disputation.[18]

Clearly, there was no future for promising students of mathematics in Berlin at the time. In fact, there was really no one teaching advanced mathematics in all of Germany with whom gifted students might study during the first quarter of the century. The example of Dirichlet is typical. When he made up his mind to study mathematics, he left Germany for Paris, and found there a lively circle of mathematicians where his talents could be developed and appreciated. For science, and certainly for mathematics, Paris was still preeminent.[19]

In 1824, however, an important change occurred at the University of Berlin. Tralles, while in London in 1822 procuring a pendulum, had died suddenly. This provided the perfect opportunity to improve the level of mathematics at the University. Gauss and Bessel were recommended to fill the vacancy. Unfortunately, Gauss could not be persudad to leave Goettingen, and Bessel was passed over largely because certain professors such as Hegel, then Dean of the University, doubted (mistakenly) that an astronomer could lecture on higher mathematics. Hegel, for administrative reasons, also opposed the appointment of an additional mathematician at the level of Docent.[20]

Eventually Enno Dirksen was appointed in 1824 as Tralles' successor. Dirksen came to Berlin with strong credentials, for he had studied with Gauss and Thibaut in Goettingen. His 'Probevortrag' had been devoted to "A Means of Computing the Opposition of Planets with the Sun." But Dirksen, who had been "shown the mysteries of analysis by Gauss," was concurrently appointed to the War College, so that his energies were not directed, full time, to the University.[21]

Not only was Dirksen recommended for the position of Ordinarius in 1824, but at the same time Martin Ohm (despite the opposition of many on the faculty) was made an Ausserordentlicher Professor. If the faculty was startled by this action of the Ministry, it must have been even more surprised at the announcement on August 28, 1824, that Jabbo Oltmanns had been named an Ordinarius for applied mathematics by the King.[22]

The circumstances leading to Oltmanns' appointment are particularly revealing, for they show how mathematics was treated – and how it was changing – in Berlin by the mid-20's. Oltmanns had studied in Paris. It was there that he had met the great German scientific entrepreneur, Alexander von Humboldt.[23] Recognizing Oltmanns' talent for computation, von Humboldt enlisted him to do the astronomical and geographical observations on Humboldt's trip to the Americas. In 1810 Oltmanns was not only elected to the Berlin Academy, but he was offered a position at the University, which he then refused, preferring instead to return to his home in West Friesland. Later, penury prompted him to seek help from friends, resulting in a favorable recommendation from von Humboldt for the position in Berlin. The Berlin Academy also recommended Oltmanns positively, but since Dirksen had already been named to Tralles' position by the Ministry, Oltmanns was given a new Ordinarius for mathematics. Unfortunately, when Oltmanns died in 1833, he was an alcoholic who had produced nothing significant during his years at the University. This, however, provided Ohm with yet another opportunity to secure a place for himself as an Ordentlicher Professor at Berlin.

Martin Ohm, in fact, is an especially instructive example, for he illustrates the types of problems mathematics faced at Berlin during the early years of the University. Like so many of his German contemporaries, Ohm was not a product of any organized mathematical instruction, but was an autodidact. As a student he had apparently heard only one lecture in mathematics on "kombinatorisches Integralkalkul", in Erlangen, where he taught as a Privatdozent from 1812 until 1817. In 1821 he habilitated in Berlin, although his examination went badly. He could hot recall formulae, and failed to respond clearly to questions Hegel had asked him. In fact, Hegel reported that Ohm answered with considerable confusion, and was of the opinion that Ohm had no qualifications to be a professor of mathematics. Tralles also gave Ohm's work a poor review.[24] As a result, it is surprising to learn that Ohm was nevertheless allowed to present his 'Probevorlesung', followed by his Habilitation in 1821. This episode seems to confirm the complete lack of acceptable standards for mathematical work at Berlin in the early 1820's.

When Ohm, newly habilitated in 1821, then applied for Tralles' position upon the latter's death in 1822, many were offended by his presumption wrote to the Faculty a year later, in 1823, noting that it was not at all clear that Ohm was suited for Tralles' position considering his poor Habilitation.[25] Ideler also submitted his opinion of Ohm, as did Dirksen, anonymously. Dirksen, who also wanted the same position, sought to eliminate Ohm as a contender.[26] His opinion, therefore, is not without self-interest. Ideler, however, did try to give an objective judgement of Ohm's abilities, although he ended his evaluation by citing passages from Ohm's works to show how Ohm managed to take clear ideas in mathematics and cloak them in a "mystical darkness."[27] Eventually, Dirksen's strategy was successful, and he, rather than Ohm, was appointed to Tralles' position.

Meanwhile, the Ministry had undertaken its own investigation of both Ohm and Dirksen. Johann Gruson, who supported Ohm, maintained that Ohm had done poorly at his Habilitation because Tralles had been unfriendly and lacked objectivity, since he and Ohm did not share similar views. Eventually the Ministry compromised; in addition to its appointment of Dirksen as an Ordinarius, it also chose to promote Ohm to the level of Ausserordentlicher Professor. Clearly, despite the negative opinions of Hegel and Tralles, Ohm had influential support in the Ministry.[28]

A decade later, when Ohm sought yet another promotion to Ordentlicher Professor, he was rebuffed by the faculty. Five years later, however, in 1839, the minister Altenstein recommended that the King make Ohm an Ordinarius, and the appointment was subsequently approved by royal fiat. Thus, as may be seen in this instance, even if the faculty had reservations about an appointment, there were always other avenues for advancement for those with the right political or social connections.

While Ohm may have been a popular lecturer, he was not especially profound. As Steiner once described him, "whoever is serious comes to Dirichlet or me - the others go to Ohm."[29] This judgment is corroborated by the experience of Emile Lampe, who had been one of Ohm's students in the 1860's. In the Winter-Semester of 1860/61 Ohm offered a course on higher equations, although to Lampe's disgust, by December Ohm had not gotten as far as cubic equations, for he was always going back to earlier points with endless repetition. A further indication of Ohm's lack of esteem among his colleagues is the fact that he was the only mathematical Ordinarius at the University who was never elected to the Berlin Academy of Sciences.[30]

The Academy, in fact, played a significant role in the support and development of mathematics in Berlin, primarily because of the special arrangement whereby members of the Academy were automatically entitled to lecture at the University.[31] Thus, by strengthening the quality of mathematicians represented in the Academy, it was possible to improve the potential teaching corps available to the University. Moreover, through a careful perusal of the letters of recommendation solicited on behalf of individual applications for membership, it is possible to trace changing attitudes, expectations and other institutional factors responsible for the changing nature of mathematics both as it was represented in the Academy and as it was taught at the University of Berlin.[32]

For example, A. L. Crelle was admitted to the Academy largely in deference to his scientific-organizational ability. His election was due to no less a promoter than Alexander von Humboldt.[33] As a result of the many years he had spent in France, von Humboldt clearly understood the desirability of developing the exact sciences in Germany. When he finally left Paris for Berlin in 1827, he brought with him a comprehensive program for the reorganization of science in Prussia, one which embraced astronomy, chemistry, biology, and of course, mathematics. As von Humboldt looked for colleagues to work with him in the promotion of science in Berlin, he could not have helped but recognize the talents and connections Crelle could offer. Only a year earlier, in 1826, Crelle had founded the famous "Journal fuer die reine und angewandte Mathematik" (often referred to simply as Crelle's "Journal"). The first volume created considerable attention owing to the appearance of papers by Abel, Jacobi and Steiner.[34] The "Journal" was of great interest in Paris, and it (and thus Crelle) may well have come to von Humboldt's attention even before the latter had left Paris for Berlin. Since both von Humboldt and Crelle were also interested in the Prussian educational system, this too brought their interests together. Thus Crelle was enlisted to help carry out that part of von Humboldt's design involving mathematics.[35]

But if Crelle was to be successful in such efforts, he required an acceptably influential position. Through von Humboldt's efforts, he was made an advisor for mathematics in the Prussian Kultusministerium. Equally significant, von Humboldt persuaded Johann Encke, who then was secretary of the section for mathematics of the Berlin Academy of Sciences, to nominate Crelle for membership. Crelle's nomination found considerable support from other members of the section as well, (including Dirksen, Eytelwein, Fischer, Gruson, Oltmanns and Poselger). Encke, in his recommendation, emphasized Crelle's potential value to the Academy, particularly through his "Journal" which might be expected to promote direct ties with French and other foreign mathematicians.

When Crelle joined the section for mathematics in 1827, it needed a thorough overhaul. None of its then-current members was in any position to give new life to mathematics, or to help in realizing von Humboldt's ambitious plans. In these matters, however, Crelle was most influential. For example, his recommendations in support of new members were aimed at bringing individuals of the first rank into the Academy. Among corresponding members he nominated

both Joseph Gergonne and Adolphe Quetelet, both editors of
specialized journals and mathematicians of international
prominence.[36]

While the Academy of Sciences was undergoing important changes, so
too was the status of mathematics at the University. If one
compares the courses being taught during the Winter-Semester
1824/25 with those advertised just seventeen years later in
1841/42, the changes are striking. In 1824/25 (which was also
Jacobi's last year as a student in Berlin), five professors
(Dirksen, Ideler, Gruson, Ohm and Lubbe) were teaching elementary
subjects like the differential and integral calculus, conic
sections, finite magnitudes and timekeeping in the old and new
world.[37] In 1841/42, just before Jacobi's return to Berlin in
1844, seven professors (Dirichlet, Dirksen, Ohm, Steiner, Gruson,
Minding and Lubbe) were teaching a wide variety of courses,
including the theory of single and multiple integrals, theories of
maxima, advanced geometry, and higher algebra.[38] However, it is
worth noting that the older professors spanning both periods,
namely Dirksen, Ohm, Gruson and Lubbe, continued to offer the same
kinds of courses they had been giving for the past seventeen
years.

Certainly one major factor in the higher level of mathematics
being offered at the University of Berlin by 1842 is reflected in
nothing more than a change in staff. But what was actually
responsible for the striking improvement in the quality of
teaching and patterns of research and publication? As Stephen
Turner has emphasized, universities in Germany (unlike other
European countries) served as major centers for both the creation
and transmission of academic knowledge.[39] This was true first in
philology and history, but later in the sciences as well, and is
intimately related to the unique value placed upon the
professoriate not only to teach, thus transmitting knowledge, but
to expand and to create new knowledge. One innovation – and once
more a uniquely German institutionalization of changing academic
standards and expectations – were the seminars first established
in philology, but later adopted by other disciplines, including
mathematics.[40] One consequence of this pattern, as Professor

Turner has argued, was the emergence of a younger, more competitive and mobile professorate with primary loyalties to a given discipline rather than to a particular institution.[41]

Teaching was also improved through von Humboldt's conscious efforts to bring talented mathematicians to Berlin. Since the University itself had few positions, Berlin was fortunate in having a number of other local institutions to employ mathematicians. In fact, had the University been the only institution in Berlin, it would have been afflicted with a severe problem of overstaffing. In 1831, for example, when there were five professors at Berlin (Dirksen, Gruson, Ohm, Dirichlet and Steiner), there was no room for any new appointments. An increase in the number of Extraordinariuses was not contemplated, as records of faculty meetings show, and thus despite several appeals to the faculty, no promotion could be obtained for Ferdinand Minding from his rank of Privatdozent.[42] Although Dirichlet did what he could to obtain a place for Minding at a higher level through the Academy, there were no places free for him there either. Consequently, so long as he could support himself through multiple positions, Minding stayed in Berlin, but eventually, in 1843, he was compelled to accept a foreign post at the University of Dorpat.[43] Nevertheless, Berlin at least afforded alternatives, and if one could not find a permanent, full-time position at the University, there were local institutions like the Bauakademie, Kriegsschule, various local Gymnasia, Technical, Real- and Gewerbeschule where mathematical talent could be placed. And there was also the Academy, from which personnel could be taken to strengthen the mathematical offerings at the University itself.

Moreover, there was an important change in career choices and employment opportunities for students, not only at Berlin, but throughout Germany towards the middle of the 19th century, and this reflects an important social change.[44] The fact that someone like Dirichlet was appointed to a professorship in Berlin is of little importance in terms of his influence upon students unless there were students in sufficient numbers who chose to study mathematics. For example, while Dirichlet was briefly in Breslau, he had very few students. Records show that his courses at Berlin in the early years attracted on the average no more than five or

six students, and sometimes as few as three. In fact, his shyness
may account for these disappointing figures, but the paucity of
students was perhaps more a result of the fact that Dirichlet
lectured on topics that were unusual for students of his day.
Dirichlet was offering courses on the frontiers of research
mathematics, including the application of infinite series to study
the physics of heat that had been pioneered by Fourier just years
before. By the time he had established his reputation in Berlin,
however, the student registers that survive indicate that his
classes swelled to as many as forty students.[45] (This is
particularly striking when one realizes that only the best, most
serious students enrolled with Dirichlet, since the others,
apparently, chose to take easier courses from Ohm, Dirksen or
Gruson. This also indicates the magnitude of increased interest –
and highter quality – of students enrolling to study advanced
mathematics at the University. Among Dirichlet's students at
Berlin, one can count such eminent mathematicians as Eisenstein,
Riemann and Kronecker). As the requirements of the Prussian
educational and examination system placed increasing emphasis upon
mathematics, more prospective teachers and consequently more
students sought accreditation in mathematics.[46]

There is a final factor as well, in explaining the remarkable
transformation mathematics had undergone from its early,
unprepossessing status in Germany at the beginning of the century.
When Dirichlet had made up his mind to study mathematics, he went
to Paris, studied with the great figures there like Fourier, and
later brought their style of mathematics, as well as their
research interests, back to Germany. Jacobi, while he did not
physically go to Paris, learned his mathematics by studying French
masters like Lagrange. Similarly, when Alexander von Humboldt
returned to Berlin from Paris in 1827, he was determined to follow
the successful example he knew from France, and thus he
consciously set out to strengthen mathematics and the sciences
generally in Berlin. As Gauss said in 1827 of Humboldt's return to
Germany, "it will bring the greatest impetus to the extension of
the exact sciences."[47]

Three years later, France was still the inspiration for reforms of
the German educational system. Crelle, in 1830, spent his vacation

in France where he studied the teaching of mathematics, especially at the 'Ecole Polytechnique'. Upon his return he filed a twenty-page report (dated September 8, 1830) with the Kultusministerium in which he characterized the 'Ecole' as an institution whose primary purpose was the traning of teachers of mathematics, a goal that Crelle emphasized in his recommendation that a local Polytechnic Institute be established in Berlin.[48] In fact, one of the few significant failures experienced by Crelle, von Humboldt and those seeking to rejuvinate mathematics in Berlin was the attempt - repeatedly made but never realized - to provide the city with such an institute, based largely on the model of its French namesake.[49] Initially, the plan to do so had found strong support from the Kultusministerium and from the Prussian Kriegsministerium, and on a number of occasions both Crelle and von Humboldt wrote vigorously in its support. Its founding, on one occasion, was unsuccessfully linked with an attempt to bring Gauss to Berlin from Goettingen. . Eventually, however, the hope of creating a new Polytechnic Institute failed. In part, financial considerations may have played a role, as did the waning support of the Kriegsministerium. Originally, endorsement from the army's General Staff, in particular from von Mueffling, presupposed that in copying the 'Ecole Polytechnique', the Institue in Berlin would be something like a high-level military academy. But as the plans for the Polytechnic Institute developed, increased emphasis was placed upon its mission to produce teachers of mathematics, physics and chemistry. As a result, the Prussian Kriegsministerium lost interest.[50]

In Paris, however, the 'Ecole Polytechnique' had been created in the aftermath of the French Revolution to teach the sciences, especially mathematics, in a newly democratized environment, for there were no other suitable institutions prepared to do so.[51] Berlin in the 19th century, unlike Paris after the Revolution, already had an established institution where mathematics had been taught since 1810, namely the University. Related institutions like the Academy and other local schools where mathematics was taught also provided considerable support for a growing community of mathematicians active in Berlin. Thus the necessity of a Polytechnic Institute was clearly not so apparent and urgent a matter in Berlin as it had been in Paris, where just the opposite had been the case in 1794 when the 'Ecole Polytechnique' was founded. As the 19th century progressed, the status of mathematics in Berlin was steadily improving, and in fact an indigenous mathematical tradition had begun to establish itself with commendable success.[52]

Although the inspiration was initially foreign, borrowing heavily upon French examples, a thriving mathematical enterprise was well-established in Prussia by the middle of the 19th century. Inevitably, it took hold in a German context, where philosophical idealism tended to deemphasize applications and placed value upon loftier, more intellectual pure mathematics. (Not long after its founding, Crelle's 'Journal' was jokingly described as the 'Journal fuer reine, unangewandte Mathematik.'[53]) Moreover, the new mathematics took hold in a special 'Berliner' context as well. Here the Academy of Sciences and other institutions of higher education strengthened the hand of mathematics. Here, too, political leverege manipulated by such individuals as Crelle and von Humboldt helped to ensure a strong place for mathematics throughout Germany. At the same time, the best mathematicians would be obtained for Berlin. As student demand for mathematics courses increased, and as the interest of graduate students to continue in research or teaching positions for mathematics grew, so too did the fortunes of mathematics in Berlin. Soon its 'Golden Age', as Kurt Biermann has called it, would commence, and the greatest figures of 19th-century German mathematics, Kummer, Kronecker and Weierstrass would all be at Berlin, constituting the justly famous and influential "Berliner mathematische Schule."[54]

Notes

1 This article is a revised version of a paper read at the conference on "Epistemological and Social Problems of the Sciences in the Early 19th Century", sponsored by the Institut fuer Didaktik der Mathematik and held at the Zentrum fuer Interdisziplinaere Forschung at the University of Bielefeld, Germany, from November 27-30. 1979. As such, it reflects the

limitations of time placed upon papers presented there, as well as constraints of length established by the editors for this published version.

The research presented here owes a great debt to the important and detailed publications of Professor Dr. Kurt-R. Biermann, Director of the Alexander-von-Humboldt-Forschungsstelle in Berlin, DDR, especially to his widely-praised Die 'Mathematik und ihre Dozenten an der Berliner Universitaet, 1810-1920'. I am grateful to the Staatsbibliothek Preussischer Kulturbesitz, Berlin, and to the archives of the Humboldt University, the Akademie der Wissenschaften der DDR, Berlin, and to the Deutsches Zentralarchiv, Merseburg, for access to material used in writing this paper.

It is with great appreciation for Biermann's scholarship that this paper is dedicated to him on the occasion of his 60th birthday, December 5, 1979. It was during a year that I spent in Berlin in 1970-71 that I first became interested in the history of the University of Berlin, largely a result of my studying research being done by Professor Biermann at the time.

2 Grattan-Guinness (1979). See also his forthcoming article, Grattan-Guinness (1980b).

3 Cf. Grattan-Guinness (1980). See also Chapter 2, Frankreich und die Ecole Polytechnique in den ersten Jahrzehnten des 19. Jahrhunderts, in: Klein (1926), pp. 63-93; Struik (1948/67), in particular pp. 144-146; Wussing (1958). On the subject of the 'Ecole Polytechnique' serving as a model for Institutes throughout Europe, see Manegold (1966), p. 183. Lorey (1916), p. 31, notes that the Prussian Ministry of Education consciously adopted the model of the 'Ecoles' as it considered educational planning and reform. Schubring (1980) remarks that it is especially ironic that not one of the many attempts to establish Polytecnic Institutes in Prussia was successful during the first half of the 19th century. This is discussed in more detail below, notes 49 and 51.

4 Crosland (1979); Daston (1980); Grabiner (1980); Shinn (1979). See also Crosland (1967) and (1976); Zwerling (1976); Fox (1973).

5 Rang (1980).

6 Engelhardt (1979); Heidelberger (1980); Lenhart (1979); Toth (1979). See also Tietze (1977).

7 Langhammer (1980); Mehrtens (1980). For a study of mathematics at Freiburg, see H. Gericke (1955).

8 For a general history of the University of Berlin, see Lenz (1910) and Smend (1961).

9 Ulmer (1961); Biermann (1973), pp. 11–18. Wilhelm von Humboldt called Tralles "eigensinnig, spitzig und nicht immer sehr artig." See his letter to F.A. Wolf, July 31, 1809, in: Harnack (1900), volume 1, p. 794, note 1.

10 The story, told by Franz Neumann, is recounted in L. Neumann (1904), p. 94. It is also repeated by Lorey (1916), p. 31; Biermann (1973), p. 12. Another student, Leopold Zunz, who was present for Tralles′ lectures on probability theory during the Wintersemester 1816/17, reported that the level of mathematics was insignificant, that the private lectures were usually never given (because féwer than three students usually appeared), and that for his public lectures Tralles had no more than seven students. See Glatzer (1964), p. 83.

11 Biermann (1973), p. 12, and Gericke (1955), p. 52. Burja is particularly interesting, for like many others in Berlin at the time, he was a member of Berlin′s French colony (as had been Euler). For details, refer to Pablo (1965), pp. 1f.

12 Biermann (1973), p. 13. See also Lenz (1910), vol. 1, p. 245.

13 On Johann Eytelwein and Ludwig Ideler, see Biermann (1973), p. 13.

14 Klein (1926), pp. 93f. For a general appraisal of the poor state of mathematics at the University of Berlin, see Lenz (1910), vol. 2, pp. 374f. Remarkably, there were some teachers at the turn of the century, like Mollweide, who despaired of ever teaching higher mathematics at university, ostensibly because it required too much writing on the blackboard! See Lorey (1916), p. 24.

15 On Zimmermann, see Biermann (1973), p. 14, and Lenz (1910), vol. 1, pp. 600f.

16 Biermann (1973), p. 14.

17 Biermann (1973), p. 14.

18 Biermann (1973), p. 15.

19 For a comprehensive introduction to the life of Dirichlet, see Biermann (1959c). In 1823, when the question of establishing a Polytechnic Institute in Berlin was being discussed, Generalleutenant von Mueffling, · Chief of the Prussian General

Staff and an honorary member of the Academy of Sciences, drew some direct comparisons between the condition of mathematics in France as opposed to Germany: "In Frankreich steht der ausgezeichnete Mathematiker in der Achtung ebenso hoch, als der ausgezeichnete Philologe ... Der oeffentliche Unterricht in der Mathematik hoert bei uns da auf, wo er in anderen Laendern anfaengt. In Deutschland ist man in der Mathematik auf Privatstudien angewiesen." Although von Mueffling was writing with vested interests in mind, his characterization of the condition of mathematics in Germany early in the 19th century seems an accurate reflection, one that is corroborated in the reports of others at the time. See Lorey (1916), p. 41.

20 Biermann (1973), p. 15; and Lenz (1910), vol. 2, pp. 375f.

21 Biermann (1973), p. 15. See also Lenz (1910), vol. 2, pp. 375f. It was noted in the official recommendation of the faculty of the University of Berlin that Dirksen, who was chosen to replace Tralles, "von seinem Lehrer, Herrn Gauss, in die Mysterien der analysis gruendlich eingeweiht worden [ist]," Biermann (1973), p. 17. The wording of this same passage is rendered somewhat differently by Lorey (1916), p. 39.

22 Biermann (1973), pp. 17f.

23 For details of Oltmanns' career, see Biermann (1973), p. 18. See also Lenz (1910), vol. 1, pp. 205, 274 and 477; vl. 2, p. 375.

24 Biermann (1973), pp. 15f. See as well the obituary by Kobell (1873).

25 Altenstein wrote to the faculty on August 5, 1823: "Bei dem wenig guenstigen Urtheile, welches die philosophische Fakultaet [...] ueber das Ergebnis der mit dem p. Ohm behufs seiner Habilitation gehaltenen muendlichen Pruefung und der von ihm eingereichten Specimina gefaellt hat, ist aber das Ministerium zweifelhaft, ob der p. Ohm die erforderliche Qualifikation zu der von ihm nachgesuchten Lehrstelle besitze," transcribed from the Archiv der Humboldt Universitaet Berlin, Philosophische Fakultaet: P-3-1, Bl. 137, in: Biermann (1973), p. 16. For a quite different evaluation, praising Ohm's teaching at Erlangen as "eine dankenswerte Hebung des mathematischen Unterrichts," see Kolde (1910), p. 231.

26 Biermann (1973), p. 16.

27 Biermann (1973), p. 17.

28 Biermann (1973), p. 17. Lorey points out that Ohm was very much interested in educational reform, and submitted several comprehensive plans concerning teacher education, the need for closer supervision and better instruction to the Prussian Ministry of Education. The Ministry, therefore, might well have been impressed and quite favorable towards Ohm as a result. Lorey also reports that Ohm was a much-admired teacher at Berlin, and suggests that he was overlooked and not well-regarded by his colleagues at the Unversity because he was self-taught. Consequently, he was not on friendly terms with the yonger mathematicians, and this, Lorey argues, accounts for his lack of influence with the new generation which eventually formed around Crelle after the mid-1820's. See Lorey (1916), pp. 35f.

29 Steiner, in fact, is reported to have said: "Wer Gruetze hat, kommt zu Dirichlet und mir, die anderen gehen zu Ohm," quoted in: Geiser and Maurer (1901), p. 329.

30 Biermann (1973), pp. 18f. For Lampe's evaluation, see E. Lampe, in: W. Lorey (1916), pp. 89f. Leo Koenigsberger provides a similar estimation, indicating that as he became older, Ohm was more and more a comic figure. See Koenigsberger (1919), pp. 27f.

31 Members of the Berlin Academy of Sciences were entitled to lecture at the University, thus adding in a very positive fashion to the quality of instruction. Among many who taught at the University by virtue of their membership in the Academy, mention should be made of Alexander von Humboldt and Albert Einstein, both "lesende Akademiemitglieder," in: Humboldt Universitaet (1960), p. 70.

32 Kurt-R. Biermann was the first to use 'Wahlvorschlaege' of mathematicians for the Berlin Academy of Sciences as serious materials of great use to the historian of science. As A.P. Juskevic, the Russian historian of mathematics said of Biermann's monograph, 'Vorschlaege zur Wahl von Mathematikern in die Berliner Akademie', such documents represent valuable histories in miniature. See Juskevic (1961). For a detailed history of the Academy, particularly in the 19th century, see Harnack (1900).

33 For details of the support v. Humboldt gave Crelle, see Section 3.8, Der Anteil A. v. Humboldts und Crelles an der Entstehung eines Zentrums mathematische Lehre und Forschung, in: Biermann (1973), pp. 21-24. For aspects of Alexander von Humboldt's support of mathematics generally, see Biermann

(1959b), and Biermann (1968).

34 Crelle's 'Journal' was perhaps more successful than earlier mathematics journals in Germany because, from the beginning, it had the full support of the Kultusministerium. In fact, the journal was permitted to print on its title page the acknowledgment, mit Unterstuetzung hoher Kgl. preussischer Behoerden." Support came in the form of a strong, official endorsement, of the journal, commending it not only for universities, but for high schools and even foreign ambassadors. The Ministry also made available copies to local schools, which served to stimulate young students, including Weierstrass for example, to study mathematics. See Lorey (1916), p.37.

35 For recent studies of Crelle, see in particular the publications of W. Eccarius (1976), (1977), and (1980). It should be noted that in 1828 Crelle was transferred from the Ministerium des Innern to the Kultusministerium. There, he immediately set to work on a comprehensive plan to reinvigorate teaching of mathematics in the Prussian Gymnasia. In 1829 a Commission was appointed to carry out the reorganization of public instruction, and among its members Crelle chose Dirichlet, who like Crelle was much impressed by the success he associated with the teaching of mathematics in France. Lorey summarizes the significance of both Dirichlet and Crelle for the advance of German mathematics as follows: "Indem Dirichlet, der seine mathemtische Ausbildung in Frankreich genossen hatte, zu den Beratungen ueber einen mathematischen Lehrplan fuer die Gymnasien hinzugezogen und zwei Jahre darauf auch zum Mitglied der wissenschaftlichen Pruefungskommission gewaehlt wurde, kommt deutlich die Absicht zutage, die den weitblickenden, von der Bedeutung der Mathematik fuer die ganze Kultur durchdrungenen Crelle leitete. Er fuehlt es, wie durch die Mathematik die Schule neues Leben bekommen wird, wenn man das Beispiel des westlichen Nachbars befolgt, dass es aber weiter vor alle Dingen noetig ist, die Lehrer mit der so herrlich aufbluehenden neuen mathematischen Forschung bekannt zu machen." Lorey (1916), p. 39.

36 For aspects of Crelle's support of individual mathematicians consult Biermann (1959a) and (1960).

37 Biermann (1973), p. 19.

38 Biermann (1973), pp. 40f.

39 Turner (1979), p. 320.

40 The most recent studies of professionalization and the establishment of seminars in the field of classical philology may be found in Turner (forthcoming a). For the first efforts to establish seminars in mathematics, following the example of the philological seminars, especially through the efforts of Scherk in Halle and Jacobi in Koenigsberg, see Lorey (1916), pp. 112-132, and Biermann (1973), pp. 41f. The establishment of the first mathematical seminar in Berlin is discussed in Biermann (1973), pp. 71-74. Although it is unclear whether Weierstrass or Kummer was the first to suggest establishing a seminar for mathematics in Berlin, Kummer drafted the first proposal on April 6, 1860. It was not until October 7, 1864, that the Finanzministerium finally endorsed the plan already approved in 1861 by the Kultusministerium.

41 Cf. Turner (1980).

42 For Minding, see Kneser (1900), and Lorey (1916), p. 40, as well as Biermann (1973), pp. 36-38, especially p. 37.

43 Minding informed the faculty of the University of Berlin that he had been offered and accepted a position as Ordentlicher Professor of applied mathematics at the University of Dorpat on July 11, 1843. See Biermann (1973), pp. 37f.

44 Walter Langhammer, in his article on the founding of the "Seminar fuer Mathematik und die gesamten Naturwissenschaften", emphasizes two conditions that were particularly important in the advance of mathematics in the early 19th century: a) the increasing "Umfang der Lehrtaetigkeit", including specialization, and the internal differentiation of the Philosophical Faculty and its various disciplines, and b) the increasing development of technology that required educated, sufficiently qualified specialists in ever greater numbers. See Langhammer (1980) in this vol..

45 For Dirichlet and the numbers of his students, see Biermann (1973), p. 30. On Dirichlet in general, see Kummer (1860), and Biermann (1959c), especially pp. 34-39.

46 For details of the effect of the Prussian educational system on the growth of mathematics in Prussia in the 19th century, see Turner (1971), especially pp. 137-148, and Turner (forthcoming b). See also Roessler (1961), pp. 95-142; O'Boyle (1968) and (1976); Mueller (1977), especially pp. 24-90; Beisenherz (1979). Lorey notes that "Wie in der frueheren IMUK-Abhandlung des

Verfassers betont wurde, ist ja das Gruendungsjahr der Berliner Universitaet, d.h. das Jahr 1810, zugleich das Geburtsjahr des Deutschen Oberlehrerstandes. Stammt doch aus diesem Jahre in Deutschland die erste Pruefungsordnung fuer das Lehramt an Hoeheren Schulen: das 'Kgl. Preussische Edikt vom 12. Julius 1810,'" in: Lorey (1916), p. 30. See also Lorey (1911). It is worth pointing out that France, as Maurice Crosland remarks, also promoted the teaching of mathematics at higher levels as a result of increasing demand for mathematics teachers. This was connected with the French examination system, especially the baccalaureat, in which, as Crosland states, "the clearest institutional encouragement on a national scale was given to mathematics. ... There were, therefore, many more positions for mathematics teachers than science teachers in the schools and these offered a clearly marked possibility of employment as well as constituting a recognised step towards positions in higher education. There was a great emphasis on mathematics as the alternative to a philosophical and literary training in the senior classes. This also had an effect on the number of students taking the license in mathematics. In Paris this number suddenly increased in 1822 and 1823; on the other hand, if one looks at the admittedly small number graduating in physical science, this dropped to zero from 1822–1829 and was generally less than the number of graduates in mathematics for the remainder of the century," in: Crosland (1979), p. 25.

Another aspect of the growing professionalization of mathematics through teaching is discussed by Volker Lenhart, who points out that early in the 19th century (from about 1800), textbooks began to address the new profession of teachers rather than educated parents and home tutors. See Lenhart (1979), p. 5. For an analysis of textbook authors, their backgrounds, professions and intended audiences, see Lenhart (1977).

47 Gauss in a letter to W. Olbers, March 1, 1827, in: Olbers (1909), p. 472. This letter is also quoted in: Biermann (1973), p. 22.

48 Lorey (1916), p. 45.

49 See section 4 of Chapter II, Plaene fuer ein Polytechniches Institut in Berlin. Der spaetere Plan von Schellbach, in: Lorey (1916), pp. 40–55; Manegold (1966); and Schubring (1980). Gert Schubring's study ist especially valuable for its use of archival

material drawing upon the former Prussian Ministerium der
Geistlichen-, Unterrichts- und Medizinalangelegenheiten,
Zentrales Staatsarchiv der DDR, Merseburg, and the
Dirichlet-Nachlass, Staatsbibliothek Preussischer Kulturbesitz,
Berlin.

50 Gert Schubring emphasizes that, had the efforts to establish
a Polytechnic Institute in Berlin been successful, it would have
represented the simultaneous professionalization and
institutionalization of mathematics in Berlin. See Schubring
(1980). In his study of the various attempts to establish a
Polytechnic Institute in Berlin, Schubring distinguishes four
phases, spanning a period of nearly thirty-five years, beginning
with the plan drafted by Tralles in 1817 for a
"Mathematisch-Technische Lehranstalt", through the last attempts
made between 1844 and 1850 by Schellbach, with the support of
Jacobi, to form an Institute. While he offers a number of
explanations for the repeated failure to found a Polytechnic
Institute in Berlin, Schubring does not mention financial
problems or the change in attitude on the part of the
Kriegsministerium towards the idea of such an Institute as
teaching was given greater emphasis at the expense of military
interests.

It should also be noted that plans to found a Polytechnic
School in Muenchen, submitted in 1824 by the engineer Georg
Reichenbach as an 'Entwurf zur Organisation einer Polytechnischen
Schule in Muenchen', also came to nothing for lack of money. Lorey
(1916), p. 58.

51 Crosland (1979), pp. 16f.

52 The increased importance of Berlin as a center for science in
Prussia upon the return of Alexander von Humboldt from Paris is
reflected in the meeting of the Gesellschaft Deutscher
Naturforscher und Aerzte, which convened in Berlin in 1828 under
the direction of Humboldt himself. See Humboldt Universitaet
(1960), p. 70, and Degen (1956).

However, as Gert Schubring points out, a mathematical seminar
would have compensated for certain shortcomings at the Unversity
of Berlin. Eventually, Berlin did establish a mathematical seminar
under the auspices of Kummer and Weierstrass. This was
successful, in part because of the Lehrerpruefungsordnung of
1866. See Schubring (1980). The founding of the Mathematical

Seminar is discussed in detail by Biermann (1973), pp. 71-74.
53 Klein (1926), p. 95.
54 Biermann (1973), p. 59. A. Kneser once called the period of mathematics at Berlin from 1864-1892 its "heroisches Zeitalter", in: Kneser (1925), p. 211.

References

Beisenherz, H.G.:   Zur gesellschaftlichen Funktion und Entwicklung der mathematisch–naturwissenschaftlichen Allgemeinbildung an den Gymnasien und Realschulen im 19. Jahrhundert, in: Bielefeld (1979), pp. 1-14

[Bielefeld:]   Epistemologische und soziale Probleme der Wissenschaftsentwicklung im fruehen 19. Jahrhundert, Bielefeld 1979 (Institut fuer Didaktik der Mathematik)

Biermann, K.-R.:   A.L. Crelles Verhaeltnis zu Eisenstein, in: Monatsbericht der Deutschen Akademie der Wissenschaften zu Berlin 1 (1959a), pp. 67-72

Biermann, K.-R.:   Ueber die Foerderung deutscher Mathematiker durch Alexander von Humboldt, in: Alexander von Humboldt Gedenkschrift, Berlin 1959b, pp. 83-159

Biermann, K.-R.:   J.P.G. Lejeune-Dirchichlet. Dokumente fuer sein Leben und Wirken, Berlin 1959c

Biermann, K.-R.:   Urteile A.L. Crelles ueber seine Autoren, in: Journal fuer die reine und angewandte Mathematik 203 (1960), pp. 216-220

Biermann, K.-R.:   Alexander   von   Humboldts
                          wissenschaftsorganisatorisches Programm
                          bei der Uebersiedlung nach Berlin, in:
                          Monatsbericht der Deutschen Akademie
                          der   Wissenschaften   zu   Berlin   10
                          (1968), pp. 142-47

Biermann, K.-R.:   Die Mathematik und ihre Dozenten an
                          der Berliner Universitaet. 1810-1920,
                          Berlin 1973

Crosland, M.:   The   Society   of   Arcueil. A View of
                          French Science at the Time of Napoleon
                          I, Cambridge (Mass.) 1967

Crosland, M.:   The   Development   of   a Professional
                          Career in France, in: Crosland, M.
                          (ed.):   The Emergence of Science in
                          Western   Europe,   New   York   1976,
                          pp. 139-159

Crosland, M.:   The Institutional Structure of Science
                          in   Early Nineteenth-Century France,
                          in: Bielefeld (1979), pp. 15-31

Dauben, J.:   Mathematical Perspectives: Essays on
                          the History of Mathematics in Honor of
                          Kurt-R. Biermann, ed. J. Dauben,
                          New York 1980

Daston, L.:   Mathematics and the Moral Sciences:
                          The Rise and Fall of the Probability
                          of Judgments,   1785 - 1840, in this
                          vol.

Degen, H.:   Die Naturforscherversammlung zu Berlin
                          im Jahre 1828 und ihre Bedeutung fuer
                          die   deutsche Geistesgeschichte, in:
                          Naturwissenschaftliche   Rundschau   2
                          (1956), pp. 333-340

Eccarius, W.:   August Leopold Crelle als Herausgeber
                          wissenschaftlicher   Fachzeitschriften,
                          in: Annals of Science 33 (1976),
                          pp. 229-261

Eccarius, W.:   August Leopold Crelle als Foerderer
                           bedeutender   Mathematiker,   in:
                           Jahresbericht   der   Deutschen
                           Mathematiker-Vereinigung 79 (1977),
                           pp. 137-174

Eccarius, W.:   August Leopold Crelle und die Berliner
                           Akademie   der   Wissenschaften,   in:
                           Dauben (1980)

Engelhardt, D.v.:   Wissenschaft   und   Bildung   in   der
                           romantischen   Naturforschung,
                           typescript circulated in conjunction
                           with Bielefeld (1979)

Fox, R.:   Scientific   Enterprise   and   Patronage
                           of Research in France, 1800-1870, in:
                           Minerva 11 (1973), pp. 442-73

Grabiner, J.:   Changing Attitudes Toward Mathematical
                           Rigor. Lagrange and Analysis in the
                           Eighteenth and Nineteenth Centuries, in
                           this vol.

Grattan-Guinness, I.:   Mathematical   Physics,   1800   -   1835.
                           Genesis in France, and Development in
                           Germany, in this vol.

Grattan-Guinness, I.:   Mathematical   Physics   in   France,
                           1800 - 1840: Knowledge, Activity and
                           Historiography, in: Dauben (1980)

Geiser, C.F. & Maurer, L.: Elwin   Bruno   Christoffel,   in:
                           Mathematische   Annalen   54   (1901),
                           pp. 329-341

Gericke, H.:   Zur Geschichte der Mathematik an der
                           Universitaet   Freiburg   i. Br.,   in:
                           Beitraege   zur   Freiburger
                           Wissenschafts-   und   Universitaetsge-
                           schichte I (1955).

Glatzer, N.:   Leopold   Zunz. Jude - Deutscher -
                           Europaer, Tuebingen 1964

Harnack, A.:   Geschichte der Koeniglich Preussischen
                           Akademie der Wissenschaften zu Berlin,
                           Berlin 1900

Heidelberger, M.:   Some   Patterns   of   Change   in   the
                           Baconian Sciences of the Early 19th
                           Century Germany, in this vol.

Humboldt Universitaet: Die Humboldt Universitaet - Gestern -
                           Heute - Morgen, Berlin 1960

Juskevic, A.:   Review of Biermann, K.-R.: Vorschlaege
                           zur   Wahl   von   Mathematikern in die
                           Berliner   Akademie,   Berlin 1960, in:
                           Deutsche   Literarische   Zeitung   82
                           (1961), pp. 1031-33

Klein, F.:   Vorlesungen ueber die Entwicklung der
                           Mathematik im 19. Jahrhundert, vol. 1,
                           Berlin 1926 (repr. New York 1956)

Kneser, A.:   Uebersicht   der   wissenschaftlichen
                           Arbeiten   Ferdinand   Mindings   nebst
                           biographischen   Notizen,   in:
                           Zeitschrift   fuer   Mathematik   und
                           Physik,   Historisch-Literarische
                           Abteilung 45 (1900), pp. 113-128

Kneser, A.:   Leopold   Kronecker,   in: Jahresbericht
                           der Deutschen Mathematiker-Vereinigung
                           33 (1925), pp. 210-228

Kobell, F.:   Nekrolog   auf   Martin   Ohm,   in:
                           Sitzungsberichte   der   Koeniglich
                           Bayerischen Akademie der Wissenschaften
                           zu Muenchen. Mathematisch-physikalische
                           Klasse 3 (1873), p. 132

Koenigsberger, L.:   Mein Leben, Heidelberg 1919

Kolde, W.:   Die   Universitaet   Erlangen unter dem
                           Hause   Wittelsbach.   1810   -   1910,
                           Erlangen and Leipzig 1910

Kummer, E.E.:   Gedaechtnisrede   auf   Gustav   Peter
                           Lejeune-Dirichlet,   in: Abhandlungen
                           der Koeniglich Preussischen Akademie
                           der Wissenschaften zu Berlin (1860),
                           pp. 1-26 (repr. in: Kronecker, L. and
                           Fuchs,   L.   (ed.):   G.   Lejeune
                           Dirichlet's   Werke,   vol. 2, Berlin
                           1897, pp. 311-344)

Langhammer, W.:   Some Aspects of the Development of Mathematics at the Unversity of Halle-Wittenberg in the Early 19th Century, in this vol.

Lenhart, V.:   Zur Wissenschaftsgeschichte der Erziehungswissenschaft. Erziehungskunst - Erziehungslehre - Erziehungswissenschaft. Die Entstehung des Programms einer wissenschaftlichen Paedagogik in Deutschland. 1750 - 1830, in Lenhart, V. (ed.): Historische Paedagogik. Methodologische Probleme der Erziehungsgeschichte, Wiesbaden 1977

Lenhart, V.:   Gesellschaftliche und institutionelle Bedingungen der Entwicklung der Erziehungswissenschaft in Deutschland von 1750 - 1830, typescript circulated in conjunction with Bielefeld (1979)

Lenz, M.:   Geschichte der Koeniglichen Friedrich-Wilhelm-Universitaet zu Berlin, Halle 1910

Lorey, W.:   Staatspruefung und praktische Ausbildung der Mathematiker an den hoeheren Schulen in Preussen und einigen norddeutschen Staaten, Leipzig, Berlin 1911

Lorey, W.:   Das Studium der Mathematik an den deutschen Universitaeten seit Anfang des 19. Jahrhunderts, Leipzig, Berlin 1916

Manegold, K.H.:   Eine Ecole Polytechnique in Berlin, in: Technikgeschichte 33 (1966), pp. 182-196

Mueller, D.K.:   Sozialstruktur und Schulsystem. Aspekte zum Strukturwandel des Schulwesens im 19. Jahrhundert, Goettingen 1977

Mehrtens, H.:   Mathematicians in Germany circa 1800, in this vol.

Neumann, L.:   Franz Neumann. Erinnerungsblaetter von
                        seiner Tochter, Tuebingen 1904

O'Boyle, L.:   Klassische Bildung und soziale
                        Struktur in Deutschland zwischen 1800
                        und 1848, in: Historische Zeitschrift
                        207 (1968), pp. 584–608

O'Boyle, L.:   Education and Social Structure. The
                        Humanist Tradition Reexamined, in:
                        Internationales Archiv fuer
                        Sozialgeschichte der deutschen
                        Literatur 1 (1976), pp. 246–57

Pablo, J.:   Die Rolle der Franzoesischen Kolonie
                        zu Berlin in der Gelehrtenrepublik des
                        18. Jahrhunderts, in: Hugenottenkirche
                        4 (1965), pp. 1–5

Rang-Dudzik, B.:   Qualitative and Quantitative Aspects
                        of Curricula in Prussian Grammar
                        Schools in the Late 18th and the Early
                        19th Century and their Relation to the
                        Development of the Sciences, in this
                        vol.

Roessler, W.:   Die Entstehung des modernen
                        Erziehungswesens in Deutschland,
                        Stuttgart 1961

Schubring, G.:   On Education as Mediating
                        Element between Development and
                        Application. The Plans for a
                        Polytechnical Institute in Berlin
                        (1817 – 1850), in this vol.

Shinn, T.:   The French Atomist Controversy. A
                        Problem of Scientific Continuity,
                        typescript circulated in conjunction
                        with Bielefeld (1979)

Smend, R.:   Die Berliner Friedrich-Wilhelms-
                        Universitaet, Goettingen 1961

Struik, D.:   A Concise History of Mathematics, New
                        York 1948 (3rd rev. ed. 1967)

Tietze, H.:	Die soziale und geistige Umbildung des Preussischen Oberlehrerstandes von 1870 bis 1914, in: Zeitschrift fuer Paedagogik, 14 (Beiheft, 1977), pp. 107-128
Toth, I.:	Metatheoretisches Selbstverstaendnis der Mathematik – am Beispiel der Entstehungs- und Rezeptionsgeschichte der nichteuklidischen Geometrie, in: Bielefeld (1979), pp. 305-318
Turner, S.:	The Growth of Professional Research in Prussia, 1818 to 1848 – Causes and Context, in: Historical Studies in the Physical Sciences 3 (1971), pp. 137-182
Turner, S.:	The Prussian Professoriate and the Research Imperative, 1790 – 1840, in this vol.
Turner, S.:	Prussian Universities and the Concept of Research, in: Internationales Archiv fuer Sozialgeschichte der deutschen Literatur (forthcoming a)
Turner, S.:	Social Mobility and the Traditional Professions in Prussia, 1770 – 1848, in: Central European History (forthcoming b)
Ulmer, F.:	Johann Georg Tralles, ein Hamburger Gelehrter, in: Hamburgische Geschichts- und Heimatblaetter 19 (1961), pp. 6-11
Wussing, H.:	Die Ecole Polytechnique – eine Errungenschaft der franzoesischen Revolution, in: Paedagogik 13 (1958), pp. 646-662
Zwerling, C.:	The Emergence of the Ecole Normale Superieure as a Center of Scientific Education in Nineteenth Century France, Boston 1976 (Ph. D. Thesis, Harvard University)

Herbert Mehrtens

MATHEMATICIANS IN GERMANY CIRCA 1800

I.

In his lectures on the development of mathematics in the 19th century Felix Klein talks of the "deutsche wissenschaftliche Renaissance",[1] which started about 1820. In mathematics, Jacobi, Dirichlet, Steiner, Pluecker and others formed a new generation, whose work brought a change in practice, style, contents, and aims of research and teaching. To provide valid historical interpretations we have to study this phenomenon from many sides. I shall, in this paper, try to cast some light on the time before this pervasive change. This, I believe, is necessary for an evaluation of possibilities and obstacles for the development of mathematical research in Germany by 1820. My question is: Who were the mathematicians around 1800 in Germany and what was their practice?

The time studied is that from about 1780 to 1820. This was the time of the French Revolution, of Prussia's collapse in 1806, of liberal reforms, of the wars of liberation, the Vienna congress, and the following political restauration. Germany was divided into hundreds of small political unities; in comparison with England and France it was industrially underdeveloped, there was hardly an economically independent bourgeoisie to back a liberal or revolutionary movement, and enlightenment had been a matter of the rational, mercantile, absolutist state, not of opposing

401

H. N. Jahnke and M. Otte (eds.), Epistemological and Social Problems of the Sciences in the Early Nineteenth Century, 401–420.

intellectuals. When talking about mathematicians and mathematics one has to be aware of this background. Differences of age, of social und geographical origin, of education and of individual character play a great role in such times. In our sample we find men as different as Gauss (1777-1855)[2] and F.W. Murhard[3] (1778-1853), who were fellow students at Goettingen. While Gauss, from lowest origin and generously supported by his duke, came to lead a life as steady as possible in those unsteady times concentrating on scholarly research, Murhard, son of an old and established family of civil servants, doubtlessly a man of strong talents, kept to mathematics only for a short period as 'Privatdozent' in Goettingen and then led a life as unsteady as the times being a traveller, journalist, editor, and politican and remebered not as a scientist but as a liberal writer. These men do not have a "collective biography". Thus I shall not try a systematic analysis of the sample of about sixty contemporary mathematicians, on which I am drawing here,[4] but rather attempt a survey by "exemplary biography".

II.

The standard account of the state of German mathematics by 1800 is about as follows: There was Gauss, "the greatest mathematician at least since Newton", who was "a transitional figure from the eighteenth to the nineteenth century".[5] Besides Gauss, however, there was hardly any other mathematician worth mentioning. The correspondants of Gauss are noted, sometimes also J. F. Pfaff. Mathematical education in the universities was elementary, research mainly confined to the unfruitful "combinatorial school" of K. F. Hindenburg. The most renowned elder mathematician was A. G. Kaestner, who had produced higly successful textbooks but hardly any creative mathematical research. With the exception of Gauss, German mathematicians disappear in the shadow of their French contemporaries. This picture is roughly correct. An attempt at an historical interpretation of this transitional period, however, needs a closer perspective.6

Of our sample about half are university professors. The rest may be divided into three roughly equal groups: Other teachers, civil servants and military, and others. Lines of demarcation are difficult to draw. University professors frequently held other

teaching positions and changes or combinations of positions as
teacher and as civil servant are found as well. To start with a
specific example right away, I may mention J. K. F. Hauff[7]
(1766-1846), who was first professor of mathematics at the
university of Marburg and Wien, then director of the polytechnical
school at Augsburg, after this "graeflich Salm'scher Berg-, Forst-
und Huettendirector" in Moravia, then mathematics professor again,
first at a gymnasium and then at the university of Gent. Hauff
published in physics, technology, astronomy, mathematics,
translated Laplace and Euclid, and edited a "Magazin fuer
Ingenieure". The mobility of Hauff is obvious, although stronger
than the average it is not at all exceptional.

After one general example let us look at the extremes, first the
practical mathematician of the day and then the best known
contemporaries. The species of the "mathematical practitioner" was
dying out with the beginning of the 19th century.[8] Before 1800
they still formed a distinct group. Other "mathematici" had for
some time been pressing for a demarcation: "MATHEMATICK-LEHRER,
Mathematicus, heisset eigentlich eine Person, welche die
Mathematick gruendlich verstehet, auch solche darin gehoerige
Wahrheiten durch eigenes Nachsinnen zu erfinden geschickt ist.
Insgemein aber wird dieser Name von Unverstaendigen sehr
gemissbrauchet, indem sie ihn allen Leuten beylegen, die einige
Sachen aus der ausuebenden Mathematick verstehen, ..."[9]. Such
"pseudo-mathematicians" may still be found in the beginning of the
19th century. Heinrich C. W. Breithaupt[10] (1775-1856) edited in
1805 a "Magazin fuer das Neueste aus der Mathematik",[11] in which
only topics of instrument-making and surveying were treated. The
journal looks very much like a company's journal of Breithaupt's
workshop which had been founded by Heinrich's father, a mechanic
at a court, and was carried on by his brother while Heinrich was a
teacher as well as a practitioner. The family enterprise stayed
alive. Heinrich's grandson, however, no longer appears in
connection with mathematics. He studied at a polytechnical school
and published in the "Zeitschrift fuer Instrumentenkunde". The
fact that technicians in the first half of the century could still
find their professional and social locus with mathematics may also
be illustrated by the 'Hamburger Mathematische Gesellschaft' which
lived through its "technical period" from 1790 to 1860.[12]

The best known professional mathematicians proper of the time are
A. G. Kaestner (1719-1800), K. F. Hindenburg (1741-1808), Gauss
and J. F. Pfaff (1765-1825). Gauss, as a mathematician of his
time, certainly deserves a more thorough treatment than I can give
here and I shall make only a few passing remarks about him. Pfaff,
respected by Gauss as his teacher, was one of the few
mathematicians who had a straightforward career and concentrated
strongly on one field of research, namely higher calculus[13].
Offspring of a Wuerttemberg family of higher civil servants and
scholars, he had an exceptionally thorough pre-university
education at the 'Hohe Karlsschule'[14]. Supported by his duke like
Gauss, Pfaff went to study mathematics with Kaestner at
Goettingen. By 1788 he had been called to the chair of mathematics
in Helmstedt and received the permission of his duke to accept the
call. When the university of Helmstedt closed, he transferred to
Halle, where he remained until his death[15]. Pfaff's younger
brother Johann (1774-1835) became a mathematician as well, "but
the rapid changes in his scientific interests prevented him from
attaining the importance of Johann Friedrich"[16]. In this respect
Johann is more representative of the average scholar. Pfaff shows
us, however, that a mathematical career with concentrated and
successful research was possible in his time in Germany.

Hindenburg, like Pfaff a student of Kaestner's, was head of the
so-called "combinatorial school"[17]. He had studied mathematics,
physics and medicine in Leipzig, then became private tutor and
followed his pupil to the university of Goettingen where he came
in close contact with Kaestner. Returning to Leipzig, he became
'Privatdozent', extraordinary, and finally (1786) ordinary
professor of philosophy and physics. He did research in physics,
but since about 1880 started with his combinatorial research
programm and concentrated more and more on mathematics, vigorously
propagating the value of his combinatorial approach to calculus. I
shall say more about his attempts at creating a specialised
research community in a moment. Hindenburg is described as a man
of exceeding self-esteem. It might be speculated, however, that it
needed a strong self-confidence to form a research school in those
days no matter how good the scientific program was.

Kaestner, a representative of an older generation, was critical of
the combinatorial approach. "Es ist nicht das Mittel, die
Mathematik in dauerhaftem Ansehen zu erhalten", he wrote to Pfaff,
"wenn sie von Unmathematikern nur als ein ihnen unerforschliches
Geheimnis soll angestaunt werden"[18]. This rejection of specialist,
esoteric mathematics as well as his demand for an obvious utility
made Kaestner especially resentful of French mathematics. In
another letter to Pfaff he wrote: "... dass eine grosse Menge
Integralformeln, die man nicht anders ausdruecken kann als in den
Zeichen, in denen sie ausgedrueckt sind, nicht mehr Werth haben
als manche Saetze der scholastischen Philosophie, die ebenfalls
wahr sind, aber nur Wahrheiten von philosophischen Kunstwoertern.
Die jetzigen franzoesischen Calculatoren treiben diese Sache sehr
ueber ihre Graenzen; was eine Mechanik ganz ohne Figuren, wie La
Grange's seine, nuetzen soll, ist nicht abzusehen, das Brauchbare
darinnen, das man laengst wusste, ist nur in abstrakten
Ausdruecken sehr unverstaendlich eingekleidet".[19] When Kaestner
wrote this in 1798 he was very old, but the basis of
misunderstanding is obviously the different aim he conceived for
mathematics. The scholar, even the mathematician, had to produce
useful science, intelligible to the broad community of
"Gelehrte".[20]

When Kaestner was called to Goettingen in 1755 he was expected to
develop a broad literary activity[21], and on such activity rested
his later reputation. This determined his approach to mathematics.
What is important is Kaestner's lasting influence. His books were
the most widely used basis for university education in
mathematics. Further, Goettingen was a university of highest
reputation and had developed by the second half of the 18th
century a scholarship of high standing, paving the way for the
neohumanistic future of German universities[22]. It is not by chance
that Gauss, Pfaff and Hindenburg, as well as most of the other
more important mathematicians of our period, received at least
part of their mathematical education at Goettingen.

III.
About two sixths of the mathematicians I have looked at were not
in teaching positions. Here amateurs are included, who did only
little work in mathematics, as well as some mathematical

practitioners. The only further distinct subgroup here is that of
civil servants and military. Here we do not find, however, a
social role allowing for scholarly research. Men, devoted to
mathematics usually attempted to get into a teaching position, be
it in the system of military education or by a change to a
university. L. Crelle (1780-1855) is in some ways a representative
case[23]. As the son of a lowly civil servant he could not afford
formal schooling and followed his father in a career in public
building administration. He taught himself mathematics and looked
for a position at a university. These attempts failed due to the
circumstances of the time. Instead, after a successful
administrative career, he came into a position where he could
display his organizational talents to the best of German
mathematics. Mathematics was part of the cameralist education, and
the educated civil servants were part of the educated public for
which the scholars wrote. Thus there were men with strong
interests in mathematics, but only by chance and with special
devotion was it possible for them to do scholarly work regularly.

The mathematicians' place was in the educational system, which
underwent great changes in the period studied here. Of the
secondary schools, few granted a reasonable mathematical
education. And it is in these few schools that we find mathematics
teachers of some scholarly productivity. E.G. Fischer[24]
(1754-1831), son of a preacher, became a teacher of mathematics
and physics first in Halle and then in Berlin. He was a member of
the Berlin academy of science and ectraordinary professor of
physics at the university. Fischer is known as the tutor of the
brothers von Humboldt, for his achievements in chemistry, and also
for his contributions to the discussion on educational reform. His
wide range of interests may be illustrated by his lectures in the
'Berliner Philomathische Gesellschaft'[25]. In mathematics Fischer
published a "Theorie der Dimensionszeichen"[26], similar to
Hindenburg's combinatorial theory, which led to a bitter
controversy with that school[27]. In 1808 Fischer published an
"Untersuchung ueber den eigentlichen Sinn der hoeheren Analysis"[28]
which starts with an "idealistische Uebersicht" of the natural
sciences and of mathematics, demanding clear and distinct
concepts, derived along the lines of Kantian philosophy. He
renounces the formalist mathematics of the Wolffian school and

conceives, e.g., the infinitesimal as "Endgraenze" being a necessary concept of human reason. The 'Untersuchung' is the attempt at a metaphysical foundation — with little technical mathematics involved. His motivation for this enterprise he gives thus: "da es aber mein Geschick gebietet, mich mit jedem Jahre wieder in den Elementen, wie in einem Wirbel, herumzudrehen, so habe ich es mir zur heiligen Pflicht gemacht, die Kraft, welche ich der Erweiterung der Wissenschaft nur selten opfern darf, wenigstens durch unablaessiges Streben nach vollendeter Deutlichkeit in den ersten Begriffen ihrer festesten Begruendung zu widmen". [29]

Questions of foundations were certainly "in the air". B. F. Thibaut, professor of mathematics in Goettingen, wrote in 1805: "Es scheint in der Bearbeitung der mathematischen Wissenschaften allenthalben ein Ruhepunkt deutlich hervorzutreten, [...] die Wissenschaft [muss] endlich den Uebergang in das maennliche Alter machen, und durch strenge Reflexion ueber sich selbst geleitet, den eigenen Geist ermessend zu einer neuen Stufe der Entwicklung fortgehen"[30]. Thibaut's analysis, namely that the weight of the host of individual results achieved since Newton is pressing and makes a new survey and a new ordering necessary, is certainly not complete. The quote by Fischer indicates another aspect. The mathematician in the school still had little chances to get a fully salaried position just as a mathematician. Further, the purely utilitarian legitimation of mathematics was no longer accepted, when the neohumanist movememt got under way. So the teacher of mathematics, who had some "Kraft fuer die Erweiterung der Wissenschaft" and who was, like Fischer[31], involved in the debates about school-reform, took to the foundations of his subject to secure an autonomous, philosophically legitimated basis for his subject to be taught as part of the 'Allgemeinbildung'. In the struggle for an accepted position for science and mathematics in the emerging new educational system the reflections on structure and foundations of the subject were part of the strategy.

The same combination as Fischer's, i.e. the position of a school teacher, strong pedagogical interests, authorship of textbooks, and a foundational rethinking of mathematics on a distinct philosophical background, we find among others also in Martin Ohm[32] (1792-1872), brother of the physicist G.S. Ohm. Their father was a locksmith who had strong interests in mathematics. Martin was autodidact in mathematics. He had studied the works of Euler and some French mathematicians and heard not more than one lecture on mathematics at the university, an introduction to combinatorial analysis.[33] After some time as 'Privatdozent' in Erlangen he became teacher at a Gymnasium, which he left for Berlin, where he finally, in 1839, became ordinary professor of mathematics, much against faculty opposition, which attested him great incompetence[34]. He seems, however, to have exerted considerable influence in the realm of school-mathematics[35], and his attempts at a "revision" of mathematics are strongly connected with pedagogical aims. Somewhat different from the elder Fischer, Ohm is looking for a foundation of mathematics in itself. He writes: "Ist aber nicht die Ausbildung des Menschen, sondern vorzueglich die Wissenschaft selbst der Zweck ihrer Behandlung, (wie dies bey einem Mathematiker von Profession der Fall seyn muss) so bekommt der Kalkuel ohnstreitig das vollkommenste Uebergewicht"[36]. Geometry is not the basis of mathematics, here spatial intution is the foundation, "einfache, naturgemaesse strenge Begruendung im Bereiche der Sinnlichkeit"[37]. The mathematics of numbers is more fundamental, and Ohm comes close to a formalist, operational conception of arithmetic and algebra, parallel to the work of Bolzano[38].

Levels of mathematical education low in standard universities did not too much differ from high standard secondary schools. The teaching of research topics is said to have started only at the end of the 1820s with Jacobi and Dirichlet. This extremely significant change in university mathematics, however, is not quite without precedents. When Ohm, e. g., lectured in 1824/25 on "Synthetische Geometrie als der eine Teil der reinen Elementarmathematik"[39] this was probably as elementary as usual, but the title indicates that Ohm structured the subject along the lines of his own foundational conceptions, which were his research matter, rather than along some standard textbook. A second example is the lecture on combinatorial analysis Ohm had heard, which had become part of university mathematics as a result of the spread of adherents to the combinatorial school over German universities.

Hindenburg himself had started this practice to add combinatorial analysis to the standard syllabus of mathematics in 1790 [40]. These were certainly exceptions to the rule that lectures remained extremely elementary and followed standard textbooks such as Kaestner's. By the turn of the century the situation was especially bad, and all major mathematicians educated up to 1830 in Germany were essentially autodidacts. University teachers were not expected to be researchers in the 18th century. To illustrate this just once more, one can quote the government of Baden, which still declared in 1807, "dass man das Erfinden im Scientifischen fuer das Geschaeft des Gelehrten, aber nicht fuer das des [Hochschul-]Lehrers halte" [41].

But what should a "Gelehrter" do, if not teach? The times, when dukes or kings would support some scholars were ending. The academies, which had institutionalized such a feudalist form of scientific practice would give a living to only very few scholars. They were, with the feudal system, in a state of decline. Thus, the scholars mainly found their place in the universities, and in the time of crisis, since about 1780, engaged strongly in debates about means and aims of reform. The question as to whether research was part of the duties of a university teacher became a subject of debate, too, but with the growing dominance of neohumanist conceptions over utilitarian enlightened positions, the universalistic conception of research became adverse to natural science and to mathematics [42] . The idealist philosophical critique of mathematics [43] was such that mathematicians, although frequently eagerly looking for philosophical foundations of their science, kept at a distance from the idealist philosophers. Only later, when a more formal "Wissenschaftsideologie" [44] had been established, devoid of philosophical prescriptions, scientists and mathematicians could easily subsume their specialist work under such a conception.

At the turn of the century, however, the situation for mathematics in the university was still bad [45]. On one hand mathematics had to give a general basic education to later professionals and a special encyclopedic education, strong in applied mathematics to the cameralists of the mercantile system. This function was reduced with the decline of this system. The new function of the philosophical faculty, education of teachers, on the other hand, developed only slowly and was dominated traditionally by theologians and then, during the reform period, by philologists and idealist philosophers. Mathematicians tended rather to take up the utilitarian, Enlightenment side in the pre-reform debate, which clearly lost ground. Thus, they had neither a self-contained social role to rely on nor a distinct epistemological and ideological basis to side effectively with the neohumanist movement.

The situation in individual universities has been described in details in some cases[46]. To illustrate some general remarks I shall briefly report on Kiel university[47]. In 1780 J.M. Ljungberg (1748-1812) left the university where he had taught mathematics and astronomy to take an administrative position at the Kopenhagen court. In 1784 J.N.Tetens (1736-1807) who already was professor of philosophy also took responsibility for mathematics. He taught the usual elementary mathematics, published some analytical studies and a treatise on mathematics "zum Nutzen des buergerlichen Lebens". He is known as a philospher of Enlightenment who influenced Kant. His practical interests in dike-construction, draining, traffic, and finance, and his travels and publications concerning those fields led to a call to the court. His successor, F. Valentiner, (1756-1813), son of a protestant minister who had first studied theology, had already been extraordinary professor of mathematics. He was also fire chief of Kiel, and published on that subject. In mathematics he had some reputation as a teacher but did not publish anything worth mentioning. In 1801 N.T. Reimer (1772-1832) was called to the chair. He was the son of a protestant minister as well, had studied in Goettingen and developed broad activities in Kiel as director of the observatory and the institute for education of forest officers, accountant of the academic hospital and the botanical garden. He published manily historical and philosophical studies on mathematics. A mathematician more of the new generation came to Kiel in 1833 – H.F. Scherk (1798-1885), who had studied with Gauss and Bessel and taught at Koenigsberg and Halle before he was called to Kiel.

The history of mathematicians in Kiel illustrates some general features of university mathematics in our period. There was no strict delimitation of subjects in teaching assignments and personal combinations of chairs within the philosophical faculty were frequent. The equation of mathematical professorship with mathematical research is valid (with exceptions) only when "mathematics" is taken in the very broad sense of the day. Changes of positions, of universities and even of professions led to a high mobility of academic professionals, not only in mathematics. This combined with a stress on professional performance in this career of social advancement. Performance, however, was not that of a disciplinary specialist but rather either that of a scientific universalist, who could build up an observatory, provide textbooks for local institutions, give educational expertise, and finally bring in some reputation as a 'Gelehrter'. Or it had to be performance in the field of civil administraton with a combination of technological, administrative, and maybe juridical expertise, which all might be centered around a basic "mathematical" education and achievement. While a professorship at a university was an aim of social advancement, it was not the ultimate aim in the traditional social structure. An administrative position at a court held higher prestige[48]. Mobility and variability in academies of the day explain much of the fact that mathematical achievement in the modern sense was very rare in universities around 1800. Textbooks, historical studies, experimental research in the natural sciences and studies in astronomy, as well as treatises on some mathematical topics of the day were extensiveley published.

IV

The last part of my paper is devoted to the contemporary "scientific community" of mathematicians. We have found two distinct "schools", the combinatorial school and Goettingen university with Kaestner. The latter is a "school" in the traditional sense, a place where many mathematicians received their professional education in a rather homogeneous way along the lines of the Kaestnerian conception of mathematics. If we compare, however, mathematicians such as Gauss, Hindenburg, Murhard, Pfaff, or Tralles we find the group of Goettingen alumni to be rather heterogeneous. This group can hardly be called a "scientific community" in the sense of T.S. Kuhn[49], that is a community of

scientists, frequently with a common education who subscribe to a
common conception of their sientific practice, the so-called
"disciplinary matrix" or "paradigm". This conception is closely
related to the concept of a "scientific school" as it is commonly
used[50]. In the time of rising idealist and historistic conceptions
of science, Kaestnerian mathematics, rooted in the Enlightenment,
was no longer strong enough to provide common commitments on the
basis of which a closely connected community could be formed.
Further, this background was bound to the broad type of scientific
practice performed by 18th century 'Gelehrte'. This is in some
sense opposed to the practice of the scientific specialist bound
to a "disciplinary matrix". Albeit specialist performance and
communication were not impossible within 18th century science, its
intellectual and social structures were certainly hindering a
development in this direction.

That such trends became stronger by the end of the century can be
seen in many fields. In mathematics the combinatorial school is
the first distinct movement towards a scientific community in
Kuhn's sense, "die eigenthuemliche, in Deutschland bisher kaum
vorgekommene Erscheinung, dass nicht nur die Schueler
Hindenburg's, sondern auch eine nicht unbedeutende Anzahl der
damaligen Mathematiker der neuen Disciplin ihre Kraefte
widmeten".[51] The combinatorialists, however, dit not produce
results of lasting historical importance. Felix Klein mentions
Hindenburg and his followers only in parentheses, "weil sie mehr
als Auslaeufer frueherer wissenschaftlicher Tendenzen (von
Lagrange u.a.), denn als Anfang neuerer wissenschaftlicher
Entwicklungen erschein[en]".[52]

H. Hankel, to whom Klein refers in this place, says that the
results of the school fell into oblivion because they were not
part of the necessary development of science[53]. The
combinatorialists, he adds, worked themselves into an enormous
formalism, forgetting that formulae are a means and not the aims
of analysis. On the other hand, Hankel ascribes to Lagrange's
stress on methods, which may be seen as a root of the
combinatorial approach, a place in the necessary development. This
is an, as yet unanalysed, contradictory situation. We find the
development of a methodological paradigm, the mathematics only for

mathematicians which Kaestner despised in Lagrange but which
certainly indicated the tendency toward an autonomous professional
research in mathematics. But the school did not leave the
traditional subject matter of analysis and, maybe because of this,
did not break way for new developments and got caught in its
formalism. Close analysis of the roots of 19th century
developments of mathematics will certainly show some of the
indirect influence of the combinatorial school. Such influences
have been found in Weierstrass' teacher Gudermann[54]. More
characteristic, it seems, is the influence via a metaconception of
pure mathematics necessary for the emergence of
professionalization of mathematical research. Gert Schubring has
analysed this connection in this volume and pointed to the
philosopher J.F. Fries (1773-1843) who was a follower of the
combinatorial school[55].

That combinatorialists did form a scientific community is
indicated by the journals which Hindenburg edited since 1781 and
which specialized more and more in mathematics alone[56] .
Combinatorial analysis found increasing emphasis here and in 1796
and 1800 he published two collections of studies which look like
"supplementary volumes" soleley devoted to combinatorial
analysis.[57] It has been mentioned above that Hindenburg started to
lecture on his subject, enlarging, with limited success, the
traditional static program of mathematical lectures. Hindenburg's
"Archiv" ceased appearance in 1800, thus sharing the fate of many
other attempts at specialised periodical publications. Public
acceptance of this type of scientific communication was still not
strong enough to overcome the economical difficulties heightened
by the crisis of the universities and by political upheavals.
Combinatorialists did not succeed in establishing such specialized
communication, nor did they change the structure of university
mathematics. In many ways they seem to have been too early. An
analysis of structure and fate of the school ought to look at the
interconnections between the mathematical program of the school as
related to the epistemological movements of the time and the
question of social legitimacy of specialized communities in
science breaking away from the "Gelehrtenkultur" of the 18th
century.

There was, however, one social locus which seems to have been more timely for the research mathematician. "In Deutschland", writes M. Ohm in 1819, "ist eigentlich die Astronomie das einzige praktische Fach, welches Mathematiker bildet"[58]. The list of those 19th century mathematicians mentioned in every history of mathematics starts with Olbers, Pfaff, Gauss, Crelle, Bessel, and Moebius (all born up to 1790). Of these six, only Pfaff and Crelle are not associated with astronomy. Olbers and Bessel were full scale astronomers, Gauss made his name first with astronomical work and became director of the Goettingen observatory, and Moebius was employed as astronomer and did research both in mathematics and astronomy. Olbers and Bessel appear in this list mainly because of the mathematical relevance of the letters Gauss wrote to them. But Bessel is well known for a series of mathematical achievements made in connection with astronomical problems, and Olbers made his name by a method to compute paths of comets, which also is in part a mathematical achievement. Obviously, astronomy posed highly technical mathematical problems. Secondly it seems that at least some astronomers had better chances to concentrate on mathematical problems than the mathematicians generally had.

Certainly there is the matter of individual talent, too. But it does not seem to be by chance that the greatest of the contemporary German mathematicians, after the rather feudalistic looking situaton of a free life supported by a dukely Maecenas, went to an observatory and not to a chair of mathematics. As we have seen, the latter position was not at all ideal. The astronomical observatory, in contrast, was in the first place not an educational institution but a scientific one. As such it provided a social role for the researching astronomer and kept him somewhat apart from the changing situation of the educational system. There was no doubt that specialist research was part of the task of the director of an observatory. And such research, at this point in history, was highly mathematical. Astronomy had to a certain extent an accepted institutional basis as a science.

This remains true even when we have to observe that astronomy shared generally the fate of mathematics and natural sciences. The ultimate professionalization of astronomy came about only with the emergence of the university observatory during the 19th century

with Bessel's new observatory in Koenigsberg and the
reconstruction of the Goettingen observatory with Gauss as
starting points[59]. Before that, university observatories were
rather neglected and part of the picture we painted for
mathematics, as illustrated by the fact that Kaestner was the
director of the Goettingen observatory, too. Private institutions
seem to have been of greater importance.

Parallel to Hindenburg we find in astronomy F. X. von Zach
(1754-1832) as an organizer of the astronomical community[60]. There
seems to have been no need in astronomy for a special paradigm to
press for professionalization. Von Zach, incidentally self-taught
like Olbers and Bessel, tried to organize in 1789 a conference on
astronomy at his observatory in Gotha, which was only partially
successful because of feudal distrust in scientific
"internationalism" within Germany and resulting political
interventions. For similar reasons Zach's attempt to found an
astronomical society was unsuccessful. More important was Zach's
"Monatliche Correspondenz" which appeared from 1800 to 1813 and
carried many mathematical articles and became an important journal
for astronomers and astronomer-mathematicians. The first lasting
journal in astronomy, Schumacher's "Astronomische Nachrichten"
started in 1821[61]. The tendency towards the formation of
specialist communities can be found in most scientific
disciplines.[62] Such attempts were mostly unsuccessful before the
establishment of a place and a role for the pure scientist in the
university system, starting in the 1820's. The fate of all
sciences in the period from 1780 to 1820 in Germany is marked by
the crisis of the universities and the beginning reform, by the
political unrest of the time triggered off by the French
revolution, and by the intellectual movement, largely in a
specific German reaction to the great political development,
towards neohumanism and idealism. In their specific historical
situations the different sciences reacted differently. Unlike
other sciences, mathematics did not have an obvious connection
with romanticism. Mathematicians were forced into opposition to
neohumanism and idealist positions because these questioned the
value of the "realist" subjects in elite education. The struggle
of mathematics with the hindrances for professional autonomization
from the side of the traditional university system as well as from

the side of the idealist mainstream of epistemological and pedagogical conceptions led to a situation which brought very few entries in the historical record of lasting mathematical achievements. But one may ask whether this period did not, under the surface of research results, accomplish much of the basic epistemological reorientation necessary to set the stage for the coming renaissance of German mathematics.

References

1 Klein, F.: Vorlesungen ueber die Entwicklung der Mathematik im 19. Jahrhundert, vol. I, Berlin 1979 (Repr. Berlin 1926), p. 17.
2 For biographical information the reader is generally referred to the Gillispie, C.C. (ed.): Dictionary of Scientific Biography, 14 vols., New York 1970-1976, and to the "Poggendorff": Poggendorff, J.C. (ed.): Biographisches-Literarisches Handwoerterbuch zur Geschichte der Exacten Wissenschaften, Leipzig 1863, repr. Amsterdam 1965 (Repr. Leipzig 1863).
3 Weidemann, W.: Friedrich Wilhelm August Murhard (1778-1853), Ein Publizist des Altliberalismus, Frankfurt 1924 (Diss.); Mueller, C.H.: Studien zur Geschichte der Mathematik, insbesondere des mathematischen Unterrichts an der Universitaet Goettingen im 18. Jahrhundert, Leipzig 1934 (Diss. Goettingen), p. 89f.
4 The sample has been collected with information from contemporary bibliographies and later biographical and historiographical works. Mathematicians selected have published in the first decade of the 19th century (not exclusively elementary or practical) and are noted in the "Poggendorff".
5 Kline, M.: Mathematical Thought from Ancient to Modern Times, Oxford 1972, p. 871.
6 A survey of mathematicians, including minor figures, gives Mueller, F.: Der mathematische Sternenhimmel des Jahres 1811, Leipzig 1911.
7 Cantor, M.: Johann Karl Friedrich Hauff, in: Allgemeine Deutsche Biographie, vol. 11, Leipzig 1880, p. 48.
8 Schneider, I.: Die mathematischen Praktiker im See-, Vermessungs- und Wehrwesen vom 15. bis zum 17. Jahrhundert, Technikgeschichte 37 (1970), pp. 210-242; Taylor, E.G.R.: The

Mathematical   Practitioners   of   Hanoverian   England   1714-1840,
Cambridge 1966.
9 Grosses vollstaendiges Universal Lexicon aller Wissenschaften
und Kuenste, vol. 19, Halle 1739, p. 2052.
10 Kirchvogel, P.A.: Die Feinmechaniker-Familie Breithaupt, in:
Schnack,   I.   (ed.):   Lebensbilder aus Kurhessen und Waldeck.
1830-1930, vol. I, Marburg 1939, pp. 39-53.
11 Breithaupt, H.C.W. (ed.): Magazin fuer das Neueste aus der
Mathematik   fuer   Ingenieur,   Militair,   Architekten,
Forstbediensteten, Markscheider und Mechaniker, vol. I, Leipzig
1805.
12 Bubendey, J.F.: Geschichte der Mathematischen Gesellschaft in
Hamburg   1690-1890,   in: Mitteilungen   der   mathematischen
Gesellschaft Hamburg 2 (1890), pp. 8-78
13 On Pfaff, see the introductory chapter to: Pfaff, C. (ed.):
Sammlung von Briefen gewechselt zwischen Johann Friedrich Pfaff
und Herzog Carl von Wuertemberg, F. Bouterwek, A.v.Humboldt, A.G.
Kaestner und anderen, Leipzig 1853.
14 Ibid., pp. 3-10.
15 Cf. Langhammer, W.: Some   Aspects of the Development of
Mathematics at the University of Halle-Wittenberg in the early
19th century, in this vol.
16 Wussing, H.: Johann Friedrich Pfaff, in: Dictionary (ref. 2)
vol. 10, p. 572.
17 On Hindenburg and the combinatiorial school see: Netto, E:
Kombinatorik, in: Cantor, M.: Vorlesungen ueber die Geschichte der
Mathematik,   vol. 4,   Stuttgart 1965   (Repr. Leipzig 1908),
chap. XXI, pp. 199-221.
18 Pfaff, Sammlung (ref. 13), p. 217.
19 Ibid., pp. 221f.
20 The present essay owes much to Steven Turner's studies on the
changing situation of scholarship in Prussia, 1760 to 1848:
Turner,   St.R.:   The Prussian Universities and the Research
Imperative, Princeton 1973 (Diss.). On 'Gelehrte' cf. his:
University Reformers and Professorial Scholarship in Germany
1760 - 1806, in: Stone, L. (ed.): The University in Society,
vol. II, Princeton 1975.
21 Mueller, Studien (ref. 3), p. 56.
22 Stichweh, R.: Ausdifferenzierung   der Wissenschaft - Eine
Analyse   am   deutschen   Beispiel,   Bielefeld   1977   (Report

Wissenschaftsforschung 8, Universitaet Bielefeld), pp. 55ff, 77.

23 Eccarius, W.:   Der Techniker und Mathematiker August Leopold
Crelle (1780-1855) und sein Beitrag zur Foerderung und Entwicklung
der Mathematik im Deutschland des 19. Jahrhunderts. Leipzig 1974
(Diss.). A summary of the dissertation (same title), in: NTM
Schriftenreihe zur Gesch. der Naturwiss. und Technik 12 (1975),
p. 38-49.

24 Cantor, M.: Ernst Gottfried Fischer, in: ADB (ref. 7), vol. 7,
Leipzig 1878, p. 62.

25 Klemm, F.:   Die   Berliner   Philomatische   Gesellschaft
(Philomathie), in: Sudhoffs Arch. 42 (1958), pp. 39-45.

26 Fischer, E. G.: Theorie der Dimensionszeichen, Halle 1792.

27 Netto, Kombinatorik (ref. 17), pp. 217f. Fischers's main
opponent, H.A. Toepfer, was also a teacher.

28 Fischer, E. G.: Untersuchungen ueber den eigentlichen Sinn der
hoeheren Analysis nebst einer idealischen Uebersicht der
Mathematik und Naturkunde nach ihrem ganzen Umfange, Berlin 1808.

29 Ibid., p. 66.

30 Mueller, Studien (ref. 3), pp. 81f.

31 Mueller, D.K.: Sozialstruktur und Schulsystem. Aspekte zum
Strukturwandel des Schulwesens im 19. Jahrhundert, Goettingen
1977, pp. 144-153.

32 Cantor, M.: Martin   Ohm, in: ADB (ref. 7), vol. 24, Leipzig
1887, pp. 203f.

33 Lorey, W.: Das   Studium der Mathematik an den deutschen
Universitaeten seit Anfang des 19. Jahrhunderts, Leipzig 1916,
p. 32.

34 Biermann, K.R.: Die   Mathematik und ihre Dozenten an der
Berliner Universitaet 1810-1920, Berlin 1973, pp. 16-19.

35 Lorey, Studium (ref. 33), pp. 31-36.

36 Ohm, M.: Kritische Beleuchtung der Mathematik ueberhaupt und
der Euklidischen Geometrie insbesondere, Berlin 1819, p. 12.

37 Ibid., p. 9.

38 Nový, L.: Origins of Modern Algebra, Prag 1973, pp. 83-92.

39 Biermann, Mathematik (ref. 34), p. 19.

40 Lorey, Studium (ref. 33), p. 27

41 Christmann, E.: Studien zur Geschichte der Mathematik und des
mathematischen Unterrichts in Heidelberg. Von der Gruendung der
Universitaet bis zur combinatorischen Schule, Heidelberg 1925
(Diss.).

42 As an example see: Schelling, F.W.J.: Vorlesungen ueber die Methode des akademischen Studiums, in: Die Idee der deutschen Universitaet. Die fuenf Grundschriften aus der Zeit ihrer Neubegruendung durch klassischen Idealismus und romantischen Realismus, Darmstadt 1956, pp. 1-123.

43 Stuloff, N.: Die Mathematik in philosophischer Kritik zu Beginn des 19. Jahrhunderts, in: XIIe Congrès International d'histoire des sciences, vol. IV (Actes), Paris 1971, pp. 171-174.

44 Turner, St.R.: The Growth of Professorial Research in Prussia, 1818 to 1848 - Causes and Context, in: Hist. Stud. Phys. Sci. 3 (1971), pp. 137-182.

45 Cf. Lorey, Studium (ref. 33), pp. 23-31. For the general situation of the universities cf. e.g. Busch, A.: Die Geschichte der Privatdozenten. Eine soziologische Studie zur grossbetrieblichen Entwicklung der deutschen Universitaeten, Stuttgart 1959, chapter 1.

46 Christmann, Studien (ref. 41); Biermann, Mathematik (ref. 34); Langhammer, Aspects (ref. 15); Gericke, H.: Zur Geschichte der Mathematik an der Universitaet Freiburg i. Br., Freiburg 1955.

47 Schoenbeck, J.: Mathematik, in: Jordan, K. (ed.): Geschichte der Christian-Albrechts-Universitaet Kiel 1665-1965, vol. 6 (Geschichte der Mathematik, der Naturwissenschaften und der Landwirtschaftswissenschaften), Neumuenster 1968, pp. 9-58.

48 Situation, background and careers of the German intellectuals are described in Gerth, H.: Buergerliche Intelligenz um 1800. Zur Soziologie des deutschen Fruehliberalismus, Goettingen 1976. Mathematicians fit well into Gerth's analysis.

49 Kuhn, T.S.: The Structure of Scientific Revolutions. Chicago 1970, 2d ed.; Mehrtens, H.: T.S. Kuhn's Theories and Mathematics, in: Historia Mathematica 3 (1976), pp. 297-320.

50 For a discussion of "schools" cf. Folta, J.: Social Conditions and the Founding of Scientific Schools. An Attempt at an Analysis on the Example of the Czech Geometric School, in: Acta hist. rer. nat. necnon tech., Special issue 10, Prague 1977, pp. 81-179.

51 Gerhardt, G.J.: Geschichte der Mathematik in Deutschland, Muenchen 1877, p. 203.

52 Klein, Vorlesungen (ref. 1), p. 113.

53 Hankel, H.: Die Entwicklung der Mathematik in den letzten Jahrhunderten, Tuebingen 1869, p. 27.

54 Manning, K.R.: The Emergence of the Weierstrassian Approach to

Complex   Analysis,   in: Arch.   Hist.   Exact   Sci.   14 (1975),
pp. 297-383.

55 Schubring, G.: On   Education as a Mediating Element between
Development and   Application. The   Plans   for   the   Berlin
Polytechnical Institute (1817-1850), in this vol.

56 Leipziger Magazin fuer Naturkunde, Mathematik und Oekonomie, 5
vols., Leipzig 1871-1885; Leipziger Magazin fuer reine und
angewandte Mathematik, 4 numbers, Leipzig 1786-1788 (edited in
collaboration with Johann III Bernoulli); Archiv der reinen und
angewandten Mathematik, 11 numbers, Leipzig 1795-1800.

57 Hindenburg, K.F.: Der polynomische Lehrsatz, das wichtigste
Theorem   der   ganzen   Analysis, Leipzig 1796; Sammlung
combinatorisch-analytischer Abhandlungen, Leipzig 1800.

58 Ohm, Beleuchtung (ref. 36), p. 10.

59 Herrmann, D.B.:   Die   Entstehung   der   astronomischen
Fachzeitschriften in Deutschland (1798-1821), Berlin-Treptow 1972
(Veroeffentlichungen der Archenhold-Sternwarte Berlin-Treptow Nr.
5), p. 32f. For a brief survey of the organization of astronomical
research cf. also: Herrmann, D.B.: Geschichte der Astronomie von
Herschel bis Hertzsprung, Berlin 1975, pp. 208-250.

60 Herrmann, D.B.:   Das Astronomentreffen im Jahre 1798 auf dem
Seeberg bei Gotha, in: Arch. Hist. Exact sci. 6 (1970),
pp. 326-344. Herrmann, Entstehung (ref. 59), p. 41 et passim.

61 Herrmann, Entstehung (ref. 59), pp. 76-94.

62 Cf., e.g. Caneva, K.: Conceptual and generational change in
German physics. The case of electricity, 1800-1846, Princeton 1974
(Diss.).

Abbé Morellet   294
Abel, N.H.   311, 331, 334f.,
  337, 340, 379
Ackerknecht, E.H.   37
Albury, W.R.   80
Alembert, J.le Rond d'   79,
  312, 314f., 318
Alexander I   100, 105
Alexandrov   339
Alibert, J.   41f.
Altenstein, K. Freiherr vom
  und zum Stein   218-221,
  246f., 274f., 278
Ampère, A.M.   12, 131, 135,
  139, 316f., 324, 351, 356,
  360
Amsterdamski, S.   xxviii, xxxv,
  xxxix
Anaxagoras   55
Apollonius   266
Arago, F.   304, 351, 355
Arbogast, L.F.A.   316, 323f.,
  361
Arfvedson, J.   132
Arsenyew, K.I.   105
Auenbrugger, d'   37, 41
Avenarius, R.   66, 72
Avogadro, A.   92, 131, 139

Bacon, F. xxv, xxviii, xxxi,
  xxxii, 55, 63
Baer, K.   94, 106
Balzac, H. de   42
Basalla, G.   273
Basedow, J.B.   166
Bayes, Th.   291-293
Bayle, A.-L.   41

Bayle, G.L.   41
Beccaria,   294
Beck, H.   159
Belanger   365
Belinsky, V.G.   102
Ben-David, J.   356
Benoit   365
Bentham, J.   304
Berkeley, G.   314, 319, 360
Bernard, C.   38, 49, 97
Bernhardi, A.F.   189-197, 276
Bernoulli, J.   5, 24, 288,
  290-292, 295, 312, 315
Bernoulli, N.   5, 288, 312,
  315
Berthollet, C.L.   127f.
Bertrand, J.   294, 231f., 304
Berzelius, I.   41, 92, 131f.,
  134, 139
Bessel,   F.W.   375,   410,
  414f.
Beuth   272
Bichat, M.F.X.   40, 42, 46-50
Biermann, K.-R.   384
Biot, J.B.   351, 356f.
Bohm, D.   xxvii
Bohr, N.   xxxvi
Bolzano, B.   78, 86f., 311,
  316, 324f., 337
Booker, P.J.   362
Bourdieu, P.   xiv, xxviii
Boyer, C.B.   82
Boyle, R.   128
Bradley, M.   364
Bredow   240
Breithaupt, H.C.W.   403
Broussais, F.J.V.   37, 41, 50

Buffon, G.-L.L., Comte de
  145, 154, 295
Burdach, K.F.   46
Burkhardt, H.F.K.   351
Burja, A.   373
Butlerov, A.M.   100

Cabanis, P.   38, 43f.
Calas, J.   294, 296
Campe, J.H.   166
Canguilhem, G.   46
Cantor, G.   254, 325
Carnap, R.   65f., 70f.
Carnot, L.N.M.   314, 316,
  322, 356f., 360, 363
Carnot, S.   355
Cassirer, E.   xx, xxvii,
  xxviii, 76f., 79
Cauchy, A.L.   93, 242, 311,
  316f., 324f., 337, 351f.,
  355-357, 360f.
Caventoux   41
Chassaigne, R. de la   37
Chaumel   41
Chebyshev, P.L.   100
Churchman, C.W.   xxxix
Clapeyron   364
Clarke, S.   xxiv
Columbus, Ch.   161
Comberousse, C. de   364
Comte, A.   49f., 83, 289,
  303f., 364
Condillac, E.B. de   xxvii,
  44, 79-83, 290
Condorcet, M.-J.-A.-N.
  Caritat Marquis de   28f.,
  83, 287f., 290-300, 302-304
Coriolis, G.G.   356, 363, 365
Corvisart, J.N.   37, 41
Coulomb, Ch.A.   11

Courtois, B.   132
Cousin, J.A.J.   356
Crelle, A.L.   244,   275,
  277f., 378f., 382-384, 406,
  414
Crosland, M.   354, 372
Cuvier, G.   47, 136-138

Dalton, J.   92, 127-130, 139
Daniell   8
Darwin, Ch.   54, 95, 97f.,
  145, 154
Daston, L.J.   372
Davy, H.   92, 132-134
Dedekind, R.   311, 325
Degen, F.   334
Delbrueck   244
Delekat, F.   170
Delorme   41
Descartes, R.   xxv, xxiii,
  xxxii-xxxi, 56-57, 63, 78,
  82
Destutt de Tracy, A.L.C.   303
Didérot, D.   xxivf., 79, 315
Dilthey, W.   60
Dirichlet,   J.P.G.   Lejeune
  278, 331, 340, 342, 373,
  374f., 378, 380-382, 401,
  408
Dirksen, E.H.   239, 375-377,
  379-382
Djadkovsky, I.E.   98
Dobereiner, J.   132
Drobisch, M.W.   85
Dubreuil   37
Duhamel, J.M.C.   356, 360
Dulong, P.   131
Dumas   365
Dupin, F.P.Ch.   300f., 356,
  360, 364

Dupuy, P.   356
Durkheim, E. xiii, xvi, xxxvii,
    32

Ebert, J.J.   xxxvi
Ehrlich 38
Eichhorn, J.A.F.   223, 251
Einstein, A.   xxxvi
Eisenstein, F.G.M.   382
Encke 379
Engelhardt, O.v.   372
Engels, F.   96
Epicur 199
Erasmus v. Rotterdam   xxv
Ernesti, J.A.   224
Euclid xxvi, 277, 403
Euler, L.   xxv, 5, 82, 93,
    312, 315, 317-320, 323f.,
    331, 337, 340-342, 360, 374,
    408
Eytelwein, J.   277, 374, 379

Faraday, M.   11
Fechner, G. Th.   66
Fermat, P. de   82, 287, 333,
    341
Feuerbach, L.   145
Fichte, J.G.   60f., 63, 110,
    165, 168, 336
Fick 66
Fischer, E.   138
Fischer, E.G.   198-204, 374,
    379, 406-408
Fleck, L.   xiv
Fontenelle, B. Le Bovier de
    318
Foucault, M.   xv, xvif.,
    xxviii, 37
Fourcroy, A.F. de   40

Fourier, J.B.   7, 10, 12,
    331, 337f., 340, 342-345,
    350-353, 356, 358-360, 382
Fox, R.   352
Francke, A.H.   244
Francoeur 356
Frankel, E.   351
Franklin 201
Fresnel, A.   133, 351, 356f.,
    359f.
Freud, S.   32
Friedrich II   322
Friedrich Wilhelm II   295
Friedrich Wilhelm III   4, 270
Fries, J.F.   277, 413
Furck, C.L.   212

Galich, A.I.   105
Galilei, G.   xxv, 55, 59, 61,
    142
Galois, E.   93, 331, 342
Galvani, L.   92, 134
Garnot, S.   97
Gartz, J.C.   239f., 242
Gauss, C.F.   15, 85, 93,
    239f., 272f., 331, 335, 337,
    340-343, 375f., 382f., 402,
    404F., 410f., 414f.
Gay-Lussac, J.L.   92, 130-132
Gedike, F.   186f., 193-195,
    197, 200, 202
Gerdil, H.S.   318
Gergonne, J.   380
Gerling, Ch.L.   239-241
Gesner, J.M.   224
Gess, G.I.   106
Gillispie, Ch.C.   3, 6, 363
Girard, A.   356, 364
Gmelin, J.F.   xxxiv
Goedel, K.   xxxv, xxxvi, 84

Goethe, J.W.v.   79, 174, 241
Grabiner, J.V.   338, 372
Grassmann, H.   255-257,
    261-263
Grassman, J.G.   93, 255-257,
    259-261, 263-266
Grattan-Guinness, I.   372
Graunt, J.   31
Grunert, J.A.   239
Gruson,   J.   374,   377,
    379-382
Gudermann, Ch.   413
Guérin, J.   42
Guerry   298
Gutsmuths,   J.   159,   166f.

Hachette, J.N.P.   356, 359f.,
    362
Hamilton, W.R.   xxvii, 93, 331
Hankel, H.   242, 412
Hardy, G.H.   336
Harnack, A.   xix
Hartley, D.   290, 302
Hauff, J.K.F.   403
Hecker, A.J.   277
Hegel,   G.W.F.   61-63,   139,
    145,   220,   223,   336f.,   375,
    377
Heidelberger, M.   372
Heinig, K.   xxx
Heisenberg, W.   xxxvi
Helmholtz, H.v.   65-72, 85,
    97
Henning, J.W.M.   166
Herbart, J.F.   xxii, 224
Herder, J.G.   170f., 224
Hering   66
Herschel, J.   92
Hertz, H.   16
Herzen, A.I.   101f., 106

Higgins, B.   128
Higgins, W.   128
Hilbert, D.   84
Hindenburg, K.F.   278, 402,
    404-406, 409, 411-413, 415
Hisinger, W.   134
Hoffmann, v.   184
Hofstadter, D.R.   xxxv
Humboldt,   A.v.   4, 137, 159,
    161,   163,   244,   274,   376,
    378f., 381-384, 406
Humboldt, W.v.   xxix, xxxvii,
    110,   165,   188f.,   194f.,
    215f., 218f., 222, 224, 406
Hume, D.   58, 65, 290
Husserl, E.   60
Hutton, J.   94
Huygens, Ch.   133, 286

Ideler, L.   374, 377, 380
Itard, G.   41
Jachmann, R.B.   215
Jacobi,   C.G.J.   238f.,   243,
    247,   251,   279f.,   331,   334,
    337, 340f., 344, 379f., 382,
    341, 408
Jacoby, B.S.   106
Jahnke, H.N.   xxviii
Jakobi   227f.
Janich, P.   173
Jean Paul [J.P.F. Richter]
    168
Jerome   238
Joerden, R.   215

Kaemtz   240, 244f., 247
Kaestner,   A.G.   241,   402,
    404f., 409, 411-413, 415

Kant, I.   xxxii; 5, 8, 11,
    14, 56, 58-62, 65f., 68f.,
    94, 123, 161, 171, 174, 185,
    216, 276, 406, 410
Kedrov, B.M.   xxvii
Kepler, J.   142, 266
Kirchhoff, G.R.   12, 16
Klein, F.   xx, 240, 332,
    337, 339, 374, 401, 412
Klein, M.   46
Kluegel, G.S.   239
Koberstein   227
Koch, J.F.W.   246, 248
Kopernikus, N.   142
Kopp, H.   xxxiv
Kronecker, L.   382, 384
Kuhn, Th.S.   xiv, 5, 76,
    356, 411f.
Kummer, E.E.   239, 331, 373,
    384

La   Barre, J.-F. Le Fèvre,
    Chevalier de   294
Lacroix, S.-F.   82, 315, 374
Ladenburg, A.   xxxiv
Laënnec   41, 50
Lagrange, J.-L.   82, 87, 241,
    311-325, 331f., 337, 350,
    352f., 356, 358-361, 374,
    405, 412f.
La Harpe, J.-F. de   303
Lamarck, J.B.A. de   45-47,
    50, 54, 94f., 97f., 136, 138
Lambert, J.H.   201
Lamé   356, 360, 364
Lampe, E.   378
Landen, J.   319f.
Lange, F.A.   68
Langhammer, W.   372

Laplace,   P.S.   Marquis   de
    23-32, 92, 95, 97, 123, 138,
    287f.,   290,   292-294,
    296-299, 304, 312, 331f.,
    336, 344, 356, 360, 403
Larrey   42
Lavallee   365
Laveran   50
Lavoisier, A.L.   xxxxii
    46f., 81f., 94, 126, 128
Le Gallois   41
Legendre, A.-M.   331, 342,
    356
Lehmus, D.   374
Leibniz, G.W.   xxv, 5, 60,
    171, 312, 314, 333, 337, 340
Lenhart, V.   372
Lepenies, W.   xiv, 161, 172
L'Hospital, Marquis de   318
L'Huilier, S.   316, 321f.
Liebig, J.v.   xxx, xxxiii,
    249
Lindner, F.W.   160
Lindt, R.   361
Linné, C.v.   230
Liouville   356, 360, 365
Littré, E.   45
Ljungberg, J.M.   410
Lobachevsky, N.I.   93, 99,
    106
Locke, J.   xxv, 81, 290
Louis   42
Lomonosov, M.V.   104
Lorenzen, P.   173
Lorey, W.   251
Loria, G.   362
Lubbe, S.   375, 380
Luedde, J.G.   161
Lundgreen, P.   271
Lyell, Ch.   94, 97, 136, 138

Mach, E.   65f., 72

Magendie, F.   38, 49f., 97

Malthus, Th.R.   30-32

Malus   351, 356

Manegold, K.H.   269, 274

Marx, K.   32, 63, 96, 145,
   147, 154

Mayer, J.R.   4

Mayer, T.   5

Mayer   41

Mehrtens, H.   372

Meierotto, J.H.L.   209f.

Mendelsohn, E.   xii

Mendelssohn, M.   201

Merz, J. Th.   67

Mill, J.St.   32, 293, 301,
   304

Minding, E.F.   380f.

Miquel   50

Mitscherlich, E.   131, 275

Moebius, A.F.   239, 331, 414

Mollweide, K.B.   239

Monge, G.   82, 331, 356, 358,
   360, 362-364

Morgagni   37

Moses   167

Mueffling, v.   383

Mueller, D.K.   212, 224

Mueller, J.   66, 68-70, 97

Murhard, F.W.   402, 411

Nagel, E.   xxvi

Napoléon I Bonaparte   138,
   297

Navier, C.L.M.H.   301, 355f.,
   360

Neumann, F.   373

Neumann, K.   240

Newton, I.   xxxii, 6f., 59,
   61, 69, 128, 133, 138, 142,
   313f., 318, 333, 337, 350,
   407

Niederer   167, 169

Niemeyer, A.H.   244

Niethammer, F.I.   224

Nikolai, I.   100, 102

Oersted, H.C.   4, 10, 14,
   132, 134f.

Ohm, G.S.   xxii, 6-16, 408

Ohm, M.   xxii, xxiv, 376-378,
   380-382, 408, 414

Olbers   414f.

Olivier, Th.   365

Oltmanns, J.   376, 379

Osipovksy, T.F.   105

Ostrogradsky, M.V.   99, 105

Otte, M.   xxviii

Parkinson   41

Pascal, B.   288

Pasteur, L.   38f., 44, 49f.

Paul, M.   xx

Paulsen, F.   209, 212

Peclet   365

Pell, J.   342

Pelletier   41

Pernice   251

Pestalozzi, J.H.   xxii,
   159f., 163, 165-175, 263

Pestel, P.I.   101

Petit, A.T.   131

Petit   41

Petrov, V.V.   106, 134

Petty, W.   31

Pfaff, Ch.H.   9-11, 404

Pfaff, J.F.   238-242, 244,
   402, 404f., 411, 414

Pfeifer, G. 162
Pinel, P.H. 40
Planck, M. xxxvi
Plato 59
Pluche, N.-A. 167
Pluecker, J. 239, 331, 401
Pohl, G.F. 8f., 11, 14
Poincaré, H. 311
Poinsot, L. 293, 300f., 303f., 357
Poisson, S.D. 287, 292f., 298–301, 305, 351, 356f., 359f.
Poncelet, J.V. 331, 356, 363f.
Popper, K.R. 144
Portal 41
Poselger 379
Praut, W. 132f. 141
Priestley, J. 128
Prochaska 97
Prony, G.C.F.M. Riche de 349, 353, 356, 358f.
Proust, J. 126f.
Puissant 356
Purkyne 97

Quesnay, F. 145, 154
Quetelet, L.A.J. 21–23, 25–32, 289, 298, 305, 380

Rabelais, F. xxiv
Rang, A. 224
Rang-Dudzik, B. 372
Ravetz, J.R. 351
Réaumur, R.-A.F. de 145
Reimer, N.T. 410
Riemann, B. 93, 382
Ritter, C. 4, 159–163, 165–168, 170–173, 175

Roenne, L.v. 221, 223, 232, 276
Rosenberger, A. 239, 242, 249, 250f.
Rouillier, K.F. 98, 106
Rousseau, J.-J. 294
Russell, B. xxxvi

Saint-Hilair, G. 97
Saint-Simon, C.H. de 32, 78
Salmon, W.C. xxxvi
Salzmann, Ch.G. 116
Sarton, G. 371
Savart 351
Schellbach, K.H. 240, 279f.
Schelling, F.W.J. xix, xxxii, 4, 13, 15, 60–63, 98, 104, 110, 133, 135, 139, 165, 336
Scherk, H.F. 239, 242, 410
Schiersmann, C. 272
Schiller, F. 162, 263–265
Schleiden, M. 94, 97
Schleiermacher, F.E.D. 83, 110, 168, 189, 239
Schlesinger, L. 85
Schmalz 239
Schoeler, W. 224
Schubring, G. 270, 273, 277, 413
Schulze, J. 220, 275f.
Schumacher 415
Schwann, T. 94, 97
Schwartz, P. 209f., 222, 228, 232
Schweigger, J.S.Ch. 8f., 242, 245f., 249
Segner, J.A. 239
Semmelweis, I. 44
Serres 41

Serturner   41

Shinn, T.   272, 372

Silliman, R.H.   357

Snethlage, B.M.   210

Sohnke, L.A.   239, 243, 245, 247, 249, 251f.

Spinoza, B. de   57f., 63

Steffens, H.   110

Stegmueller, W.   xiv

Steiner, J.   280, 331, 335, 378-381, 401

Steinhaeuser   239, 242

Stromeyer, F.   132

Struik, D.J.   332, 334, 339

Strueve, V.Y.   106

Struwe, W.   xxix

Sturm, L.C.   354, 360

Suevern, J.W.   219

Sylvius   xxxiii

Tarski, A.   144

Taylor, B.   313f., 316-318, 321-323

Tennant, S.   132

Tennard, L.   132

Tetens, J.N.   408

Thibaut, B.F.   240f., 373, 405

Thiersch, F.W.   224

Thomasius, Ch.   237

Thompson-Rumford, B.   133

Thomson, W.[Lord Kelvin]   15

Thomson, T.   129

Timirjasev, K.A.   97

Tobler   160

Toth, I.   370

Tralles, J.G.   269, 371, 373-375, 409

Trapp, E.Ch.   166

Tréviranus   46f., 54

Trommsdorf, J.B.   xxix-xxxiv

Turchin, V.F.   xxxvi

Turgot, A.-R.-J., Baron de l'Aulne   30

Turner, St.J.   378f.

Valentiner, F.   408

Varenius   162

Velikowsky, I.   347

Villers, Ch.   168

Virchow, R.   38, 48

Volladon   363

Volta, A.   7f., 11, 92, 134

Voltaire [F.-M. Arouet] 292, 294

Voskresensky, A.A.   100

Wackernagel, Ph.   223

Wallaston. W.   130, 132

Wallis, J.   342

Weber, M.   32

Weber, W.   15, 242

Weierstrass, K. 309, 323, 371, 382, 411

Weingart, P.   xxxviii

Weyel, H.   87

Wheatstone   8

Whittaker, E.   350

Wilden, A.   xxxvi

Williams, R.   vi

Wittgenstein, L.   65

Woehler, F.   131

Woellner, J.Ch.v.   186

Wolf, F.A.   238f.

Wolff, Ch.   94, 171, 237, 239, 404

Wussing, H.   78

Zach, F.X.v.   413
Zedlitz, K.A. Freiherr v.
  218
Zeleny, J.   xxxix
Zeno   xxxiv
Zimmermann, C.G.   197
Zimmermann, Ch.   372
Zinin, N.N.   100, 106
Zwerling, C.S.   354

LIST OF PARTICIPANTS

K. BAYERTZ, Bremen

H.G. BEISENHERZ, Muenchen

B. BEKEMEIER, Bielefeld

D. BROADY, Stockholm

P. BUCK, Cambridge (Mass.)

M. CROSLAND, Canterbury

P. DAMEROW, Berlin

L.J. DASTON, Cambridge (Mass.)

J.W. DAUBEN, New York

M. DE MEY, Gent

W. DIEDERICH, Bielefeld

H. DINGES, Frankfurt

A. DRESS, Bielefeld

Y. ELKANA, Jerusalem

D.v. ENGELHARDT, Heidelberg

P. GAJDENKO, Moscow*

J.V. GRABINER, Dominguez Hills

I. GRATTAN-GUINNESS, Enfield

K.P. GROTEMEYER, Bielefeld

M. HEIDELBERGER, Muenchen

G. HEINEMANN, Kassel

E.N. HIEBERT, Cambridge (Mass.)

H.N. JAHNKE, Bielefeld

Ph.S. JONES, Ann Arbor

D. KALLOS, Lund

U. KNAUER, Oldenburg

W. KROHN, Starnberg

L. KRUEGER, Bielefeld

K.J. KRYSMANSKI, Muenster

R. KUENZLI, Kiel

G. KUEPPERS, Bielefeld

W. KUYK, Antwerpen

L. LAESKER, Berlin (GDR)

W. LANGHAMMER, Halle (GDR)

V. LENHART, Heidelberg

A.C. LEWIS, Austin

I. LOHMANN, Muenster

R. LORENZ, Bielefeld

P. LUNDGREEN, Bielefeld

U.P. LUNDGREN, Stockholm

H. MEHRTENS, Berlin

E. MENDELSOHN, Cambridge (Mass.)

S.R. MIKULINSKY, Moscow*

Th. MIES, Bielefeld

C.U. MOULINES, Mexico

D.K. MUELLER, Bochum

H. NOWOTNY, Wien

M. OTTE, Bielefeld

H.W. PAUL, Gainesville

A. RANG, Berlin

B. RANG-DUDZIK, Berlin

K. ROETTGERS, Bielefeld

L. ROGERS, London

C. SALOMON-BAYET, Paris*

H.J. SANDKUEHLER, Bremen

W. SCHARLAU, Muenster

B. SCHMINNES, Bielefeld

I. SCHNEIDER, Muenster

E.-C. SCHROEDER, Bielefeld

G. SCHUBRING, Bielefeld

T. SHINN, Paris

J.D. SNEED, Albany (N.Y.)

H.G. STEINER, Bielefeld

I. STENGERS, Brussels

R.J.K. STOWASSER, Bielefeld

R.H. STUEWER, Minneapolis

I. TOTH, Regensburg

R.St. TURNER, Fredericton

W. VESPER, Braunschweig

P. WEINGART, Bielefeld

M. WOLFF, Bielefeld

* unable to come

430